Beginning Objective-C

James Dovey
Ash Furrow

Apress·

Beginning Objective-C

Copyright © 2012 by James Dovey and Ash Furrow

This work is subject to copyright. All rights are reserved by the Publisher, whether the whole or part of the material is concerned, specifically the rights of translation, reprinting, reuse of illustrations, recitation, broadcasting, reproduction on microfilms or in any other physical way, and transmission or information storage and retrieval, electronic adaptation, computer software, or by similar or dissimilar methodology now known or hereafter developed. Exempted from this legal reservation are brief excerpts in connection with reviews or scholarly analysis or material supplied specifically for the purpose of being entered and executed on a computer system, for exclusive use by the purchaser of the work. Duplication of this publication or parts thereof is permitted only under the provisions of the Copyright Law of the Publisher's location, in its current version, and permission for use must always be obtained from Springer. Permissions for use may be obtained through RightsLink at the Copyright Clearance Center. Violations are liable to prosecution under the respective Copyright Law.

ISBN-13 (pbk): 978-1-4302-4368-7

ISBN-13 (electronic): 978-1-4302-4369-4

Trademarked names, logos, and images may appear in this book. Rather than use a trademark symbol with every occurrence of a trademarked name, logo, or image we use the names, logos, and images only in an editorial fashion and to the benefit of the trademark owner, with no intention of infringement of the trademark.

The use in this publication of trade names, trademarks, service marks, and similar terms, even if they are not identified as such, is not to be taken as an expression of opinion as to whether or not they are subject to proprietary rights.

While the advice and information in this book are believed to be true and accurate at the date of publication, neither the authors nor the editors nor the publisher can accept any legal responsibility for any errors or omissions that may be made. The publisher makes no warranty, express or implied, with respect to the material contained herein.

President and Publisher: Paul Manning
Lead Editor: Steve Anglin
Developmental Editor: Douglas Pundick
Technical Reviewer: Felipe Laso
Editorial Board: Steve Anglin, Ewan Buckingham, Gary Cornell, Louise Corrigan, Morgan Ertel, Jonathan Gennick, Jonathan Hassell, Robert Hutchinson, Michelle Lowman, James Markham, Matthew Moodie, Jeff Olson, Jeffrey Pepper, Douglas Pundick, Ben Renow-Clarke, Dominic Shakeshaft, Gwenan Spearing, Matt Wade, Tom Welsh
Coordinating Editor: Katie Sullivan
Copy Editor: Mary Behr
Compositor: SPi Global
Indexer: SPi Global
Artist: SPi Global
Cover Designer: Anna Ishchenko

Distributed to the book trade worldwide by Springer Science+Business Media New York, 233 Spring Street, 6th Floor, New York, NY 10013. Phone 1-800-SPRINGER, fax (201) 348-4505, e-mail orders-ny@springer-sbm.com, or visit www.springeronline.com.

For information on translations, please e-mail rights@apress.com, or visit www.apress.com.

Apress and friends of ED books may be purchased in bulk for academic, corporate, or promotional use. eBook versions and licenses are also available for most titles. For more information, reference our Special Bulk Sales–eBook Licensing web page at www.apress.com/bulk-sales.

Any source code or other supplementary materials referenced by the author in this text is available to readers at www.apress.com. For detailed information about how to locate your book's source code, go to www.apress.com/source-code/

For the bookends of the process: Clay Andres, who started the ball rolling three years (!) ago, and J'aime Ohm, on whose birthday this is released.

—James Dovey

Contents

About the Authors

Jim Dovey has been writing software exclusively for the Macintosh (and later iOS) for 12 years now. A British expat, he works at Kobo in Toronto, Canada, where until recently he was the lead architect on the company's iOS applications, but these days he works as a liaison with the publishing industry and various standards committees and in the office carries a big stick labeled "Implement ePub 3" (no really; it looks kind of like Mallett's Mallet— Google that). Under the nom-de-hackuerre (is that a thing? can we make it a thing please?) he's the creator of many open source projects, including AQGridView, the original grid view control for iOS; AQXMLParser, the best event-based XML parser for the iPhone; and the original third-party development kit for the Apple TV. He also worked on Outpost, the original Basecamp client for iPhone and created an Apple TV-based digital signage system. This is his first book, but he hopes to churn out many more in the future.

Ash Furrow has been writing iOS application since the days of iOS 2. While completing his undergraduate degree, he worked on iOS applications for provincial elections and taught iOS development at the University of New Brunswick. He has also developed several of his own applications (for sale on the App Store) and contributes to open source projects. In 2011, Ash moved to Toronto to work with 500px to create their now wildly popular iOS application.

Currently, Ash works at 500px as the lead developer of the iOS team. He also tweets, blogs, and photographs.

About the Technical Reviewer

Felipe Laso Marsetti is a self-taught software developer specializing in iOS development. He is currently employed as a Systems Engineer at Lextech Global Services. Despite having worked with many languages throughout his life, nothing makes him happier than working on projects for iPhone and iPad. Felipe has over two years of professional iOS experience. He likes to write on his blog at http://iFe.li, create iOS tutorials and articles as a member of www.raywenderlich.com, and work as a technical reviewer for Objective-C and iOS related books. You can find Felipe on Twitter as @Airjordan12345, on Facebook under his name, or on App.net as @iFeli. When he's not working or programming, Felipe loves to read and learn new languages and technologies, watch sports, cook, or play the guitar and violin.

Acknowledgments

None of this would have come to pass without a chance meeting with Jeff LaMarche at Macworld 2009, who subsequently introduced me to Clay Andres of Apress at WDC that year. The authors and editors of the Apress family have all been a great help and inspiration, especially Felipe Laso Marsetti, whose assistance has been invaluable in ensuring the navigability of the mine of information within these pages; and editors Katie Sullivan, Douglas Pundick, and Steve Anglin, who should particularly be rewarded for putting up with my Douglas-Adams-like approach to deadlines over the last year.

—James Dovey

I've had a lot of help, both in the content I wrote for this book and with getting to a position where I had enough experience to write it. No one gets where they are on their own; everyone has help along their way. There are simply too many friends, teachers, and mentors to thank. I ran ideas and passages past two friends in particular who have always been invaluable in helping me perfect my writing; thank you to Jason Brennan and Paddy O'Brien for their discerning eyes.

My wife was absolutely supportive during my work on this book. She helped me keep working through late nights and weekends, and I couldn't have done this without her.

— Ash Furrow

Chapter 1

Getting Started with Objective-C

The Objective-C programming language has a long history, and while it has languished in the fringes as a niche language for much of that time, the introduction of the iPhone has catapulted it to fame (or infamy): in January 2012, Objective-C was announced as the winner of the TIOBE Programming Language Award for 2011. This award goes to the language that sees the greatest increase in usage over the previous twelve months; in the case of Objective-C, it leaped from eighth place to fifth on the index during 2011. You can see its sudden, sharp climb in Figure 1-1.

The Objective-C programming language was created in the early 1980s by Brad Cox and Tom Love at their company StepStone. It was designed to bring the object-oriented programming approach of the Smalltalk language (created at Xerox PARC in the 1970s) to the existing world of software systems implemented using the C programming language. In 1988, Steve Jobs (yes, that Steve Jobs) licensed the Objective-C language and runtime from StepStone for use in the NeXT operating system. NeXT also implemented Objective-C compiler support in GCC, and developed the FoundationKit and ApplicationKit frameworks, which formed the underpinnings of the NeXTstep operating system's programming environment. While NeXT computers didn't take the world by storm, the development environment it built using Objective-C was widely lauded in the software industry; the OS eventually developed into the OpenStep standard, used by both NeXT and Sun Microsystems in the mid-1990s.

In 1997, Apple, in search of a solid base for a new next-generation operating system, purchased NeXT. The NeXTstep OS was then used as the basis for Mac OS X, which saw its first commercial release in early 2001; while libraries for compatibility with the old Mac OS line of systems were included, AppKit and Foundation (by then known by the marketing name Cocoa) formed the core of the new programming environment on OS X. NeXT's programming tools, Project Builder and Interface Builder, were included for free with every copy of Mac OS X, but it was with the release of the iPhone SDK in 2008 that Objective-C began to really take off as programmers rushed to write software for this exciting new device.

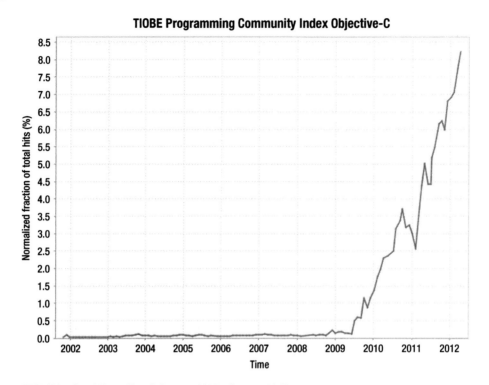

Figure 1-1. TPCI Objective-C Usage Trend, January 2002–January 2012

In this chapter you will learn how to use the Xcode programming environment to create a simple Mac application, including work on the UI and user interaction. After that you'll look at some of the details of the Objective-C language itself: the keywords, structure, and format of Objective-C programs, and the capabilities provided by the language itself.

Xcode

Programming for the Mac and iPhone is done primarily using Apple's free toolset, which chiefly revolves around the Xcode integrated development environment (IDE). Historically, Xcode shipped with all copies of OS X on disc or was available for download via the Apple Developer Connection web site. In these days of the App Store, however, Xcode is primarily obtained through it. Fire up the App Store application on your Mac, type "Xcode" into the search field, and hit Enter. You'll find yourself presented with the item you see in Figure 1-2.

Figure 1-2. *The latest version of Xcode is freely available from the Mac App Store*

Click to download it, and (admittedly some time later) you'll have a copy of Xcode in your Applications folder ready to use.

Xcode comes with a lot more than just its namesake IDE application. It also contains many useful debugging and profiling utilities, and provides optional downloads for command-line versions of the GCC and LLVM compiler suites. Among the available tools you will find are the following:

- *Instruments*: An application for generating detailed runtime profiling information for your applications—probably the most useful tool in your arsenal for a Mac or iOS developer.

- *Dashcode*: An HTML and JavaScript editor designed to help you to easily construct Dashboard widgets and Safari plug-ins.

- *Quartz Composer*: An application that enables the creation of complex graphical transformations, filters, and animations using a no-code patch-bay assembly technique.

- *OpenGL Apps*: A full suite of apps are provided to work with OpenGL (and OpenGL ES on iOS). Here you'll find profilers, performance monitors, shader builders, and an OpenGL driver monitor.

■   *Network Link Conditioner*: A dream come true for network-based software engineers, this handy little tool lets you simulate a host of different network profiles. It comes with defaults for the most commonly encountered environments, and you can create your own, specifying bandwidth, percentage of dropped packets, latency, and DNS latency. Want to debug how your iOS app handles when it's right on the very edge of a Wi-Fi network? That becomes nice and easy with this little tool.

Those are a few of our favorites, but it's by no means an exhaustive list. As you will see later in the book, the technology underlying a lot of the Xcode tools is if anything even more impressive.

Creating Your First Project

Upon launching Xcode for the first time, you will find yourself presented with the application's Welcome screen. The following steps will guide you through the creation of the new project.

1.   Click the button marked "Create a new Xcode project." You will be asked which type of project you would like to create.

2.   From the Mac OS X section, select Application, then the Cocoa Application icon in the main pane.

3.   Click Next to be presented with some options to define your project. Enter the details shown in Figure 1-3, then click Next again and choose where to save your project.

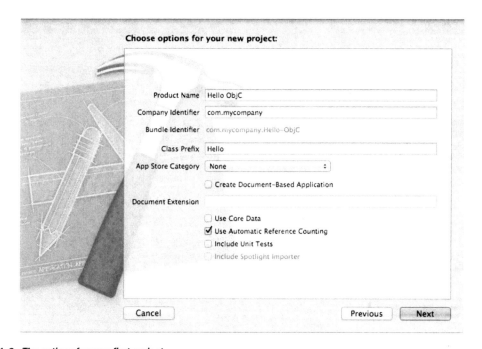

Figure 1-3. The options for your first project

Let's go through the layout of Xcode and the new project. On the left of the window you can see the Navigator, shown in Figure 1-4. This is where you can browse your project's source code files, resources, libraries, and output. The Navigator will also let you browse your project's class hierarchy, search and replace across your entire project, and browse build logs.

Figure 1-4. *The Xcode Navigator pane*

In the center pane of the Xcode window is the editor. Here's where you'll work with your code and your user interface resources.

On the right hand side is the Utilities pane. The upper part is context-sensitive and displays different choices of tabs depending upon the content currently focused in the editor pane. Below this is a palette from which you can drag user interface elements, new files based on templates, code snippets, and media. You can add your own templates and snippets here, too.

The Application Template

The Cocoa Application template generated a lot of information for you already. In fact, you already have a fully-functional application here. In the Navigator, switch to the browser tab (the leftmost option) and look inside the Hello ObjC folder. Here you'll see your primary source files and the user interface definition (a .xib file). Also in here is a Supporting Files folder; it contains the application's main.m file, which is responsible for kicking off the application itself, and the prefix header, which is included automatically into every file you add to the project. You'll also see Hello ObjC-Info.plist, which contains metadata about your application, and InfoPlist. strings, which holds localized versions of the data in the .plist file. You usually won't need to change these directly, as the Info.plist is most commonly edited through the target editor, to which you will be introduced in a later chapter.

The one item here that you might want to change is `Credits.rtf`. The contents of this file will be displayed within the application's About dialog; and as it's an `.rtf` file, you can style this as you like. The contents will be placed in a scrollable multi-line text field on the About dialog.

Below this is the `Frameworks` folder. It contains a list of all the frameworks and dynamic libraries upon which your application relies. Note that this is not an automatically-managed list: you need to add frameworks and libraries to the project yourself as you need them. Lastly, the `Products` folder contains a reference to the compiled application. Right now its name is likely in red, since it hasn't yet been built.

Click once on `HelloAppDelegate.h` to open it in the editor pane. Right now it looks a little bare, as seen in Listing 1-1. The code declares the structure and interface of a *class*, in this case named `HelloAppDelegate`. It tells the system that it implements all required methods defined in a *protocol* called `NSApplicationDelegate`, and that it has one property called `window`. You'll look into the details of this syntax in the next chapter, but for now just take it on trust that this works as expected.

Listing 1-1. HelloAppDelegate.h

```
#import <Cocoa/Cocoa.h>

@interface HelloAppDelegate : NSObject <NSApplicationDelegate>

@property (assign) IBOutlet NSWindow *window;

@end
```

Next is the implementation file, seen in Listing 1-2. This is similarly terse right now: in between some delimiters declaring the implementation of the `HelloAppDelegate` class all you can see is a directive named `@synthesize`, which seems to refer to the `window` property you saw a moment ago. This is, in fact, exactly the case: this directive tells the Objective-C compiler to synthesize getters and setters for the `window` property, saving you the need to write them yourself. It also specifies that the *instance member variable* used to store the property should be called `_window`; the compiler will create that member variable for you, too, again saving on the need to write it out explicitly.

Listing 1-2. HelloAppDelegate.m

```
#import "HelloAppDelegate.h"

@implementation HelloAppDelegate

@synthesize window = _window;

- (void)applicationDidFinishLaunching:(NSNotification *)aNotification
{
    // Insert code here to initialize your application
}

@end
```

Hello Interface Builder

If you select the `MainMenu.xib` file, the editor changes into Interface Builder mode, so named because the task of building user interfaces was until recently the domain of a separate (though integrated) application titled, appropriately enough, Interface Builder. You can see what this looks like in Figure 1-5.

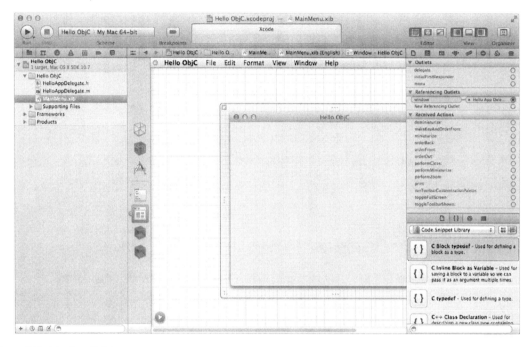

Figure 1-5. *Interface Builder*

In here you can see the application's menu, and down the left side of the editor is the document outline. All the objects in the interface document are listed here: at the top are the "inferred" objects, which are present in all (or almost all) `.xib` documents. Below the divider are objects explicitly added to the `.nib` file. The second item in this list is the application's window. Select that to make it appear in the editor.

Now that it's selected, the upper part of the Utilities pane on the right side of Xcode's window gains a lot more tabs. Click through these to see what they present; hovering the mouse over a tab selector will show a tooltip informing you of that tab's name.

Now, thanks to a lot of behind-the-scenes cleverness in the Interface Builder, you can build a nice application with user input and dynamically-updating feedback. What's more, you'll add only three lines of code to the project to do so!

User Interface Controls

First of all, you want to have somewhere for the user to type. Fetch your controls from the object palette in the lower half of the utilities pane; you can see all the items you'll use in Figure 1-6.

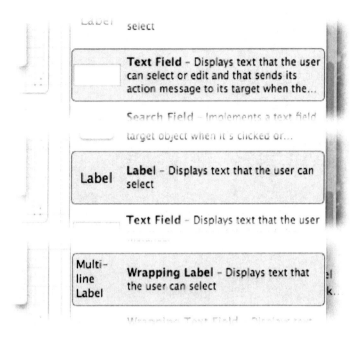

Figure 1-6. The Text Field, Label, and Multi-Line Label controls

1. In the lower part of the Utilities pane, select the second tab from the right (the box icon) to switch to the user interface Object Palette.

2. Pull down the Object Library pop-up menu and select Controls to limit the contents of the palette to just the standard controls for the moment (see Figure 1-6).

3. The first item you need is a text field. Scroll down a little way to find it.

4. Now drag that row from the palette straight out and onto the window in the editor. You'll notice that it changes into a real text field as it does so.

5. Move it up towards the top-right of the window's content area and blue lines will appear, helping snap the field into place. Position it there, at the top-right, as in Figure 1-7.

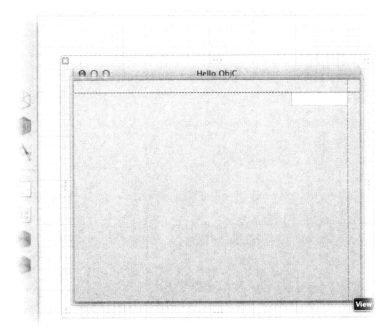

Figure 1-7. *Placing the text field*

6. Next you'll look for a label (a non-editable text field with no special background).

7. Drag this up to the top left, but notice that, while it can click into the top-left corner happily enough, guides also appear that cause it to align with the bottom edge of the text field you've already placed, or with the baseline of the text within that text field. This latter is the one you want to use: drop the label there, as shown in Figure 1-8.

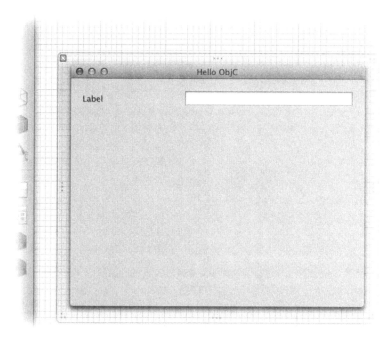

Figure 1-8. Positioning the label

8. To edit the label's text, double-click it. Type "Your Name:" and press Enter to store the change. Now clip the label's size to that of its text by pressing ⌘+=.

9. Select the text field and move the mouse cursor over the leftmost edge of the text field until the cursor changes to resize mode (a pair of arrows pointing both left and right). Click and drag the edge of the field over towards the label, and stop when the blue guide appears.

10. Lastly, look for the Wrapping Label control in the Object Library, and drag it into the center of the window, a little below the text field. More guides will appear to help snap it into the horizontal center of the window and to keep it well positioned below the text field itself. We suggest moving it a little further down so it has a nice amount of space around it.

11. Drag its edges out to meet the guides near the left and right edges of the window; this means the text can grow nicely. Now click on the handle in the center of the window's bottom edge and drag that up a little, shrinking the window so there's not quite so much empty space there.

Interface Bindings

If you're coming to Objective-C from another language, you might be used to the idea of handling your UI by hooking up variables referencing the various UI elements for manipulation. In Cocoa, however, that isn't always necessary. Instead, there is a system called *key-value coding* (KVC), which allows observation of a given value contained in a given object, which is referenced by a key. The key is either a method name or a member variable name—most commonly a method. The property declaration you saw earlier actually generates code that conforms precisely to that required by KVC, so that's how you'll be referencing and storing your values.

We will cover KVC in more depth in a later chapter, but for now you'll take advantage of a technology built on top of it: bindings. The essence of the idea is that certain properties of a user interface element can be *bound* to a value specified using KVC. This means that when one changes, the other does, too: editing a text field will change the value to which it's bound, and vice versa. Many properties of UI elements can be bound in this manner, but here you'll focus on arguably the most important one: the element's *value*.

In the case of a text field, the element's value is a string. So, first of all, you must create a string property somewhere to which you'll bind your interface. To do so, open up `HelloAppDelegate.h` and enter a new line under the existing property (see the line in bold in Listing 1-3).

Listing 1-3. The userName Property

```
@interface HelloAppDelegate : NSObject <NSApplicationDelegate>

@property (assign) IBOutlet NSWindow *window;
@property (copy) NSString * userName;

@end
```

This tells the world at large that `HelloAppDelegate` has a property called `userName` and that it is a string. It also states that the string is *copied* rather than *referenced* when set. Don't worry if you're not sure what that means yet: you soon will. For now, just accept it as a Good Thing.

This only declares the property, however. To actually implement it requires one more step. Open `HelloAppDelegate.m` and enter the highlighted line in Listing 1-4.

Listing 1-4. Synthesizing the userName Property

```
@implementation HelloAppDelegate

@synthesize window = _window;
@synthesize userName;

@end
```

Here you have asked the compiler to synthesize the implementation for you. Note that, unlike the `window` property, you have opted not to provide a name for the property's backing member variable; by convention, this means that the member variable's name matches the property's name exactly.

The next steps both happen in the Interface Builder: click `MainMenu.xib` to open it once more.

SYNTHESIZED VARIABLE NAMING

There are a number of different approaches to the naming of properties and their corresponding instance variables. Each developer no doubt has their own preference: we like to let the compiler handle the instance variables itself.

The following are the two most commonly seen approaches:

- *No name specified:* The compiler uses the exact same name for the creation of the backing variable.

- *An underscored name:* This matches Apple's internal naming scheme for instance variables. We and many other programmers follow this scheme, although Apple has, at times, recommended against it due to a potential clash with any instance variable names they might add to a class in the future.

A number of people argue that you should always explicitly supply a variable name when synthesizing properties, but we take the opposite approach as we believe it encourages the use of the accessor methods rather than directly accessing the underlying variable. This becomes especially important when using atomically accessed properties: the accessors are locked and synchronized, so nothing can read a variable mid-modification from a secondary thread. Accessing the instance variable directly has no such guarantees, however.

Binding User Input

1. Select the text field.

2. In the Utilities pane you'll see some of its attributes appear; the fourth tab contains the Attributes inspector where you can adjust the field's attributes: its font, colors, and some behavior. The fifth is the Size inspector where you can adjust the field's size and its placement, as well as its behavior when resizing its containing view (in this case, the window). The sixth is the Connections inspector, which you will see later in the book. Following that is the Bindings inspector, which is what you'll use to hook up the field's value.

3. At the top of the Bindings inspector is a pop-open row titled "Value." Open it to see a lot of options.

4. At the top is the "Bind to:" pop-up menu. In here you can see references to the application itself, the file's owner (the object that handles the interface definition in this .xib file at runtime), the global font manager and user defaults, and your app's delegate object, Hello App Delegate.

> ## DELEGATES
>
> The concept of a *delegate* is not peculiar to Objective-C, but due to the language's dynamic nature it is one of the core techniques used by the system libraries. A *delegate object* is an object that conforms to some predefined protocol—a list of methods it agrees to implement—by which another object can request that it undertake some actions or make some decisions on the other's behalf. For instance, a text field's delegate might check the text being entered and tell the text field to reject certain characters.
>
> Delegation is a very powerful tool and is the reason why Objective-C applications rarely tend to subclass classes such as the `Application` class: instead, a delegate object is created to make the important decisions and leaves the `Application` instance alone to handle the guts of making the app "go."

---

5. Select `Hello App Delegate` from the pop-up menu. In the Model Key Path field enter `self.userName`.

6. Check the "Continuously Updates Value" checkbox. The result should look like that in Figure 1-9.

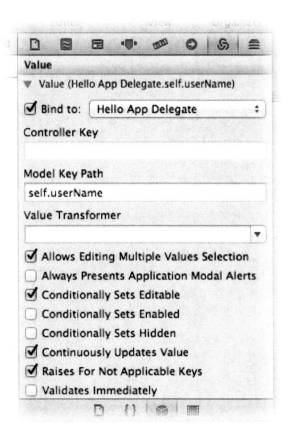

Figure 1-9. Binding the text field's value

This field's value is now bound to the property created earlier; as the user types in the field, the property's value will be updated to match.

The next step is to make some output from that value.

1. Select the Multiline Label and open the Bindings inspector once more. Here you'll not just set the value, however: you'll provide a pattern, similar to a format string, which will be augmented by a bound value.

2. Open the "Display Pattern Value1" item; it looks quite similar to Figure 1-9, with the addition of a Display Pattern value. By default this field contains %{value1}@, which is the way in which the Value1 binding created here will be applied to the label. You're going to bind to the same property here that you did before.

3. Select Hello App Delegate from the pop-up menu, and type self.userName into the "Model Key Path" field.

4. Now edit the Display Pattern field slightly, so it reads 'Hello, %{value1}@!' This will cause the field to display "Hello, *user*!" for a given value of user. Your input should leave the inspector looking similar to Figure 1-10.

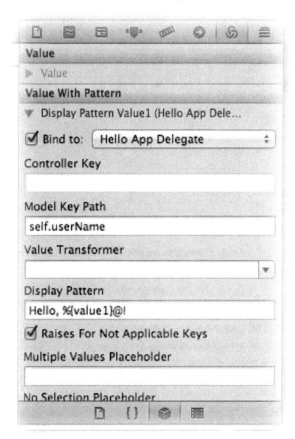

Figure 1-10. Formatting the output field

5. Lastly, switch to the Attributes inspector (the fourth tab on the sidebar) and change the field's alignment to centered, as in Figure 1-11.

Figure 1-11. Centering the output field

Running the App

It might come as a pleasant surprise to note that the application is now all but finished. You can compile and launch it right now by clicking the Run button in Xcode's toolbar. As you type in the text field, the output field below it updates dynamically.

However, it looks a bit strange at first launch. The text field doesn't contain anything, so the output field reads "Hello, !" and that doesn't really seem very impressive. It might be better to provide a default value when the application launches. In fact, it might be useful to preset the content with the current user's full name. Let's do that.

Open HelloAppDelegate.m once more. You're going to fill in the empty method here, which is part of NSApplication's delegation protocol. It currently looks like the code in Listing 1-5.

Listing 1-5. Delegating the App Launch

```
@synthesize userName;

- (void)applicationDidFinishLaunching:(NSNotification *)aNotification
{
    // Insert code here to initialize your application
}

@end
```

This method is called by NSApplication on its delegate once the application has finished launching and is ready to begin showing windows and processing user input. This is where you'll likely set up the initial state for any applications you write. In this instance, you'll fetch the user's name using the handy C function NSFullUserName() and assign it to the userName property. Assigning and referencing properties uses a structure-like syntax to differentiate it from regular method calls; the compiler swaps in the real Objective-C method calls when compiling the project. Enter the highlighted code from Listing 1-6.

Listing 1-6. Fetching the User Name

```
@synthesize userName;

- (void)applicationDidFinishLaunching:(NSNotification *)aNotification
{
    // Fetch the current user's name as a default value
    self.userName = NSFullUserName();
}

@end
```

Now run the application again to see the result of your changes (you can see mine in Figure 1-12). Your name is pre-filled in the text field!

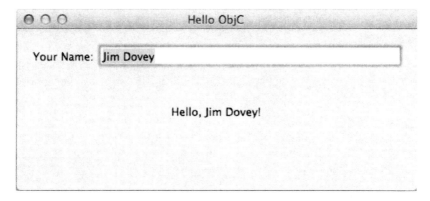

Figure 1-12. The finished application

That's the end of your whistle-stop tour through using Xcode. We will cover some parts of this process again later in the book, but from now on the focus is going to be strongly oriented towards the language itself rather than the toolset: there are other books out there that can teach you everything you need to know about Xcode and much more information is on the Internet.

Language Fundamentals

This section will provide a short recap of the core facets of the C programming language. It won't teach you everything about C or how to be a great C programmer, but it will provide enough of a basis so that you can understand the remainder of this book. You will also see how Objective-C keywords were added to the C language—specifically how to determine whether what you're looking at is pure C or Objective-C.

In the following definitions, text within square brackets "[ ]" denotes *optional* elements and text within angle brackets "< >" denotes a *required* element.

Types and Variables

The C language (and thus Objective-C) is a *statically-typed* and *imperative* language. This means that each variable must have its type declared before it can be used. The values of variables can change (this is, after all, why we call them "variable") but their types cannot.

```
double d = 4.789203;
int x = 78;
d = d + 10.0;
x = x + 5;
x = x + 8.3; // invalid-- a type error!
```

C defines a number of built-in scalar types; however, the sizes of some of these types change depending upon the system in use. Since we're targeting OS X and iOS, there is only one difference to bear in mind, that of the `long int` type.

- `int`: A 32-bit signed integer value.

- `short int` (or just `short`): A 16-bit signed integer value.

- `char`: An 8-bit signed integer value, commonly used to represent an ASCII character using single quotes (e.g., `char c = 'a';`).

- `long int` (or just `long`): On 32-bit systems (such as iOS) and smaller, it's a 32-bit signed type (the same as `int`). On 64-bit OS X, this is a 64-bit signed type.

- `long long int` (or `long long`): A 64-bit signed integer type.

- `float`: A 32-bit single-precision floating-point value.

- `double`: A 64-bit double-precision floating-point value.

- `long double`: A 128-bit double-precision floating-point value.

- `void`: No type specified. Can only be used as a return type for a function ("function returns nothing") or as the type of data referenced by a pointer.

All of the integral types above are *signed* by default, meaning that one bit of information is used to record whether they are positive or negative. Using the `unsigned` keyword prior to the type (e.g., `unsigned int`) can reclaim that bit. This will give a full *n* bits of precision, at the expense of only handling positive values.

C also provides the concepts of *structures* and *arrays*. Structures are larger types that consist of smaller types arranged in a specific order.

```
struct telephone
{
    unsigned int area_code;
    unsigned int number;
    unsigned int extension;
};
```

Arrays refer to contiguous blocks of a single type stored in sequence.

```
int n[10];
struct telephone directory[100];
```

Pointers

Pointers in C are a powerful concept. A pointer variable is a *reference* type rather than a *value*. When a value is copied, a new variable is created and set to the input value. When a reference is copied, the underlying value remains the same, and only the details of its location changes hands. A C pointer is actually a register-sized variable containing the address of another variable. As such, it is important to note that the size of a pointer variable depends upon the target CPU; on iOS a 32-bit ARM CPU is used, so pointers are 32-bits in size. Modern OS X computers, on the other hand, use 64-bit CPUs, so pointers there are 64-bits in size. The & (ampersand) operator obtains the address of a variable or other symbol, while the * (asterisk) operator fetches the value referenced by a pointer.

```
int  i = 100;    // a regular integer variable
int *p = &i;     // a pointer to i
i = 42;          // change the value of i
int x = *p;      // x is assigned 42
*p = 200;        // i is assigned 200
```

In C, a string is simply a pointer to an array of char elements. The shorthand for the declaration of a string is to enclose multiple characters within double quotes.

```
char * name = "Ernest Hemingway";
```

It is also worth noting that arrays are simply pointers with a little syntactic sugar about them, and the types are therefore interchangeable. When declaring int a[10], the type of a is actually int *. Additionally, array subscript access (i.e. a[5] = 7) works on any pointer type with the exception of void *, which just means "pointer to something".

Functions and Declarations

Functions are declared in a manner similar to variables: their type (or *return type*, the type of the variable to which the function will evaluate) comes first, followed by the name. *Parameters* (or *arguments*, if you prefer) follow the name, enclosed in parentheses. The statements that make up the function itself then follow, enclosed in a pair of curly braces (see the "Scope" section next).

```
int mean_average(int a, int b)
{
    return ( (a + b) / 2 );
}

int x = mean_average(12, 4);
```

Functions must be declared before they can be used. This means that they must be declared somewhere above the point at which they are used in any given file. In C, defining a function also has the effect of declaring it; thus the previous example is able to work. However, once a program is broken into multiple files then it is common for each implementation file (something.c in C, something.m in Objective-C) to also declare a header *file*, like something.h, to contain those declarations. When explicitly declaring something, whether a function or a variable, the content is omitted and replaced with a semicolon.

```
int mean_average(int a, int b);
int x;
```

These statements simply announce the existence, form, and name of some external symbol that can then be referenced by the compiler. The header file can then be imported into an implementation file using the #include (or in Objective-C, #import) directives.

```
#include "something.h"

int r = mean_average(12, 14);
```

The scope of declared items is by default external, meaning it can be referenced anywhere that sees its declaration.

Scope

Scope in C refers to the visibility of a symbol (such as a variable or a function). There are two ways of determining scope. Firstly, there is *file scope*; anything typed inside a file, with no other means of limiting its scope, is scoped at the file level. The second way is by using curly braces: { and }. Anything placed in between a pair of curly braces is visible only within those braces. These are used to scope the contents of functions and loops in C, and are used to enclose the contents of certain types such as structures or, in Objective-C, a class's instance variables.

In C, the keywords extern and static are the only built-in scope qualifiers.

- extern specifies that a symbol has external visibility; this provides that the symbol is accessible at runtime from outside the current compilation unit (the current file and its included headers). This is the default: omitting this qualifier will result in a symbol with external visibility.

- static specifies that a symbol is private; that is, it is only visible from within the current scope. The symbol will not be visible to the linker following the compilation of a single compilation unit.

- This means that a static symbol declared at the root scope of a file is visible to everything within that file, or within anything that includes that file. Within a function or other lexical scope enclosure such as a loop, if/ else, or suchlike, the variable is only visible within that narrower scope. For variables, the static keyword also provides that the storage for that variable is located in a predefined (by the compiler) location within memory, usually mapped directly from the output binary. As such, a static variable will exist only once in memory, even if declared within a function: a new copy will not be created on the stack, but by declaring it within a function, the scope of that variable will be limited to only that one function.

Conditions

Evaluating conditions in C is done primarily using the `if` and `else` keywords.

```
if (value == 1)
{
    // do something
}
else
{
    // error!
}
```

Note that the curly braces can be omitted when only a single statement is performed as the result of a condition test. However, it is often considered cleaner and more readable to always use curly braces, even when not absolutely required.

The C language also provides the switch statement to handle larger groups of conditions. Within a switch block, the case statement provides a value and the actions to take, the break statement leaves the switch block, and the default statement provides actions to take if no case matches the inspected variable.

```
switch ( value )
{
    // with optional braces
    case 1:
    {
        result = "yes";
        break;
    }

    case 0:
        result = "no";
        break;
    default:
        result = "maybe";
        break;
}
```

In case statements, the curly braces are almost entirely optional: they are only required if a new variable is declared within the case block. It is idiomatic to indent the contents of case blocks for clearer reading, even when omitting braces.

Note that the break keyword is always used in this example. This is because, without it, program execution would continue to the next case statement's contents as if that had matched, in what is termed *fall-through*. Consider the following example:

```
switch ( value )
{
    case 0:
        result = "no";
    case 1:
        result = "yes";
    default:
        result = "maybe";
}
```

In this code, the result would always be set to "maybe". If the value matched zero, then the result would first be set to "no", then would fall through to set it to "yes", and then again to the "maybe". By placing a break statement at the end of each case, however, the entire switch block exits after the first case has been matched.

Loops

Loops in C are implemented using the for, while, and do keywords. For-loops are used to specify the initialization, test, and step instructions for the loop internally, leaving the loop definition clean of such things. This pattern is commonly used for looping over the contents of arrays.

```
for (int i = 0; i < 10; i++)
{
    x = x + array[i];
}
```

The while and do keywords both refer to the while-loop, which has two forms. The first checks a condition at the start of each loop iteration, while the latter checks at the end. The difference is that the latter will always run through the code once and is therefore more suited to handling retries of a section of your code.

```
while ( has_more_data() )
{
    append(data, read());
}
process_data(data);

int sent_data = 0;
do
{
    sent_data = try_to_send(data);

} while (sent_data == 0);
```

Objective-C Additions

Objective-C adds only a few small items to the C language, and virtually all of them begin with the @ (ampersat) symbol. Objective-C string literals (instances of the NSString class) are declared by placing an ampersat before a regular C-string declaration: @"A string value". Similarly, NSNumber-based numbers can be created using a similar format: @42 or @812.90731 will produce NSNumber instances with the supplied integer or floating-point values.

All of Objective-C's new keywords also begin with ampersats in order to distinguish them from regular C code, where the ampersat is not a valid character with which to begin a symbol name. Examples include @try/@catch/@finally for exception support and the @class, @interface, and @implementation keywords used to define classes. The only remaining change Objective-C makes to plain C is the addition of square braces around Objective-C method calls: [someObject doSomething]. Since no valid pure-C statement can begin with an opening square brace, this allows the Objective-C compiler to easily compartmentalize and identify Objective-C method calls.

You will see these and a whole lot more in the next chapter when you dive straight into the heart of the Objective-C language itself.

Summary

In this chapter you looked at the creation of a simple Mac application in Xcode and you were introduced to the primary tools with which you'll spend your time as a Mac and/or iOS developer. You've seen how Interface Builder teams up with technologies such as bindings to provide almost code-free creation of interactive applications and you've taken a tour of the fundamental building blocks of the Objective-C language itself.

In the next chapter you will delve further into the world of Objective-C by learning the concepts of object-oriented programming and how they are applied in Objective-C itself.

Chapter 2

Object-Oriented Programming

Object-oriented programming is not new; today it's probably the most widely used programming paradigm on the planet. Its history goes back to the late 1950s and early 60s with the first use of classes and instances in the Simula 67 language. This concept was then expanded upon at Xerox PARC in the 1970s with the creation of the Smalltalk language, which introduced the term *object-oriented programming* to describe the pervasive use of objects and messages throughout the system; everything in Smalltalk was an object, even constant scalar values such as "62." Objective-C was created in the 1980s as a means to merge the object-oriented approach (and some of the syntax) of Smalltalk with the imperative programming of C.

This chapter will teach you about the fundamentals of object-oriented programming and will introduce you to the means in which the Objective-C language implements OOP. By the end of the chapter you should be familiar with all the relevant terminology and concepts necessary to work through the remainder of this book, as well as any other text on the Objective-C language.

Objects: Classes and Instances

In iterative programming languages, sequences of instructions are broken into methods to provide a form of encapsulation of those instructions. Programmers further break down collections of functions into separate files or libraries, providing interfaces via header files that other groups of methods can use. Object-oriented programming (or OOP) takes this a step further by providing a means of encapsulating data along with associated methods and giving a first-class language construct to define that encapsulation.

The reasoning behind the encapsulation of data is a fairly simple one: non-OOP programs, having no means to encapsulate data beyond explicitly passing that data around between many functions, often place some of that data at *global scope*, making it accessible from (almost) anywhere. This leads to problems as the non-OOP program grows in size, leaving the programmer to try and prevent simultaneous access to these shared resources because not doing so could easily lead to bugs with quite disastrous effects.

Encapsulation

Object-oriented programming places data within objects along with the *methods* that operate on that data. The data itself is commonly not accessible by the rest of the program, save through use of the prescribed methods themselves. Objects themselves can also be created and copied, making it a simple matter to have multiple groups of similar data in flight at any one time, reducing the likelihood of the kind of bugs that are caused by using globally-accessible data.

Each object in an OOP program is typically designed to represent a single *concept*. For example, an object could represent a window, a label, the interface to a printer, or a network data stream. Each of these concepts is defined as a *class*—literally a classification (in the linguistic sense) of a resource type. The class describes the structure and meaning of an object, specifying the data it contains and the methods it provides for interacting with that data. When a program wishes to make use of such an object, an object of a given class is then *instantiated*, meaning that it is allocated in memory and its internal state is initialized. The resulting object is then usable as a discrete entity in its own right, separate from any other instantiations of the same class of object.

In OOP, an object's data is usually considered internal to the object. An external actor can only modify an object's state by calling specific methods provided by that object, which serves a few key purposes.

- *Privacy*: It keeps private data hidden where no-one else can interfere or otherwise corrupt it.

- *Safety*: It ensures that any linked variables and common state can be appropriately kept in sync.

- *Simplicity*: By keeping all data and methods together, it enforces a strictly modular approach, resulting in greater maintainability.

Inheritance

Another important component of object-oriented programming is the concept of *inheritance*. The idea is that one class might be a specialization of another class. For instance, a circle, a rectangle, and a cube are all types of shape. Therefore, you might have a single class representing a Shape, and the classes for Circle, Rectangle, and Cube would all be *subclasses* of Shape. You can see this idea broken down in Figure 2-1.

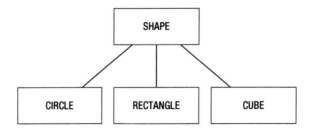

Figure 2-1. An example class hierarchy: the Shape class with Circle, Rectangle, and Cube subclasses

By subclassing Shape, the three new classes still behave in every way as if they were a Shape. Anywhere that a Shape object might be used, any instance of Circle, Rectangle or Cube will also suffice.

The subclasses can adjust the behavior of methods and interfaces provided by the Shape class. For instance, a Shape might have properties indicating the number of edges and faces it has. Each of the three subclasses would return different values for these properties, but they would be the same properties themselves. Therefore, one need only declare that a Shape has a numberOfFaces property: the Circle class and its siblings will all inherit that property because they **are** shapes, so they **also** have all the same properties and methods. The *implementation* of those methods and properties might be different (a Circle would have one edge, while a Cube would have twelve), but their availability would remain the same. This means that one can write code that deals with Shape objects and it would automatically also be able to deal with Circle, Cube, or Rectangle objects.

USEFUL TERMINOLOGY

- *Class*: An object's type. A class describes the methods and data that comprise an object.

- *Superclass/subclass*: A given class's parent or child in the class hierarchy.

- *Instance*: An object in the running application. An instance of an object of a particular class is a separate unit from the others.

- *Member*: A method or property of an object instance. A *data member* refers to data associated with a particular instance; a *member function* or *method* refers to a method that operates upon an instance.

- *Instance variable/method*: A synonym for member, it refers to data or methods that are part of an individual object instance.

- *Interface*: The list of methods and properties made available by an object for external use.

- *Implementation*: The definitions of an object's functions and data members.

- *Override*: To implement a method in a class that is present in a parent class in order to replace the superclass' implementation within instances of your class.

Another key part of the subclassing paradigm is that not only does your new class inherit the data and methods (and thus behaviors) of its superclass, but it can also replace any method by implementing it again. In some languages such as Java or C++, only methods marked using certain keywords (those two languages use the virtual keyword) can be overridden by subclasses. In Objective-C, any method can be overridden.

For instance, a Circle class might implement a Draw method, but its subclass, SkewedCircle, would re-implement Draw to behave differently. In this way, the subclass overrides the inherited behavior with its own. This is one of the most powerful aspects of object-oriented programming: entirely new and complex classes can be created simply by taking an existing class and overriding only certain small parts of its behavior.

Many popular object-oriented languages follow the Simula model, which performs a lot of work at compile-time. As a result, the code generated to call a method within an object is specific to that particular implementation. A call to Draw on a Shape is not interchangeable with a call to Draw on a Label unless the method is declared through a shared superclass.

By contrast, the Objective-C language defers as many decisions as possible from compile-time and link-time to runtime. It dynamically infers the class of an object while running, and it determines whether an object implements a given method at runtime also. This means that methods and even instance variables don't need to be set up explicitly during compilation or linking, but can be determined at runtime as they are accessed. Any object, regardless of ancestry, can implement a Draw method and it will be called just like any other object's Draw method.

This dynamism is at the heart of the Objective-C language and is known as *message passing*. You will learn all about this in the remainder of this chapter.

Objects in Objective-C

In Objective-C, as in other languages, an object associates data with the operations that make use of them. This data is known as *instance variables* in Objective-C; in other environments you might have heard them referred to as *ivars* or *member variables*, but all these terms refer to the same underlying concept. By default, Objective-C objects do not make their instance variables available for others' use; how this is specified will be covered later when we discuss *scope*.

Objective-C also provides a single data type, id (rhymes with "did"). It refers to any object type regardless of its class, and for both instances and classes themselves. It is actually implemented as a pointer to the underlying C type used as the basis for all Objective-C objects, as shown in Listing 2-1.

Listing 2-1. The Definition of id in Objective-C

```
typedef struct objc_class * Class;
struct objc_object {
    Class isa;
};
typedef struct objc_object * id;
```

In Objective-C, the default return type of an object method (i.e. that assumed by the compiler if none is explicitly given) is always id, while for regular C constructs it remains int. Additionally, Objective-C objects have an explicit "zero" value, which is defined as nil. Any method that returns an object instance can instead return nil as a zero or failure value.

Message-Passing and Dynamism

In Objective-C, the concept of a method is implemented using a system known as *message passing*. This refers to the fact that the compiler doesn't generate code that directly calls some object's method in memory; it instead passes a message to an object, and the object itself determines the actual compiled function to call. In essence, the compiler records only the name of the message being passed (in Objective-C parlance, this is called a *selector*) and generates a function call that passes this selector to the object, which will then respond if it is able. The concept of message passing was one of the core tenets of the Smalltalk language; sometimes it and Objective-C are referred to as *message-oriented* languages. Henceforth, when you read "message" you can usually consider that term interchangeable with "method."

It is worth noting that in Objective-C a class is also a type of object; the compiler creates exactly one object for each class at compile-time. By convention, class names begin with an uppercase letter, such as MyObject, while the names of instances begin with a lowercase letter, such as myObject. Class objects also have their own type, Class, and their own zero value, Nil. Note that these names also follow the capitalization convention mentioned previously.

So if you have an instance of a class called String, you can send messages to it. You can also send messages directly to the String class, rather than a particular instance. It is common in Objective-C to implement *factory methods* on classes, which return an initialized instance of that class. From the point of view of the runtime library, there is no difference between sending a message to an object instance and sending a message to a class. The only difference to you as the programmer is that each class exists only once, as itself, and is accessed through its name—in this case String—rather than through a typed variable.

Objective-C programs usually conform to some specific programming paradigms designed to assist with the encapsulation of data and logic. All of these will be explored in more detail in later chapters of this book, but for now here's a brief introduction to each of the patterns you're likely to encounter and later use when writing Objective-C code.

- *Delegation*: The Delegation pattern specifies that one logical unit (commonly an object) can pass off some decisions about its behavior to another object and this object is referred to as a *delegate*. It implements a number of methods corresponding to the decisions in which it wishes to partake.

- *Observation*: This pattern allows any interested object to receive and respond to status updates from any other part of the system. In particular, Objective-C's dynamic binding allows this to happen in a completely decoupled way: it allows for the handling of discrete events without needing to explicitly forge a connection between the observer and the source of the event.

- *Model-View-Controller*: The Objective-C UI frameworks (AppKit on the Mac, UIKit on iOS) use this pattern extensively. It provides for a separation between the management of data (the Model) and the presentation of that data (the View). In between sits the Controller and its job is to provide the bridge between the two; here is where the application's logic resides. This pattern helps prevent inter-dependencies between presentation and data code and modules, allowing for much greater re-use of those components.

- *Proxying*: Objective-C's dynamic handling of messages and types at runtime allows for the use of *proxy objects* as intermediaries. These proxies forward messages on to a "real" object internally, which the caller can't otherwise access. Proxies can be implemented in order to enforce additional interface alterations upon existing objects, such as implementing a form of synchronization over shared resources, or to provide a reference to an object present within another system (you will see this when you learn about XPC later in this book). A system API might return a proxy for an internal object that implements a restricted interface, for example.

As you can see, these patterns are particularly well suited to a language with a dynamic runtime. Common paradigms in other languages do not so often appear in Objective-C, such as the Iterator pattern used frequently in the C++ standard template library. Iterators, as an example, are of less use when the concept of "any object" is available in the language and when method calls are implemented using message-passing: the knowledge of an object's type is rarely necessary for most iteration, sorting, or enumeration operations.

Writing Objective-C

This section covers the syntax and use of Objective-C objects. There are a few parts to this, which we'll address in the following order:

- Object allocation and initialization.
- Passing messages to objects.
- The rules surrounding memory management.

Then you will learn how to define your own object classes in the following ways:

- Declaring a class's interface.
- Explicitly defining instance data.
- Implicitly defining instance data through properties.
- Declaring class and instance methods.
- Lastly, the implementation of all of this.

To start with, however, there is a simple yet important lesson to learn: in Objective-C, all objects are *pointer types*. That is, you will never refer to a String alone, you will refer to a String *. All Objective-C objects are allocated on the *heap*, never on the *stack* (there's one exception to this rule—isn't there always?—which you'll encounter later). The compiler will helpfully alert you if you declare a *statically allocated* object rather than a pointer, as shown in Listing 2-2.

Listing 2-2. Objective-C Objects Are Always Pointer Types

```
String aString;    // Semantic Issue: "Interface type cannot be statically allocated."
String *aString;   // Correct.
```

Allocation and Initialization

In Objective-C on the Mac and iOS, all objects[1] descend from the NSObject class[2]. This root class implements the basic allocation and initialization methods, which are inherited by all other

---

[1] Well, almost all; you will meet the (very few) exceptions later on.
[2] If you're using "pure" Objective-C without the major frameworks, there is an equivalent (but much older, and not really maintained) Object class defined by the runtime headers.

Objective-C objects. Among these are the +alloc and -init methods, which are used together to create new instances of a given class.

POSITIVE, NEGATIVE, OR INDIFFERENT?

You might look at the method names above and wonder just what those plus and minus signs are doing there. Is this something to do with that as-yet-nebulous "reference counting" thing about which you've heard so many horror stories? Are these hints to the compiler of some kind? An indication of a return value, perhaps?

The answer is (relatively) simple. When defining a class, not only can you create methods that are handled by *instances* of that class, but you can define methods to be handled *by the class itself*[6]. Instance methods are identified by a preceding hyphen, class methods by a preceding plus. Thus, a message described as -doSomething would be sent to an object instance, for example [nameString doSomething], while +doSomething would be sent to a class, for example [String doSomething].

The first method, +alloc, is sent to a class object to ask that it allocate a new instance of its class on the heap; this is the most common function of class objects within Objective-C. Allocation, however, is only part of the story. The +alloc method will allocate memory and fill it with zeroes, and will return the newly allocated instance. That instance then needs to be *initialized*, which is done using the -init method. A class will set up its instance variables, properties, and associated state here.

The -init method is the basic initializer; it is usually useful to include it when creating your own objects, and most (if not all) of the system objects will initialize themselves appropriately when it's called. Most classes, however, implement more specific initializers, which take parameters. These all begin with "init" to mark them as initializers but can take any other forms beyond that, so -initWithString:, -initWithOrigin:andSize: and so on are all valid examples of initializer methods.

Both +alloc and -init return id types, and the calls are typically chained together: the result of +alloc is immediately passed the -init message, and the result of that call is kept as a variable— the result of +alloc is otherwise unused. Either function may return nil if it was unable to perform its function; in the case of -init, however, the method would also deallocate the memory apportioned by +alloc. The code in Listing 2-3 illustrates the creation of a new object using the alloc/init methods and leads us nicely into the syntax of *message passing*.

Listing 2-3. Allocating and Initializing a New Object Instance

```
MyObject * obj1=[[MyObject alloc] init];
NamedObject * obj2=[[NamedObject alloc] initWithName: "aName"];
if ( obj2 == nil )
{
    // error allocating or initializing NamedObject instance
}
```

---

[3] Readers familiar with C++ or Java will know these as *static member* methods.

Sending Messages

As shown in Listing 2-3, Objective-C message-send operations are enclosed within square braces. The target of the message, the *receiver*, is placed to the left, and the *message*, interspersed with its *arguments*, is placed to the right. This is on one level similar to the system used in other object-oriented languages such as C++, Ruby, or Java, and slightly different due to the inline placement of arguments within the message name. Figure 2-2 shows how these two paradigms map to one another, with Objective-C's messaging syntax on top, and the C-style method calls below.

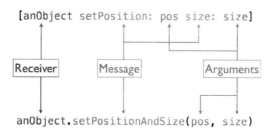

Figure 2-2. Messaging (top) vs. method-calling (bottom)

Unlike function names in C-style languages, the Objective-C message name is broken up with its arguments interspersed, each preceded by a colon character. It is important to note that no sub-parts of an Objective-C message name are optional, nor can their order be changed. While some languages implement a concept known as *named parameters* or *keyword parameters*, which might look similar, those concepts suggest that certain arguments can be reordered or omitted at runtime and that some arguments might have predefined default values. None of these characteristics apply to Objective-C messages: the placement of arguments within the message name is simply provided as a syntactic aid to the programmer where long lists of parameters might be required. Consider Listing 2-4, where similar functions are called using Objective-C and C++.

Listing 2-4. Contrasting Method Invocations

```
[myObject drawLineFromX: 100 Y: 120 toX: 140 Y: 120 weight: 2 color: redColor];
myObject.drawLine(100, 120, 140,  120, 2, redColor);
```

In the Objective-C example, the meaning of each parameter is immediately clear. Reading the C++ example, however, this isn't as clear without visiting a header file or documentation page to read up on the method's arguments.

The unusual syntax of Objective-C's messages do not preclude anything you might be used to from other languages, however: the results of functions or other messages can be placed directly inline as arguments or receivers. The latter is typified by the [[MyObject alloc] init] sequence; the former could be any result, nested to any level, as in Listing 2-5. Note that the indenting is only for formatting purposes: Objective-C, like C, effectively treats all groups of whitespace the same as a single space.

Listing 2-5. Deeply-Nested Messages

```
[myView addSubview:
    [[LabelView alloc] initWithTitle:
        [[String alloc] initWithCString: "title"]]];
```

Now, you might feel like you're trapped somewhere not unlike the setting of *Inception*, tumbling through calls within calls within calls. Well, that's actually a fairly apt analogy: the nested dreams within the movie perform in exactly the same manner as the nested methods shown previously. Within the first call, you dive into another, and then into another, and so on. Then, as the last one completes, its result is fed back into the former, which feeds its own result back up until everything has resolved.

In places like this, Objective-C's bracketed syntax actually makes things easier; each opening brace indicates the start of a new method call. When a closing brace appears, the result of that bracketed statement will appear to become part of the surrounding statement. In the previous example, there are the following steps:

1. In looking at [myView addSubview:, you see an opening brace. Dive down a level.

2. Another opening brace, followed by another, which wraps [LabelView alloc]. So that method is evaluated.

3. The result is followed by initWithTitle: and more opening braces, down another level.

4. Here you see the same construct again: you evaluate [String alloc] and the result is paired with initWithCString:"title".

5. Now you've found a closing brace: evaluate the initWithCString: call and go back up a level.

6. This is followed by another closing brace: the result is passed to -initWithTitle:.

7. The last closing brace: the result of the previous step is applied to -addSubview:, and you step up again out of the entire expression.

Memory Management

Having covered the basics of objects' creation and use, let's now look at memory management. After all, as you saw earlier, all Objective-C objects are allocated on the heap, so they must therefore be deallocated somewhere if you are not to run out of resources.

Back in the dim and distant past of the 1980s and the early 1990s, Objective-C used a memory management model quite similar to that of C: if you allocated something, you had to remember to deallocate it. And you needed to be careful about what you were given, too. Something returned an object? It needed to be deallocated using the -free message[4].

---

[4]For example, see the source for the original web browser, written in Objective-C in 1991, at www.w3.org/History/1991-WWW-NeXT/Implementation/.

This gave way to the *reference counting* method, which is still used today: each object keeps count of any references held to it. If you receive an object and you want to keep it, you *retain* that object, incrementing its reference count. When you are done with it, you *release* it, which decrements its reference count. Once that count reaches zero, it is inferred that no one is referencing the object and it is automatically deallocated using the -dealloc method.

Additionally, an object could be told to "release at some point in the (hopefully) near future" using *autorelease pools*. The idea is that somewhere on the stack (typically at the start of a thread or while responding to input events) an autorelease pool is created and pushed onto a stack. Any object can then be sent an -autorelease message, and it is assigned to that pool. When the pool object is deallocated, it simply sends a -release message to all its assigned objects. That way, any objects that are no longer used (i.e. they haven't been explicitly retained) are then deallocated.

Until fairly recently (specifically, until the release of OS X 10.7 Lion and iOS 5) this was implemented as part of the Foundation framework of Objective-C classes, primarily by NSObject and NSAutoreleasePool. Now, however, it has been made a canonical part of the language runtime itself, and its implementation has been moved into the runtime code. This allows the runtime and compiler to make much more educated decisions about the lifetime of objects, and it allows the runtime to heavily optimize the handling of reference counting and autorelease pools in general.

Today, you might see any of three different memory management techniques in use in Objective-C code.

- *Manual reference counting*: This refers to the use of -retain, -release and -autorelease messages by the programmer to manage the reference count of individual objects. This has been the standard style on iOS until iOS 5.0 and on OS X since its inception.

- *Garbage collection (GC)*: Similar to many more modern languages, Objective-C gained a garbage collector for automatic memory management with the advent of OS X 10.4. This made reference counting unnecessary, and it could be applied to any memory allocation made by any C code in the system. It also provided a very useful "zeroing weak reference" system, whereby a weak reference to an object (or any allocated memory) could be held, which would not affect any reference counts; once the object in question was deleted, all weak references would be set to zero. However, garbage collection required significant resources, and it was too resource-intensive to be deployed on the iPhone or iPad platforms. As a result, use of garbage collection on OS X is now officially deprecated in favor of the next item on the list.

- *Automatic reference counting (ARC)*: Introduced in OS X 10.7 Lion and iOS 5.0 (and available to a degree in OS X 10.6 and iOS 4), ARC moved the reference counting mechanisms into the language runtime itself and beefed up the LLVM compiler's knowledge of it (see sidebar "Compilation Complication" for more information on LLVM and other compilers on OS X). This led to a compiler that could determine exactly where objects should be retained, released, and autoreleased, meaning that this work could be inserted silently by the compiler rather than the programmer. ARC also includes the same zeroing weak reference system that was available through OS X's garbage collector. The prime difference between ARC and GC is that while GC would let objects accumulate and then clean them up after a certain interval, ARC simply inserts the relevant retain/release calls for you. As a result, there is no memory build-up, no expensive collection phase, and in fact, the compiler can seriously optimize the entire retain/release cycle.

In this book, we will be using ARC code throughout because it's more approachable for those accustomed to languages with automatic memory management and it's more idiomatic to use such code these days. Additionally, using ARC will enable us to use zeroing weak references, which makes a lot of code much more stable and error-free, especially once we get into the later chapters of this book.

Don't think that you are entirely off the hook, however! While you might not actually *type* retain and release any more, it is still going on, and it is still possible to run into problems such as the dreaded *retain cycle* (dynamic pipe-organ stab, lightning flashes, and a blood-curdling scream echoes from off-stage!). We will look at what's really going on, and how to debug any issues that might arise, in the next chapter.

COMPILATION COMPLICATION

Objective-C is a *compiled* language, meaning that your source code is converted into highly-optimized machine code. The software that performs this task is the *compiler*.

Historically, both Xcode and its predecessor, Project Builder, made use of the GNU GCC compiler (GNU Compiler Collection). Apple made many adjustments and contributions to this compiler over the years, but in 2007 a new, modern compiler system was created, called LLVM (Low Level Virtual Machine). It was originally used as part of Apple's graphics library, as it enables source code to be compiled into a highly-efficient bytecode format that can be very quickly compiled just prior to runtime into machine code for a CPU or a GPU. Apple used this to enable their graphics runtime to execute on any GPU or CPU without requiring specific manual tweaking for each target.

LLVM has other strengths, perhaps the chief of which is that its mid-compilation format retains a lot of information about the source code from which it was derived—much more than GCC or other compilers. This allows it, for example, to track exactly when variables are used and discarded and then make decisions based on their use; this is the feature that enables ARC to work. Essentially, the compiler can tell when exactly a variable is no longer used and can determine its memory characteristics so it can insert the appropriate memory management method calls automatically.

LLVM has proven to be very powerful and much easier to extend than GCC, which has its roots in 1970s compiler design. As a result, Apple has moved its compiler efforts wholeheartedly behind the LLVM project, even hiring the project's leader and main contributors to work on it full-time. Having laid the groundwork, Apple is now bringing more and more compiler-supported features into the Objective-C language as a result, such as ARC and the new object literal statements introduced in OS X 10.8 and iOS 6.0.

Class Interfaces

The first task in creating a new class of object is to define its interface. This is done using an @interface ... @end block. Instance variables can be declared within this block by placing them within curly braces immediately following the @interface keyword (as in Listing 2-6), or alternatively they can be kept "invisible" and declared instead as part of the class's implementation, as you'll see shortly.

Listing 2-6. A Class Interface

```
@interface MyObject
{
    int var1;
}

...

@end
```

If you were to actually use this class in an application, however, the compiler would issue a reasonable number of warnings. The reason for this concerns the use of a *root class* in the class hierarchy; a lot of the common methodology in Objective-C is implemented by the NSObject class. Historically (prior to OS X 10.7 and iOS 5.0), this included the entire reference-counted memory management system; now it contains many default function implementations for things like comparisons, hashing, and more. As a result, you will almost never create a class that does not have a superclass, and NSObject will be at the root of that class hierarchy in almost every situation.

A superclass is specified by placing it after your class's name, following a colon, as seen in Listing 2-7.

Listing 2-7. A Subclass of NSObject

```
@interface MyObject : NSObject
{
    int var1;
}

...

@end
```

Instance variables in object-oriented languages are usually intended to remain sealed away from use by anything but the methods defined in an object itself; Objective-C is no exception. Several scopes are provided to specify the level of access to individual variables. Each of these is specified using a single keyword, and any variables following that keyword have that scope. The options are mostly similar to those used in other popular object-oriented languages.

- ▓ @public: The following instance variables are accessible by all.

- ▓ @protected: The following variables are accessible only within the defining class and any of its subclasses. This is the default scope if none is otherwise specified.

- @private: The following variables are only accessible within the defining class. Subclasses do not inherit access.

- @package: A special case, instance variables are accessible as though in @public scope from within the same executable image (such as a framework or plug-in), but are considered @private from without. This is mostly used by Apple for tightly-coupled framework classes where instance variable access is shared but should not be exported outside that framework.

Methods

Method declarations in Objective-C are quite different from those you already know. For one thing, the only items that are parenthesized are types (the return type and the types of each argument). The arguments themselves are also interspersed within the method name in a manner similar to when passing a message (see Figure 2-3). You can see the structure of an Objective-C method declaration in Figure 2-3.

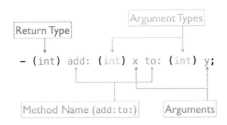

Figure 2-3. Breaking down an Objective-C method declaration

One thing to note is that the colon characters that precede each argument are part of the method name. In Figure 2-3, the method name recorded by the compiler (and used by the runtime to call it) is add:to:, not addto. You might also note that, unlike languages such as C++ that provide *function overloading*, the method name does not make note of the return type or argument types. This means that methods can be referred to in code in the most obvious and direct manner; contrast that with the intricately mangled method names generated by the C++ compiler.

The one item not explicitly called out in Figure 2-3 is the hyphen at the start of the method. This is the same hyphen you encountered earlier when learning about allocation and initialization. When defining a method, you start the line with a hyphen to denote that this is an instance method, and you use a plus to denote a class method. The layout is otherwise the same as that used in message passing; the only other additions are the parenthesized return and argument types placed before the method and argument names, as in Listing 2-8.

Listing 2-8. A Class with Both Class and Instance Methods

```
@interface MyObject : NSObject
{
    int var1;
}
```

```
// a class factory method, equivalent to [[MyObject alloc] initWithValue: value]
+ (id) objectWithValue: (int) value;

// an initializer which takes an initial value
// this is the designated initializer
- (id) initWithValue: (int) value;

// you can also call -init, which will use a starting value of zero

@end
```

Note that you don't need to explicitly declare that the object supports the +alloc or -init methods; those are inherited from the superclass, NSObject. MyObject might implement its own version of those methods, but the fact that NSObject declares them means that you don't need to duplicate that information here.

There's also a new term hiding in one of the comments in the last listing—did you see it? A *designated initializer* is the initializer that is guaranteed to be the one that does the "real" initialization of an object; in other words, all other initializers ultimately call this one. This makes it much simpler (and arguably safer) to subclass another object: rather than overriding all the superclass's initializer methods in order to cover all bases, you can implement only the designated initializer and rest easy in the knowledge that the others now call your override of that method.

Properties

In addition to explicitly defined data members and the methods that act upon them, Objective-C provides the concept of *properties*. A property refers to a piece of data that can be accessed or altered from outside the object through a specific getter/setter interface. In Objective-C, this provides for the definition of complex interactions during the fetching or setting of a property, all of which is hidden behind a very simple structure-based syntax. The idea is to distinguish the use of methods that primarily exist to adjust data from those that perform complex calculations or functions. It also allows the programmer to offload some of the work of creating getter and setter methods by letting the compiler synthesize these accessors automatically. The compiler can even synthesize the member variables used to store the properties' values, leaving the class interface clean and sparse.

Properties are declared using the @property keyword within an @interface block, alongside any method declarations. At its simplest, a property declaration looks quite like a variable declaration, as in Listing 2-9.

Listing 2-9. A Simple Property Declaration

```
@interface MyObject : NSObject

@property id anotherObject;

@end
```

Properties in Objective-C can also accept a number of qualifiers that define how they can be used. These are placed in parentheses following the @property keyword and include the following:

- *Access* (readonly, readwrite): Denotes whether a property is settable or read-only. The default is readwrite. Only one of these may be specified on a single property.

- *Thread-safety* (atomic, nonatomic): By specifying the atomic keyword (the default) all synthesized accessors for this property will be locked and synchronized for thread-safety. The nonatomic keyword disables this and is commonly used on iOS where large amounts of locking can degrade performance.

- *Storage* (assign, retain, copy, strong, weak): Scalar variable types default to the assign storage type, while objects default to using retain to increment the value's reference count (and similarly release it when the value is changed or unset). If an object value supports it, you can use copy to indicate that the object should be copied wholesale, not simply retained (useful for mutable values). The strong and weak qualifiers are new with ARC: the former denotes a strong (retained) reference to an object, while the latter is a non-retained zeroing reference. If the value is deallocated, the value of the property is automatically set to nil. Only one of these may be specified for a single property.

- *Methods* (getter=, setter=): These options allow the specification of custom message selectors for a property. By default, a property named myProperty would have a getter method named myProperty and a setter named setMyProperty:. This is most commonly used for Boolean properties: a property hidden could use isHidden and setHidden: as its methods.

Some more idiomatic property declarations can be seen in Listing 2-10.

Listing 2-10. More Idiomatic Property Declarations

```
@interface MyObject : NSObject

@property (nonatomic, assign, getter=isHidden) BOOL hidden;
@property (weak) id myParent;
@property (nonatomic, copy) String * title;

@end
```

Since property declarations carry a lot of information, the compiler can synthesize everything about them, including the accessor methods and the instance variables backing them. As a result, if a class's data members are intended to be accessible, it is common (and indeed idiomatic) to declare them using only the property syntax and let the compiler worry about the implementation details.

Protocols

An additional component of many class interfaces is the *protocol*. Protocols in Objective-C are similar in concept to interfaces in Java or .NET, but there are a few differences.

A protocol is declared in a manner similar to a new class, albeit using the `@protocol` keyword in place of `@interface`. A protocol doesn't have a superclass (or a super-protocol); instead, it can state that it *conforms to* another protocol to say effectively the same thing. The syntax for declaring conformance to a protocol is the same for both protocol and class declarations: the names of any protocols are placed in angled-braces following the class/protocol name and the name of any superclass (as shown in Listing 2-11).

Listing 2-11. Using a Protocol

```
@protocol MyProtocol<AnotherProtocol>
...
@end

@interface MyObject : NSObject<MyProtocol>
...
@end
```

A protocol declaration can include anything that can go inside a class interface with the exception of instance variables. A protocol can specify properties and any class and instance methods using the same syntax used to declare a class itself. The only additions are a pair of keywords similar to those used to provide access scope for instance variables: `@optional` and `@required`. The `@required` keyword states that any item following it **must** be implemented by any class that claims to conform to this protocol; this is the default behavior if neither `@required` nor `@optional` is specified. Conversely the `@optional` keyword states that the following items are **not** required in order to properly conform to this protocol. Optional protocol methods (also known as *informal protocols*) are often used to define interfaces for delegation where a delegate object might choose to only take part in one or two decisions without being required to implement a large number of potential delegate methods. Keeping this codified as a protocol allows the compiler to ensure that a delegate assigned to an object does indeed conform to the required protocol while still allowing flexibility in the implementation.

Formal protocols (where everything is required) are used to declare and delimit certain pieces of functionality that a class might implement. Examples include the ability to perform a full copy of an object, to serialize it in a known manner, and similar activities. In the case of the `copy` storage attribute on a property, copying is performed using the methods prescribed by the `NSCoding` protocol. As a protocol, any object can choose to implement the methods it describes, regardless its class hierarchy. The dynamic nature of Objective-C message passing means that a `-copy` method on one object is called in the same way as on any other object. The declaration and implementation of a protocol provides a way at runtime and at compile time to determine whether a given object (even when its class is unknown) does implement a known set of functionality.

Implementation

Lastly, we come to the implementation of an object's code. The definition of an object's class and instance methods is placed within an `@implementation` ... `@end` block.

Additionally, an object's instance variables can also be declared within this block in a manner similar to that used within the @interface block seen earlier. Note, however, *all* variables must be placed together in the same place. You can't put some variables in the @interface block and some in the @implementation. Listing 2-12 shows this in action.

Listing 2-12. A Sample Object Implementation

```
@implementation MyObject
{
    int aValue;
}

@synthesize value = aValue;

+ (id) objectWithValue: (int) value
{
    return ( [[self alloc] initWithValue: value] );
}

- (id) initWithValue: (int) value
{
    self = [super init];
    if ( self == nil )
        return ( nil );

    aValue = value;

    return ( self );
}

- (id) init
{
    // call through to the designated initializer
    return ( [self initWithValue: 0] );
}

@end
```

Here you can see the definitions of a class method and two initializers, as well as a few new keywords.

First is the @synthesize statement: this is the counterpart to a @property declaration in the class's interface. Following the keyword is either a comma-separated list of property names or a list of property-name/variable-name pairs. In the former case, the compiler pairs the property to an identically-named instance variable. If one has been specified already, it uses that; otherwise it will create one for you at runtime. In the latter case, an instance variable has already been declared, and the @synthesize statement simply tells the compiler to use that variable to store the property's value. These must have the exact same type or the compiler will complain. In Listing 2-12 the value property is told to use the aValue instance variable as its storage.

Most programmers prefer to explicitly name the backing variables for their properties, using @synthesize myVar = _myVar or similar. We recommend using this only when exposing an internal computation variable. When a property simply acts as a container for some value that is primarily used from the outside, we prefer to let the compiler handle it for us, using only `@synthesize myVar`. This reminds us of the use we had in mind for the property, by forcing us to use property accessor syntax to work with it.

Below this is a class method implementing a factory function. This introduces another new keyword, `self`. In an Objective-C method implementation, `self` is used to refer to the object receiving the message. This is similar in use to the `this` keyword in C++ or C# or the similarly named `self` keyword in Ruby. Its type is always that of a pointer to the correct class instance (or class object)—the compiler knows enough to provide that much context—and it can be messaged just like any object. Since this is a class method, `self` here refers to the `MyObject` class itself. This means that any messages you pass to it must also be class methods; `+alloc` is one such method and is called here. This returns a newly allocated instance, which is then sent the `-initWithValue:` message to initialize it and the result of that call is then returned.

The next method implements the object's *designated initializer*. As discussed, this is the initializer method through which all other initialization routines will funnel. Note that the concept of the designated initializer is something that is up to the programmer, not the compiler. It is part of the API contract, specifically informing subclasses that if they implement this one initializer then it is guaranteed to execute, no matter which of the superclass's initializers is actually called at runtime.

Inside the initializer is another new keyword: `super`. This keyword, like `self`, is valid only within an Objective-C method definition and is a special object receiver. It acts in a manner almost identical to `self` except that any message handling is undertaken by the current class's superclass. Therefore, by using `[super init]` here, you are in fact calling the `-init` implementation provided by the `NSObject` class, **not** the one provided here. This facility allows subclasses to defer implementation behavior up to their superclasses or, as in this case, to allow their superclasses to initialize any instance variables and other state that was inherited from them.

SELF = WHAT NOW?

You'll have noticed that the value of `self` is set to the result of the superclass's initializer method. This is a **very** important step—important enough that the compiler will complain quite vocally should you omit it. The reasoning behind this is that any object's initialization could do anything, up to and including returning a different instance than the one which received the `-init` message. This is done in some implementations of the *singleton* design pattern (more on this later in the book), but a particularly useful concrete example actually comes from the Objective-C garbage collection subsystem.

In order to speed up the performance of the collector, the allocations of some objects are performed in batches. For example, many strings are created and released all the time. The runtime therefore allocates enough memory for a few string objects at once, and upon a string becoming eligible for collection it is placed into a pool of recently used strings. Then, the next time a string is allocated, an existing, discarded one is fetched from the pool at very little cost instead of allocating memory for a new one from scratch. Strings can be complicated beasts. Are they mutable? What encoding do they have? Is this string small enough that its characters are stored inline as an array, or long enough that a separate allocation must be made to hold them all? As a result, the `+alloc` method of the string class may return memory suitable for the storage of a small string using inline storage, but the value passed to `-initWithCharacters:length:` may conceivably be quite large. Then the initializer releases the allocated instance (thereby returning it to the pool) and allocates the correct storage structure for a large string using out-of-line character data.

That might sound quite far-fetched, but it's exactly the sort of thing that happens all the time. In fact, there are quite a lot of different string classes in the Objective-C Foundation framework, all of which appear to use programmers as a single class: NSString. Creating an NSString can result in the allocation of one of a number of different private NSString subclasses, any one of which might implement any number of different optional ways to store its data. After all, strings, like arrays, are used *very, very often* and so benefit from a *lot* of very careful optimization.

Now, since -init could conceivably return nil (unlikely in this case, you might think, but you never know), the result of this is checked. If it returned nil, then you do the same, immediately, because any initializer that fails (thereby returning nil) must also deallocate itself. These days, this is enforced by the compiler as one of the benefits of ARC, so there's really *no excuse* for not handling it cleanly. Attempting to access any member variables after a call to [super init] has returned nil is going to result in an invalid memory access, and then where will you be? Nowhere good, that's where...

Once the superclass's initialization has proven successful, you can initialize your own instance variables and/or properties, and finally you return self.

The last method in Listing 2-12 shows how the basic no-parameter initialization function calls through to the designated initializer, simply passing it a default value. This pattern ensures that any subclass of MyObject can intercept all initialization by overriding that single initializer.

Summary

This chapter has been a long one—and heavy on the theory to boot. You've looked at the fundamental building blocks of object-oriented programs and how these are provided and implemented by the Objective-C language. You now know about classes and instances, variables and properties; you can both declare and implement protocols.

After a long chapter like this one, you might think to yourself, "But what can I **do** now?" The answer is that the information you've absorbed here is going to serve as the bedrock for the remainder of the book. Objective-C is nothing without its frameworks, which are extensive, flexible, and powerful. In the next chapter, you'll start working with the objects and classes with which you'll begin to implement your own applications. After that, you'll return to the language to learn the method behind the madness and to discover some of the more intricate and useful tools the language has to offer.

Chapter 3

Foundational APIs

Foundational APIs include strings, collections, class introspection, threading, and basic object persistence. Foundational APIs are defined in the Foundation library, which your application is linked against. These APIs are shared across iOS and OS X applications.

NSLog, while not strictly an API, is a part of a foundational knowledge of Objective-C. It prints a format string (discussed shortly) to the Xcode console during debug (or the system log during normal execution). It is helpful for debugging and logging purposes.

In this chapter, you will learn about the core classes provided for working with the Objective-C language. You'll see strings, arrays, sets, and more, and you will learn about threading, run loops, and data serialization and deserialization.

Strings

Strings in the Foundation library are represented as NSString objects. In code, string literals are represented by text surrounded by quotation marks and prefixed with an @ sign, as shown in Listing 3-1.

Listing 3-1. String Literals

```
NSString *aString = @"this is a string";
NSString *anotherString = @"and this is another one";
```

Non-literal string instances can be created using two methods.

- *Allocation and initialization*: Allocate memory for an instance of a string object and initialize it with one of NSString's initialization methods.

- *"Convenience" methods*: Use one of the convenience class methods of NSString to return an initialized object.

> **Note**   These two different methodologies for creating strings are common across all Foundation classes.

Each has its own small advantages and disadvantages, but the latter requires less typing and fits in better with ARC, so this chapter will mostly discuss these methods. For illustration, the two lines of code in Listing 3-2 produce identical functionality when compiling with ARC.

Listing 3-2. String Object Initialization

```
NSString *aString = [[NSString alloc] initWithString:@"some string literal"];
NSString *aString = [NSString stringWithString:@"some string literal"];
```

The only caveat to using the convenience class methods alone is that there are a few methods for creating string objects that don't have equivalent class methods, such as initWithData:encoding:.

Strings are often created using *format strings*, which will feel very familiar to any readers with experience in C or C++. Format strings are used to define a string into which the formatted values of a list of variables can be inserted, as shown in Listing 3-3.

Listing 3-3. Format Strings

```
int theValueOfPi = 3;
//produces the string "pi is exactly 3!"
NSString *aString = [NSString stringWithFormat:@"pi is exactly %d!", theValueOfPi];
```

Format specifiers are itemized in the format string and are prefixed by a percent sign. See Table 3-1 for examples.

Table 3-1. Common Format Specifiers in Objective-C

Variable Type	Format Specifier
int (32-bit)	%d
unsigned int	%u
long (32-bit or 64-bit)	%ld
unsigned long	%lu
float	%f
NSObject subclass instance	%@

> **Note**   Foundation provides a pair of customized integer types, which it favors over the use of int and long: NSInteger and NSUInteger. They have a small caveat with regards to format strings, however: in 32-bit code (such as on iOS) these are based on the int type using %d and %u, whereas in 64-bit code on OS X they are based on the long type and are specified with %ld and %lu. The compiler will alert you, however, if your format string doesn't match its arguments.

The last item in Table 3-1 is interesting: Objective-C extends the common C format specifiers with one of its own, %@. This specifier invokes the descriptionWithLocale:method (or the description method if descriptionWithLocale: is not available) of an object at runtime. This method, by default, returns a string specifying an object's type and its location in memory. However, in the case of NSString, the %@ format specifier specifies the text contents of the string object. Many other classes provide custom description implementations to provide more information about their contents; collection classes and views, for example, return a lot of useful information about the instance's state.

> **Note**   The description method is a method that any class may override. While doing so can make debugging easier, it is usually unwise to include the contents of an object's description as text to the user.

Listing 3-4 illustrates use of the object format specifier.

Listing 3-4. Object Format Specifiers

```
NSString *aString = @"criminals";
NSString *anotherString = [NSString stringWithFormat:@"When you %@ strings, only %@ will
use strings.", @"criminalize", aString];
```

Comparing strings is, as is typical with most languages, not as simple as using the equality operator. As with plain C, a function is required to correctly look at the *contents* of the string objects, rather than their addresses. In this case, you use -isEqualToString:, as shown in Listing 3-5.

Listing 3-5. Correct String Comparison

```
NSString *aString = @"hello";
NSString *anotherString = @"hello";
BOOL stringsAreEqual = ([aString isEqualToString:anotherString]);
```

> **Note**   In Objective-C, the Boolean primitive is represented by the type BOOL which can either be YES or NO (equivalent to true or false, respectively).

If you were to use the equality operator alone, you would be comparing the values of two pointer variables, not the character data within the objects they reference. Listing 3-6 would return NO.

Listing 3-6. Incorrect String Comparison

```
NSString *aString = @"hello";
NSString *anotherString = @"hello";
BOOL stringsAreEqual = (aString == anotherString);
```

Even though the text contents of the string objects are identical, stringsAreEqual is NO. This is because using the equality comparison operator compares the values of the *pointers* to the string objects; since there are two objects with two distinct pointers, the comparison fails.

The -isEqualToString: method on NSString is based upon a more generic object-comparison API defined on NSObject: -isEqual:. NSString and some other core classes provide special versions of this function to avoid the potential overhead of checking the type of the argument. This is unlikely to be a concern for your own objects, but strings, arrays, and such are used and compared so often in Objective-C applications and the core frameworks that this sort of optimization makes quite a difference.

The implementation of -isEqual: in NSObject compares an object's pointer values; other classes need to provide their own implementations to look at their internal state to implement the comparison.

> **Note** It is safe to call isEqual: on a string instance even if it is nil. This is because any messages passed to nil will return a value of nil. This return value is interpreted as the BOOL value NO. Note, however, that it is not necessarily safe to pass a nil value as the argument to -isEqual:, as the method may not check for that and attempt to access it, causing your application to crash.

Table 3-2 lists some common methods invoked on string objects.

Table 3-2. Common NSString Instance Methods

Method Name	Behavior
length	Returns an int specifying the number of characters in the string.
hasSuffix:	Returns a BOOL specifying if the receiver begins with the parameter string.
hasPrefix:	Returns a BOOL specifying if the receiver ends with the parameter string.
stringByAppendingString:	Returns a new string instance created by appending the parameter to the receiver.
stringByAppendingFormat:	Returns a new string instance created by appending the formatted string specified in the parameter to the receiver.
upperCaseString	Returns a new string instance identical to the receiver except all letters are in upper case.
intValue	Returns an int specifying integer value represented by the string.

Mutable Strings

As in many popular languages, such as Java, string objects are immutable in Objective-C. As we discuss in the remainder of this chapter, classes in the Foundation library are immutable by default and typically have mutable subclasses. This immutability is for the sake of performance.

NSMutableString is a subclass of NSString that implements several methods that allow mutation of the receiver. You can get a mutable copy of any NSString instance by calling mutableCopy on the instance.

A common use of NSMutableString is to append a new string to the existing instance. Listing 3-7 shows examples of how to do this and Listing 3-8 shows an example of how *not* to do this.

Listing 3-7. Appending to NSMutableString

```
NSString *aString = @"milk";
NSMutableString *aMutableString = [NSMutableString stringWithString:@"Remember to buy apples"];
[aMutableString appendString:@", orange juice"];
[aMutableString appendFormat:@", and of course, %@", aString];
```

It is critically important to note that the code in Listing 3-8 does not instantiate a mutable string instance.

Listing 3-8. Incorrect Instantiating of NSMutableString

```
NSMutableString *aMutableString = @"this string is not mutable at all!";
```

Looking closely at Listing 3-8, you'll notice that you have indeed defined aMutableString to be a pointer to an NSMutableString instance. However, it's a classic blunder: since NSMutableString instances are still valid NSString objects, string literals assigned to NSMutableString pointers are perfectly valid.

The code in Listing 3-8 would have compiled (albeit with a warning) but caused a runtime exception if any NSMutableString messages were passed to the aMutableString instance. These types of errors, since they are not caught at compile-time, are a common source of bugs in Objective-C code. Any experienced Objective-C developer is all too familiar with the runtime exception "unrecognized selector sent to instance." See Listing 3-9.

Listing 3-9. Instantiating NSMutableString

```
NSString *aString = @"some string";
NSMutableString *aMutableString = [someString mutableCopy];
```

Another use of the NSMutableString class is to delete strings within a certain range of characters. To accomplish this, you use the NSRange C struct (see Listing 3-10). NSRange contains two fields, a location and a length, and it is typically created with the NSMakeRange function.

Listing 3-10. Deleting Characters with a Range

```
NSMutableString *aMutableString = [NSMutableString stringWithString:@"abcdefghijk"];
NSRange range = NSMakeRange(0, 4);
[aMutableString deleteCharactersInRange:range]; //string is now "efghijk"
```

Substring substitutions can be accomplished with NSMutableString by editing the instance "in place" or by creating a new instance of NSString (which is immutable), as shown in Listing 3-11.

Listing 3-11. Replacing Characters with a Range

```
NSString *aString = @" abcdefghijk";
NSString *replacedString = [aString stringByReplacingOccurrencesOfString:@"ABC"
    withString:@"XYZ"
    options:NSCaseInsensitiveSearch
    range:NSMakeRange(0, aMutableString.length)]; //string is now "XYZefghijk"
```

```
NSMutableString *aMutableString = [NSMutableString stringWithString:@"abcdefghijk"];
[aMutableString replaceOccurrencesOfString:@"ABC"
    withString:@"XYZ"
    options: NSCaseInsensitiveSearch
    range:NSMakeRange(0, aMutableString.length)]; //string is now "XYZefghijk"
```

While the two substring replacement techniques in Listing 3-11 produce identical results, they use dramatically different methods. The first example sees a new string instance created, which is fast (due to performance enhancements afforded by immutability) but takes up additional memory. The second example is slower, editing a mutable string in place but doesn't require any additional memory.

The distinctions between immutable and mutable Foundation classes may see like pedantic nonsense, but it cuts to the heart of the classic tradeoff in computer science of speed vs. space. While the differences between NSString and NSMutableString seem inconsequential, when applied to the collections libraries, the issues surrounding the use of mutable types makes this distinction much more important.

Numbers

Like Java, C#, and many other modern programming languages, Objective-C provides a wrapping class for number primitives. Programming language frameworks provide these wrapping classes because collections libraries can typically only contain object instances, not primitives. In this regard, Objective-C is no different. It is different, however, in the way it includes all primitives in a single class: NSNumber.

NSNumber encapsulates all manner of integer, floating point, and Boolean values. Like NSString, it provides both the traditional allocate-and-initialize and convenience methods for creating instances.

The convenience methods for creating NSNumber instances follow the pattern of numberWithType:, where *Type* is whatever type of variable you're passing as a parameter. The convenience methods are as follows:

- numberWithBool:
- numerWithChar:
- numberWithDouble:
- numberWithFloat:
- numberWithInt:
- numberWithInteger:
- numberWithLong:
- numberWithLongLong:
- numberWithShort:
- and unsigned versions of the above.

> **Note**   The distinction between numberWithInt: and numberWithInteger: comes down to
> what platform the code is compiled for. numberWithInt: expects a 32-bit int primitive, while
> numberWithInteger: expects an NSInteger. NSInteger is used to describe an integer value
> irrespective of platform; on iOS and 32-bit OS X applications, it is an int and on 64-bit OS X
> applications, it is a 64-bit long.

Listing 3-12. Uses of NSNumber

```
NSNumber *aNumber = [NSNumber numberWithInt:3];
NSLog(@"I have %@ apples" aNumber);
NSLog(@"I have %d apples", [anumber intValue]);
```

Both of the NSLog statements in Listing 3-12 produce the same output.

When calling boolValue on an NSNumber instance, there are some semantics that define how
the value is interpreted. As developer familiar with C would expect, anything other than 0 is
interpreted as YES.

As discussed, passing a message to nil will return nil, which is true with any message sent to
any type of object; here the result is interpreted as NO. This means that it is safe to call boolValue
(or, in fact, any method) on a nil instance of NSNumber as long as you expect the default value to
be 0 or NO.

Numeric Object Literals

Introduced with version 4.0 of Apple's LLVM compiler (provided with Xcode version 4.4 for OS X
10.8 and iOS 6.0) is a new set of literals that evaluate to new Objective-C objects. You already saw
something like this before when you looked at NSString: the @"string" syntax is a *string object
literal*. In the case of NSString it functions similarly to plain C string literals (such as "a string") in
that the string is created once by the compiler and referenced as static data. For numeric literals,
the compiler swaps out the literal with the appropriate call to create a new NSNumber object.

For numbers, the syntax is very simple: you just place an @ symbol in front of the number and
you have an object. The compiler will figure out what type of number you're using (32-bit,
64-bit, float, double, BOOL) and will generate the appropriate method call. Note that it recognizes
numeric object literals in the exact same manner it does regular numerics: their type and size is
determined by a suffix. Table 3-3 shows a few examples.

Table 3-3. Examples of Numeric Object Literals

Literal Syntax	Equivalent Code
`@'Z'`	`[NSNumber numberWithChar: 'Z']`
`@42`	`[NSNumber numberWithInt: 42]`
`@42U`	`[NSNumber numberWithUnsignedInt: 42U]`
`@42LL`	`[NSNumber numberWithLongLong: 42LL]`
`@3.14159254F`	`[NSNumber numberWithFloat: 3.14159254F]`
`@3.1415926535`	`[NSNumber numberWithDouble: 3.1415926535]`
`@YES`	`[NSNumber numberWithBool: YES]`

> **Note**   If you want to check for the availability of numeric literal support at compile-time, you can use the `__has_feature(objc_bool)` preprocessor macro to determine this.

Data Objects

The Foundation framework provides a class to interact with raw byte data (instead of using a C array bytes). The class is called NSData and it contains two important instance methods: bytes, a void* pointer to the binary data encapsulated by the data object, and length, the length of that data. Typically, you don't interact directly with these methods.

NSData is useful for loading contents of files and URLs (over a network) and parsing later. It can also be used to persist binary data to files stored in the filesystem.

Listing 3-13. Example of NSData and the Filesystem

```
NSData *data = [NSData dataWithContentsOfFile:@"/path/to/some/file"];
[data writeToFile:@"/path/to/some/other/file" atomically:YES];
```

The code in Listing 3-13 loads data bytes from one location and write them to a new location. There are other, more advanced methods for reading and writing data to and from files and URLs.

NSData is immutable, like NSString, NSArray, and the others discussed in this chapter. Like the other classes, it has a subclass that allows developers to change the contents of those classes. NSMutableData is useful for receiving chunks of data from a network request. It is possible to use the appendData: method to append newly received bytes to the existing data before finishing and using the data in its entirety for some purpose, such as decompressing a JPEG or decoding a large block of text. While the use of NSURLConnection is beyond the scope of this chapter, the code in Listing 3-14 should illustrate the use of NSMutableData.

Listing 3-14. NSData and the Filesystem

```
NSData *downloadMutableData;
NSURLConnection *activeURLConnection;
```

```
-(void)startDownload
{
    downloadMutableData = [NSMutableData dataWithLength:0];
    NSURLRequest *request = [NSURLRequest requestWithURL:[NSURL URLWithString:@"http://path/to/
some/block/of/text]];
    activeURLConnection = [NSURLConnection connectionWithRequest:request delegate:self];
    [activeURLConnection start];
}

- (void)connection:(NSURLConnection *)connection didReceiveData:(NSData *)data
{
    [activePurchaseDownloadData appendData:data];
}

- (void)connectionDidFinishLoading:(NSURLConnection *)connection
{
    NSString *downloadedString = [[NSString alloc] initWithData:downloadMutableData
encoding:NSUTF8StringEncoding];
    NSLog(@"downloaded string: %@", downloadedString);
}
```

Collections

The Foundation framework provides a comprehensive set of collection classes: arrays, sets, dictionaries, and mutable versions of each.

> **Note** Memory management and ARC are discussed in the following chapter. However, it is important to note that collections classes maintain a strong reference to the objects they contain. In other words, if you put an object in an array, you can be sure that it will still be there when you come back for it and that it will continue to take up memory at least until the array is deallocated.

Arrays

Arrays are used to hold a list of objects in a fixed order. This list of objects may contain repeated objects (that is, an individual instance of an object can appear several times in an array).

The array class in Foundation is NSArray and, like NSString and NSNumber, you can create instances of this class using both allocate-and-initialize and convenience class methods (see Table 3-4).

Table 3-4. Equivalent Array Creation Methods

Initialization Method	Class Method
init	arrayWithObject:
initWithObjects:...	arrayWithObjects:...
initWithArray:	arrayWithArray:
initWithArray:copyItems:	

The "..." in some of the table items denotes a variable argument list. This is a variable-length, nil-terminated list of comma-separated values you can pass to the method.

Listing 3-15. Examples of NSArray Creation

```
NSArray *emptyArray = [NSArray array];
NSArray *shoppingList = [NSArray arrayWithObjects:@"apples", @"bananas", @"milk", nil];
NSArray *anotherShoppingList = [[NSArray alloc] initWithObjects:@"apples", @"bananas",
@"milk", nil];
NSArray *yetAnotherShoppingList = [NSArray arrayWithArray:anotherShoppingList];
```

> **Note** Variable-length lists must be terminated with nil, as demonstrated in Listing 3-15. If you forget to end your list with nil, a compiler warning is generated and you will likely receive a runtime exception that will crash your application.

The method arrayWithObject: seems rather odd until you start using some of the other Cocoa (or Cocoa Touch) frameworks that expect an array of objects as parameters. This method is a convenience method to create an array with only one object. The class method array can be used to create an empty array, though this is far less common.

The initialization method initWithArray:copyItems: has a second parameter, a BOOL. If YES is passed in, a deep copy is made of the items in the first parameter array. Each object in the first array has a special -copy method invoked to create a second copy of it to be placed in the second array. Note that this method is not provided for you; you need to adopt the NSCopying protocol and implement -copy or -copyWithZone: to implement it. Typically, you won't require this behavior and either passing NO as the second parameter, or calling initWithArray: or arrayWithArray:, will be sufficient.

> **Note** Objects contained within an NSArray, and in fact all Foundation collection classes, must be objects and not primitives. This includes nil. If you try to use nil as an object to an array, a runtime exception is generated. If necessary, use the singleton NSNull to represent nil values in collections.

In the latest version of Xcode, immutable arrays can also be created using a new form of literal syntax. The code in Listing 3-16 shows the creation of an immutable NSArray containing three objects.

Listing 3-16. Array Literal Syntax

```
NSArray * array = @[ @"Hello", NSApp, [NSNumber numberWithInt: 3] ];
```

Classically, arrays are only a place to store and access objects. In this regard, NSArray is more than adequate. The method count returns an unsigned NSInteger (an NSUInteger) that specifies the number of objects contained within the array. Similarly, objectAtIndex: accepts as a parameter an NSUInteger representing the index of an object in the array, which is returned. This method returns an object of type id. Naturally, if you try to access an object at an index that does not exist, a runtime exception is generated.

The return value of objectAtIndex: has an interesting implication: an array can be a heterogeneous list. Unlike Java, C++, or C#, Objective-C does not include a strict templating system because the collections libraries can contain any type of object. An array instance typically only holds one type of object, but the code in Listing 3-17 is perfectly valid.

Listing 3-17. Heterogeneous Arrays

```
NSArray *array = [NSArray arrayWithObjects:@"a string", [NSNumber numberWithBool:YES], nil];
```

New in OS X 10.8 and iOS 6.0 with the latest LLVM compiler is a collection subscription syntax. This provides a much simpler (and arguably more readable) way of accessing an array's contents, shown in Listing 3-18.

Listing 3-18. Array Subscripting

```
NSString * str = myArray[3];
```

> **Note**   We said "OS X 10.8 and iOS 6.0" rather than just "with the latest compiler," as for numeric object literals. The reason for this is that array subscripts evaluate not to a call to -objectAtIndex:, but to a new method called -objectAtSubscriptedIndex:. This is only implemented on NSArray in the new operating systems, hence the requirement. You can check for the existence of this method at runtime using -respondsToSelector: or [NSArray instancesRespondToSelector:].

If NSArray only provided functions to store and access a list of objects, we would stop here. Fortunately, the Foundation collection libraries are rich with functionality.

You can create an array by appending an object, or objects, to an existing array, as shown in Listing 3-19.

Listing 3-19. Appending to Existing Arrays

```
NSArray *myNewArray = [myOldArray arrayByAddingObject:myObject];
NSArray *myOtherNewArray = [myOldArray arrayByAppendingObjectsFromArray:myOtherOldArray];
```

It's important to reiterate that these new ways to create arrays don't copy the objects they contain; the new array points to the same objects in memory as the first array does.

Displaying the contents of an array to users can be accomplished using the method componentsJoinedByString:.

Listing 3-20. Formatting an Array's Contents

```
NSArray *array = [NSArray arrayWithObjects:@"apples", @"bananas", @"milk", nil];
textField.text = [array componentsJoinedByString:@", "];
```

The code in Listing 3-20 generates the string "apples, bananas, milk" to appear in the text field.

If you want to test for inclusion of an object in an array, the typical approach is to iterate over the array contents until either you reach the end (not found) or the object is located. In NSArray (as well as NSSet), there is a convenience method called containsObject:. This method iterates over the contents of the array and passes isEqual: to each object until the message returns YES.

Listing 3-21. Testing for Inclusion within an Array

```
NSArray *array = [NSArray arrayWithObjects:@"apples", @"bananas", @"milk", nil];
if ([array containsObject:@"apples"])
    NSLog(@"found it!");
```

In Listing 3-21, even though the string object in the array and the string literal passed to containsObject: are different pointers, the method still works as expected. The containsObject: method uses isEquals: instead of pointer comparison.

Testing for inclusion may not be enough; maybe you want to access the specific object in the array. In this case, you can use the indexOfObject: method. This method returns the index of the first occurrence of the object in the array (since, remember, you can have duplicates objects in the array) or the constant NSNotFound if the object isn't present.

Say you have an array with mutable strings and you want to change the occurrence of one of the objects. You can implement the code shown in Listing 3-22.

Listing 3-22. Example of indexOfObject:

```
NSArray *array = [NSArray arrayWithObjects:[NSMutableArray arrayWithObject:@"apples"], ...,
nil];
NSUInteger index = [array indexOfObject:@"apples"];
if (index != NSNotFound)
    [[array objectAtIndex:index] insertString:@"green" atIndex:0];
```

This code changes the mutable string containing the text "apples" to "green apples".

Of course, testing for inclusion takes linear time with respect to the length of the array. Most of the time, this won't matter, but if you're looking at an array with, say, 10,000 objects, it may be wise to defer the search to a background thread (discussed shortly).

Sometimes it is useful to access the last index of an array. Typically, you find the length of the array, subtract one, and access the object at the resulting index. NSArray has a convenience method called -lastObject that performs this mundane operation. Additionally, the -lastObject method can be called even on an empty array: it simply returns nil. This is in contrast to -objectAtIndex:, which throws a range exception in that case.

Finally, the Objective-C language defines a method for fast enumeration of an array.

Listing 3-23. Enumerating the Contents of an NSArray

```
NSArray *array = [NSArray arrayWithObjects:@"apples", @"bananas", @"milk", nil];
for (NSString *item in array)
```

```
{
    NSLog(@"%@", item);
}

for (NSInteger i = 0; i < [array count]; i++)
{
    NSLog(@"%@", [array objectAtIndex:i]);
}
```

The two loops in Listing 3-23 perform identical operations.

Mutable Arrays

Mutable arrays can be created by typical allocate-and-initialize or convenience class methods. Additionally, a mutable copy of an existing NSArray instance can be created with the mutableCopy message.

> **Note**   The mutability of an array only refers to the references that array holds to other objects. Properties of the objects in an immutable NSArray instance can change, though the list of specific objects held in the array cannot.

It is possible to add or remove objects from an NSMutableArray using a few different instance methods. Adding an object to the end of a mutable array is accomplished with the addObject: method; the removeLastObject method removes the object at the end of the array.

Any attempt to remove the last object from an empty array will raise a runtime exception. The convenience methods for adding and removing objects from a mutable array make implementing a stack almost trivially easy, as shown in Listing 3-24.

Listing 3-24. Simple Stack Implementation

```
@interface Stack : NSObject
{
    NSArray *theStackArray;
}
@end

@implementation Stack

-(void)push:(id)theObject
{
    [theStackArray addObject:theObject];
}

-(id)pop
{
    if ([theStackArray count] == 0)
        return nil;
    id lastObject = [theStackArray lastObject];
```

```
    [theStackArray removeLastObject];
    return lastObject;
}
```

@end

Removing and inserting objects at specific index is achieved using the insertObject:atIndex: and removeObjectAtIndex: methods, respectively. Naturally, any attempt to remove an object from an index that does not exist or to insert an object at an index that does not existing within the bounds of the array will raise a runtime exception. With these new methods, implementing a queue is only slightly different from implementing the stack. Listing 3-25 shows one way to do this.

Listing 3-25. Simple Queue Implementation

```
@interface Queue : NSObject
{
    NSArray *theQueueArray;
}
@end

@implementation Queue

-(void)enqueue:(id)theObject
{
    [theQueueArray addObject:theObject];
}

-(id)dequeue
{
    if ([theQueueArray count] == 0)
        return nil;
    id firstObject = [theQueueArray objectAtIndex:0];
    [theQueueArray removeObjectAtIndex:0];
    return lastObject;
}
```

@end

If you ever want to remove all objects from a mutable array, use removeAllObjects.

The final method for changing the contents of a mutable array is the replaceObjectAtIndex:withObject:. As you should expect, replacing an object at an index that doesn't exist within the array will raise a runtime exception.

Since there is a performance hit for using mutable arrays compared to their immutable superclass, you should only use mutable arrays when the contents change often. As an alternative to using mutable arrays, you can create a new, immutable array with any changes you need. The instance methods arrayByAddingObject: and arrayByAddingObjectsFromArray: can be used to create new arrays with expanded contents.

The final use of mutating arrays is sorting, a common practice in software development. NSArray provides methods for returning sorted versions of existing arrays while NSMutableArray provides methods for sorting existing arrays in place.

Listing 3-26. Examples of Sorting Arrays

```
NSArray *array = [NSArray arrayWithObjects:@"cat", @"bat", @"antelope", @"dog", nil];
NSArray *sortedArray = [array sortedArrayUsingSelector:@selector(compare:)];

NSArray *mutableArray = [array mutableCopy];
[mutable sortUsingSelector:@selector(compare:)];
```

By the end of Listing 3-26, both `mutableArray` and `sortedArray` contain the strings "antelope", "bat", "cat", and "dog", in that order. The difference is that `mutableArray` has been sorted in place while the `sortedArray` is a new array object that is pointing to the existing string objects.

These two sorting methods require a selector parameter. Selectors behave similarly to function pointers; the selector is a method passed to objects in the array to determine their order. The selector, in this case, must return an `NSComparisonResult`, a C enumeration. The `compare:` method of `NSString` returns `NSOrderedAscending`, `NSOrderedSame`, or `NSOrderedDescending` depending on the result of comparing the receiver to the parameter.

Sets

At a high level, sets are similar to arrays in that they contain a list of objects. However, sets have no implicit ordering and cannot contain duplicate references to the same object instance.

If sets impose these restrictions on their composition and limitations of their use, it's natural to wonder why they are included in the Foundational APIs.

Sets offer constant-time testing for inclusion, which is *far* faster than the linear-time testing for arrays. This is one of the biggest reasons to choose to use sets over arrays. In other words, the time it takes to test for inclusion in an array grows in a linear fashion as the size of the array grows; testing for inclusion in a set always takes the same amount of time.

To use a set from the Foundation framework, use the `NSSet` class. Creating sets is accomplished using methods similar to `NSArray` creation, as shown in Table 3-5.

Table 3-5. Equivalent Set Creation Methods

Initialization Method	Class Method
init	Set
N/A	setWithObject:
initWithObjects:...	setWithObjects:...
initWithSet:	setWithSet:
initWithSet:copyItems:	
initWithArray:	setWithArray:

As with arrays, initialization methods offer no real benefit when compiling with ARC, so using the class convenience methods is recommended. Additionally, as with arrays, `initWithSet:copyItems:` can be used to perform a deep copy of the items contained within the first parameter, but is typically not necessary.

Testing for inclusion of an object in a set looks similar to testing for inclusion in an array. There are two methods: one returns a BOOL indicating whether or not an object is in a set, and the other returns the object itself. It is a fine distinction, but important. The two methods are containsObject: and member:.

Listing 3-27. Testing for Inclusion in Sets

```
NSSet *set = [NSSet setWithObjects:@"apples", @"milk", @"bananas"];
NSString *string = @"apples";
if ([set containsObject:string])
    NSLog(@"This is printed because the set contains an object that matches the parameter
string");
NSString *stringContainedInSet = [set member:string];
```

After the code in Listing 2-27 has finished executing, stringContainedInSet points to the actual instance contained in the set.

If you need any object contained within a set, use the anyObject method; it will return an object within the receiver.

Since you cannot access specific objects in a set based on their index (they have no index), enumerating over a set directly using a for loop is impossible. Instead, call allObjects on an NSSet instance to generate an NSArray containing the same objects that are in the set. The order of the objects in the array is undefined; do not rely on a specific order.

Listing 3-28. Testing for Inclusion in Sets

```
NSSet *set = [NSSet setWithObjects:@"apples", @"milk", @"bananas"];
NSArray *array = [set allObjects];
for (NSString *string in array)
{
    NSLog(@"%@", string);
}
```

The code in Listing 3-28 prints out the words "apple", "milk", and "bananas" in some order to the console log.

It's possible to test for more than just inclusion of a particular object in a set. The methods intersectsSet:, isEqualToSet:, and isSubsetOfSet: allow you to test if a receiving set intersects with, is equal to, or is a subset of another set, respectively.

Mutable Sets

Mutable sets are to set as mutable arrays are to arrays. The mutable set object in the Foundation framework is NSMutableSet and it extends NSSet. The two most simple methods provided by NSMutableSet are addObject: and removeObject:. By now, you should expect that any attempt to remove an object that does not exist in a mutable set generates a runtime exception (luckily, testing for inclusion in a set is a performed in constant-time, so you have no excuse not to check first!).

If you want to add more than one object to a set at a time, use the addObjectsFromArray: method.

Remember that sets do not allow duplicate object references, so any objects that were already in the set and are added to a mutable set will still only appear once in the set.

Developers with a background in mathematics may find sets interesting; sets in the Foundation framework behave similarly to sets in mathematics. This brings us to the final methods for changing the contents of a mutable set, shown in Table 3-6.

Table 3-6. Mutable Set Methods

Set Operation	Instance Method
Intersection of two sets	`insertsectSet:`
Difference of two sets	`minusSet:`
Union of two sets	`unionSet:`

Listing 3-29 demonstrates the power of mutable sets; while sets are not found in many APIs, they are an efficient and useful data structure to keep in your Objective-C toolbox.

Listing 3-29. Mutable Sets

```
NSMutableSet *mutableSet = [NSMutableSet setWithObjects:@"apple", @"bananas", @"milk", nil];
[mutableSet intersectSet:[NSSet setWithObject:@"apple"]];
    //mutableSet contains only @"apple" now

[mutableSet unionSet:[NSSet setWithObjects:@"bread", @"jam", @"apple", nil];
    //mutableSet now contains @"apple", @"bread", and @"jam"

[mutableSet minusSet:[NSSet setWithObject:@"bread"]];
    // mutableSet now contains @"apple" and @"jam"

[mutableSet minusSet:[NSSet setWithObject:@"pasta"]];
    // mutableSet is unchanged; it still contains @"apple" and @"jam"
```

Dictionaries

The final member of the collections library in Foundation is `NSDictionary`. A dictionary is a list of key-value pairs. Keys are typically `NSString` instances and the values are `id`. Dictionaries are often used to pass a variable number of optional parameters to an API, such as Core Text. They are also used heavily with `NSNotification` and `NSError`.

Keys within a dictionary must be unique. Creating a dictionary with two identical keys will cause a runtime error.

Creating a dictionary is possible with both the allocate-and-initialize and convenience class methods. Table 3-7 details the common dictionary creation methods, although this is not a complete list.

Table 3-7. *Equivalent Dictionary Creation Methods*

Initialization Method	Class Method
init	dictionary
initWithObject:forKey:	dictionaryWithObject:forKey:
initWithObjects:forKeys:	dictionaryWithObjects:forKeys:

The class methods provide better readability and operate identically when compiled under ARC and will be used in this section.

The final method, `dictionaryWithObjects:forKeys:` accepts two parameters, both NSArray instances. The two arrays must have the same count; a runtime exception will be raised if this is not the case. The first object in the first parameter is the object that corresponds to the first object in the second array, and so on for each element in each array.

The count method returns an integer corresponding to the number of key-value pairs in the dictionary. You can access an object for a specific key by invoking the `objectForKey:` method. If the key specified is not contained in the dictionary, the value nil is returned.

`objectForKey:` looks for keys based on an object's hash value. It isn't important to understand the mechanics of dictionary lookup except that the lookup *does not* rely on pointer comparison. Notice in Listing 3-30 that dictionary lookups are performed with *different* string instances that contain the *same* text. Two equivalent NSString instances have the same hash value, so the lookup is successful.

Listing 3-30. *Using Dictionaries*

```
NSArray *keys = [NSArray arrayWithObjects:@"name", @"identificationNumber", nil];
NSArray *values = [NSArray arrayWithObjects:@"Bob", [NSNumber numberWithInt:123], nil];
NSMutableSet *dictionary = [NSDictionary dictionaryWithObjects:values forKeys:keys];

NSLog(@"dictionary count: %d", [dictionary count]); //prints the count as 2
NSLog(@"object for name key: %@", [dictionary objectForKey:@"name"]); //prints Bob
NSLog(@"object for birthday key: %@", [dictionary objectForKey:@"birthday"]); // prints nil
```

You can extract independent lists of the key and values in a dictionary with the allKeys and allValues methods. Since the only access method is objectForKey: and not keyForObject:, it is uncommon to use allValues.

The most common reason to use the allKeys method is to enumerate over the contents of the dictionary, demonstrated in Listing 3-31.

Listing 3-31. *Enumerating over a Dictionary*

```
NSArray *keys = [NSArray arrayWithObjects:@"name", @"identificationNumber", nil];
NSArray *values = [NSArray arrayWithObjects:@"Bob", [NSNumber numberWithInt:123], nil];
NSMutableSet *dictionary = [NSDictionary dictionaryWithObjects:values forKeys:keys];

for (NSString *key in [dictionary allKeys])
{
    NSLog(@"%@ => %@", key, [dictionary objectForKey:key]);
}
```

The code in Listing 3-31 prints each key-value pair in the dictionary. The *order* of the keys is undefined, so do not rely on the order in your code.

Similar to the NSArray examples earlier, the latest OS and LLVM compiler provides literal expression support for dictionaries, too. Listing 3-32 shows an alternative means of creating an NSDictionary.

Listing 3-32. A Dictionary Literal

```
NSDictionary *dictionary = @{
    @"name" : NSUserName(),
    @"date" : [NSDate date],
    @"processInfo" : [NSProcessInfo processInfo]
};
```

As with the NSArray example, this dictionary creation syntax evaluates to a standard creation method call, which is available on any OS version. The dictionary subscripting syntax, however, again requires a custom method similar to that on NSArray: -objectForKeyedSubscript:. This method is only implemented in OS X 10.8 and iOS 6.0, so dictionary subscript access requires those operating system versions. An example can be seen in Listing 3-33.

Listing 3-33. Dictionary Subscripting Syntax

```
id key = ...;
id value = object[key];
```

Mutable Dictionaries

The NSMutableDictionary class, which extends the NSDictionary class, offers methods to add, replace, and remove key-value pairs in the dictionary.

To remove an object for a specific key, use the removeObjectForKey: method. To add or replace an object in a mutable dictionary, use the setObject:forKey: method. If there was previously a different object associated with an equivalent key, then the old object is replaced with the new one. Otherwise, the new object is added to the mutable dictionary.

Similar to NSMutableSet and NSMutableArray, you can remove all objects in a mutable dictionary with removeAllObjects. To remove specific key-value pairs, use the removeObjectsForKeys: method, which accepts an array as a parameter of keys to remove.

Finally, it is possible to add the key-value pairs from another dictionary with addEntriesFromDictionary:.

Rolling Your Own

There is a from-scratch implementation of an array object with full source available at www. apress.com. This section highlights some features of the APSortingArray implementation, including fast enumeration, copying, mutable copying, and subscripted indexing.

Recall that fast enumeration is a language construct for enumerating each object in an array. The NSFastEnumeration protocol is defined in Listing 3-34.

Listing 3-34. NSFastEnumeration Protocol

```
typedef struct {
    unsigned long state;
    id __unsafe_unretained *itemsPtr;
    unsigned long *mutationsPtr;
    unsigned long extra[5];
} NSFastEnumerationState;

@protocol NSFastEnumeration
- (NSUInteger)countByEnumeratingWithState:(NSFastEnumerationState *)state objects:
(id __unsafe_unretained [])buffer count:(NSUInteger)len;
@end
```

Implementing NSFastEnumeration in your APSortingArray involves implementing the method in Listing 3-35.

Listing 3-35. Fast Enumeration

```
- (NSUInteger) countByEnumeratingWithState: (NSFastEnumerationState *) state objects:
(__unsafe_unretained id []) buffer count: (NSUInteger) len
{
    NSUInteger count = 0;

    if ( state->state == 0 )
    {
        // first time into here-- let's fill out the basics
        state->mutationsPtr = &_mutationCounter;
        state->state = 0;
    }

    if ( state->state < _length )
    {
        // still some items to return
        for ( NSUInteger i = state->state, j = 0, max = MIN(len, _length-i); i < max;
i++, count++ )
        {
            buffer[j] = _array[i];
        }
    }

    return ( count );
}
```

This method is used to store pointers to objects in the buffer C array. The count of the number of items stored in that array is returned. Using this method, the Foundation library does not need to be aware of the internal working of APSortingArray to provide fast enumeration. You are only responsible for placing objects in the buffer.

NSCopying is a protocol that defines behavior of copying objects. Copying occurs when copy is called on an object. The system will invoke this during deep copies of objects in an array during certain set and array initialization methods. In these cases, copying references to objects is not enough; the objects themselves (and the data they encapsulate) need to be copied. Let's think about why you might want to do this.

If you have a property in a class, you want to be sure that after your property is set, the values defined in the object stored in your property can't be modified. To illustrate, consider the code in Listing 3-36.

Listing 3-36. Use of Copy Properties

```
@interface Employee : NSObject
@property (nonatomic, strong) NSString *employeeName;
@end
```

. . .

```
Employee *employee = ...;//some employee object
NSMutableString *mutableName = [@"James Dovey" mutableCopy];
employee.employeeName = mutableName;
[mutableName setString:@"Ash Furrow"]; //employeeName is now "Ash Furrow"
```

This code demonstrates how setting properties with mutable subclasses can be a problematic source of bugs and security holes. Instead, if you had defined employeeName as a copy parameter, the string would have been copied on assignment and its contents would not be accessible to outside methods.

NSMutableCopying is a similar protocol that returns a mutable copy of the receiver. It is useful for quick access to mutable copies of existing classes. The APSortedArray conforms to both of these protocols.

Listing 3-37. Use of Copy Properties

```
-(id) copyWithZone: (NSZone *) zone
{
    // immutable objects just return a new reference to themselves (retained automatically by ARC)
    return ( self );
}


- (id) mutableCopyWithZone: (NSZone *) zone
{
    // allocate and initialize a mutable variant
    // we know that our object array is sorted, so we can short-circuit it a bit
    APMutableSortingArray * mutable = [[APMutableSortingArray alloc] initWithCapacity:
_capacity];
    mutable->_length = _length;
    mutable->_array = (__strong id *)malloc(_capacity*sizeof(id));
    for ( NSUInteger i = 0; i < _length; i++ )
    {
        mutable->_array[i] = _array[i];
    }
    mutable->_comparator = _comparator;
    mutable->_selector = _selector;
    mutable->_sortFunction = _sortFunction;
    return ( mutable );
}
```

Listing 3-37 demonstrates that, for immutable types, simply returning self is sufficient. Mutable instances, however, require a more complex implementation. First, you allocate and initialize a new, mutable instance. Afterwards, you perform a shallow copy of the contents of your array (that is, you don't call copy on each object, since those objects may not conform to the NSCopying protocol) and set up the new instance to reflect your own internal state.

As previously noted, the LLVM 4.0 and clang 3.1 compilers introduced a new Objective-C language feature that permits C-style subscript syntax for access elements of arrays, available on OS X 10.8 and iOS 6.0. It's possible to provide access to your APSortedArray using this syntax by implementing the methods detailed in Listing 3-38.

Listing 3-38. Implementing Subscripted Array Access

```
- (id) objectAtIndexedSubscript: (NSInteger) index
{
    if ( index > _length )
        [NSException raise: NSRangeException format: @"Index %lu is outside bounds %@.",
(unsigned long)index, NSStringFromRange(NSMakeRange(0, _length))];

    __block id result = nil;
    dispatch_sync(_q, ^{
        result = _array[index];
    });
    return ( result );
}
```

The code in Listing 3-38 uses blocks to avoid concurrency issues. The functionality of the C-style subscript notation is provided by invoking this method at runtime.

Reflection and Type Introspection

Objective-C has a dynamic runtime; object instances can be inspected at runtime. This is particularly helpful if you have a heterogeneous collections instance where the collection contains different object types. Passing a message to an instance that can't respond to it will raise a runtime exception that will likely crash your application.

Every NSObject subclass instance returns a Class object that defines what kind of class it is. Additionally, the class itself defines a class method (which can be called on the class itself and not on an instance). Given these two tools you can inspect instances and make a determination of different code to execute depending on their type, as demonstrated in Listing 3-39.

Listing 3-39. Type Introspection

```
NSString *string = @"I am a string";
NSNumber *number = [NSNumber numberWithInt:4];
NSArray *array = [NSArray arrayWithObjects:string, number, nil];
for (id object in array)
{
    if ([object isKindOfClass:[NSString class]])
        NSLog(@"%@ is a string", object);
    else if ([object isKindOfClass:[NSNumber class]])
        NSLog(@"%@ is a number", object);
}
```

The isKindOfClass: method also respects class hierarchies. Observe the relationship between NSMutableString and NSString in Listing 3-40.

Listing 3-40. Example Type Introspection with Subclasses

```
NSMutableString *mutableString = [NSMutableString stringWithString:@"I am a string"];
if ([mutableString isKindOfClass:[NSString class]])
    NSLog(@"mutableString is a string");
```

The log statement confirms that invoking isKindOfClass: with a superclass' Class object as a parameter still returns YES.

In addition to testing whether or not an instance happens to be an instance of a particular class, you can test for the ability to respond to selectors.

Listing 3-41. Reflection with Selectors

```
NSArray *array = ... //some array of objects
for (id object in array)
{
    if ([object responseToSelector:@selector(mySelector)])
        NSLog(@"object %@ responds to mySelector");
    if ([object responseToSelector:@selector(mySelector:)])
        NSLog(@"object %@ responds to mySelector:");
}
```

In Listing 3-41, note that the second if statement uses a selector with a colon at the end of the selector name. This indicates a selector that accepts a single parameter and makes this selector distinct from the first. Omitting colons from the end of selector names in this fashion is a common mistake when writing Objective-C code because there is no compile-time check. This is an important distinction, so we'll state it again for clarity.

> **Note**   Objective-C message selectors *include the colons.* This means that getData and getData: are two distinct selectors.

A selector can also be invoked directly on an object, as demonstrated in Listing 3-42.

Listing 3-42. Invoking a Selector Programmatically

```
id object = @"this is a string";
NSUInteger length = (NSUInteger)[object performSelector:@selector(length)];
NSLog(@"length is %d", length); //prints that the length is 16
```

Beyond these basics, you're playing with fire. Adding and removing methods to objects at runtime can be dangerous, but sometimes useful. If possible, use an Objective-C category or class extension instead.

> **Note**   If you choose to use ARC in your project, you will see compiler warnings for every use of
> -performSelector: as the compiler doesn't know the reference-counting characteristics of the API
> you're calling at this point. The best solution to this warning we've found is to use NSInvocation to
> implement the method call instead.

Listing 3-43 provides an example of how to add a method to the NSObject class.

Listing 3-43. Adding an Instance Method at Runtime

```
#import <objc/runtime.h>

id myNewMethod (id self, SEL _cmd)
{
    NSLog(@"I was added at runtime!");
}

void installMyMethod(void)
{
    IMP implementation = (IMP)myNewMethod;
    SEL selector = sel_registerName("myNewMethod");
    // We need a string defining the return and argument types for the method
    // Let's copy one from another (void) -noArgs method somewhere.
    Method from = class_getInstanceMethod([NSObject class], @selector(dealloc));
    const char *types = method_getTypeEncoding(from);

    // add the new method
    class_addMethod([NSObject class], selector, implementation, types);

    // it's also possible to add a method based on a Block:
    selector = sel_registerName("myBlockMethod");
    implementation = imp_implementationWithBlock(^{ NSLog(@"I'm a block method!"); });
    class_addMethod([NSObject class], selector, implementation, types);

    NSObject *object = [[NSObject alloc] init];
    [object myNewMethod]; //prints "I was added at runtime!" to the debug console
    [object myBlockMethod]; // prints "I'm a block method!" to the debug console
}
```

As you can see, the code to add new methods to classes at runtime is very low level compared
to most of Objective-C.

MAKING IT USEFUL

You could be forgiven for wondering just how useful this is. So here's a prime example: supporting old and new APIs
in the same code.

Let's say that you're using a system class that has a useful API in the latest OS X or iOS version, but you have to
support older versions, too. You have your own implementation of the same function, but it's fairly slow, and you'd

like to use the better version when that's available. Or worse, perhaps the older API actually performs differently on older systems (UIViewController.parentViewController, I'm looking at you).

You could work around it by calling -respondsToSelector: everywhere in your code, but that's not a graceful way to handle it. Instead, you create two methods, like so:

```
- (void) doSomething
{
    // legacy code goes here...
}
- (void) doSomethingWithNewAPI
{
    // do the same thing, but using the new API
}
```

Now, rather than selectively calling the appropriate method, you can just use the ObjC runtime to swap them around—effectively to swap the contents of the two methods, so that -doSomething contains the code from -doSomethingWithNewAPI and vice versa. The Objective-C runtime even gives you a nice and simple one-shot function that does this for you. So, rather than checking for the new API at every potential call site, you can put it somewhere like the object's +initialize method (+initialize gets called by the runtime immediately before the first message dispatch is sent to a class), like so:

```
 + (void) initialize
{
    // this gets called for my class and all its superclasses, so check:
    if (self != [MyObject class] )
        return;

    if ( [[SomeSystemClass instancesRespondToSelector: @selector(theNewAPI)] == NO )
        return;    // running the old system, leave the legacy code in place

    // get the two methods:
    Method legacy = class_getInstanceMethod(self, @selector(doSomething));
    Method newAPI = class_getInstanceMethod(self, @selector(doSomethingWithNewAPI));

    // swap the implementations of those two methods:
    method_exchangeImplementations(legacy, newAPI);
}
```

Now your newAPI code will run whenever you call -doSomething on a recent OS version, while the older versions will still run the legacy code. Neat, huh?

Threading and Grand Central Dispatch

OS X and iOS provide a number of different APIs for handling multi-threading and concurrency. The basic NSThread class is older and doesn't allow as much flexibility as the new Grand Central Dispatch concurrency API, which was introduced in Mac OS X 10.6 and iOS 4. Both GCD and the Objective-C NSOperation and NSOperationQueue classes provide a queue- and task-based metaphor for performing concurrent operations, which can be a lot simpler and more flexible to work with than a plain thread creation/consumption API.

Long-running tasks such as large computations or synchronous network activity should not take place in the main thread. Doing so will stall user interface interactions until the long-running activity completed. This is *especially* important when dealing with the network, as there's no guarantee that a network resource won't become temporarily unavailable, resulting in potentially very long wait times.

NSThread wraps execution of a selector in a background thread. It is possible to start and cancel thread execution from the main thread. Listing 3-44 shows an example of starting up a background thread.

Listing 3-44. NSThread

```
-(void)performLongRunningTask
{
    @autoreleasepool
    {
        //perform some kind of long-running task
        //maybe fetching from a network store or intense computation
        [self performSelectorOnMainThread:@selector(taskFinished) withObject:nil
waitUntilDone:NO];
    }
}

-(void)taskFinished
{
    //perhaps update the user interface
}

-(void)startTaskInBackground
{
    [NSThread detachNewThreadSelector:@selector(performLongRunningTask) toTarget:self
withObject:nil];
}
```

The semantics are straightforward with the exception of the @autoreleasepool directive. Autorelease pools are covered in Chapter 4, but what's important to note is that background threads do not have autorelease pools, so you should create one if you're using background threads.

Updating the user interface of an application, whether on OS X or iOS, should always occur on the main thread. This is a common source of runtime errors; they can be difficult to identify and intermittent in nature, so always be sure to update the user interface from the main thread.

Grand Central Dispatch, or GCD for short, provides a way to enqueue anonymous functions for execution on GCD queues. A GCD queue is, fundamentally, a wrapper for POSIX threads. GCD is an incredibly efficient and flexible way to add threading to your application. The code in Listing 3-44 can be expressed using GCD queues, as shown in Listing 3-45.

Listing 3-45. Grand Central Dispatch

```
-(void)startTaskInBackground
{
    dispatch_async(dispatch_get_global_queue(DISPATCH_QUEUE_PRIORITY_LOW, 0), ^{
        // perform some kind of long-running task
        // maybe fetching from a network store or intense computation

        dispatch_async(dispatch_get_main_queue(), ^{
            // perhaps update the user interface
        });
    });
}
```

Dispatch queues are first-in-first-out (FIFO) queues that accept GCD blocks. There are a number of default background queues that can be retrieved using the C method `dispatch_get_global_queue`. The first parameter is a constant defined in GCD and is one of the constants listed in Table 3-8. The second parameter is meant for possible expansion of the API later and, at the writing of this book, is always 0.

Table 3-8. GCD Background Queues

Dispatch Queue Priorities
DISPATCH_QUEUE_PRIORITY_HIGH
DISPATCH_QUEUE_PRIORITY_DEFAULT
DISPATCH_QUEUE_PRIORITY_LOW
DISPATCH_QUEUE_PRIORITY_BACKGROUND

It is possible to create your own dispatch queues as well, but these advanced GCD techniques are beyond the scope of this chapter.

Block objects are anonymous functions that capture the scope around them. They are covered in more depth in Chapter 4. For now, it is sufficient to know that the execution of code between the ^{ and } symbols is deferred to the specified queue.

Enqueuing a block ensures that its execution will take place before any subsequently enqueued blocks and after any preceding enqueued blocks. Blocks enqueued on the same GCD queue will execute simultaneously unless the GCD queue is marked as concurrent; this is an advanced technique not covered in this chapter.

GCD is more than a way to easily execute code in the background; it takes full advantage of multiple CPU cores for incredibly efficient code execution.

The NSOperation and NSOperationQueue APIs are built on top of Grand Central Dispatch and provide an Objective-C paradigm of queues and tasks. Operations are typically created by subclassing NSOperation, and these are then enqueued on an NSOperationQueue. As you've seen previously, the GCD API is very minimal. There is very little boilerplate code required to make some of your code run asynchronously. While this is not true for NSOperation (you actually have to subclass objects and more) you do have more control; the NSOperation API provides the ability to cancel individual operations and to provide some priority ordering between them, while a GCD queue is a strict FIFO queue. You can also explicitly wait (blocking the current thread) for a given NSOperation to complete, or for all operations on a queue to complete, while GCD provides no means of determining even whether a given queue has any blocks enqueued at a given time.

We will cover NSOperation and GCD in more detail in a later chapter, since there's a lot of information to cover there.

Run Loops

Run loops, or NSRunLoop objects, are used to implement asynchronous behavior. At their core, run loops use Mach microkernel messages. These messages are designed for inter-process communication and are a very fast, safe, and efficient way to have marshal messages from one thread to another.

The basics of this marshaling involve accepting messages posted from sources and delivering them to their destinations. The sources can be any event, such as a timer, a user interaction event, or a network event. Run loops are the destinations.

The Foundation class, NSRunLoop, is actually a wrapper for a lower-level API class called CFRunLoop (the CF stands for "Core Foundation"). Run loops operate based on run loop modes, which are string constants assigned to them. The mode of a run loop defines *which sources* the run loop can handle and, by extension, which messages it marshals.

The most famous run loop, the one you've implicitly used already, is the main run loop; it is used to update user interface elements on the screen. The main run loop is used to update elements on the screen, but is *not used* to handle interaction events. Another run loop, whose mode is UITrackingRunLoopMode on iOS and on NSEventHandlingRunLoopMode OS X, accepts user interaction events like tapping or clicking a button.

Implementing a synchronous, long-running task on the main thread (which will stall the main run loop) will stop all user interface updates (animations and other UI updates will stop until the operation has completed). Stalling the UI tracking run loop, which you can do by holding you finger down while scrolling a web view, stops other UI tracking. Divorcing these two operations (interface updates and interface interaction tracking) allows content in the web view to be updated as another run loop handles the event tracking.

There is another run loop that you may become familiar with as you begin to load resources from the network. All network requests are processed in their own run loop—even the synchronous ones! The difference between synchronous and asynchronous network requests is that the synchronous ones wrap equivalent asynchronous requests and stall whatever run loop they are called from until the request completes.

Run loops, by default, do not automatically have autorelease pools. While ARC frees Objective-C developers from many hassles associated with memory management, this is one area you still need to be very much aware of if you're using run loops. Autorelease pools are covered in Chapter 4.

Coders and Decoders

The Foundation library provides a protocol that defines how objects can be serialized and deserialized to and from the disk. The NSCoding protocol has two required methods. encodeWithCoder: is used to serialize an object and initWithCoder: is used to deserialize an object instance that has been previously encoded. Both are passed a single parameter, an instance of NSCoder, which is responsible for the serialization and deserialization of the object instance.

NSCoder is a class that is not often instantiated by the developer; instead, the Foundation framework manages the NSCoder object for the developer, typically used with NSKeyedArchiver and NSKeyedUnarchiver.

Essentially, objects save their internal state and unarchive it later. Listing 3-46 provides a complete example of the NSCoding protocol.

Listing 3-46. NSData and the Filesystem

```
@interface Employee : NSObject <NSCoding>
{
    NSInteger employeeID;
    NSString *name;
    NSArray *currentProjects;
}
@end

@implementation Employee

-(void)encodeWithCoder:(NSCoder*)aCoder
{
    [aCoder encodeInt:employeeID forKey:@"id"];
    [aCoder encodeObject:name forKey:@"name"];
    [aCoder encodeObject:currentProjects forKey:@"current projects"];
}

-(id)initWithCoder:(NSCoder*)aCoder
{
    self = [self init];
    if (!self)
        return nil;

    employeeID = [aCoder decodeIntForKey:@"id"];
    name = [aCoder decodeObjectForKey:@"name"];
    currentProjects = [aCoder decodeObjectForKey:@"current projects"];

    return self;
}

@end
```

Any object can be used with NSCoder as long as that object also conforms to the NSCoding protocol. All of the objects stored in the currentProjects array must also conform to this protocol.

Using an NSCoder object is similar to using an NSMutableDictionary object. The convenience methods for encoding and decoding primitives are demonstrated in Listing 3-36. Each encode has a matching decode; in this fashion, the internals of an object can be packed and unpacked using NSCoder.

Any custom class that conforms to the NSCoding protocol can be persisted with the aide of NSKeyedArchiver. Extending the example in Listing 3-47, you can create a binary archive file on disk.

Listing 3-47. Property Lists

```
NSArray *employeeArray = ...;//some array of Employee instances
NSString *path = [[NSBundle mainBundle] pathForResource:@"Employees" ofType:@"archive"];

[NSKeyedArchiver archiveRootObject:employeeArray toFile:path]
```

> **Note**   The file path retrieved with pathForResource:ofType: must refer to a file that already exists. Otherwise, nil is returned.

The contents of the archive file don't concern you; Employees.archive is a binary file and should not be edited directly.

Unarchiving an existing file is demonstrated in Listing 3-48.

Listing 3-48. Property Lists

```
NSString *path = [[NSBundle mainBundle] pathForResource:@"Employees" ofType:@"archive"];
NSArray *employeeArray = [NSKeyedUnarchiver unarchiveObjectWithFile:path];
```

Another way to persist small pieces of information across application launches is with the use of NSUserDefaults. These defaults are stored in a plist file specific to your application. On iOS, this file is stored in your application bundle and on OS X, it is stored in the user's Library folder.

You can create your own NSUserDefaults object, but typically you interact with the standard user defaults, accessed with the standardUserDefaults class method. While this is an easy place to store user data, it should be reserved for small bits of preference data. It is appropriate to store small settings or information about the application; it is not appropriate to store any user data in this location.

The NSUserDefaults class is used in a way very similar to mutable dictionaries. It implements a key-value store in which you can store strings, numbers, data, and collections of these objects, as well as primitives like int and BOOL, as shown in Listing 3-49.

Listing 3-49. NSUserDefaults

```
[[NSUserDefaults standardUserDefaults] setBool:YES]
    forKey:@"shouldLaunchAtLoginKey"];
...
BOOL shouldLaunchAtLogin = [[NSUserDefaults standardUserDefaults]
    boolForKey:@"launchAtLoginKey"];
```

Property Lists

Property lists are a hierarchy of key-value pairs stored in XML format. They can be serialized, creating an NSData instance that is writable to disk.

Listing 3-50. Property Lists

```
NSArray *stringArray = [NSArray arrayWithObjects:@"some string", @"another string", nil];
NSString *error = nil;
NSString *path = [[NSBundle mainBundle] pathForResource:@"Strings" ofType:@"plist"];

id plistData = [NSPropertyListSerialization dataFromPropertyList:stringArray
    format:NSPropertyListXMLFormat_v1_0
    errorDescription:&error];
if (plistData) //short hand for if (plistData != nil)
{
    [plistData writeToFile:path atomically:YES];
}
else
{
    NSLog(@"Could not create plist data: %@", error);
}
```

The code in Listing 3-50 creates an NSData object and persists it to disk in the main application bundle as the file Strings.plist. In the case of an error during serialization, the NSError object is logged.

The contents of the actual file written to disk (see Listing 3-51 for the example output) don't typically matter to you as a developer; while it is possible to edit the XML file directly, in code only the Foundation framework should be used to read or write the file to disk. We know you're eager to write your own XML parser, but just use the Foundation framework and save yourself a lot of time.

Listing 3-51. A Property List File

```
<?xml version="1.0" encoding="UTF-8"?>
<!DOCTYPE plist PUBLIC "-//Apple//DTD PLIST 1.0//EN"
"http://www.apple.com/DTDs/PropertyList-1.0.dtd">
<plist version="1.0">
<array>
        <string>some string</string>
        <string>another string</string>
</array>
</plist>
```

Accessing a property list that has already been written to disk looks very similar (see Listing 3-52).

Listing 3-52. Property Lists

```
NSString *error = nil;
NSString *path = [[NSBundle mainBundle] pathForResource:@"Strings" ofType:@"plist"];

NSData *plistData = [NSData dataWithContentsOfFile:path];
NSPropertyListFormat format;
id plist;
```

```
plist = [NSPropertyListSerialization propertyListFromData:plistData
                                    mutabilityOption:NSPropertyListImmutable
                                              format:&format
                                    errorDescription:&error];
if(!plist)
{
    NSLog(@"%@", error);
}
else
{
    NSLog(@"deserialized plist: %@", plist);
}
```

The code in Listing 3-52 prints the description of the `plist` object to the console. This `plist` object is an `NSArray` instance.

The only objects that can be persisted to property lists are the Foundation classes discussed in this chapter.

`NSKeyedArchiver`, `NSKeyedUnarchiver`, and property lists are suitable tools for persisting small amounts of data to disk in binary and XML formats. For complex object graphs, use Core Data, covered in Chapter 8.

Summary

Whew! Are you tired after getting through all that? If so, we don't blame you one bit. There was a lot of information packed in there.

- You met the basic string, number, and data types, and learned how to use them.

- You learned how to make use of the primary collection classes in the Foundation framework and how to subclass them and implement their features in your own collections.

- You looked at the threading APIs available to you, including a quick glance in the direction of Grand Central Dispatch, which is, in our not-so-humble opinion, just about the greatest thing a programmer could want.

- You know what run loops are now, so they won't scare you when they start to make more frequent appearances later in the book.

- You've seen how to serialize and deserialize data, both using `NSCoder` for arbitrary structured data types and objects, and using property lists for storing nested groups of the more basic data types.

You'll be putting all this, and more, into proper use very soon indeed. With that in mind, now might be a good time to take a coffee break…

Chapter **4**

Objective-C Language Features

Now that we have covered the Foundation framework in Chapter 3, you should be familiar with reading Objective-C code and should have an intuitive mental model of how the runtime operates. This chapter takes a closer look at the language and its semantics; it breaks that mental model down from the intuition you've developed and presents the rules that form the mechanics of Objective-C.

Strong and Weak References

A large part of writing Objective-C is managing the references that executing code holds to objects, as well as the references objects hold to one another. Previous to ARC, Objective-C used manual memory management on iOS and, optionally, garbage collection on OS X. Both of these approaches have their advantages and disadvantages. Now it uses ARC, which combines the best aspects from both methods.

ARC, or Automatic Reference Counting, is a compile-time mechanism that inserts the calls for manual memory management into the code as it is compiled. The compiler is very smart and ARC code is very well optimized. While ARC has freed developers from having to write manual memory management code, it cannot break reference cycles, like platforms using garbage collection can. For this reason, developers need to give the compiler some direction for avoiding reference cycles.

Once an object has no more *incoming* strong references, it is deallocated. If it was the last object to have a strong reference to some other object, that other object is also deallocated, and so on. Figure 4-1 shows a reference cycle.

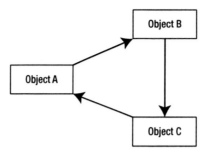

Figure 4-1. *A reference cycle*

Object A can't be deallocated until Object C is, and Object C will never be deallocated as long as Object B has a strong reference to it. Finally, Object B will never be deallocated until Object A is deallocated. This is a reference cycle and it will cause memory in an application to leak.

In Figure 4-2, the strong reference Object C had to Object A (symbolized by a solid line) has been replaced with a weak reference (symbolized by a dashed line).

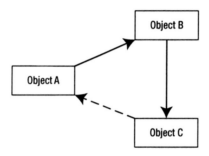

Figure 4-2. *Breaking a reference cycle*

Weak references do not prevent objects from being deallocated, so Object A is deallocated, then Object B, and finally Object C.

If you're familiar with C or C++, you'll likely notice a problem with weak references. If an object can be deallocated at any moment, and you have a weak reference to that object, then you can end up with a dangling pointer. With ARC compiling for iOS 5 and OS X 10.7 (or higher), weak references to objects become nil once those objects are deallocated; these are therefore known as *zeroing weak references*.

iOS 4 and OS X 10.6 do not support the __weak keyword used to denote weak references so you must use __unsafe_unretained instead. As its name implies, it is unsafe to rely on a reference to an unsafe, unretained object. This may seem dangerous, but as long as you are aware of this limitation, the application code you write should be fine.

Let's take a quick review of the different types of variables in Objective-C. There are local variables, which belong to their enclosing scope (simply: the surrounding pair of curly braces, whether a function, if statement, for statement, etc.) and are only in scope during the execution of that scope. Additionally, there are instance variables, which belong to object instances and are valid until the object instance is deallocated.

By default, both local and instance variables are strong references. Properties, defined with the @property directive, are also strong by default. Marking variables as weak is done using the __weak keyword (or, when declaring properties, by using the weak keyword in the qualifier list).

The compiler figures out how objects are returned from methods based on their names. Methods of the types alloc, copy, init, mutableCopy, or new return objects that transfer ownership to the invoking method. All other methods return objects that do not transfer ownership of the object. The compiler uses this naming convention to insert the appropriate memory management code; see Listing 4-1 for an example.

Listing 4-1. ARC References

```
id instanceVariable;
...
-(void)performLongRunningTask
{
    //ARC transfers ownership from copy to the local variable
    id obj = [someObject copy];

    //ARC makes a new strong reference to obj
    id anotherObj = obj;

    //Transferring to instance varable doesn't require any memory management code
    //instanceVariable is strong and init returns a strong reference
    instanceVariable = [[SomeObject alloc] init];

} //anotherObj goes out of scope and its reference is removed
```

The code in Listing 4-1 isn't **exactly** what goes on under the hood; there are a lot of optimizations ARC uses to eliminate redundant memory management code. As a developer, however, this is the appropriate mental model you should form.

A common pattern is to think of strong and weak references as "owned" and "owned by," respectively. If an object owns another object, then it uses a strong reference. If an object is *owned by* another object and has a reference to its owner, it uses a weak reference. While this is insufficient reasoning for *all* references, it is a helpful trick for remembering Objective-C's memory management conventions.

As a concrete example, let's take a look at NSArray. Arrays have strong references to all of the elements they contain. You can think of an array *owning* those objects, even though other objects might own them, too.

Another example is the Delegation pattern in Objective-C. Delegation is a way of using weakly coupled callbacks and is very common, especially in user interface code. A common delegation example in iOS is the UITableViewDataSource protocol. Table views, owned by a view controller, need to know what to display to the user. The view controller is responsible for providing this information to the table view. The table view's reference to the view controller is weak (see Figure 4-3).

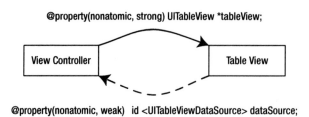

Figure 4-3. Weak references in UITableViewDataSource

Autorelease Pools

Autorelease pools were first used in Objective-C to transfer ownership of an object from one method to another.

In Figure 4-4, Method B has created an object to which it holds a strong reference. It needs to break that reference so it doesn't leak memory, but it has to do it *only after* Method A has had a chance to establish a strong reference to it. If Method B released the object before Method A captured the object in its scope, the object could be deallocated between the handover of ownership and the application might crash.

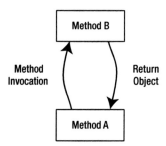

Figure 4-4. Transferring ownership with autorelease

Autorelease is a way to mark objects as needing to be released at some time in the future. When? Well, when an object is marked as autoreleased, it's added to the current autorelease pool. At some point in the future, the pool is drained and all of the objects are released. When, exactly? The current autorelease pool is drained at the end of the current run loop.

When compiling with ARC, you no longer have to worry about using NSAutoreleasePool objects explicitly. Actually, you can't use these objects in code compiled with ARC at all; you will get a compiler error if you try to create an explicit NSAutoreleasePool object or if you try to mark an object as autoreleased manually.

> **Note** In fact, ARC is clever enough that it often doesn't even need to mark objects as autoreleased. It can infer the transfer of ownership and optimize away the need for Method B to release and Method A to capture the strong reference.
>
> ARC manages this by inspecting the call stack at runtime. A function returning an autoreleased object actually returns the result of a call to `objc_autoreleaseReturnValue()`. That function, at runtime, looks up the stack to see if the next operation in the caller is a call to `objc_retainAutoreleasedReturnValue()`. If it is, the object is dropped into thread-local storage momentarily and is *not* autoreleased. `objc_retainAutoreleasedReturnValue()` then checks whether the same value is in thread-local-storage and if so, it does *not* issue a retain. This then skips the whole `x = [[object autorelease] retain]` step, resulting in just `x = object`, which is *significantly* faster.

Under ARC, there are two main reasons for using autorelease pools: in detached threads (using `NSThread`, for instance), or for keeping the "high-water mark" of memory usage down. Let's take a look at both.

Recall from Chapter 3 that when using `NSThread` to perform long-running tasks in the background, you used the `@autoreleasepool` directive, as shown in Listing 4-2.

Listing 4-2. NSThread and Autorelease Pools

```
-(void)performLongRunningTask
{
    @autoreleasepool
    {
        //perform some kind of long-running task
        //maybe fetching from a network store or intense computation
        [self performSelectorOnMainThread:@selector(taskFinished) withObject:nil
waitUntilDone:NO];
    }
}

-(void)taskFinished
{
    //perhaps update the user interface
}

-(void)startTaskInBackground
{
    [NSThread detachNewThreadSelector:@selector(performLongRunningTask) toTarget:self
withObject:nil];
}
```

You want to make sure that any objects that are autoreleased will actually be released when the `performLongRunningTask` method is finished. If you neglected to use this directive, the code would probably execute fine, since ARC is usually smart enough to optimize autoreleases.

However, if an object is marked as autoreleased when there is no autorelease pool available, the autorelease is *ignored* and memory is leaked.

The second case for using autorelease pools is keeping the high-water mark of your application memory low. When your application is executing, it creates and destroys objects which use memory. The high-water mark is the most memory that your application is using at once.

Consider a for loop that creates many objects. It would be ideal for any objects that have been marked as autoreleased to be released at the end of each iteration, since they're out of scope anyway. This is exactly what autorelease pools can be used for (see Listing 4-3).

Listing 4-3. NSThread and Autorelease Pools

```
for (id obj in array)
{
    @autoreleasepool
    {
        //some operation that creates a lot of temporary objects
    }
}
```

In Listing 4-3, any temporary objects that are marked as autoreleased are released at the end of each loop iteration, instead of waiting until the end of the current run loop.

Memory consumption is very critical, particularly on iOS devices with very limited RAM. Consider the graph of memory usage in Figure 4-5, which demonstrates a for loop like the one in Listing 4-3 without and with the @autoreleasepool directive.

Figure 4-5. Comparing loops with and without autorelease pools

The graphs in Figure 4-5 represent two loops with identical code iterating four times. The only difference is the second loop uses @autoreleasepool to keep its high-water mark down. Implementing this in your code makes you a good memory-management citizen and will help prevent your app from being terminated due to low memory conditions.

Using @autoreleasepool essentially creates a new scope for objects to be created in. These directives can even be stacked (see Listing 4-4)!

Listing 4-4. NSThread and Stacked Autorelease Pools

```
for (NSArray *subArray in array)
{
    @autoreleasepool
    {
        //some operation that creates a lot of temporary objects
        for (id obj in subArray)
```

```
        {
            @autoreleasepool
            {
                //some other operation that creates a lot of temporary objects
            }
        }
    }
}
```

Any object marked for autorelease in the inner loop is released at the end of each inner loop iteration, as you expect.

Exceptions

Exceptions in Objective-C are just like exceptions in any other language that supports them. What makes exceptions in Objective-C unusual is *how and when* they are used.

Exceptions, encapsulated in an NSException object, represent *truly exceptional* circumstances. If it is possible to foresee the circumstances that would cause an exception, don't use exceptions. Exceptions are reserved for serious problems, such as a disk becoming disconnected during a write operation, an accidental division by zero, or accessing an out-of-bounds array element. Most exceptions encountered during development are due to developer error. In fact, that's what Apple says they should be used for: to notify developers that they're doing something wrong.

Nevertheless, no book on Objective-C would be complete without at least a summary of how exceptions work.

Throwing exceptions is accomplished by instantiating an NSException objecting and then calling its raise method. Alternatively, NSException defines a convenience class method for raising exceptions. The two methods are demonstrated in Listing 4-5.

Listing 4-5. NSException Examples

```
NSException * exception = [NSException
    exceptionWithName:@"DiskBecameUnavilableDuringWrite"
    reason:@"Disk Became Unavailable During a Write Operation"
    userInfo:nil];
[exception raise];

[NSException raise: @"DiskBecameUnavilableDuringWrite"
    format:@"Disk Became Unavailable During a Write Operation"];
```

The latter example uses a format string for its second parameter. Also note that the former example specifies a userInfo parameter. This parameter is an NSDictionary instance that can be used to provide details about the exception.

NSException.h provides several built-in exception names that can be used by any developer. They are listed in Table 4-1.

Table 4-1. Generic Exception Names Listed in NSException.h

Generic Exception Names
NSGenericException
NSRangeException
NSInvalidArgumentException
NSInternalInconsistencyException
NSMallocException
NSObjectInaccessibleException
NSObjectNotAvailableException
NSDestinationInvalidException
NSPortTimeoutException
NSInvalidSendPortException
NSInvalidReceivePortException
NSPortSendException
NSPortReceiveException

Catching exceptions should look familiar; see Listing 4-6 for an example.

Listing 4-6. Catching Exceptions

```
@try {
    //attempt some dangerous action
}
@catch (NSException *exception) {
    NSLog(@"Caught %@: %@", [exception name], [exception  reason]);
    @throw;
}
@finally {
    //perform any cleanup
}
```

In the @catch block, invoking @throw will raise the same exception again.

If exceptions are eschewed in Objective-C, then how should developers perform error handling? The easiest way to avoid exceptions is to check for circumstances that might cause them and write code that will adapt to avoid them. If something *does* go wrong, the common pattern is to pass a pointer to an NSError object into a method that might fail. If the error object is still nil after the method returns, then nothing went wrong.

To illustrate how to write adaptable code, let's take a look at code that divides a string based on a character you expect to be present. In Listing 4-7, you've retrieved a string from the network (the name of a podcast, for example) and you want to divide the name of the podcast from the name of the episode.

Listing 4-7. Non-Adaptive Code

```
NSString *podcastString = ...;// Retrieved from an API, this is "Some Podast - Episode 8"
NSArray *array = [podcastString componentsSeparatedByString:@"-"];
NSString *podcastName = [array objectAtIndex:0];
NSString *podcastEpisodeName = [array objectAtIndex:1];
```

The componentsSeparatedByString: method returns an array of strings by splitting the receiver into substrings based on the parameter as a delimiter.

The problem with the code in Listing 4-7 is that it assumes that the "-"character will be present in the string. It's completely possible for the podcast provider to change the "-"character to a longer em-dash like "–". If there is no dash character present, array only contains one element and calling [array objectAtIndex:1] will crash the application.

Rather than wrap this code in a @try/@catch block, you should check for the number of elements first. The code in Listing 4-8 avoids use of exceptions entirely; it is more cohesive and makes for a less coupled architecture (since no other code needs to be aware of this problem); and it is easy to read and understand, explicitly, what this code does.

Listing 4-8. Adaptive Code

```
NSString *podcastString = ...;// Retrieved from an API, this is "Some Podast - episode 8"
NSArray *array = [podcastString componentsSeparatedByString:@"-"];
NSString *podcastName = nil;
NSString *podcastEpisodeName = nil;
if ([array count] < 2)
{
    podcastName = nil; //we'll use nil as a sentinel value for "not found"
    podcastEpisodeName = [array lastObject];
}
else
{
    podcastName = [array objectAtIndex:0];
    podcastEpisodeName = [array objectAtIndex:1];
}
```

There are times when you need to handle errors that are unpredictable, like a failed write to a file or database. Listing 4-9 provides an example of writing an NSData instance to a file.

Listing 4-9. NSError

```
NSError *error = nil;
NSData *someData = ...;//some data, maybe a compressed jpeg
if (![someData writeToFile:path options:nil error:&error])
{
    //writeToFile:options:error: returns NO in case of failure
    NSLog(@"Could not write data to file %@: %@", path, error);
}
```

NSError provides a cleaner, more elegant way to handle errors than exceptions and you should employ it whenever is appropriate in the code you write.

Synchronization

Cross-threaded synchronization is a critically important feature in supporting multiple threads. When employing multiple threads in your application, extreme care must be taken to avoid accessing shared resources simultaneously. These race conditions can put your application in an invalid state. Discovering the cause of errors in multithreaded programs is difficult and the best strategy is to avoid them by properly synchronizing threads.

Since Objective-C is a strict C superset, you can use pthread mutexes. However, Objective-C defines its own locking mechanisms, so this book won't cover pthread locking. Instead, we'll cover the Foundation locking objects and protocol plus the built-in language constructs provided for synchronization of parallel code.

NSLock is a part of the Foundation framework described in Chapter 3. It defines a simple-to-use mutex for locking and unlocking, allowing developers to ensure multithreaded correctness. Using the NSLock class is very simple, as you can see in Listing 4-10.

Listing 4-10. NSLock

```
NSLock *sharedLock = [[NSLock alloc] init];

...

[sharedLock lock]; //blocks current thread

//perform some critical section

[sharedLock unlock];
```

In addition to the simple lock and unlock, NSLock provides two other useful methods: tryLock and lockBeforeData:. As its name suggests, tryLock attempts to acquire a lock on the mutex but does not block the thread it is called from. The other method, lockBeforeDate: blocks the main thread, but automatically gives up trying to acquire the lock if it can't do so by a given date. See Listing 4-11 for an example.

Listing 4-11. NSLock

```
NSLock *sharedLock = [[NSLock alloc] init];
...
while (calculationsLeft) {
    /* Do another iteraction of calculation */
    if ([sharedLock tryLock]) {
        /* Update display used by all threads. */
        [sharedLock unlock];
    } else {
        /* Wait or break from the loop here. */
    }
}
```

Listing 4-11 demonstrates how to use tryLock to update user interface components if the lock is available, but not to block the calculations if not.

Objective-C also defines a language directive for synchronizing multithreaded programs. The @synchronized directive behaves the same as any other mutex; it provides mechanisms for locking and unlocking critical sections of code, but it does so without creating an explicit lock object.

The code in Listing 4-12 uses the @synchronized directive to lock out other threads for accessing the critical section. Any two threads using @synchronized with the same object instance will be unable to perform their critical sections at the same time; the second one to attempt to do so will block until the first reaches the end.

Listing 4-12. @synchronized

```
-(void)performCriticalMethod
{
    @synchronized(self)
    {
        //perform critical section here
    }
}
```

Remember that Objective-C classes are actually objects themselves; these Class objects are singletons that can also be used with the @synchronized directive. This can be used to not only synchronize on a specific object instance but an entire object type. If you want to block out all instances of an object from accessing their critical path, you could modify the code in Listing 4-12 to look like that in Listing 4-13.

Listing 4-13. Modified Example of @synchronized

```
-(void)performCriticalMethod
{
    @synchronized([self class])
    {
        //perform critical section here
    }
}
```

No two instances of that object could perform the critical section at the same time.

Listing 4-14 demonstrates how you can take advantage of this locking technique to implement your own singleton objects. Notice the plus sign in front of the sharedInstance method and recall that this indicates a class method.

Listing 4-14. Singleton in Objective-C

```
static MySingleton *sharedInstance = nil;

+(MySingleton *)sharedInstance
{
    @synchronized(self)
    {
        if (!sharedInstance)
```

```
            {
                sharedInstance = [[self alloc] init]; //or other initialization
            }
        }

    return sharedInstance;
}
```

Even calling sharedInstance on two different threads will guarantee retrieving the same object instance.

If an exception is generated during a @synchronized block, the Objective-C runtime will catch the exception and release the underlying semaphore before re-throwing the exception. This allows other threads waiting to execute the protected code to continue their execution.

NSConditionalLock is yet another way to synchronize multithreaded programs. This conditional lock maintains an internal state, represented as an integer. Locking an NSConditionalLock requires a condition; the lock will block until the internal state of the lock is the same as the condition. Unlocking also accepts a condition; an unlock provides a new state the conditional lock should assume. A pending lock waiting for this condition will stop blocking and enter their critical section.

Conditional locks are important when certain operations must take place in a specific order. The simplest example is a producer-consumer scenario. Consider a producer that places some data to be processed in a queue and a consumer that dequeues some data to process. The producer should not add more data if the consumer hasn't finished yet and the consumer cannot consume anything if the queue is empty. Listing 4-15 details a fully synchronized implementation of the producer-consumer pattern.

Listing 4-15. Producer-Consumer Pattern

```
enum { NO_DATA_IN_QUEUE = 0, HAS_DATA_IN_QUEUE};
...
NSConditionalLock *conditionalLock;
...
conditionalLock = [[NSConditionalLock alloc] initWithCondition: NO_DATA_IN_QUEUE];
//conditionalLock set up before processing begins
...
while (YES) //Producer
{
    [conditionalLock lockWhenCondition: NO_DATA_IN_QUEUE];
    //produce some data and place it in the queue
    [conditionalLock unlockWithCondition: HAS_DATA_IN_QUEUE];
}
...
while (YES)
{
    [conditionalLock lockWhenCondition: HAS_DATA_IN_QUEUE];
    //remove some data from the queue and consume it
    [conditionalLock unlockWithCondition: NO_DATA_IN_QUEUE];
}
```

Let's discuss implicit locking mechanisms in Objective-C. By default, all properties of an object defined with the @property directive are atomic in nature; there is an implicit lock when setting or getting the value of the property. This is to prevent a race condition between two threads trying to set a value to the same property of the same instance. However, excess locking can cause performance problems (particularly on iOS), so it is usually a good idea to specify properties as nonatomic if the object won't be used in a multithreaded environment.

Properties are atomic by default and their getters/setters cannot be overridden unless they are specified as nonatomic. Specifying a property to be nonatomic is helpful if you want setting or getting a property to have some side effects, such as marking an object as dirty. However, you should avoid doing any "heavy lifting" such as long-running computations in getters and setters. Typically, having profound or unnecessary side effects in getters and setters is frowned upon.

In-Depth: Messaging

In Objective-C, communicating between objects is done via messaging, a mechanism borrowed from the programming language Smalltalk. Let's take another look at how messages are passed.

Messages are determined by selectors. In Listing 4-16, the selector is performSomeActionWithAParameter:. The *receiver* of the message is receiver and the message returns some value, which is stored in returnValue.

Listing 4-16. Basic Message Passing

```
id returnValue = [receiver performSomeActionWithAParameter:someParameter];
```

Referring to selectors by the textual, English-readable names would be slow. Objective-C binds selector names to specific IDs at runtime (not at compile time). Invoking the count method on an array uses the *same selector* as invoking the count method on a set. No two different selectors have the same ID and no two selectors with the same name have a different ID.

Selectors have a type of SEL and are accessible via the @selector() directive. You can call the same init selector on the two aforementioned arrays and set objects (see Listing 4-17).

Listing 4-17. Message Passing using performSelector:

```
SEL countSelector = @selector(count);
[array performSelector:countSelector];
[set performSelector:countSelector];
```

It is also possible to obtain the SEL selector with a string (not necessarily a string literal) using the NSSelectorFromString method. Generally, this is not very peformant and is unnecessary most of the time. It is interesting to note that you can also get the string equivalent of the selector name at runtime using the NSStringFromSelector method, which can be helpful for debugging purposes.

Message Orientation

Objective-C borrows its (some would say) peculiar syntax for invoking methods from the programming language Smalltalk. It's arguable that, while Objective-C certainly has a concept of objects in the modern programming language sense, it's not strictly an *object-oriented* language in the same vein as Smalltalk and Ruby. The distinction here is that in "true" object-oriented languages, *everything* is an object, including number literals, character literals, and more. In Objective-C (and others, such as C++, C# and Java), there are literal types that are *not* objects. In Smalltalk you can type something like 3 timesDo: [drawSomething], because typing "3" actually gives you an object. That isn't true in Objective-C, although with the new literal syntax this sort of behavior is becoming available; for instance, [@3 description] yields @"3".

The term "object-oriented programming" first appeared amidst a revelation in the software industry that procedural programming was not sufficient for *every* software project. At that time, any language that supported a concept of objects was "object-oriented." Today, with the exception of new functional languages, most new languages are called object-oriented solely because they have a built-in extensible object system based on the concepts of classes, subclassing, and interfaces or protocols.

Objective-C and Smalltalk have another defining feature: messaging. The concept of messages and message passing is so baked-in to Objective-C and Smalltalk that it's useful to think of them as message-oriented programming languages. To see how they're different from other object-oriented languages you may have seen, let's take a look at message passing in more detail.

Sending Messages

From a developer's perspective, messages are sent to receivers using the square bracket syntax. In reality, the compiler converts the Objective-C square bracket syntax to a C function call. Though the two lines of code in Listing 4-18 are equivalent, you should *never* need to call objc_msgSend yourself.

Listing 4-18. Behind the Scenes of Objective-C Messaging

```
[receiver someSelector];
objc_msgSend(receiver, @selector(someSelector));
```

The objc_msgSend function can accept selectors with parameters in the form of a variable list, such as objc_msgSend(receiver, selector, arg1, arg2, ...). This function is responsible for dynamically binding the message call to the method implementation. This is a three-step process.

1. Locate the specific implementation (procedure) of the selector in the receiver's Class object.

2. Invoke the implementation, passing a reference to self as well as any parameters.

3. Pass any return value onto the invoking procedure.

Every Class structure has a dispatch table mapping the selectors to which the class can respond to the address of the implementation in memory. The class also has a pointer to its superclass, which defines the class hierarchy.

Each class instance has an isa pointer to its Class object, which holds the dispatch table. When passing a message to an instance, the runtime examines the isa pointer and traverses up the class hierarchy until it finds a class that responds to selector it is passing. Since traversing an entire class hierarchy for every message-passing operation is expensive, each Class object caches the locations of its selectors.

In step 2 of objc_msgSend, notice that a reference to self is passed to the procedure. This is one of two "hidden parameters" included in all Objective-C messages. The self parameter defines the context for how the procedure operates.

This concept of lazily-loaded procedure lookup based on a class hierarchy stands in contrast to other object-oriented languages. These languages hold large tables of method locations and an invocation just jumps the program counter to that memory location. (This is certainly a simplification, but bear with us.) The static, rigid nature of other compiled languages like C++ (or even Java) make class reflection difficult and slow. In message-oriented languages like Objective-C, reflection is easy and built into the language.

The procedure implementation belongs to the Class object of the instance; copying the same executable code to each instance of an object would be incredibly wasteful. Since the code being executed belongs to the Class object, and not the instance of the class, it *must* have a reference to self passed in with each procedure invocation. Having to explicitly define this parameter would be tedious for the programmer, so the compiler takes care of it.

In the source code for any method, using the self keyword is actually accessing this hidden parameter. In addition to this hidden parameter, there is a second, which is the selector currently being invoked. This isn't typically much use to the developer, since it's obvious which selector is being invoked anyway. You can access this second, hidden parameter with the _cmd keyword.

Proxies and Message Forwarding

If you tried to compile the code in Listing 4-19 under ARC, you would get, at best, a compiler warning or, at worst, a compiler error, depending on the compiler version.

Listing 4-19. Invoking Non-Existent Methods Under ARC

```
NSString *someString = @"this is a string";
[someString doSomething];
```

The doSomething is not defined anywhere visible to the compiler at this time. The solution to the compiler errors and warnings is to *declare* the methods belonging to string instances, as shown in Listing 4-20.

Listing 4-20. Invoking Non-Existent Methods Under ARC

```
@interface NSString (Something)

-(void)doSomething;

@end

...

NSString *someString = @"this is a string";
[someString doSomething];
```

This declaration can be anywhere—in any header file that's been #imported where this method is declared. The compiler needs to know about the doSomething method. If the compiler can't see the declaration, it will try to infer that all parameters are of type id and the return type is id, too. Under ARC, this can cause serious problems (remember that the compiler needs to determine whether to retain, release, or autorelease objects based on their usage), hence the compiler error.

But declaring the method is not enough. It is only enough to get the code to *compile* but not necessarily run. At this point, calling doSomething on the string instance will generate a runtime exception specifying that this string instance does not respond to the selector. When the runtime searches the object hierarchy for the selector doSomething, it won't find it.

There are three message-forwarding steps that are taken when the runtime cannot locate a selector. If none of these three are successful, a runtime exception is generated.

1. The runtime tries to resolve the selector at runtime and give the object a chance to add an instance method to its Class object. For instance methods, resolveInstanceMethod: is called on the Class object; for class methods, resolveClassMethod: is called instead. Both of these methods have a parameter—a SEL selector—that gets added to the Class.

> **Note**   This lazy-loading approach isn't strictly "forwarding" anything, but it is fast. Subsequent messages with this selector will invoke the method (which was added on the first call).

2. The runtime looks for an implementation of forwardingTargetForSelector:. This method returns a new object to which the message, unchanged, can be forwarded. It can also return nil to skip to step 3 (helpful if you only want to forward *some* of the messages). Returning self might force the code into an infinite loop, so be careful!

3. The runtime looks for an implementation of both methodSignatureForSelector: and forwardInvocation: in your instance. These are methods for (possibly) modifying the original message and forwarding it onto another object.

   The process takes two steps. First, methodSignatureForSelector: is called to obtain an NSMethodSignature object that defines the return type and parameter list of the selector. Subsequently, the runtime calls forwardInvocation: with an NSInvocation object that wraps the NSMethodSignature. The NSInvocation object can be invoked by calling invokeWithTarget: with the object to which you want to forward the message as a parameter.

   If this final step fails to properly handle the message, the runtime will send doesNotRecognizeSelector: and a runtime exception is raised.

Naturally, implementing any or all of these steps is possible and different actions can be taken depending on the selector in question.

This is quite a complex topic; Listing 4-21 provides a complete (though somewhat pedagogical) example of using all three methods.

Listing 4-21. Three Message Forwarding Techniques

```objc
@implementation NSArray (MessageForwarding)

-(void)methodAddedAtRuntime
{
    NSLog(@"This method was added at runtime");
}

// Step 1
-(BOOL)resolveInstanceMethod:(SEL)name
{
    if (name != @selector(methodAddedAtRuntime))
        return NO;

    struct objc_method newMethod;
    newMethod.method_name = sel_registerName("methodAddedAtRuntime");
    newMethod.method_imp = methodAddedAtRuntime;

    struct objc_method_list *methodList;
    methodList = malloc(sizeof(struct objc_method_list));
    methodList->count = 1;
    methodList[0] = newMethod;

    class_addMethods ([self class], methodList);

    return YES;
}

// Step 2
-(id)forwardingTargetForSelector:(SEL)name
{
    if (name != @selector(methodWithForwardedTarget))
        return nil;
    return sharedObject; //sharedObject is the object the method is forwarded to.
}

// Step 3
// let's see forward the message onto the items in us - we are an array, remember!
-(NSMethodSignature *)methodSignatureForSelector:(SEL)name
{
    //may return nil, that's OK.
    return [[self lastObject] methodSignatureForSelector:sel]))
}

// will forward all other messages onto our obkects
-(void)forwardInvocation:(NSInvocation *)invocation
{
    for(id obj in self)
    {
        if (![obj respondsToSelector:[invocation selector]])
        {
            [self doesNotRecognizeSelector: [invocation selector]];
            return;
        }
```

```
        [inv invokeWithTarget:obj];
    }
}

@end
```

To reiterate, this is only pedagogical code to demonstrate how message forwarding works.

There is a problem with this code in step 3; if NSArray responds to the selector, like count, then the array instance will trap the message and the forwarding mechanism will never be triggered.

What you need is a more reliable way to forward messages. For this reason, you use NSProxy, which is a lightweight, abstract class that you subclass. Since it responds to so few selectors, it won't interfere with messages forwarding.

To use proxies, define a category (of the object from which messages are to be forward) that creates an instance of your proxy subclass. All the message forwarding (step 3) is then performed by the proxy object instead of whatever class it is proxying.

Listing 4-22 demonstrates a common use of NSProxy: forwarding messages to all elements in an array. As you'll see in the next section discussing blocks, this pattern has been replaced in Objective-C, but it's still useful to illustrate how proxies work.

Listing 4-22. NSProxy

```
@implementation NSArray (MessageForwardingWithProxies)

-(id)do
{
    return [[MyProxy alloc] initWithArray:self];
}

@end

...

@interface MyProxy : NSProxy
{
    NSArray *array;
}

-(id) initWithArray:(NSArray *)theArray

@end

@implementation MyProxy

-(id) initWithArray:(NSArray *)theArray
{
    //explicitly *not* calling [super init]
    array = theArray;
    return self;
}
```

```
-(NSMethodSignature *)methodSignatureForSelector:(SEL)name
{
    NSMethodSignature *sig = nil;

    for(id obj in self)
    {
        sig = [obj methodSignatureForSelector: name];
        if(sig)
            break;
    }
    return sig;
}

-(void)forwardInvocation:(NSInvocation *)invocation
{
    for(id obj in array)
        [invocation invokeWithTarget:obj];
}

@end
```

> **Note**   NSProxy is a root class that does not inherit from NSObject (though it does conform to the
> NSObject protocol, an interesting Objective-C curiosity). If you call [[NSProxy alloc] init], a
> runtime exception is generated.

Luckily, Objective-C has introduced the concept of first-class functions called blocks. For many
purposes, these blocks replace the need for NSProxy subclasses.

Blocks

Blocks are the Objective-C construct for anonymous functions. You can declare, create, and
invoke blocks like you would normal methods, but you can do it inline. Additionally, while blocks
are actually implemented at the C level (and are therefore usable in C or C++ code), when in
an Objective-C application they are actually set up as Objective-C objects, and so they can be
retained, copied, released, and autoreleased just like other objects.

The code in Listing 4-23 demonstrates how to declare, assign, and invoke blocks. The ^ symbol
is used as the "block operator" because it is an operator that cannot be overridden in C++.

Listing 4-23. Block Declaration, Assignment, and Invocation

```
-(void)blocksExample
{
    void (^exampleBlock)(int); //declaration
```

```
exampleBlock = ^(int theInt) { //assignment
    NSLog(@"I'm in a block with an int: %d", theInt);
};

exampleBlock(13); //invocation
}
```

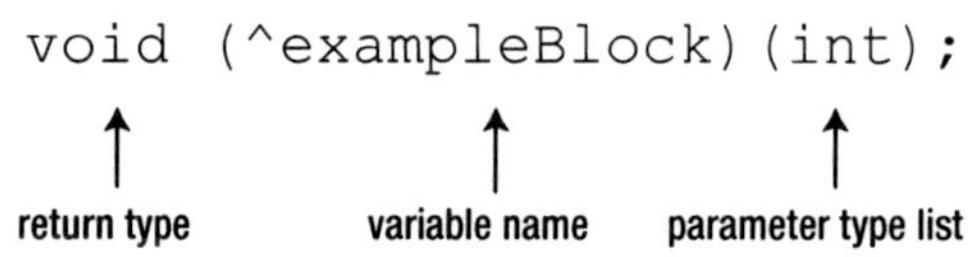

$$void\ (\verb|^|exampleBlock)(int);$$

↑   ↑   ↑

return type   variable name   parameter type list

Figure 4-6. Block declaration

The parameter list only defines types, not parameter names in the declaration. This list of types must match the list in the assignment exactly (see Figure 4-6).

Blocks without parameters must specify void in the parameter list and may omit the parameter list during assignment of the block object, as shown in Listing 4-24.

Listing 4-24. Blocks with No Parameters

```
void (^exampleBlock)(void);

exampleBlock = ^ {
};

exampleBlock();
```

Since blocks are just Objective-C objects, they can be used as return values of methods. A block that takes no parameters and returns no result can be represented with the C type dispatch_block_t.

Blocks are, in fact, quite special objects. Unlike every other Objective-C object, they aren't created on the heap, but they initially start out allocated on the stack. As a result, they can disappear immediately once execution leaves the scope in which they were declared.

Creating blocks on the stack means that they are very cheap to create and use when passing a block into a function that will use it (for instance, see the block-based enumerators later in this chapter). However, if you want to keep one around, calling -retain on a block isn't enough to ensure this because retaining an object only updates its reference count. Instead, to ensure that a block always stays around, use the -copy method, which copies the block to the heap, *along with any captured variables*. If a block is already on the heap, calling -copy simply updates its reference count as if you had called -retain instead.

As a result of this, you cannot return a block object directly; you need to copy it so that it is guaranteed to exist on the heap. ARC automatically copies the block if you explicitly define the return type of the method. Otherwise, you need to call copy on the block object explicitly. Listing 4-25 demonstrates both techniques.

Listing 4-25. Blocks as Return Values

```
-(dispatch_block_t)methodWithExplictReturnValue
{
    return ^{ NSLog(@"I am in a block"); };
}

-(id)methodWithIdReturnValue
{
    return [^{ NSLog(@"I am in a block"); } copy];
}
```

You can use blocks as parameters, too. The code in Listing 4-26 demonstrates how blocks can be used to enumerate over the contents of an array without using a for loop.

Listing 4-26. Array Enumeration Using Blocks

```
NSArray *array = ...; //some array

[array enumerateObjectsUsingBlock:^(id obj, NSUInteger idx, BOOL *stop) {
    NSLog(@"Array index %d is %@", idx, obj);
}];
```

If you take a look in NSArray.h, you can find the declaration for this method. Listing 4-27 includes a naïve implementation of how this method might work.

Listing 4-27. Block Declaration, Assignment, and Invocation

```
- (void)enumerateObjectsUsingBlock:(void (^)(id obj, NSUInteger idx, BOOL *stop))block
{
    for (NSInteger i = 0; i < self.count; i++)
    {
        __block BOOL stop;
        block([self objectAtIndex:i], i, &stop);
        if (stop)
            return;
    }
}
```

This brings us to another important feature of blocks: lexical closures.

Lexical Closures

Block objects can use variables that are in lexical scope when they are declared. The variables are captured by the block and can be accessed from within the block code, as shown in Listing 4-28.

Listing 4-28. Blocks as Lexical Closures

```
void (^exampleBlock)(void);

if (YES) //just to create a new lexical closure
```

```
{
    id obj = ...; //some object
    NSInteger someInteger = 13;
    exampleBlock = ^(void) {
        NSLog(@"I captured the object %@ and the int %d from my lexical scope!", obj,
someInteger);
    };
}
```

```
exampleBlock();
```

While blocks can access the variables they capture from the lexical scope they are defined in, these variables are *read-only*. Writing to a variable from the block will generate a compiler error (see Listing 4-29).

Listing 4-29. Blocks Cannot Write to External Variables

```
void (^exampleBlock)(void);

NSInteger someInteger = 13;
exampleBlock = ^(void) {
    someInteger = 11; //generates a compiler error
};

exampleBlock();
```

In order to write to local variables captured in the block's scope, the variable declaration must use the qualifier __block. Variables declared with the __block keyword, such as those seen in Listing 4-30, are stored and accessed through a hidden level of indirection. If these variables are declared on the stack, then they still exist on the stack, but if any block that references them is copied to the heap, the storage for these block variables will also be moved to the heap.

Listing 4-30. __block Variables

```
void (^exampleBlock)(void);

__block NSInteger someInteger = 13;
exampleBlock = ^(void) {
    someInteger = 11;
};

//someInteger is 13
exampleBlock();
//someInteger is now 11
```

A clever and cunning trick at the runtime level even ensures that all references to the block variable are updated to refer to its new location, including any blocks still on the stack and even any surrounding references inside the original function. Listing 4-31 shows this in action.

Listing 4-31.   __block Variables and Copied Blocks

```
- (void) myMethod
{
    // this variable exists on the stack
    __block NSUInteger someInteger = 0;

    // pass it to a method which copies the block
    [self.someObject doSomethingWithBlock: ^{
        someInteger++;
    }];

    // ... wait a while ...

    // now 'someInteger' is on the heap, and we can still use it.
    NSLog(@"After a while, someInteger is %u", (unsigned)someInteger);
}
```

It's also worth noting that any global variables or method-static variables referenced by blocks are neither copied nor seen as read-only: they're global so they exist only once in memory and can be accessed from anywhere, including any blocks, without any special help from the compiler.

The block objects you've seen so far have only ever been local variables. Naturally, it's possible to store blocks as instance variables, too. This looks something like the code in Listing 4-32. Note that this code has a very subtle, very serious bug.

Listing 4-32. Block Reference Cycles

```
@implementation MyObject
{
    void (^exampleBlock)(void);
}

-(void)someMethod
{
    NSLog(@"This is an instance method");
}

-(id)init
{
    if (!(self = [super init]))
        return nil;

    exampleBlock = ^(void) {
        [self someMethod];
    };

    return self;
}

@end
```

Remember that blocks maintain strong references to the Objective-C objects they captured in their lexical context and copy any primitive values from the stack. The code in Listing 4-33 forms a strong reference to the block object, and the block object forms a strong reference to the object. This is a reference cycle and will leak memory!

These kinds of reference cycles are very easy to miss when writing your code. Any reference to a property or instance variable will cause the block to make a strong reference to `self`. Consider the flawed code in Listing 4-33.

Listing 4-33. Block Reference Cycles with Instance Variables

```
@interface MyObject
@end

@implementation MyObject
{
    void (^exampleBlock)(void);
    NSString * _someString;

}

-(id)init
{
    if (!(self = [super init]))
        return nil;

    exampleBlock = ^(void) {
        // the variable reference here means the block implicitly
        // references 'self', causing a retain cycle.
        NSLog(@"%@", _someString);
    };

    return self;
}

@end
```

What you *think* you're making a reference to is the string stored in the property, but what's actually being referenced is *self*. The solution is to explicitly use a weak reference to self instead. Consider the code from Listing 4-34, rewritten to avoid reference cycles.

> **Note**   Remember that zeroing weak references in ARC code are only available from OS X 10.7 and iOS and later. Other ARC features will work (with a little compiler help) on OS X 10.6 and iOS 4, but this particular feature relies on changes across the system frameworks in the newer operating systems, so it's not backwards-portable.

Listing 4-34. Block Reference Cycles with Properties

```objc
@interface MyObject

@property (nonatomic, strong) NSString *myString;

@end

@implementation
{
    void (^exampleBlock)(void);
}

@synthesize someString;

-(id)init
{
    if (!(self = [super init]))
        return nil;

    __weak MyObject * weakSelf = self;

    exampleBlock = ^(void) {
        __strong MyObject * blockSelf = weakSelf;
        if ( blockSelf != nil )
            NSLog(@"%@", blockSelf.someString);
    };

    return self;
}

@end
```

The block only captures the weakSelf variable, which is a weak reference to self, so the reference cycle is broken. Then within the block a new strong reference (thus, retained by the ARC-ready compiler) is created. If the weakly-referenced object has been deallocated, it will be nil, so you can check for this before doing any work. If you're ever debugging problems like this, the static analyzer in Xcode can be a great help.

> **Note**   The practice of creating a new strong reference within the block is *very* important. The weak reference is set to zero as soon as the object it references is deallocated, and this can happen *at any time*. As a result, it might disappear half-way through some long-running set of operations. When the compiler sees a strong reference created from a weak reference, it knows to obtain *and retain* the object and to release it when it goes out of scope. This therefore keeps the object in memory until such time as it's no longer needed.

Grand Central Dispatch

You've seen how blocks can be used to store arbitrary functions, passed as parameters in useful ways, and used to capture variables in a lexical closure. What makes block *really useful* is Grand Central Dispatch, or GCD for short.

GCD was introduced by Apple, alongside blocks, as a way to easily use multiple threads in your applications. The traditional way to think about multithreaded programming is in terms of threads of execution (line by line of code). Instead, GCD has us look at threads in terms of queues. Work is dispatched onto a queue and dequeued for eventual execution.

Dispatch queues actually wrap POSIX thread work queues (a form of thread pool), and GCD is very clever about how it uses these. Dispatch queues are very cheap to create and use. Let's first focus on how to use the built-in queues and later look at more advanced techniques like making your own dispatch queues.

Queues are represented by the dispatch_queue_t data type, an opaque data structure whose internal state you should not access. The main queue, representing the main thread, is accessible via dispatch_get_main_queue(). There are other global queues built into the system, which you saw in Chapter 3, and they are accessible via the dispatch_get_global_queue method. See Listing 4-35 for a reminder.

Listing 4-35. dispatch_async

```
dispatch_queue_t targeQueue =  dispatch_get_global_queue(DISPATCH_QUEUE_PRIORITY_HIGH, 0);
dispatch_async(targetQueue, ^{
    //perform some high-priority task in the background
    dispatch_async(dispatch_get_main_queue(), ^{
        //update the UI from the main queue
    };
});
```

The code in Listing 4-36 demonstrates how to enqueue blocks onto a dispatch queue in an asynchronous way. When you use dispatch_async, the method call returns immediately and the block is eventually executed on its target queue.

In contrast, using the method dispatch_sync causes the thread it is called on to block until the block has been dequeued from its target queue and execution has finished.

> **Note**   Since the calling thread will block on a call to dispatch_sync(), calling this method with the same target queue it is being invoked from will hang your application indefinitely.

In addition to synchronous and asynchronous dispatches, block dequeuing can be triggered after a certain time interval.

Listing 4-36. dispatch_after

```
double delayInSeconds = 2.0;
dispatch_time_t popTime = dispatch_time(DISPATCH_TIME_NOW, delayInSeconds * NSEC_PER_SEC);
dispatch_after(popTime, dispatch_get_main_queue(), ^(void){
    NSLog(@"Executed after 2 seconds");
});
```

Use dispatch_queue_create to create your own dispatch queue; this method requires a C string name for the queue (typically associated with a bundle identifier) and an attribute. Currently, the only attributes are DISPATCH_QUEUE_SERIAL, which is defined as NULL, for normal FIFO queuing behavior and DISPATCH_QUEUE_CONCURRENT, which allows blocks to be dequeued and executed concurrently with respect to other blocks on the same queue (see Listing 4-37).

Listing 4-37. dispatch_queue_create

```
dispatch_queue_t backgroundQueue = dispatch_queue_create("com.myApp.backgroundQueue", NULL);
dispatch_async(backgroundQueue, ^{
    NSLog(@"Some code to execute in the background");
});
dispatch_release(backgroundQueue);
```

Any call to dispatch_queue_create or dispatch_retain must be matched by a call to dispatch_release with the created queue. Queues contain a retain count of how many times they've been retained, which is set to 1 when they're created. Once this retain count reaches zero, the queue is reused by the system. In this respect, they are very similar to Objective-C objects; in fact, in OS X 10.8 and iOS 6 and above, they *are* Objective-C objects, at least in Objective-C programs. This means that, provided you target those operating systems or later, ARC will automatically retain and release your dispatch objects for you.

When queuing a block for execution, the queue is retained by the block and released when the block has finished executing. This indicates that the code in Listing 4-37 is completely correct; even though the dispatch queue is released immediately after enqueueing a block, the block has already retained the queue.

Dispatch objects such as queues can be suspended and resumed with the dispatch_suspend and dispatch_resume functions, respectively. These suspensions can be nested, too. Each queue keeps a counter of how many times it has been suspended. For each suspend, it is incremented, and for each resume, it is decremented. Calls to these methods *must* be balanced. Do not try to suspend any of the global queues, including the main queue; these queues cannot be suspended.

Suspending a queue stops the queue from dequeuing any subsequent blocks until the queue has been resumed. It does not stop the execution of any currently executing blocks. Listing 4-38 shows how this can be done.

Listing 4-38. dispatch_resume and dispatch_suspend

```
dispatch_queue_t backgroundQueue;
...
dispatch_async(dispatch_get_global_queue(DISPATCH_QUEUE_PRIORITY_HIGH, 0), ^{
    dispatch_suspend(backgroundQueue);
    //perform some action here, possibly even enqueue more blocks onto backgroundQueue
    dispatch_resume(backgroundQueue);
});
```

Since queues are FIFO and do not allow parallel execution of blocks, it's possible to implement thread synchronization without using expensive locks. Access to a shared data structure can be synchronized by accessing it only in a special queue, as shown in Listing 4-39.

Listing 4-39. Using GCD for Thread Synchronization

```
@implementation MyThreadSafeObject
{
    dispatch_queue_t lockQueue;
    id obj;
}

-(id)init
{
    if (!(self = [super init]))
        return nil;

    lockQueue = dispatch_queue_create("com.myApp.lockQueue", NULL);

    return self;
}

-(void)dealloc
{
    dispatch_release(lockQueue);
}

-(void)setObject:(id)theObj
{
    dispatch_sync(lockQueue, ^{
        obj = theObj;
    });
}

-(id)obj
{
    __block result;

    dispatch_sync(lockQueue, ^{
        result = obj;
    });

    return result;
}
```

This allows any queue to access the variable obj in a completely thread-safe way; all writes and reads are guaranteed to occur on the same thread.

When using concurrent background queues, it is sometimes necessary to submit a block that cannot be executed concurrently. Use dispatch_barrier_sync and dispatch_barrier_async to wait for already enqueued blocks to finish their execution. The newly enqueued block is then executed by itself before any subsequently enqueued blocks are executed (see Listing 4-40).

Note that calling these barrier methods has no effect on a non-concurrent dispatch queue. All calls to enqueue blocks on serial queues are like barrier calls on concurrent queues.

Listing 4-40. dispatch_barrier_async

```
dispatch_queue_t backgroundQueue = dispatch_queue_create("com.myApp.concurrentQueue",
DISPATCH_QUEUE_CONCURRENT);
...
dispatch_barrier_async(backgroundQueue, ^{
    //code here will *not* be executed concurrently, despect being on a concurrent queue.
});
```

If you need to repeat a task some number of iterations, you can use concurrent dispatch queues to take advantage of multiple cores on the system. The method `dispatch_apply` accepts a block to be executed some number of times. The code in Listing 4-41 demonstrates a trivial example of using `dispatch_apply`.

Listing 4-41. dispatch_apply

```
dispatch_queue_t concurrentQueue = dispatch_queue_create("com.myApp.concurrentQueue",
DISPATCH_QUEUE_CONCURRENT);

size_t count = 100;

dispatch_apply(count, concurrentQueue , ^(size_t i) {
    NSLog(@"iteration %d", i);
});
```

A call to `dispatch_apply` is a synchronous call and will block the thread it is called on until all iterations have been completed.

> **Note** There is no guaranteed ordering implied by `dispatch_apply`; it will actually break up the provided counter into a few separate chunks and will hand each chunk to a different thread. This means that thread 1 might perform iterations 1-10 in serial order while thread 2 performs 11-20, thread 3 performs 21-30, and so on. Listing 4-42 shows a sample of the result of running the code in Listing 4-41 so you can see this happening.

Listing 4-42. Partial Output of Listing 4-41

```
2012-05-10 13:25:28.889 SimpleHTTPServer[1535:2703] Iteration 16
2012-05-10 13:25:28.889 SimpleHTTPServer[1535:2303] Iteration 19
2012-05-10 13:25:28.936 SimpleHTTPServer[1535:2f03] Iteration 25
2012-05-10 13:25:28.936 SimpleHTTPServer[1535:403] Iteration 24
2012-05-10 13:25:28.936 SimpleHTTPServer[1535:2603] Iteration 23
2012-05-10 13:25:28.936 SimpleHTTPServer[1535:2903] Iteration 28
2012-05-10 13:25:28.936 SimpleHTTPServer[1535:2803] Iteration 27
2012-05-10 13:25:28.936 SimpleHTTPServer[1535:2303] Iteration 30
2012-05-10 13:25:28.936 SimpleHTTPServer[1535:2703] Iteration 29
2012-05-10 13:25:28.936 SimpleHTTPServer[1535:2503] Iteration 26
```

Though dispatch queues are where you enqueue blocks for execution, custom queues are not responsible for executing the actual blocks. At runtime, queues use their *target queue* to actually execute blocks.

By default, all dispatch queues target the default priority global queue. You can change a target queue using the `dispatch_set_target_queue` method.

There are several reasons you may want to change the target queue of a custom queue. You may want blocks submitted to your custom queue to be executed on the higher priority global queue. Or maybe you'd like them executed on main queue. You can even set custom queues as targets of other custom queues, creating a hierarchy of queue targets.

> **Note**   Defining a target queue hierarchy with a loop will lead to undefined behavior.

If you suspend a queue, any queues that target that queue will also be suspended. This is an easy way to suspend and resume a large number of queues at once.

> **Note**   Do not try to set the target queue of the main queue or a global queue.

The final feature of Grand Central Dispatch is the idea of one-time invocation of a block. Recall the singleton pattern implementation in Objective-C (Listing 4-43).

Listing 4-43. Singleton in Objective-C

```
static MySingleton *sharedInstance = nil;

+(MySingleton *)sharedInstance
{
    @syncronized(self)
    {
        if (!sharedInstance)
        {
            sharedInstance = [[self alloc] init]; //or other initialization
        }
    }

    return sharedInstance;
}
```

The lock used to synchronize the initialization is only really needed once, but it must be locked and unlocked during every invocation of `sharedInstance`. This is relatively expensive and can be replaced by a block that is guaranteed to only ever be executed once. Listing 4-44 is a much more efficient and elegant solution to initializing the shared instance of a singleton.

Listing 4-44. A More Elegant Singleton Solution

```
static MySingleton *sharedInstance = nil;

+(MySingleton *)sharedInstance
```

```
{
    static dispatch_once_t predicate;
    dispatch_once(&predicate, ^{
        sharedInstance = [[MySingleton alloc] init];
    });

    return sharedInstance;
}
```

Summary

In this chapter, you learned a great deal about the workings of the Objective-C runtime and the features it offers you as a programmer, even without the attendant libraries and frameworks. You now know all about blocks and how to use them, about the exception handling and synchronization primitives provided by the languages, and how messaging really works. You also took a quick look at Grand Central Dispatch, which, while not Objective-C itself, provides such a fundamental set of tools that its use is going to become more and more important in the future.

In later chapters you will put this new knowledge to work as we expand on some of the topics introduced here.

Chapter 5

Using the Filesystem

The filesystem has been around for a long time. Pretty much every general-purpose computer of the last 40 years has had a filesystem of some description, so it would be fairly safe to assume that the APIs for interacting with it are all clean and simple, right? I mean, for something that's been around for so long, there can't really be any complications that haven't already been ironed out already. Right? Anyone?

Bueller...?

Ah, if only that were the case... The filesystem is usually, from the user point of view, a fairly simple construct, and that hasn't really changed. Sure, there are newer types of filesystem out there, but they all export these things called files, which allow reading and writing, and includesome sort of permissions system.

What *has* changed over the years are our demands of this clean and simple interface. Now we have multiprocessor computers running concurrent software, all of which is trying to do something with the filesystem. Then there is the media involved: when working with memory or a solid state drive (SSD), the physical location of a file isn't a concern. However, on a rotary disk (such as the still-common hard disk), a single program reading from one file and writing to another can run quickly or slowly based entirely on the physical location of its two files: if the read/write heads on the disk have to move a long way between these files, everything will be slow. Now, that could be solved if only one program were accessing the disk, but what about when several are accessing files from all over the place? What if many programs are accessing the same file?

This chapter looks at the basic filesystem APIs and the various other pieces of the puzzle that Apple has provided to solve such problems as those outlined above.

Files, Folders, and URLs

The filesystem in Mac OS X and iOS is based upon the now-standard idea of *files* and *folders* (also called *directories*). If you're coming from the world of Windows computers, then you will also be familiar with the concept of a *drive*, commonly denoted by a single letter and a colon, for example C: or E:, which would appear at the start of each full path. You should know that OS X and iOS don't use this form of notation, instead using the UNIX format of simple paths preceded by a forward-slash character: '/'. Instead of Windows' approach of making each drive the root of its own filesystem, OS X unifies everything under a single root.

A *file* is a single container of data on the disk. The data can be anything; as far as the filesystem is concerned, it's just a collection of raw bytes. A *folder* is an item that acts as a container for other items, be they folders or files, and these can be nested to a reasonably high level (although not infinitely). For example, in the path /Users/jim/Desktop/, there are four folders specified, in order of containment. These are enumerated in Table 5-1.

Table 5-1. Folder Path Components

Folder	Description
/	The root of the filesystem; all full paths start with this folder.
Users	A folder called Users within the root folder.
jim	A folder called jim within the Users folder.
Desktop	A folder called Desktop within the jim folder.

You can tell in this case that the path refers to a folder because you can see a trailing forward-slash character. This is not necessary, but it can save the system some work, as it would have to inspect the filesystem to determine whether the last item in the path was a file or a folder. Note that there is no way to directly specify that something is a file in the same manner.

URLs

Historically, files have been identified using only their path, normally specified using a string variable. In Objective-C, this need be no different; in fact, you'll find a lot of places where a file or folder is specified using an NSString variable—NSData's +dataWithContentsOfFile:, for example, takes a path parameter specified using an NSString. In recent years, however, Apple has begun to move towards the URL (specifically, the NSURL class) as its locator of choice.

UNIFORM RESOURCE LOCATORS

The Internet Engineering Task Force (IETF) created the URL in 1992 as a means of combining communications protocol and Internet domain information with a standard filesystem path. It consists of two major parts: a *scheme* and a *context*, separated by a colon. For e-mail URLs, the scheme is "mailto," resulting in the following URL:

    mailto:jimdovey@me.com

For filesystem-based URLs, the context was adapted from an existing ad-hoc standard that prepended a hostname to a path, prepending the whole thing with two slashes (i.e. //jims-imac/Users/jim/Desktop/), resulting in the following, more familiar format:

    afp://jims-imac/Users/jim/Desktop/

This format is used again for local files, with a scheme of "file," and there are two formats you'll likely encounter. The first is the more correct version, specifying a hostname of "localhost" to indicate the computer itself, and is the format you'll see used by NSURL:

```
file://localhost/Users/jim/Desktop/
```

The other format makes use of a shorthand for "localhost," which is an empty string. This format is most frequently used by people typing or otherwise quickly converting a path to a file URL:

```
file:///Users/jim/Desktop/
```

There are, of course, other URL schemes with which you'll be familiar, beginning with `http://` and maybe even `ftp://`. You'll look at those later in the book when you look at network resources.

There are a few reasons for this decision. First, a file is a resource, and a URL is, literally, a *Uniform Resource Locator*. Another reason is that since a URL can represent locations outside of the local filesystem, its use can provide many objects with a simple means of accessing data across the network or other storage medium.

Chiefly, however, is the matter of *metadata*. There is a lot of extra data associated with files and folders—their size, access permissions, and more—which are often accessed quite frequently. As a path string is passed through a number of different APIs, each one of those methods might want to know something about the file to which it refers; well, each request involves a round-trip to the operating system kernel to obtain that information. This isn't amassed and passed around between different methods, as they are only expecting a string of characters to refer to the file.

In a talk given at Apple's Worldwide Developers' Conference (WWDC) in 2009, Apple engineers showed how they tracked all the filesystem calls made by the Preview application as it opened. Their data showed that the file's information was accessed a great many times just while the app was launching. As a result, they updated the NSURL class to provide APIs for directly accessing particular resources, and to cache those values so that they could be quickly fetched again without the same round-trip to the filesystem. As a result of this and some other refactoring, the number of filesystem events dropped dramatically and the Preview application's launch time was greatly reduced.

Creating and Using URLs

The NSURL class provides a few different initializers, shown in Table 5-2, although for local filesystem access the +fileURLWithPath:isDirectory: class method is likely the most useful.

Table 5-2. NSURL Initializers

Initializer	Description
-initWithScheme:host:path:	Initializes a URL of the form [scheme]://[host][path]
+fileURLWithPath:	Creates a URL referencing a local file or folder. A filesystem call is placed to determine whether the path references a file or a folder.
+fileURLWithPath:isDirectory:	Creates a URL referencing a local file or folder. The caller specifies the type of the item, avoiding the filesystem call.
+URLWithString:	Creates a URL from a string representation of a full URL, such as http://www.apple.com/index.html.
+URLWithString:relativeToURL:	Creates a URL relative to another URL; used for referencing items by relative paths, for example in HTML documents, or referencing a file within a folder for which you already have a URL.

In this chapter I will use only the -fileURLWithPath: and -fileURLWithPath:isDirectory: methods; the others I'll detail in a later chapter when dealing with network resources. These two methods are used to initialize a URL using a standard string-based file path. You can always check whether a given URL references a local file using the -isFileURL method, which simply checks for the presence of a file: URL scheme.

It's easy to create and adjust path URLs on OS X and iOS, too. The NSURL class provides a number of routines designed to work with path components in a number of different ways: adding and removing components and extensions, or building paths from a list of components. In fact, this way of building paths is often considered much cleaner than hard-coding the UNIX path separator (the solidus, or forward-slash character '/') into a string. A lot of programmers haven't adopted this technique to the extent that perhaps they should due to the amount of code required to create an array of path components in the first place. With the new array literals in Objective-C, however, it becomes very quick and easy to type, so now there's really no excuse. The most commonly-used methods can be seen in Listing 5-1.

> **Note**   While I am focusing on NSURL at this point, it should be noted that the same path manipulation routines are available on the NSString class as well.

Listing 5-1. URL Path Manipulation

```
// build a URL for a new document
NSURL * homeFolder = [NSURL fileURLWithPath: NSHomeDirectory() isDirectory: YES];
NSURL * base = [NSURL fileURLWithPathComponents: @[homeFolder, @"Documents", @"MyApp"]];
NSURL * document = [[base URLByAppendingPathComponent: @"MyDocument"]
URLByAppendingPathExtension: @"mydoc"];

// ...

// check the URL for validity
NSURL * userURL = self.userSelectedURL;
```

```
if ( [[userURL pathExtension] isEqualToString: @"mydoc"] == NO )
    return ( NO ); // not a valid document extension

// see if it's in the user's home folder (/Users/someone)
NSArray * components = [userURL pathComponents];
if ( [[components subarrayWithRange: NSMakeRange(0, 2)] isEqual: [NSHomeDirectory()
    pathComponents]] == NO )
    return ( NO );  // only support documents within the user's home folder

// get the name of the file out of the path
NSString * fileName = [userURL lastPathComponent];

// etc...
```

More of these methods can be found in `<Foundation/NSURL.h>`, in the `NSURLPathUtilities` category on `NSURL`.

Resources

There is a lot of metadata associated with a file or folder. They have names (well, *duh*) and also creation/modification/last-access dates, they have sizes (both in terms of contents and the space allocated on disk for them), they can have permissions and security information, and a lot of other metadata. These are all accessed in a keyed-value format similar to a dictionary. A few of the most common items are listed in Table 5-3.

Table 5-3. URL Resource Specifiers

Resource Specifier	Description
NSURLLocalizedNameKey	Returns a localized (or extension-hidden) form of the item's name, suitable for display to the user.
NSURLIsRegularFileKey, NSURLIsDirectoryKey, NSURLIsVolumeKey	Used to determine the type of item referenced by the URL.
NSURLCreationDateKey, NSURLContentAccessDateKey, NSURLContentModificationDateKey	Obtains the dates at which the item was created, accessed, or modified.
NSURLVolumeURLKey	Obtains the URL for the volume upon which the item resides.
NSURLTypeIdentifierKey, NSURLLocalizedTypeDescriptionKey	Used to determine the programmatic and user-visible type of the referenced item respectively.
NSURLEffectiveIconKey, NSURLCustomIconKey	Returns an NSImage instance for the item's current icon, or only the custom icon if one has been set.
NSURLVolumeTotalCapacityKey, NSURLVolumeAvailableCapacityKey	Returns the total size and available size of the volume referenced by the URL.

There are, of course, many more resource values available through the NSURL API— see
`<Foundation/NSURL.h>` for the full list and their descriptions.

You typically access resource values using four primary functions, described in Table 5-4. You
will notice that the single-resource accessor, `-getResourceValue:forKey:error:`, returns its value
through a by-reference parameter rather than in its return value, and you may think that this is
unwieldy. You would, of course, be right—it *is* unwieldy. However, this is not only the best (and
most idiomatic) way to distinguish between a stored value of nil and an unavailable value, its
awkwardness underlines an important point which underlines the reason for this API's existence:
it's better to request multiple resources all at once than in multiple passes. As a result, the better
way to work is to determine *all* the resources in whose values you might be interested and request
all of them at once using the `-resourceValuesForKeys:error:` method. This allows the system to
use the most optimal method of accessing the resource's data and avoids potential disk-thrashing
behavior should you request these values while the disk is in use by another process.

Table 5-4. NSURL Resource Access APIs

Method	Description
- (BOOL)getResourceValue:(out id*)value forKey:(NSString*)key error:(out NSError**)error	Loads a single resource value either from the NSURL's cache or from the filesystem itself, returning it by reference through the value parameter. If the method returns YES and the value contains nil, then the resource does not contain the requested value. The method will only return NO if an error occurs while accessing the value.
- (NSDictionary*)resourceValuesForKeys:(NSArray*) keys error:(NSError**)error	Reads a list of resource values corresponding to the supplied array of keys. The returned dictionary contains any non-nil values found, accessed by their usual resource keys.
- (BOOL)setResourceValue:(id)value forKey:(NSString*)key error:(NSError**)error	Sets a single resource value on the item referenced by the URL. Attempts to set read-only or unsupported properties will fail silently, but are not considered errors (the method will still return YES).
- (BOOL)setResourceValues:(NSDictionary*) keyedValues error:(NSError**)error	Sets multiple resource values on the URL's referenced item. As with the other setter, if a particular property is not supported or read-only, that property's set will silently fail. Should an error occur, the keys of any items whose values could not be set are available from the error's userInfo dictionary using the key NSURLKeysOfUnsetValuesKey.

Access Permissions

Files on OS X and iOS have two sets of permissions data. The first is the standard UNIX
permission field, which specifies whether the file can be *read*, *written*, or *executed* by the file's
owner, the owner's *group*, and *other* users. Additionally, the *execute* permission when applied

to folders is used to specify *search* permission, namely the ability to obtain a list of the folder's contents. Search permission is not required to test for the existence of a named file, but it is required in order to scan the contents of a given folder.

UNIX (or more correctly POSIX) permission information is typically provided by the programmer using a bitfield represented using octal numbers (where each digit can be between 0 and 7, using three bits per digit). Each permission has a single bit associated with it, and each digit refers to the user, group, and other. Within each digit, the three bits represent, from left to right (so, most to least significant bit), the read, write, and execute permissions. Therefore the value 0755 (remember that to type octal values in C and Objective-C you type the number with a leading zero) sets all three bits (7 octal = 111 binary) for the user, meaning the user can read, write, and execute the file. The *group* and *other* sections set only the read and execute bits (5 octal = 101 binary), so you can see that only the owner of the file can change its contents.

This information is visible from the command line using the ls -l command (ls = list, -l = long format), where it is presented in a more readable format, as shown in Listing 5-2. The first entry on each line describes the file's type, permissions, and some attributes.

Listing 5-2. File and Folder Attributes on the Command Line

```
LP-347 ~ " ls -l
total 8
drwx------+ 12 jdovey  204937174   408  3 Jun 20:12 Desktop
drwx------+ 38 jdovey  204937174  1292  2 Jun 14:50 Documents
drwx------+  4 jdovey  204937174   136  3 Jun 19:20 Downloads
drwx------@ 31 jdovey  204937174  1054  2 Jun 13:29 Dropbox
drwx------@ 43 jdovey  204937174  1462  4 Jun 08:24 Library
drwx------+  3 jdovey  204937174   102  1 Jun 16:01 Movies
drwx------+  3 jdovey  204937174   102  1 Jun 16:01 Music
drwx------+  8 jdovey  204937174   272  1 Jun 23:54 Pictures
drwxr-xr-x+  4 jdovey  204937174   136  1 Jun 16:01 Public
drwxr-xr-x@  4 jdovey  204937174   136 23 Aug  2010 Scripts
LP-347 ~ "
```

The first letter tells you the type of the item; in this case d indicates that the item is a directory (folder). A regular file has a type of -, symbolic links use l, sockets use s, and there are others that you are even less likely to encounter. Following this is a group of nine characters, in three groups of three. These specify the read (r), write (w), and execute/search (x) privileges for the user, group, and other users respectively. If a privilege is granted, its letter appears in the appropriate slot; otherwise its slot contains a hyphen (-) character. You can see that most items in Listing 5-2 are folders that are only readable, writable, and searchable by their owner. The last two items, Public and Scripts, are also readable and searchable by members of the same group and any other users.

Following the permissions fields is one more character, which is used to denote extra information available. In this case, some items specify the @ character, denoting *extended attributes* are set (more on those shortly), while others have the + character, informing you that an *access control list* is set on that item, which leads nicely into the next type of permission data.

Access Control Lists (or *ACLs*) are used to specify a larger number of permissions in a much more granular manner. For instance, you can use ACLs to grant or deny privileges to specific users and groups, and you can grant or deny privileges not just for reading, writing, and executing, but deletion, adding or removing items from folders, and much more. You can view this at the command line using `ls -le`, as in Listing 5-3.

Listing 5-3. Access Control Lists on the Command Line

```
LP-347 ~ " ls -le
total 8
drwx------+ 12 jdovey  204937174    408  3 Jun 20:12 Desktop
 0: group:everyone deny delete
drwx------+ 38 jdovey  204937174   1292  2 Jun 14:50 Documents
 0: group:everyone deny delete
drwx------+  4 jdovey  204937174    136  3 Jun 19:20 Downloads
 0: group:everyone deny delete
drwx------@ 31 jdovey  204937174   1054  2 Jun 13:29 Dropbox
drwx------@ 43 jdovey  204937174   1462  4 Jun 08:24 Library
 0: group:everyone deny delete
drwx------+  3 jdovey  204937174    102  1 Jun 16:01 Movies
 0: group:everyone deny delete
drwx------+  3 jdovey  204937174    102  1 Jun 16:01 Music
 0: group:everyone deny delete
drwx------+  8 jdovey  204937174    272  1 Jun 23:54 Pictures
 0: group:everyone deny delete
drwxr-xr-x+  4 jdovey  204937174    136  1 Jun 16:01 Public
 0: group:everyone deny delete
drwxr-xr-x@  4 jdovey  204937174    136 23 Aug  2010 Scripts
LP-347 ~ "
```

Access Control Lists can have an arbitrary number of privileges stated, and they are processed in order—a later privilege overrides an earlier one. In Listing 5-3, you can see that the members of the group "everyone" (which literally means everyone, unless a computer administrator has exempted someone from that group) have been denied the right to delete the item. This is designed to prevent any software from removing the preconfigured home folder contents on OS X. A more complex example is available by looking at the root of your system disk, excerpted in Listing 5-4.

Listing 5-4. A More Complex ACL

```
drwxrwxrwt@  4 root  admin       136  3 Jun 19:45 Volumes
 0: group:everyone deny add_file,add_subdirectory,directory_inherit,only_inherit
```

Here you can see that the everyone group has again been denied some privileges, specifically the ability to add files and subfolders to the Volumes folder. The `directory_inherit` privilege specifies that any subfolders inherit this ACL entry. The last item, `only_inherit`, is a special one: it tells the ACL processor that this particular privilege rule should *only* be used to define privileges inherited by items within this folder, but should *not* affect the item itself. As a result, the whole "deny" rule seen here doesn't apply to the Volumes folder itself but will be automatically applied to any other folder created within it.

Access Control Lists and permissions can be accessed through NSURL's resource API. Effective permissions for the current user (i.e. whether your app can read/write/execute an item) can be obtained using the keys `NSURLIsReadableKey`, `NSURLIsWritableKey`, and `NSURLIsExecutableKey`. Full POSIX permissions and Access Control Lists are accessible with `NSURLFileSecurityKey`, which returns an instance of NSFileSecurity. The one hitch to this otherwise nice API is that the NSFileSecurity class defines no methods or properties at all. Instead, to make use of it you have to cast it to its toll-free bridged CoreFoundation counterpart, CFFileSecurityRef. Having done so, you'll be able to make use of it to read and potentially modify the file's user/group/other POSIX permissions and any access control lists, although the latter uses an even lower-level plain C API, which is beyond the scope of this book. For your delight and edification, however, I respectfully submit Listing 5-5, which shows how to list all the relevant information from an NSFileSecurity object.

Listing 5-5. Using NSFileSecurity

```
NSFileSecurity * sec = ...;
CFFileSecurityRef cfSec = (__bridge CFFileSecurityRef)sec;
CFUUIDRef tmpUUID = NULL;
uid_t owner = (uid_t)-1;
gid_t group = (gid_t)-1;
mode_t mode = 0;
acl_t acl = NULL;

if ( CFFileSecurityCopyOwnerUUID(cfSec, &tmpUUID) )
    NSLog(@"Owner UUID = %@", CFBridgingRelease(tmpUUID));
if ( CFFileSecurityCopyGroupUUID(cfSec, &tmpUUID) )
    NSLog(@"Group UUID = %@", CFBridgingRelease(tmpUUID));

if ( CFFileSecurityGetOwner(cfSec, &owner) )
    NSLog(@"Owner       = %s (%u)", getpwuid(owner)->pw_name, owner);
if ( CFFileSecurityGetGroup(cfSec, &group) )
    NSLog(@"Group       = %s (%u)", getgrgid(group)->gr_name, group);

if ( CFFileSecurityGetMode(cfSec, &mode) )
    NSLog(@"Mode        = %#o", mode);

if ( CFFileSecurityCopyAccessControlList(cfSec, &acl) )
{
    char * aclStr = acl_to_text(acl, NULL);
    NSLog(@"ACL         = %s", aclStr);
    acl_free(aclStr);
    acl_free(acl);
}
```

File Reference URLs

Along with path-based URLs, a local file or folder can also be referenced using a special type of file URL known as a *file reference URL*. The theory goes like this: a path-based URL specifies a location in terms of a path through various folders to a location. The item at that location is known by the filesystem through a unique identifier. When that file moves elsewhere or is renamed, its identifier doesn't change, nor does the storage allocated for that file on disk. The only change that takes place is that the reference to it in its current parent folder is removed, and a similar reference is placed into its new parent folder. A file reference URL identifies the file by its reference number rather than its position in the folder hierarchy, meaning that it doesn't matter where the file resides, or whether it moves—as long as it exists, it can be found.

Any file path URL can generate a file reference URL referencing the same resource (assuming it currently exists; file path URLs can reference items you've yet to create, after all) using the -fileReferenceURL method and can be identified using -isFileReferenceURL. Once you have a file reference URL, the user can gleefully move or rename the file as they wish, and your software will still be able to locate it. This makes them ideal for keeping references to user-visible documents.

Now, file reference numbers aren't static. They are only valid until the next time you reboot your computer. This makes them less than useful for storage. For that purpose, URLs have the ability to generate something called a *bookmark*. A URL bookmark is similar to an *alias file* in the Finder application; it contains enough data to locate the file again through various means, and it even includes information on accessing any volumes necessary. This last means that you can create a bookmark to a file on a shared filesystem and any attempt to access—or *resolve*—that bookmark when its volume isn't currently mounted will prompt the system to do so automatically, prompting the user for authentication if necessary. Bookmarks can also cache any resource value associated with a URL and can be specified in a relative format. Relative bookmarks might sound strange at first, but when you consider that you might want to reference a file on an external backup, you would NOT want your bookmark to match your local copy during resolution. As a result, providing a relative bookmark means you can specifically tell the bookmark that it is based off the URL for the external volume, providing some useful context to the lookup later on which will help the system avoid false matches.

A bookmark is provided as a blob of opaque data and can be generated from any file path or file reference URL using the method -bookmarkDataWithOptions:includingResourceValuesForKeys :relativeToURL:error:. Any of the provided parameters can be zero (or nil). Listing 5-6 shows how bookmark data can be generated and placed into the application preferences for later access.

Listing 5-6. Caching Bookmark Data

```
NSURL * myURL = [NSURL fileURLWithPath:@"/Users/jim/Documents/Chapter05.doc"];
NSArray * keys = @[ NSURLLocalizedNameKey, NSURLVolumeLocalizedNameKey ];
NSError * error = nil;

NSData * bookmark = [myURL bookmarkDataWithOptions:
                                    NSURLBookmarkCreationPreferFileIDResolution
                    includingResourceValuesForKeys: keys
                                     relativeToURL: nil
                                            error: &error];
if ( bookmark == nil )
{
    // handle the error
}
else
{
    [[NSUserDefaults standardUserDefaults] setObject: bookmark forKey: @"LastItemURL"];
}
```

Caching resource values within the bookmark can be useful to keep track of values such as the item's localized name or its volume's localized name. A document-based application could then show this information to the user based directly on the bookmark without having to resolve it, which is very important if a list of files is being displayed. Resource values cached as part of a bookmark can be accessed directly from the bookmark data using the NSURL class method +resourceValuesForKeys:fromBookmarkData:.

A URL itself can be created from stored bookmark data using the method -initByResolving BookmarkData:options:relativeToURL:bookmarkDataIsStale:error: or its class factory method, as detailed in Listing 5-7.

Listing 5-7. Resolving a Bookmark

```
NSData *bookmark = [[NSUserDefaults standardUserDefaults] objectForKey: @"LastItemURL"];
BOOL isStale = NO;
NSError * error = nil;

NSURL *url = [NSURL URLByResolvingBookmarkData: bookmark
                                       options: 0
                           bookmarkDataIsStale: &isStale
                                         error: &error];
if ( url == nil )
{
    // handle the error
}
else if ( isStale )
{
    // the bookmark data needs to be updated: create & store a new bookmark
    // ...
}

// now use the URL...
```

Security Scope

One last component in the security capabilities of NSURL involves bookmarks and the app sandbox. The sandbox itself is something I'll discuss in more detail later in the book; for now, think of the sandbox as an environment in which your application has a very limited set of privileges to access and interact with the rest of the computer system. A sandboxed process gains access to files selected by the user in Open or Save dialogs, but otherwise can only access the contents of its own special storage area, separate from the rest of the system—its *sandbox*. In OS X 10.7.3, new APIs were introduced so that applications that required access to certain user-selected folders could retain access privileges across application launches. Prior to this, such privileges would only be allowed by asking the user to (again) select the item in an Open dialog. This could be problematic for applications such as clients for revision control systems, which require access to folders rather than files, yet do not treat those folders as their documents per se.

The way in which this shortcoming was addressed was to add the ability to store some of the sandbox-provided access privileges as part of a bookmark. These privileges are called *security scope*. The idea is that after a sandboxed application gains access to a folder or file, it can create a bookmark and specify some options to record its security scope information. The way to do this is by specifying one or two options in the options parameter to the bookmark creation APIs: NSURLBookmarkCreationWithSecurityScope adds the security information to the generated bookmark data, and NSURLBookmarkCreationSecurityScopeAllowOnlyReadAccess states that you only wish to gain read access to the bookmarked item, not write access.

When resolving a bookmark, you specify the NSURLBookmarkResolutionWithSecurityScope option to have the relevant access privileges prepared by the sandboxing system. After this, you wrap any use of the item at the URL with calls to -startAccessingSecurityScopedResource and -stopAccessingSecurityScopedResource, which together actually obtain and return the relevant access privileges from the system.

Filesystem Metadata

OS X and iOS both have a filesystem-level metadata system based around the concept of *extended attributes*. These attributes use string-based names in UTF-8 format, and the data associated with that name can be anything at all. Finder information (the locations of icons in the grid view, visibility status, and others) is stored using extended attributes, for example, and Time Machine backups track a lot of information using them, too.

You can see details of extended attributes easily from the Terminal application. For example, if you open the Terminal app and change to the root directory (type cd / at the prompt) you can use ls -l@ to view extended attributes for all files and folders there. The output will look something like that in Listing 5-8. The FinderInfo entries on most of these items are used to specify that these items be hidden in the Finder.

Listing 5-8. Extended Attributes on the Command Line

```
LP-347 / " ls -l@
total 30453
drwxrwxr-x+ 70 root   admin     2380  2 Jun 15:00 Applications
drwxr-xr-x+ 64 root   wheel     2176  3 Jun 22:54 Library
drwxr-xr-x@  3 root   wheel      102  2 Jun 13:29 Network
        com.apple.FinderInfo           32
drwxr-xr-x+  4 root   wheel      136  1 Jun 20:06 System
lrwxr-xr-x   1 root   wheel       60  4 Apr 14:05 User Guides And Information ->
/Library/Documentation/User Guides and Information.localized
drwxr-xr-x   6 root   admin      204  1 Jun 16:01 Users
drwxrwxrwt@  4 root   admin      136  3 Jun 19:45 Volumes
        com.apple.FinderInfo           32
drwxr-xr-x@ 39 root   wheel     1326  1 Jun 20:04 bin
        com.apple.FinderInfo           32
drwxrwxr-t@  2 root   admin       68 16 Aug  2011 cores
        com.apple.FinderInfo           32
dr-xr-xr-x   3 root   wheel     4417  2 Jun 13:28 dev
lrwxr-xr-x@  1 root   wheel       11 18 Nov  2011 etc -> private/etc
        com.apple.FinderInfo           32
dr-xr-xr-x   2 root   wheel        1  3 Jun 19:52 home
-rw-r--r--@  1 root   wheel 15567576  9 Apr 22:34 mach_kernel
        com.apple.FinderInfo           32
dr-xr-xr-x   2 root   wheel        1  3 Jun 19:52 net
drwxr-xr-x@  6 root   wheel      204 18 Nov  2011 private
        com.apple.FinderInfo           32
drwxr-xr-x@ 62 root   wheel     2108  1 Jun 20:04 sbin
```

```
        com.apple.FinderInfo        32
lrwxr-xr-x@  1 root   wheel      11 18 Nov  2011 tmp -> private/tmp
        com.apple.FinderInfo        32
drwxr-xr-x@ 14 root   wheel     476  3 Jun 22:54 usr
        com.apple.FinderInfo        32
lrwxr-xr-x@  1 root   wheel      11 18 Nov  2011 var -> private/var
        com.apple.FinderInfo        32
```

While some NSURL resource specifiers actually refer to items stored in extended attributes, the only available API to interact with arbitrary extended attributes exists at the C level, shown in Table 5-5.

Table 5-5. The Extended Attribute API

Function	Description
ssize_t getxattr(const char *path, const char *name, void *value, size_t size, u_int32_t position, int options);	Obtains a single extended attribute value by name from the file at a given path. The value is written into the value buffer provided by the caller, and the size of the value is returned.
int setxattr(const char *path, const char *name, const void *value, size_t size, u_int32_t position, int options);	Sets a new value for a named extended attribute on the file at a given path.
int removexattr(const char *path, const char *name, int options);	Removes a single extended attribute from a given file.
ssize_t listxattr(const char *path, char *namebuff, size_t size, int options);	Obtains a list of extended attribute names from a file, returning the size of the attribute list. The attribute names themselves are separated by null characters.

These methods leave a little to be desired when compared to the APIs provided by NSURL. For that reason, I offer the category in Listing 5-9, which provides an NSURL-style API for accessing extended attribute data.

Listing 5-9. An NSURL Category for Accessing Extended Attributes

```objc
#import<sys/xattr.h>

@interface NSURL (ExtendedAttributes)
- (NSData *) extendedAttributeDataForKey: (NSString *) key error: (NSError **) error;
- (BOOL) setExtendedAttributeData: (NSData *) data forKey: (NSString *) key error: (NSError **)
error;
- (NSSet *) extendedAttributeNames: (NSError **) error;
@end

@implementation NSURL (ExtendedAttributes)
```

```objc
- (NSData *) extendedAttributeDataForKey: (NSString *) key error: (NSError **) error
{
    if ( [self isFileURL] == NO )
    {
        if ( error != NULL )
            *error = [NSError errorWithDomain: NSPOSIXErrorDomain
                                         code: EINVAL
                                     userInfo: nil];
        return ( nil );
    }

    const char * path = [[[self filePathURL] path] fileSystemRepresentation];
    ssize_t size = getxattr(path, [key UTF8String], NULL, SIZE_MAX, 0, 0);
    if ( size == 0 )
        return ( nil );
    if ( size < 0 )
    {
        if ( error != NULL )
            *error = [NSError errorWithDomain: NSPOSIXErrorDomain
                                         code: errno
                                     userInfo: nil];
        return ( nil );
    }

    NSMutableData * data = [[NSMutableData alloc] initWithLength: size];
    if ( getxattr(path, [key UTF8String], [data mutableBytes], size, 0, 0) == -1 )
    {
        if ( error != NULL )
            *error = [NSError errorWithDomain: NSPOSIXErrorDomain
                                         code: errno
                                     userInfo: nil];
        return ( nil );
    }

    return ( [data copy] );
}

- (BOOL) setExtendedAttributeData: (NSData *) data forKey: (NSString *) key error: (NSError **)
error
{
    if ( [self isFileURL] == NO )
    {
        if ( error != NULL )
            *error = [NSError errorWithDomain: NSPOSIXErrorDomain
                                         code: EINVAL
                                     userInfo: nil];
        return ( NO );
    }

    const char * path = [[[self filePathURL] path] fileSystemRepresentation];
    if ( setxattr(path, [key UTF8String], [data bytes], [data length], 0, 0) < 0 )
```

```objc
    {
        if ( error != NULL )
            *error = [NSError errorWithDomain: NSPOSIXErrorDomain
                                        code: errno
                                    userInfo: nil];

        return ( NO );
    }

    return ( YES );
}
- (NSSet *) extendedAttributeNames: (NSError **) error
{
    if ( [self isFileURL] == NO )
    {
        if ( error != NULL )
            *error = [NSError errorWithDomain: NSPOSIXErrorDomain
                                        code: EINVAL
                                    userInfo: nil];

        return ( nil );
    }

    const char * path = [[[self filePathURL] path] fileSystemRepresentation];
    ssize_t size = listxattr(path, NULL, 0, 0);
    if ( size == 0 )
        return ( nil );

    if ( size < 0 )
    {
        if ( error != NULL )
            *error = [NSError errorWithDomain: NSPOSIXErrorDomain
                                        code: errno
                                    userInfo: nil];

        return ( nil );
    }

    NSMutableSet * result = [NSMutableSet new];
    NSMutableData * buffer = [[NSMutableData alloc] initWithLength: size];
    if ( listxattr(path, [buffer mutableBytes], size, 0) < 0 )
    {
        if ( error != NULL )
            *error = [NSError errorWithDomain: NSPOSIXErrorDomain
                                        code: errno
                                    userInfo: nil];

        return ( nil );
    }

    const char * p = [buffer bytes];
    const char * e = p + size;
    while ( p < e )
    {
        [result addObject: [NSString stringWithUTF8String: p]];
    }
```

```
    return ( [result copy] );
}
```

```
@end
```

Managing Folders and Locations

When it comes to managing the contents of folders or moving items around, copying them, or deleting them, your go-to API will be NSFileManager. This class, typically used through a single instance obtained by calling +defaultManager, provides all the methods you'll need to make changes to the filesystem beyond the scope of a single file. It also provides a means of locating various standard locations in the filesystem, such as the folder for cache data, the user's Documents folder, the Applications folder, and more.

OS X, like its predecessors Mac OS and NeXTstep, utilize a well-defined folder hierarchy with standard locations for the placement of different types of items. Preferences for all applications go in a certain place, as do shared libraries and frameworks, plug-ins, and more. On top of this, it provides a *domain* system. Many of these folders exist in a number of different domains: the *user* domain (for a single user, inside the user's home folder), the *local* domain (applicable to all users, based at the root of the system volume), the *system* domain (system default values, inside /System on the system volume), and the *network* domain (network administrator-set items, on filesystems mounted from an OS X Server, but rarely used these days). For instance, the Library folder exists in all four domains: there's one in your home folder, one at the root of the system volume, one inside /System, and (if you have anything there) one inside the Network folder. These domains also have a set order of precedence: User, Local, Network, and System. This means that when searching for preferences, the system will first check the preferences stored in the user's home folder, then those in the root Library folder, then inside the Network folder, and finally in the System folder, where Apple-provided default values reside.

Many system folder types are defined; they are all specified using integer constants defined in <Foundation/NSPathUtilities.h>, and the most commonly used examples are enumerated in Table 5-6.

Table 5-6. Standard System Folders

Identifier	Description
NSLibraryDirectory	The Library folder, containing documentation, support, and configuration files.
NSDocumentDirectory	The user's Documents folder—only applicable in the User domain.
NSCachesDirectory	A subfolder of Library, where cached (but replaceable) data is stored for quicker access.
NSApplicationSupportDirectory	Another subfolder of Library, where applications commonly store non-user data.
NSApplicationScriptsDirectory	The folder where AppleScripts for the current application should be stored (only in the User domain).

(continued)

Table 5-6. (continued)

Identifier	Description
NSItemReplacementDirectory	The location of a directory used as part of an atomic file-swap operation, thus somewhere on the same volume as a provided URL. Atomic file swaps are performed by writing the new data to a new file and then exchanging the on-disk storage blocks associated with each file.
NSTrashDirectory	The location of the Trash folder as appropriate for a given other URL. There is typically one Trash folder for the system volume located in the user's home folder and others located on each other volume so items can be placed in the trash without moving them between volumes. Available in OS X 10.8.

NSFileManager provides two methods for locating such folders. The first method, -URLsForDirectory:inDomains:, returns a list of URLs for a given directory type in their search order across a number of specified domains. The domains are specified using a bitfield; multiple values can be bitwise-OR'd together to handle multiple domains. The returned list of URLs are based on the path for the requested item within the chosen domains, but it's important to note that there is no guarantee that these folders actually exist on disk; you may have to create them.

That method is good for when you expect to search through user-specific, computer-specific, network-based, and default items in order. When you're looking for a single directory, however, there's another API that fits better, and additionally provides the ability to specify a URL with which this one will be used. This allows you to easily locate the appropriate volume-specific Trash location to move an item into the trash, or to provide a canonical URL for item replacement, used to implement atomic file exchanges. It also allows you to request that the directory be created if it does not already exist. This API is -URLForDirectory:inDomain:appropr iateForURL:create:error:, and a few examples of its use can be seen in Listing 5-10.

Listing 5-10. Using URLForDirectory:inDomain:appropriateForURL:create:error:

```
// locate the appropriate Trash folder for an item we want to move to the trash
// this will return the URL of a user-specific folder on the same volume as the
// item to be trashed.
NSURL * trashFolder = [[NSFileManager defaultManager] URLForDirectory: NSTrashDirectory
                                                     inDomain: NSUserDomainMask
                                            appropriateForURL: itemURL
                                                       create: YES
                                                        error: &error];
// move the item to the trash
NSURL * trashedItemURL = [trashFolder URLByAppendingPathComponent:
                                              [itemURL lastPathComponent];
[[NSFileManager defaultManager] moveItemAtURL: itemURL
                                        toURL: trashedItemURL
                                        error: &error];

. . .
```

```
// Get a temporary folder to write out our new data ready to swap out with the old
NSURL * swapFolder = [[NSFileManager defaultManager] URLForDirectory:
                                                  NSItemReplacementDirectory
                                         inDomain: NSUserDomainMask
                                    appropriateForURL: itemURL
                                              create: YES
                                               error: &error];
NSURL * tmpItemURL = [swapFolder URLByAppendingPathComponent:
                                           [itemURL lastPathComponent]];


// Generate the new content
[self generateContentAtURL: tmpItemURL];

// now swap the new item with the old
[[NSFileManager defaultManager] replaceItemAtURL: itemURL
                                  withItemAtURL: tmpItemURL
                                 backupItemName: nil
                                        options: 0
                             replacementItemURL: NULL
                                          error: &error];
```

Aside from these very useful methods are those found in Table 5-7, for moving items around
on the filesystem and for accessing their attributes. The attributes available through the
NSFileManager API are fewer in number than those available from NSURL, however, and are
not cached like those obtained from a URL object. It is also worth noting that NSFileManager
has a delegation protocol that allows you to confirm many operations before they happen
and to gracefully handle any errors that might occur. For more details on that,
see <Foundation/NSFileManager.h>.

Table 5-7. More NSFileManager APIs

Method	Description
copyItemAtURL:toURL:error:	Makes a copy of a given item at the target URL.
moveItemAtURL:toURL:error:	Moves an item to a new location.
removeItemAtURL:error:	Deletes the file or folder at a given URL.
linkItemAtURL:toURL:error:	Creates a *hard link* between an existing item and a new location.
trashItemAtURL:resultingItemURL:error:	Moves the specified item to the user's Trash folder.
	Available in OS X 10.8
createSymbolicLinkAtURL:withDestinationURL: error:	Creates a *symbolic link* to a given URL at the specified location.
createDirectoryAtPath:withIntermediateDirec tories:attributes:error:	Creates a new folder with the given attributes, optionally creating any missing parent folders.
attributesOfItemAtPath:error:	Obtains an NSDictionary containing various attributes of the file at the given path.

LINKS, HARD AND SYMBOLIC

When the methods in Table 5-7 refer to *links*, they are talking about the ability of the filesystem to create a file which, rather than containing data itself, simply references another file.

There are two types of links on OS X and iOS:

- *Hard links* are essentially the same thing as regular files—both the link's target and the link itself refer directly to the same blocks of storage on the physical media.

- *Symbolic links* are regular files that contain an absolute or relative path; they are automatically traversed by the core filesystem APIs.

Hard links are actually identical to regular files. When a file is placed in a folder, a hard link is created to attach the folder entry describing the file to the actual storage on disk. Creating a hard link to an existing file just created another folder entry which links to the same storage. These links are counted at the filesystem level such that the underlying storage blocks are only made available for reuse by the system once all hard links to them have been removed. Thus you can create a hard link to A from B, and upon deleting A, the file will remain on disk. Only when B is also deleted will the storage space be reclaimed.

A symbolic link contains a filesystem-encoded absolute or relative path that is read transparently by the low-level filesystem APIs. The file itself is tagged with a special mode flag that tells the system to treat it differently. As a result, any attempt to interact with a symbolic link file will, unless using a special non-link-following API, determine the path to its target and instead interact with that.

Note that hard links will remain valid if the target file is moved or renamed while symbolic links, being path-based, will fail to resolve should this happen. Despite this, symbolic links are usually preferred to hard links as they are easier to identify as links. Hard links are indistinguishable from real files, and as a result, any filesystem traversal would calculate the size of a file twice upon seeing two hard links to it. If file A is 4GB in size and file B is a hard link to it, then (without delving into *very* low-level filesystem-format-specific details) these would be indistinguishable from two *copies* of the same file, taking up 8GB of storage space between them.

In addition to these APIs, NSFileManager provides a number of ways of inspecting the contents of folders themselves. You can obtain the contents of a single folder as an array using -conte ntsOfDirectoryAtPath:error:, but the most flexible means of working with folder contents is through an NSDirectoryEnumerator. An enumerator can be created while specifying some find-grained options on how deeply it should enumerate and whether any NSURL properties should be prefetched for you. It provides means of fetching the next item, obtaining its attributes, and choosing to skip particular subfolders during the enumeration. An example of its usage is shown in Listing 5-11, and the code's output can be seen in Listing 5-12.

Listing 5-11. Enumerating Folder Contents

```
NSURL * myURL = [NSURL fileURLWithPathComponents: @[ NSHomeDirectory(), @"Pictures" ]];
    NSArray * properties = @[ NSURLLocalizedNameKey, NSURLLocalizedTypeDescriptionKey,
NSURLFileSizeKey ];
NSDirectoryEnumerationOptions options = NSDirectoryEnumerationSkipsPackageDescendants;
```

```
NSDirectoryEnumerator * dirEnum = [[NSFileManager defaultManager] enumeratorAtURL: myURL
        includingPropertiesForKeys: properties options: options
        errorHandler: ^BOOL(NSURL *url, NSError *error) {
    NSLog(@"Error looking at URL '%@': %@", url, error);
    // continue enumerating
    return ( YES );
}];

while ( (url = [dirEnum nextObject]) != nil )
{
    NSDictionary * attrs = [url resourceValuesForKeys: properties error: NULL];
    NSNumber * size = [attrs objectForKey: NSURLFileSizeKey];
    NSString * sizeStr = nil;
    if ( size != nil )
        sizeStr = [NSString stringWithFormat: @", %@ bytes", size];

    NSString * relativePath = [self relativePathOfURL: url
                                    forEnumerationLevel: [dirEnum level]];

    NSString * msg = [NSString stringWithFormat: @"%@: %@, %@%@",
                    [attrs objectForKey: NSURLLocalizedNameKey], relativePath,
                    [attrs objectForKey: NSURLLocalizedTypeDescriptionKey], sizeStr];
    fprintf(stdout, "%s\n", [msg UTF8String]);
}
```

Listing 5-12. Folder Enumeration Sample Output

```
dlanham- Tea for Two: Pictures, Folder
dlanham- Tea for Two iPad.jpg: Pictures/dlanham- Tea for Two, JPEG image, 345792 bytes
dlanham- Tea for Two.jpg: Pictures/dlanham- Tea for Two, JPEG image, 1293586 bytes
dlanham-TeaforTwo_iPhone.jpg: Pictures/dlanham- Tea for Two, JPEG image, 200843 bytes
patt-tea43.gif: Pictures/dlanham- Tea for Two, Graphics Interchange Format (GIF), 419 bytes
Send a Thanks.URL: Pictures/dlanham- Tea for Two, Web site location, 119 bytes
UsageTerms.rtf: Pictures/dlanham- Tea for Two, Rich Text Format, 968 bytes
dlanham-Full Moon: Pictures, Folder
dlanham-Full Moon.jpg: Pictures/dlanham-Full Moon, JPEG image, 353181 bytes
dlanham-FullMoon-iPhone.jpg: Pictures/dlanham-Full Moon, JPEG image, 86943 bytes
dlanham-FullMoon_iPad.jpg: Pictures/dlanham-Full Moon, JPEG image, 180853 bytes
dlanham-FullMoon_iPhone.jpg: Pictures/dlanham-Full Moon, JPEG image, 143928 bytes
Send a Thanks.url: Pictures/dlanham-Full Moon, Web site location, 119 bytes
UsageTerms.rtf: Pictures/dlanham-Full Moon, Rich Text Format, 968 bytes
iChat Icons: Pictures, Alias, 47 bytes
Jim_crop: Pictures, Portable Network Graphics image, 54046 bytes
Photo Booth Library: Pictures, Photo Booth Library
```

Accessing File Contents

There are a number of ways in which you can access the contents of files in Objective-C. The simplest is to use the provided initializer and factory methods on the various data classes: NSArray, NSDictionary, NSString, NSData and more all have -initWithContentsOfURL: methods or similar. These methods (and their companion -writeToURL: methods) provide the simplest means of getting standard property-list types written to disk (arrays and dictionaries are written as property list files and may contain numbers, dates, strings, data, and more arrays or dictionaries). These methods are all synchronous, however, which makes them less desirable for large amounts of work.

Random-Access Files

The standard way to gain random access to a file is to use NSFileHandle. Instances of this class enable you to open a file, seek to various positions within it, and read or write data in descrete packages. You can also choose to read data in the background, being notified when the operation is complete. NSFileHandle also provides some simple methods to gain access to the UNIX standard input, standard output, and standard error file handles, allowing you to read input sent from another program on the command line, or to send data to another program in the same manner. As you will see when you look at networking, NSFileHandle is also able to work with BSD sockets, receiving and transmitting data across the network.

Obtaining a file handle is as simple as calling its initializer or factory methods. Reading and writing are also simple. Note that there are three *modes* of access with which you can open a new file handle:

- *Reading:* The file will be readable and you can seek to different locations within it, but any attempt to write data will result in an exception being thrown.

- *Writing:* The file will be automatically emptied of data, and new data can be appended to the file, but seeking and reading will cause an exception to be thrown.

- *Updating:* Both reading/seeking and writing are allowed on the file, making it possible to append data to any already in place.

Listing 5-13 shows an example logging method, which writes out a message to both standard error and to a separate log file.

Listing 5-13. Writing to a File Using NSFileHandle

```
- (void) writeLogMessage: (NSString *) message
{
    NSData * stringData = [message dataUsingEncoding: NSUTF8StringEncoding];

    NSFileHandle * logFile = [NSFileHandle fileHandleForUpdatingAtURL: self.logURL];
    [logFile seekToEndOfFile];
    [logFile writeData: stringData];
    [logFile synchronizeFile];   // ensure data is pushed out to disk NOW
    [logFile closeFile];

    // standard error is write-only stream: no seeking, just writing
    [[NSFileHandle fileHandleWithStandardError] writeData: stringData];
}
```

If you're reading large amounts of data, or if you're reading from a pipe such as standard input, you likely don't want to hold up your user input processing while waiting for something to happen. NSFileHandle provides both -readDataOfLength: and -readDataToEndOfFile methods, but these will block the calling thread until they have completed their task. Particularly when dealing with standard input or when the disk is under heavy use by other applications, these methods can take a while to return. For this reason, NSFileHandle provides notification-based variants of these methods. Listing 5-14 contains a simple program that echoes user input back out again using these methods.

Listing 5-14. A Simple Echo Application

```
#import<Foundation/Foundation.h>

int main(int argc, char * const argv[])
{
    @autoreleasepool
    {
        // get hold of standard input
        NSFileHandle * input = [NSFileHandle fileHandleWithStandardInput];

        // register to receive the 'read complete' notification first
        NSString * name = NSFileHandleReadToEndOfFileCompletionNotification;
        NSOperationQueue * queue = [NSOperationQueue mainQueue];
        [[NSNotificationCenter defaultCenter] addObserverForName: name
            object: input queue: queue usingBlock: ^(NSNotification *note) {
            // get the data from the notification's userInfo
            NSData * data = [[note userInfo] objectForKey: NSFileHandleNotificationDataItem];
            if ( data == nil )
                data = [@"No Input!" dataUsingEncoding: NSUTF8StringEncoding];

            // write the input data to standard output
            NSFileHandle * output = [NSFileHandle fileHandleWithStandardOutput];
            [output writeData: data];

            // append a newline character too
            [output writeData: [NSData dataWithBytes: "\n" length: 1]];

            // all done now, so stop the runloop
            CFRunLoopStop(CFRunLoopGetMain());
        }];

        // book-keeping: handle Control-C to kill the app
        dispatch_source_t sigHandler =
            dispatch_source_create(DISPATCH_SOURCE_TYPE_SIGNAL, SIGINT, 0,
            dispatch_get_main_queue());
        dispatch_source_set_event_handler(sigHandler, ^{
            CFRunLoopStop(CFRunLoopGetMain());
        });
        dispatch_resume(sigHandler);

        // read all data and notify us when it's done
        [input readToEndOfFileInBackgroundAndNotify];
```

```
    // run the main runloop to wait for the data
    // the notification handler will stop the runloop, exiting the app
    CFRunLoopRun();
    }

    return ( 0 );
}
```

To try this, create a new OS X command line tool in Xcode using `Foundation`, and copy the contents of the `main()` function above into the `main()` function in the application, and compile it (⌘B). Run the application in a terminal, sending text to it via standard input through the system echo command, as in Listing 5-15.

Listing 5-15. Running the SimpleEcho App

LP-347 Products/Debug » echo "This is a test." | ./SimpleEcho
This is a test.

LP-347 Products/Debug »

Tip   To quickly find a built application in Xcode, pop open the Products group in the Project Navigator, right-click (or Control-click) the built application in there, and choose "Show in Finder" (the topmost option) in the pop-up menu. Then you can open the Terminal application, type cd and a space, and drag the containing folder (in this case Debug) from the Finder onto the Terminal window to have its path entered for you. Press Enter and you'll be ready to run the application.

Streaming File Contents

If you don't need to jump around within a file but simply need to read or write data in an ordered, start-to-finish fashion, the `NSStream` API is your best friend. `NSStream` is frequently used for transmitting data across the network, too, as you'll see in a later chapter, but its principles apply just as well to handling files on the local system, particularly large files that could take up a lot of memory if read into memory all at once.

Streams work asynchronously based on delegation. After creating a stream, you assign it a delegate, attach it to a run loop, and open it; this is shown in Listing 5-16. The stream then calls its delegate, telling it about any status changes: open complete, bytes ready to read, space available to write, end-of-file, or any errors. The method implemented by the delegate is described by the `NSStreamDelegate` protocol.

Listing 5-16. Initializing an Input Stream

```
NSInputStream * stream = [[NSInputStream alloc] initWithURL: inputURL];
[stream setDelegate: self];
[stream scheduleInRunLoop: [NSRunLoop currentRunLoop] forMode: NSDefaultRunLoopMode];
[stream open];
```

An opened input stream can then be monitored for events describing data availability. For example, a simple encryption/decryption application can be written using an NSInputStream. In its -stream:handleEvent: method, the stream delegate can read data from the stream itself and encrypt or decrypt that data, and also report any alarming situations that occur, as in Listing 5-17, writing the encrypted/decrypted data to an NSFileHandle.

Listing 5-17. Encrypting Data from an Input Stream

```
- (void) stream: (NSStream *) aStream handleEvent: (NSStreamEvent) eventCode
{
    switch ( eventCode )
    {
        case NSStreamEventHasBytesAvailable:
        {
#define BUFLEN 8192 h
            uint8_t buf[BUFLEN];
            NSInteger numRead = [_inputStream read: buf maxLength: BUFLEN];
            if ( numRead < 0 )
            {
                // signal an error and exit
                fprintf(stderr, "Unknown error reading from file!\n");
                CFRunLoopStop(CFRunLoopGetMain());
                break;
            }

            NSData * data = [[NSData alloc] initWithBytesNoCopy: buf length: numRead
freeWhenDone: NO];
            if ( _encrypt )
                [_outputHandle writeData: [_cryptor encryptData: data]];
            else
                [_outputHandle writeData: [_cryptor decryptData: data]];

            break;
        }

        case NSStreamEventErrorOccurred:
        {
            // report the error and exit
            fprintf(stderr, "Error reading from file: %s\n", [[[aStream streamError]
localizedDescription] UTF8String]);
            CFRunLoopStop(CFRunLoopGetMain());
            break;
        }

        case NSStreamEventEndEncountered:
        {
            // stop processing
            [_inputStream close];
            NSData * finalData = [_cryptor finalData];
            if ( [finalData length] != 0 )
                [_outputHandle writeData: finalData];
            [_outputHandle synchronizeFile];
```

```
            [_outputHandle closeFile];
            CFRunLoopStop(CFRunLoopGetMain());
            break;
        }

        default:
            break;
    }
}
```

A working command-line application based on this example can be found online in the FileEncryptor project.

Rolling Your Own Streams

It is also possible to create your own streams. For example, you can define a special output stream class that encrypts all the data written to the stream before sending it elsewhere: this is what you'll create in this section. You can see the finished project in the EncryptingOutputStream project online.

Now, looking at the definition of NSOutputStream your first thought might be to subclass it and override its -write:maxLength: method and initializer. If you try this, however, you'll find that it doesn't work. Instead, you'll see some errors such as -[EncryptingOutputStream initWithURL:append:]: unrecognized selector sent to instance 0x104033650, which doesn't make a lot of sense: the headers explicitly state that NSOutputStream responds to -initWithURL:append:, so what's wrong?

The answer lies in the class-cluster nature of the Foundation streams API. NSOutputStream is in fact only an abstract class. If you call +alloc on either the NSOutputStream or NSInputStream classes, then you'll actually be returned an instance of a private subclass: NSCFOutputStream or NSCFInputStream respectively. The publicly declared interfaces for the output and input stream classes are actually the interfaces of those two internal classes. However, because you're allocating your custom subclass, the +alloc method is smart enough not to substitute a new class and allocates an instance of your subclass directly.

The requirement, then, for rolling your own stream classes, is to implement the entire NSStream interface manually (yes, it's abstract all the way up to NSObject). Thus your new subclass must implement the methods to open and close the stream, to obtain its status and error, to get and set its delegate, and to add it to or remove it from a run-loop.

The first few of these are, for your encrypting stream, fairly simple. You can store the values in member variables, and all is fine. The run-loop integration is a little trickier though: how does one signal a run-loop in Objective-C? You could keep a list of all run-loop/mode pairs and use NSRunLoop's -performSelector:target:argument:order:modes:, but if a stream is attached to multiple run-loops (which is perfectly valid) then you could end up messaging your target multiple times, which is hardly the correct behavior.

The correct approach is to use a *run-loop source*; these are event sources for run-loops, and no matter to how many run-loops a source has been attached, it will only be processed by exactly one loop. Sadly, this requires dropping down to the level of CoreFoundation, since no Objective-C counterpart exists. The type you want is CFRunLoopSourceRef, and there are two versions. The first (version 0) uses a semaphore-style signaling paradigm: you signal a source and wake up its associated run-loops to get it processed. The second (version 1) uses a low-level inter-process communication facility to send complex data to the source, to be handled on whichever run-loop is activated by the arrival of that message.

For this project let's stick with the simpler version 0 sources. Additionally, I have provided a simple Objective-C wrapper for such a source, available online as part of the EncryptingOutputStream project. Its interface can be seen in Listing 5-18.

Listing 5-18. The SimpleRunLoopSource Interface

```
@interface SimpleRunLoopSource : NSObject

- (id) initWithSourceHandler: (void (^)(void)) handler;

- (void) signal;
- (void) invalidate;

- (void) addToRunLoop: (NSRunLoop *) runLoop forMode: (NSString *) mode;
- (void) removeFromRunLoop: (NSRunLoop *) runLoop forMode: (NSString *) mode;

@end
```

As you can see, the API lives up to its name—it's very simple. You initialize your instance with a handler block, which will be run when the source is signaled. You can signal it and invalidate it (invalidation means that any run-loops to which it has been attached will forget about it in future). Lastly, this object handles all the details of being added to and removed from run-loops, including waking them up when it is signaled.

With this fiddliness out of the way, you can now start thinking about your stream subclass in earnest. You'll be using the standard NSOutputStream interface, so the only interface you need to define is a custom initializer to take a passphrase. This is shown in Listing 5-19.

Listing 5-19. The EncryptingOutputStream Interface

```
@interface EncryptingOutputStream : NSOutputStream
- (id) initWithFileURL: (NSURL *) fileURL passPhrase: (NSString *) passPhrase;
@end
```

The implementation is a little more involved. First of all, you'll tackle the basic getter/setter methods required by the NSStream and NSOutputStream APIs, in Listing 5-20.

Listing 5-20. EncryptingOutputStream's NSOutputStream API Implementation

```
#import "EncryptingOutputStream.h"
#import "SimpleRunLoopSource.h"
#import <CommonCrypto/CommonCryptor.h>

@implementation EncryptingOutputStream
{
    CCCryptorRef            _cryptor;
    NSFileHandle *          _output;
    SimpleRunLoopSource *   _source;
```

```objc
    id<NSStreamDelegate>    _delegate __weak;
    NSStreamEvent           _currentEvent;
    NSStreamStatus          _status;
    NSError *               _error;
}

- (id) initWithFileURL: (NSURL *) fileURL passPhrase: (NSString *) passPhrase
{
    ...
}

- (void) dealloc
{
    ...
}

- (void) open
{
    _status = NSStreamStatusOpening;
    _currentEvent = NSStreamEventOpenCompleted;
    [_source signal];
}

- (NSInteger) write: (const uint8_t *) buffer maxLength: (NSUInteger) len
{
    ...
}

- (void) close
{
    ...
}

- (void) setDelegate: (id<NSStreamDelegate>) delegate
{
    _delegate = delegate;
}

- (id<NSStreamDelegate>) delegate
{
    return ( _delegate );
}

- (void) scheduleInRunLoop: (NSRunLoop *) aRunLoop forMode: (NSString *) mode
{
    [_source addToRunLoop: aRunLoop forMode: mode];
}

- (void) removeFromRunLoop: (NSRunLoop *) aRunLoop forMode: (NSString *) mode
{
    [_source removeFromRunLoop: aRunLoop forMode: mode];
}
```

```
- (NSStreamStatus) streamStatus
{
    return ( _status );
}

- (NSError *) streamError
{
    return ( _error );
}
```

Next I'll walk through the initializer, wherein you'll have to create a few things:

- *The encryption interface*: You'll use the CoreCrypto API for this.

- *The run-loop source*: This will use the aforementioned SimpleRunLoopSource class.

- An NSFileHandle *used to write the data to the provided URL*: I chose this over another output stream for simplicity (so you don't have to worry about buffering data while a stream asynchronously pushes it to the filesystem).

In addition, you'll have to implement a -dealloc method since you're using some non-Objective-C resources. Listing 5-21 shows the implementation of the initializer and deallocator.

Listing 5-21. EncryptingOutputStream Initialization and Deallocation

```
- (id) initWithFileURL: (NSURL *) fileURL passPhrase: (NSString *) passPhrase
{
    NSParameterAssert([fileURL isFileURL]);
    NSParameterAssert([passPhrase length] != 0);

    self = [super init];
    if ( self == nil )
        return ( nil );

    // get the password as data, padded/truncated to the AES256 key size
    NSMutableData * passData = [[passPhrase dataUsingEncoding: NSUTF8StringEncoding]
mutableCopy];
    [passData setLength: kCCKeySizeAES256];

    // create the encryptor
    if ( CCCryptorCreate(kCCEncrypt, kCCAlgorithmAES128, kCCOptionPKCS7Padding,
                        [passData bytes], [passData length], NULL, &_cryptor) != kCCSuccess )
    {
        return ( nil );
    }

    // NSFileHandle can't open a file that isn't there. Ensure the destination exists.
    if ( [[NSFileManager defaultManager] fileExistsAtPath: [fileURL path]] == NO )
        [[NSData data] writeToURL: fileURL options: 0 error: NULL];
```

```
    // open the output file
    _output = [NSFileHandle fileHandleForWritingToURL: fileURL error: NULL];

    // create the runloop source, with a simple handler
    _source = [[SimpleRunLoopSource alloc] initWithSourceHandler: ^{
        if ( _currentEvent == NSStreamEventOpenCompleted )
            _status = NSStreamStatusOpen;

        [_delegate stream: self handleEvent: _currentEvent];

        // always signal space-available for NSFileHandle-based streams, since
        // NSFileHandles can always be written to
        _currentEvent = NSStreamEventHasSpaceAvailable;
        [_source signal];
    }];

    // the initial status of the stream
    _status = NSStreamStatusNotOpen;

    return ( self );
}

- (void) dealloc
{
    if ( _cryptor != NULL )
        CCCryptorRelease(_cryptor);
}
```

> **Note** Remember that when you're using ARC you still need to implement -dealloc methods to release any objects not handled by ARC, such as C arrays and structures allocated on the stack, CoreFoundation objects, and the like. You don't need to call [super dealloc], however: the compiler will handle that for you.

One item of interest in the initializer is the content of the source's handler block. My strategy for posting delegate messages is to set an instance variable to the event I want to post and then signal the source. The source handler block then checks that event and posts it to the stream's delegate. The first thing it does is check whether the event is "open completed," at which point it sets the appropriate stream status before calling the delegate. Then, as the comment notes, it sets the "has space available" event and signals the source again, since NSFileHandle's blocking I/O means that you don't need to check for asynchronous writability here.

Next up are the -write:maxLength: and -close methods. I group these together since, when encrypting data using a block cipher such as AES, there is often some extra data appended to the output after all the input data has been passed through, and I use the -close method to append that to the output file. Listing 5-22 shows how the encryption takes place. When writing, you run each chunk of data through the encryptor. It then returns a block of encrypted data, which you write out to the filesystem. When closing, you ask the encryptor for a final data block.

If there is such a block (there may not be, for some ciphers and input data sizes) you write it to the output file and close it. In both these methods you use an NSMutableData object to allocate and manage the memory buffer to receive the encrypted data; this is purely to have ARC take over the duty of deallocating those buffers when they are no longer needed.

Listing 5-22. Writing to and Closing the EncryptingOutputStream

```
- (NSInteger) write: (const uint8_t *) buffer maxLength: (NSUInteger) len
{
    // update our status to indicate we're in the middle of a write operation
    _status = NSStreamStatusWriting;

    // encrypt the data
    NSMutableData * encrypted = [[NSMutableData alloc] initWithLength: len];
    size_t numWritten = 0;
    CCCryptorStatus status = CCCryptorUpdate(_cryptor, buffer, len, [encrypted mutableBytes],
len, &numWritten);
    if ( status != kCCSuccess )
    {
        // an error occurred-- note it, signal the condition, and return -1
        _error = [NSError errorWithDomain: @"CoreCryptoErrorDomain" code: status userInfo: nil];
        _status = NSStreamStatusError;
        _currentEvent = NSStreamEventErrorOccurred;
        [_source signal];       // tell the delegate about it
        return ( -1 );
    }

    // write this data out via the superclass
    [_output writeData: encrypted];

    // reset our status to open and return the length of data we wrote
    // (we wrote all of it)
    _status = NSStreamStatusOpen;
    return ( len );
}

- (void) close
{
    // write any final data first
    NSMutableData * final = [[NSMutableData alloc] initWithLength: kCCBlockSizeAES128];
    size_t numWritten = 0;
    if ( CCCryptorFinal(_cryptor, [final mutableBytes], [final length], &numWritten) ==
kCCSuccess && numWritten != 0 )
            [_output writeData: final];

    // flush any filesystem buffers to the disk and close the file
    [_output synchronizeFile];
    [_output closeFile];

    // update our status
    _status = NSStreamStatusClosed;
}
```

With that last change, you're done. You now have a custom NSOutputStream subclass that encrypts the data passing through it.

Filesystem Change Coordination

When dealing with data in files and folders there is a potential hazard lurking around the corner, ready to strike—any file you're working with could be read or written at any time. While you're writing out changes to a file, the Finder might request a QuickLook preview of it. The user might rename a file that you're working with or move it to another location. The user might even move some ancestor folder of your file to a different place on disk. These situations can all lead to data corruption or even loss. The Foundation framework provides two types which implement a nuanced approach to this topic: NSFileCoordinator class and the NSFilePresenter protocol.

The primary actor in file coordination is the NSFileCoordinator class. This class defines methods that allow you to provide discrete file operations as blocks. The file coordinator waits synchronously until it is safe to execute the block implementing the requested operation and then does so, while ensuring that all conflicting access is suspended until the block finishes running. The class then handles all the intricate details of the coordination itself leaving you free to concentrate on your data.

The NSFilePresenter protocol defines methods that your file-handling object can implement to be informed of other processes' attempts to read or modify the content it's presenting to the user. You would be notified when something else is about to read from the content so that you could, for example, ensure that the latest data is written out to the filesystem (so that any unsaved changes will show up in, for example, a Finder preview). You would also be notified when a file is about to be modified by another process, so that you can ensure your application will handle those changes gracefully. In both of these situations, you will be able to pass the coordination system a block of code to run once the actual operation completes. So you could, for example, auto-save your document before a reader accesses it and disable auto-save until such time as the other process has finished reading it.

Some applications work on a folder basis. iTunes, for example, stores many different documents within the Music/iTunes Music folder in your home directory. Such an application could register an NSFilePresenter for that parent folder and it would be alerted to any changes that would affect not only that folder but any item within it. The NSFileCoordinator also handles changes at the folder level. As an example, the Finder uses a coordinator to manage the movement of files and folders from one place to another. Rather than use the coordinator to manage the individual copying of thousands of files in a hierarchy, however, it need only inform the system of the root folder or folders being moved; NSFileCoordinator automatically handles any coordination necessary for files and folders within that hierarchy.

File Presenters

Let's start out by looking at the file presenter interface. Most of it is optional, but there are two read-only properties that all adopters of the protocol must implement: presentedItemURL and presentedItemOperationQueue. The first of these properties returns the URL of the item this presenter is handling, whether it is a file or a folder. The value itself can be nil, however, as a presenter might be associated with a document which has not yet been saved to disk. The file coordination system keeps track of this fact and will refetch the URL after the presenter completes any coordinated file operations, in case the item was just created.

The `presentedItemOperationQueue` value, on the other hand, *cannot* be nil. All messages sent to the presenter will take place on this queue. In very simple cases you might be able to return [NSOperationQueue mainQueue] here, but ordinarily this would be an invitation to deadlocks.

The methods of the `NSFilePresenter` protocol fall into three groups.

- *Coordinating Access:* These methods enable the presenter to ensure that readers get access to the latest updates by writing out any unsaved content and provide notifications so a presenter can avoid interrupting any other processes' reads and writes. Your presenter will also be notified if its content file is renamed, deleted, or moved to a new location.

- *File Changes:* Any modification to the file's contents or attributes, whether that modification was done through file coordination or otherwise, will trigger a message to the presenter. Your presenter can then check to ensure that it has an up-to-date copy of the file's data. On OS X 10.7 and iOS 5, you may also be notified of versioned changes to the file, whether a new version was added, removed, or a conflict was resolved.

- *Folder Changes:* When your file presenter is presenting an entire folder, you will be informed of any changes to the contents of that folder and its subfolders. You will be able to react to pending deletion of a sub-item, and you'll be notified of any new sub-items appearing, any move or rename operations, and any versioning information similar to that provided for presenters of individual files.

Trying It Out

To properly illustrate the use and capabilities of file coordination, I'll walk you through the creation of a fairly contrived example: a command-line app that monitors the file size and allocated size of the contents of a folder and writes this data to a nearby log file. It will update the log file using two separate file presenters, which will have to coordinate their updates to the file between themselves. As a result, both file presenters will wind up working with the same data, with potentially some different unsaved content at any time. Each time something in the folder changes, one of the log file's presenters will be informed of the new totals and will record them. Whenever another presenter (such as the Finder or QuickLook) wishes to read from an item, the presenters will record any unsaved changes, being sure to load any new content from the file first.

The full source code is available as an Xcode project named `FileCoordinationExample` online. In the book, I will skip over some details and focus on the implementation of the major file coordination API elements.

Watching a Folder

The first task is to create an object that will watch an individual folder and keep track of its size. You can use the `FolderInfoPresenter` class for this purpose, which has the very simple interface seen in Listing 5-23.

Listing 5-23. The FolderInfoPresenter Interface

```
@interface FolderInfoPresenter : NSObject <NSFilePresenter>
- (id) initWithFolderURL: (NSURL *) folderURL;
@end
```

Instances of `FolderInfoPresenter` are initialized with the URL of the (existing) folder that it will monitor. You'll notice that it declares that it conforms to the `NSFilePresenter` protocol.

The class's instance variables, declared as part of its implementation block, can be seen in Listing 5-24.

Listing 5-24. The FolderInfoPresenter Class's Instance Variables

```
@implementation FolderInfoPresenter
{
    NSURL *               _folderURL;

    // a pair of presenters, updated in alternation
    InfoFilePresenter * _infoFiles[2];
    NSUInteger            _whichFile;

    NSOperationQueue * _queue;

    NSUInteger            _totalFileSize;
    NSUInteger            _totalAllocatedSize;

    BOOL                  _suspended;
}

@end
```

First of all, you'll see that it keeps track of its URL; as outlined above, an `NSFilePresenter` is expected to return the URL of its presented item on demand.

Next come the two log file presenters I mentioned, along with a variable referencing the array location of the next one to be messaged. After this is a private `NSOperationQueue` instance, again to be returned as required by the `NSFilePresenter` protocol.

Lastly you'll see the two variables for the folder's file size and disk allocation size plus a Boolean flag you'll use to determine whether you should avoid scanning the folder hierarchy for a while due to file operations from other actors.

The initializer sets up some of these variables, as seen in Listing 5-25.

Listing 5-25. FolderInfoPresenter's Initialization Method

```
- (id) initWithFolderURL: (NSURL *) folderURL
{
    self = [super init];
    if ( self == nil )
        return ( nil );
```

```
    // our private operation queue upon which the NSFilePresenter methods are called
    _queue = [NSOperationQueue new];

    _folderURL = [folderURL copy];

    NSURL * infoURL = [[[folderURL URLByDeletingLastPathComponent]
                            URLByAppendingPathComponent: @"folder-info.txt"] copy];
    _infoFiles[0] = [[InfoFilePresenter alloc] initWithFileURL: infoURL queue: _queue];
    _infoFiles[1] = [[InfoFilePresenter alloc] initWithFileURL: infoURL queue: _queue];

    // register with the file coordination system
    [NSFileCoordinator addFilePresenter: self];

    [self updateFolderInfo];

    return ( self );
}
```

The log file is created in the parent of the watched folder, with a name of folder-info.txt. The two presenters for this file are created and placed into a two-element array.

Next comes a very important part: this file presenter is registered with the file coordination system by calling [NSFileCoordinator addFilePresenter: self]. This should technically be balanced by a call to [NSFileCoordinator removeFilePresenter: self] when this object goes away, but ARC handles this for you when this instance is deallocated. When using manual memory management, however, you must perform this task yourself in your -dealloc implementation.

Lastly the initializer calls -updateFolderInfo to set its state according to the current contents of the folder. This task is performed using the appropriate NSFileCoordinator methods to synchronize access to the contents of the folder with other presenters, readers, and writers, and can be seen in Listing 5-26.

Listing 5-26. Updating Folder Information

```
- (void) updateFolderInfo
{
    if ( _suspended )
        return;

    // create a file coordinator to synchronize our access to the folder's contents
    NSFileCoordinator *coordinator = [[NSFileCoordinator alloc]
                                                    initWithFilePresenter: self];

    // enumerate the file sizes and total allocated file sizes for all items
    // within the folder. We'll ask the enumerator to prefetch these resource values.
    NSArray * properties = @[ NSURLFileSizeKey, NSURLTotalFileAllocatedSizeKey ];

    // perform the read operation through the coordinator
    [coordinator coordinateReadingItemAtURL: _folderURL
                                    options: NSFileCoordinatorReadingWithoutChanges
                                      error: NULL
                                 byAccessor: ^(NSURL *newURL) {
```

```
        // we use the URL passed into this block rather than the _folderURL variable in case it
has changed
        NSDirectoryEnumerator * dirEnum = [[NSFileManager defaultManager]
                                enumeratorAtURL: newURL
                    includingPropertiesForKeys: properties
                                        options: 0
                                   errorHandler: ^BOOL(NSURL *url, NSError *error) {
            // ignore any errors for now
            return ( YES );
        }];

        _totalFileSize = 0;
        _totalAllocatedSize = 0;

        NSURL * subItemURL = nil;
        while ( (subItemURL = [dirEnum nextObject]) != nil )
        {
            // update our data with the item's size attributes
            NSDictionary * attrs = [subItemURL resourceValuesForKeys: properties
                                                               error: NULL];
            _totalFileSize += [[attrs objectForKey: NSURLFileSizeKey]
                                                          unsignedIntegerValue];
            _totalAllocatedSize += [[attrs objectForKey: NSURLTotalFileAllocatedSizeKey]
                                                          unsignedIntegerValue];
        }
    }];

    // update our log file
    [self updateInfoFile];

    // the file coordinator instance doesn't stay around, since it retains the presenter
    // we let ARC release it for us when this method exits
}
```

The first thing you'll notice is that you won't touch anything if you're in a suspended state—this means that another actor is working with the folder or one of its sub-items. Next, you create an NSFileCoordinator instance through which you'll synchronize your operation with the rest of the system. The coordinator object is provided a reference to this instance so that it can exclude it from any messages it would otherwise send to NSFilePresenter instances interested in the folder or its contents, thus avoiding potential deadlocks or infinite loops.

You perform the operation by handing a block to the file coordinator's -coordinateReadingIt emAtURL:options:error:byAccessor: method. The options available allow you to specify how the file coordinator handles your read operation. One option is to request that the coordinator resolve symbolic links before sending out coordination messages, or if it leaves them as-is. In this case you pass the other available option, telling the coordinator that you don't want to see any pending changes to items. This prevents it from asking any relevant file presenters to save any updates to disk before your read operation executes.

The read block itself receives a URL, and it is important that the block use that URL to access its content item rather than the value it passed into the coordinator. The reason for this is that there may have been a pending movement operation that took place between your calling the coordinator and the reader block being executed. The passed-in URL is guaranteed to be up-to-date with any such moves or renames. In this instance, you obtain a directory enumerator and use the URLs it returns to total up the file sizes for your data. The coordinator blocks until the reader block has run (or an error has occurred prior to running it), so after your call completes you know you have the most up-to-date statistics for the presented folder.

Lastly, you send your new data to one of your log file presenters. You'll see how those objects work shortly.

The first few presentation methods are simple to implement: -presentedItemURL just returns your _folderURL instance variable, and -presentedItemOperationQueue returns the _queue variable. The remaining items are more interesting. Firstly, the file-access coordination methods can be seen in Listing 5-27.

Listing 5-27. Folder Access Coordination

```
- (void) relinquishPresentedItemToReader: (void (^)(void (^reacquirer)(void))) reader
{
    _suspended = YES;
    reader(^{ _suspended = NO; });
}

- (void) relinquishPresentedItemToWriter: (void (^)(void (^reacquirer)(void))) writer
{
    _suspended = YES;
    writer(^{ _suspended = NO; });
}

- (void) accommodatePresentedItemDeletionWithCompletionHandler: (void (^)(NSError *))
completionHandler
{
    fprintf(stdout, "Presented item was deleted, shutting down now.\n");
    completionHandler(NULL);

    // stop this application now, as the item we're presenting has been deleted
    CFRunLoopStop(CFRunLoopGetMain());
}

- (void) presentedItemDidMoveToURL: (NSURL *) newURL
{
    _folderURL = [newURL copy];
    fprintf(stdout, "Presented item moved to %s\n", [[newURL path] UTF8String]);
}
```

The first two methods are called when another process wants to either read or write to the folder you're presenting. In this instance, this would refer to modifications of the folder's attributes or either adding or removing items inside this folder itself (not inside one of its sub-folders). Since you don't have a read/write view of the folder in this class, you handle this by marking yourself as suspended so you don't inadvertently try to traverse the folder structure while something else is going on. You then call the provided reader or writer block and pass that yet another block. When the read/write operation is complete, this block will be executed, allowing you to reclaim your view of the item. Since you don't look at any attributes of the presented folder itself, you only have to remove the suspension at this point.

The next method deals with the deletion of the presented folder. In this case, you print a message to the console and stop the main run-loop, causing the application to exit. Next comes a handler for the case when your presented folder is either moved or renamed; here you take the opportunity to update your _folderURL instance variable to the new value.

When new items are added inside your folder, the file coordination system will inform you. Your reaction is fairly simple: rather than iterate through the folder's contents again to build up the totals from scratch, you can simply look at the size of the new item and add it on its own. The call should still be made using file coordination, however, so use an NSFileCoordinator instance to do so.

> **Note**   Remember that NSFilePresenter notification messages are sent via the file presenter's queue, so the file coordination system is not waiting for these methods to return. This means that you can safely call NSFileCoordination APIs directly from within any of these notification methods without fear of causing a deadlock.

The implementation of the above logic can be seen in Listing 5-28.

Listing 5-28. Handling the Appearance of a New Sub-Item

```
- (void) presentedSubitemDidAppearAtURL: (NSURL *) url
{
    // handled very simply: add the new item's sizes to our totals
    // Apple recommends that this occur via NSFileCoordinator coordinateReading...
    NSFileCoordinator * c = [[NSFileCoordinator alloc] initWithFilePresenter: self];
    [c coordinateReadingItemAtURL: url options: NSFileCoordinatorReadingWithoutChanges error:
NULL byAccessor: ^(NSURL *newURL) {
        NSDictionary * attrs = [url resourceValuesForKeys: @[NSURLFileSizeKey,
NSURLTotalFileAllocatedSizeKey]
                                                   error: NULL];
        _totalFileSize += [[attrs objectForKey: NSURLFileSizeKey] unsignedIntegerValue];
        _totalAllocatedSize += [[attrs objectForKey: NSURLTotalFileAllocatedSizeKey]
unsignedIntegerValue];
    }];

    // send the new details to the info file
    [self updateInfoFile];
}
```

The method of dealing with a deleted sub-item is very similar; instead of adding the details, you remove them. However, since you are being messaged prior to the sub-items actual deletion, you are provided a block to call when you're done. The implementation of this method looks almost identical to that in Listing 5-28, except that you subtract the file sizes from your totals and you call the provided completionHandler block before returning.

You are also told when sub-items change their content/attributes somehow and when they are moved or renamed. In Listing 5-29, you log movements and rescan your folder when items change.

Listing 5-29. Handling Sub-Item Changes

```
- (void) presentedSubitemDidChangeAtURL: (NSURL *) url
{
    // we don't know the prior state of this sub-item, so we have to rebuild
    // from scratch.
    [self updateFolderInfo];
}

- (void) presentedSubitemAtURL: (NSURL *) url didMoveToURL: (NSURL *) newURL
{
    // not used in our info file, but we can log it to stdout
    fprintf(stdout, "Sub-item moved from %s to %s\n", [[url path] UTF8String],
                    [[newURL path] UTF8String]);
}
```

Presenting and Coordinating Files

The `InfoFilePresenter` class can help you manage your folder-info file. This is initialized with a URL and an `NSOperationQueue`. As you saw in Listing 5-25, there are two instances created by the folder presenter, which hands its own operation queue to the two file presenters. In the interest of brevity, I won't walk through the entire implementation of the file presenter class itself, as a large part of its implementation is based around the handling of multiple log lines as discrete objects and the parsing of the info file into those objects when it reads. Instead I'll focus on the `NSFilePresenter` methods it implements and how these work.

One interesting facet, however, is that since these classes are reading data from a file, they need to accommodate changes made by applications that do not adopt the file coordination APIs. As a result, even though content will be loaded each time you're informed of a change and immediately after a coordinated write completes, you must still be careful to reload the file's data before writing out any modifications. This is best implemented using one of `NSFileCoordinator`'s multi-operation APIs, which enables you to perform both operations in a single block, with no other coordinated access taking place between them as might otherwise happen. Listing 5-30 shows how to implemented this.

Listing 5-30. Coordinating a Multiple-Step Operation

```
- (void) writeFile
{
    ...
    // read the existing content before pushing out our changes
    NSFileCoordinator * coordinator = [[NSFileCoordinator alloc]
                                            initWithFilePresenter: self];
    [coordinator coordinateReadingItemAtURL: _fileURL options: 0
            writingItemAtURL: _fileURL options: 0 error: NULL
            byAccessor: ^(NSURL *newReadingURL, NSURL *newWritingURL) {
```

```
    // read the file to ensure we have the latest data
    NSString * content = [[NSString alloc] initWithContentsOfURL: newReadingURL
                                    encoding: NSUTF8StringEncoding error: NULL];


    @synchronized(self)
    {
        [self importEntriesFromString: content];

        // write out the new data
        NSMutableString * output = [NSMutableString new];
        ...
        [output writeToURL: newWritingURL atomically: YES
                encoding: NSUTF8StringEncoding error: NULL];
    }
  }];
}
```

The -coordinateReadingItemAtURL:options:writingItemAtURL:options:error:byAccessor:
method is primarily designed to assist with applications that are, for example, copying content
from one item to another. In this case, however, it helps you to avoid any race conditions between
this instance and any others. Note also that the coordinator provides you with new URLs for both
reading and writing, as either item could potentially have been moved or renamed in the interim.

As in the FolderInfoPresenter class, the -presentedItemURL and -presentedItemOperationQueue
methods simply return the URL of the info file and the operation queue provided during
initialization respectively. It gets more interesting when working with readers and writers in other
processes: you mark the instance as suspended to prevent any reads or writes going through,
but you keep track of any such operations while suspended and perform them when you
reacquire the item. Listing 5-31 shows this in action.

Listing 5-31. Synchronizing Access to the File

```
- (void) relinquishPresentedItemToReader: (void (^)(void (^reacquirer)(void))) reader
{
    fprintf(stdout, "Relinquishing file to reader.\n");
    _suspended = YES;
    reader(^{
        _suspended = NO;
        if ( _deferredRead )
        {
            _deferredRead = NO;
            [self loadFile];
        }
        if ( _deferredWrite )
        {
            // there was a request to write the file while we were suspended
            // fire off the operation now
            _deferredWrite = NO;
            [self writeFile];
        }
    });
}
```

```
- (void) relinquishPresentedItemToWriter: (void (^)(void (^reacquirer)(void))) writer
{
    fprintf(stdout, "Relinquishing to writer.\n");
    _suspended = YES;
    // load the new data after the writer's complete
    writer(^{
        _suspended = NO;

        if ( _deferredRead )
        {
            _deferredRead = NO;
            [self loadFile];
        }

        if ( _deferredWrite )
        {
            // there was a request to write the file while we were suspended
            // fire off the operation now
            _deferredWrite = NO;
            [self writeFile];
        }
    });
}
```

As described above, you chose to load content immediately before writing out your changes, rather than doing so immediately after another process' write operation has completed. As a result, you only load in this situation if a load was deferred while you were waiting for the other write to complete.

The remaining NSFilePresenter methods implemented here deal with the coordinator asking you to save any modifications you have and properly handling the item being moved, renamed, or deleted. You handle movement in the same manner as FolderInfoPresenter, by updating your _fileURL instance variable.

When the item is deleted, you load up all its content first to ensure you don't miss anything added by an external process. The reasoning here is that while your presenter is still loaded into memory, the data is still live, and it should be possible to save it again whether the user has deleted the underlying file or not. Changes are handled by explicitly reloading the data from the file. The implementation of these methods can be seen in Listing 5-32.

Listing 5-32. Handling Presented File Changes

```
- (void) savePresentedItemChangesWithCompletionHandler: (void (^)(NSError *)) completionHandler
{
    fprintf(stdout, "Saving changes.\n");
    [self writeFile];

    // call the completion handler to tell the world we're done
    completionHandler(NULL);
}
```

```objc
- (void) accommodatePresentedItemDeletionWithCompletionHandler: (void (^)(NSError *))
completionHandler
{
    fprintf(stdout, "FolderInfo file being deleted.\n");
    // deletion is relatively simple for us to handle-- we'll ensure we've got the latest
contents cached in memory
    // and let it go
    [self loadFile];
    completionHandler(NULL);
}

- (void) presentedItemDidMoveToURL: (NSURL *) newURL
{
    // store the new URL
    _fileURL = [newURL copy];
}

- (void) presentedItemDidChange
{
    // load the new contents
    [self loadFile];
}
```

Thus ends your whistle-stop tour of the NSFileCordinator APIs. I strongly encourage you to read through the very extensive documentation provided by Apple to get a thorough understanding of the likely situations in which file presenters and the file coordination system work together. This API provides a wonderfully simple and clean way to handle some very thorny problems, and if everyone adopts it, then it will make everyone else's tasks that much easier.

Searching with Spotlight

So far just about everything I've talked about has been based around the concepts of files and folders. However, with folder hierarchies getting deeper and more complicated, and with disk sizes and their contents growing in tandem, a manual trawl through the filesystem isn't the simple task it once was. Apple's solution to this revolves around a metadata searching utility called Spotlight.

You are likely already familiar with Spotlight. It's always accessible on the Mac through the magnifying-glass icon at the top right of the screen. As you type into the search field revealed by clicking on that icon, results appear almost instantly, matching against file names, the content of recently visited links, e-mails, and even the contents of certain types of documents. This technology isn't only available through the OS X menu bar, however; a full and rich API underlies it and provides developers with the ability to execute queries (in a properly asynchronous fashion, of course) against the Spotlight metadata and content database.

There are a lot of different metadata attributes upon which you can search, and you can specify different queries to help locate some items. For example, to locate all if the files in your home folder that were modified within the last five minutes, you can open the Terminal application and type 'mdfind -onlyin ~ 'kMDItemContentModificationDate > $time.now(-300)'. An example result is shown in Listing 5-33.

Listing 5-33. Searching for Items Modified in the Last Five Minutes

```
LP-347 ~ " mdfind -onlyin ~ 'kMDItemContentModificationDate > $time.now(-300)'
...
/Users/jdovey/Dropbox/Books/BeginningObjC
/Users/jdovey/Dropbox/Books/BeginningObjC/978-1-4302-4368-7_dovey_ch05_usingthefilesystem.doc
...
LP-347 ~ "
```

Gosh, look what was being modified just then!

The Metadata API

The core API used to interact with the metadata server is, naturally, written in C using CoreFoundation-style "objects." On top of that, however, is a pretty well-equipped Objective-C API, which you can find in `<Foundation/NSMetadata.h>`. A complete listing of all Apple-defined metadata attributes is available in the `MDItem.h` header, which is part of the `CoreServices` framework on Mac OS X (import `<CoreServices/CoreServices.h>`). On iOS, only the items specified in `NSMetadata.h` are presently supported, and it is only possible to execute Spotlight searches on iOS against an iCloud ubiquitous store, as you'll see later in this chapter.

Before you can properly investigate the Spotlight searching APIs, however, you must look at the means of specifying search criteria. On OS X and iOS, this is implemented using *predicates*.

Predicates

Search and matching criteria are specified using instances of the `NSPredicate` class. An `NSPredicate` is used to describe both individual clauses and a complete compound expression (a collection of multiple clauses). The individual clauses consist of two *expressions* and a single *comparison operation*. The operations are specified using enumerated values, and expressions are instances of `NSExpression`.

The simplest way to create an `NSPredicate` is by specifying a format string. You will note, if you look at the headers, that `NSPredicate` also offers a `+predicateWithBlock:` method allowing you to specify a block to run to evaluate that predicate against some data. While this is very useful for filtering collections, it can't be used for Spotlight searches, as these searches must be converted to a different type to be sent to the metadata indexing engine for processing. Thus the only applicable creation methods for this purpose are those that use format strings or build the predicate explicitly using `NSExpression` instances.

Format strings are specified in a manner similar to C compound clauses, such as you might use in an `if` or `while` statement. For example, to search based on the file name property you would use a format string of `kMDItemFSName == 'MyFile.doc'`. The constant `kMDItemFSName` is a predefined metadata attribute name that refers to a file's name on disk. An alternative would be `kMDItemDisplayName`, which might be localized or have its extension hidden—the file's name as shown in the Finder. There are many, many attributes for which you can search, and it's entirely possible to specify your own metadata attribute names (whose values you would import using a Spotlight plug-in, as you'll see in the final chapter where I will guide you through the creation of a working application). Another commonly used attribute name is `kMDItemTextContent`, which is the attribute used by the Spotlight search menu to locate files based on their content.

A number of different operators are supported by Spotlight, listed in Table 5-8.

Table 5-8. NSPredicate Operators

Operator	Description
==, !=, <=, >=, <>	These match their C counterparts, with the exception of <> which is a synonym for !=.
BETWEEN { A, B }	Matches if the located value is between the two values A and B, which can be dates or numbers.
LIKE	A string comparison similar to the LIKE operator in SQL databases. The test value can include the wildcard characters ? (matches any 1 character) and * (matches any number of characters).
BEGINSWITH, CONTAINS, ENDSWITH	A string comparison that matches values that begin with or end with a given string or those that contain the given string anywhere in their content.

As you can see, the format strings when using NSPredicate are a little different from the ones used with the mdfind command in the Terminal. Where the pure Spotlight syntax would use 'kMDItemDisplayName == 'MyDoc*'', a typical NSPredicate would use 'kMDItemDisplayName LIKE 'MyDoc*'' or the more easily-evaluated 'kMDItemDisplayName BEGINSWITH 'MyDoc''. An example of creating an NSPredicate with a Spotlight format string can be seen in Listing 5-34, where you can see a compound predicate being created based on the Spotlight menu's format of '(* == 'search-term*'wcd || kMDItemTextContent == 'search-term*'wcd)'.

Listing 5-34. Creating an NSPredicate with a Format String

```
NSString * searchTerm = "Cupertino*";
NSPredicate * predicate = [NSPredicate predicateWithFormat:
                        @"* LIKE[cd] %@ || kMDItemTextContent LIKE[cd] %@",
                        searchTerm, searchTerm];
```

An alternative way to create the same predicate would be to use raw Objective-C objects to define its expressions and clauses. This can be a useful optimization if your application makes heavy use of predicates, as interpreting a predicate format string like that in Listing 5-34 can be quite expensive. Instead, you might use the code in Listing 5-35, which avoids this expense by building the predicate manually from the constituent objects. Note that for Spotlight queries the left expression *must* be a key-path expression, as Spotlight only supports clauses of the form 'KEY operator VALUE'. In regular use, an NSPredicate will happily allow any type on either side, since it can still internally evaluate equality between the expressions.

Listing 5-35. Creating an NSPredicate from NSExpression Objects

```
NSExpression *lhs, *rhs;
NSPredicate *predicate = nil;
NSMutableArray *subpredicates = [[NSMutableArray alloc] initWithCapacity: 2];
NSString *searchTerm = "Cupertino*";
```

```
lhs = [NSExpression expressionForKeyPath: @"*"];
rhs = [NSExpression expressionForConstantValue: searchTerm];
predicate = [NSComparisonPredicate predicateWithLeftExpression: lhs rightExpression: rhs
        modifier: NSDirectPredicateModifier type: NSLikePredicateOperatorType
        options: NSCaseInsensitivePredicateOption|NSDiacriticInsensitivePredicateOption];

[subpredicates addObject: predicate];

lhs = [NSExpression expressionForKeyPath: (__bridge id)kMDItemTextContent];
// rhs remains unchanged
predicate = [NSComparisonPredicate predicateWithLeftExpression: lhs rightExpression: rhs
        modifier: NSDirectPredicateModifier type: NSLikePredicateOperatorType
        options: NSCaseInsensitivePredicateOption|NSDiacriticInsensitivePredicateOption];

[subpredicates addObject: predicate];

// now create the compound predicate using an OR provision
predicate = [NSCompoundPredicate orPredicateWithSubpredicates: subpredicates];
```

The rabbit-hole goes much deeper than this, of course. Not only are there comparison and compound predicates, there are expressions that are based upon the results of evaluating another predicate, expressions that perform built-in mathematical operations, or expressions that perform selectors provided by you—and all of these can be fairly arbitrarily nested.

Querying the Metadata Store

To search for items using Spotlight you construct a query to send to the metadata store. The first part of this you've already seen—it's the predicate used to test whether an item matches your query. The NSMetadataQuery object handles the query itself.

A metadata query has a number of attributes and abilities beyond the basic matching predicate. You can specify a means of ordering the results, for example, and can choose to group results by certain common attributes. You can also limit the search to a certain domain (home folder, local volumes, or iCloud) or ask the metadata server to return values for some attributes along with the query to save yourself another round-trip to the server to fetch those attributes later.

As an example, the code in Listing 5-36 creates a new metadata query that searches the current user's home folder for items with content of "search." It then tells the query to sort by relevancy and the returned items' paths (in that order), and to group all results by type. Note that most of these methods take arrays of options; Listing 5-36 uses the *wonderful* new array literal syntax to define these inline.

Listing 5-36. Creating a Metadata Query

```
NSMetadataQuery * query = [[NSMetadataQuery alloc] init];
[query setPredicate: predicate];

// limit search to local volumes, not across the network
[query setSearchScopes: @[NSMetadataQueryUserHomeScope]];
```

```
// sort results by path
[query setSortDescriptors: @[[NSSortDescriptor sortDescriptorWithKey:
NSMetadataQueryResultContentRelevanceAttribute ascending: YES], [NSSortDescriptor
sortDescriptorWithKey: NSMetadataItemPathKey ascending: YES]]];

// group results by their type-- this attribute is a Uniform Type Identifier
// to display the UTI we'll fetch its description
[_query setGroupingAttributes: @[(__bridge id)kMDItemContentType]];
```

Once a query has been created, it can be launched asynchronously by calling its -startQuery method. To receive information about its progress and completion, however, you need to register for the notifications described in Table 5-9.

Table 5-9. NSMetadataQuery Status Notifications

Notification Name	Description
NSMetadataQueryDidStartGatheringNotification	The metadata query has begun to acquire details of matching items.
NSMetadataQueryGatheringProgressNotification	Sent periodically as more results are gathered but before the complete list is ready.
NSMetadataQueryDidFinishGatheringNotification	Sent to indicate that the initial search has completed.
NSMetadataQueryDidUpdateNotification	Sent after initial gathering is complete as new items appear that match the query, or previously matched items no longer do so.

The query itself operates in two phases. The first phase, *gathering*, obtains a list of matching items and returns them. The second phase is optional, and is called *live update*. At this point you'll receive notifications whenever the contents of the gathered list change based on updates to files or the creation of new ones. If you're only doing a one-time search, you can skip the live update phase by sending -stopQuery to your NSMetadataQuery object after processing the results from the gathering phase.

Once you receive the gathering-complete notification, you can iterate across all available items. To ensure that live updates don't interrupt this, call -disableUpdates and -enableUpdates either side of the operation. In Listing 5-37, you can see this in action: a matched list of items is printed out in groups, with each group's type printed in its localized display form. This sample is available in a full Xcode project online as PerformSpotlightSearch.

Listing 5-37. Listing the Results of an NSMetadataQuery

```
- (void) gatherComplete
{
    // pause live updating
    [_query disableUpdates];

    // iterate through the groups
    for ( NSMetadataQueryResultGroup * group in [_query groupedResults] )
```

```
    {
        // fetch the type identifier from the group, and ensure it's presentable
        NSString * groupValue = [group value];
        NSString * type = CFBridgingRelease(
                            UTTypeCopyDescription((__bridge CFStringRef)groupValue));
        if ( type == nil )
        {
            // doesn't have a nice description, so make one
            CFStringRef tag = UTTypeCopyPreferredTagWithClass(
                        (__bridge CFStringRef)groupValue, kUTTagClassFilenameExtension);
            type = [NSString stringWithFormat: @"Unknown type (.%@ file)",
                                                        CFBridgingRelease(tag)];
        }
        else
        {
            // some descriptions aren't properly capitalized
            type = [type capitalizedString];
        }

        // print the type as a header
        fprintf(stdout, "%s:\n", [type UTF8String]);

        // iterate through the items in the group
        for ( NSUInteger i = 0, max = [group resultCount]; i < max; i++ )
        {
            NSMetadataItem * item = [group resultAtIndex: i];

            // print out the item's path
            fprintf(stdout, "  %s\n", [[item valueForAttribute: NSMetadataItemPathKey]
            UTF8String]);
        }
    }

    fflush(stdout);

    // resume live updates but stop the query in general
    [_query enableUpdates];
    [_query stopQuery];
}
```

As discussed earlier, NSPredicate and its friends offer the ability to create some very intricate and powerful matching rules. When these are combined with Spotlight's deep content and metadata indexing engine, your application can locate many different types of files anywhere on the system in a flash. That's not all it's useful for, as you're about to find out…

Files in the Cloud

With iOS 5 and OS X 10.7.2, Apple introduced iCloud to the world. iCloud is Apple's cloud-based data store and associated services. It provides synchronization of media and data across all a user's devices and naturally comes with a complete API. It is possible to mark items as stored on iCloud, at which point they will be synchronized automatically between devices. Developers can also store preference-like data directly on iCloud in a key-value store. Even the mighty Core Data framework, which you'll meet later in this book, has deep iCloud integration, allowing complex data stores to be synchronized to cloud storage in an optimal manner.

iCloud's primary API operates in terms of *ubiquitous items*. A ubiquitous item is, essentially, something that is accessible from anywhere, regardless of device or system. The idea is that you can edit a document on your Mac, save it, and pick up your iPad and immediately see the changes reflected there. As a result, there are a number of considerations to be made when working with such content:

> ▩ *Coordination:* All modifications to files should be done in a coordinated manner with regards to other processes reading from those items. Essentially, any number of things might read an item at the same time, but any modification operation should be exclusive of all other access.

> ▩ *Synchronization:* An item might change at any time based on updates that arrive from the iCloud servers. Any devices currently using an item must be made aware of these changes when they happen, so that they can update their view of the item appropriately.

> ▩ *Location:* The cloud isn't like a networked disk that can be attached to a device programmatically and traversed like a regular folder structure. Instead it deals in terms of data types and accessors. Each application has its own associated store into which its content goes, and that content could be user data or it could be application data. It could also be available on the local system or stored only in the cloud. Beyond those distinctions, the physical organization of items is of little concern.

> ▩ *Privilege Management:* A user might choose to disable document synchronization either across the board or for individual applications, and the system needs to be able to manage such changes.

You've already dealt with one of these items in this chapter—the matter of location. Finding files in iCloud is typically done using NSMetadataQuery; in fact, the metadata API was added to iOS 5 for precisely this reason (on iOS this is the metadata API's *only* use case). Using Spotlight searches of your application's iCloud store is the primary way to locate content stored there.

Likewise you've already seen the API used for coordinating changes made by other devices: the NSFileCoordinator APIs. When your items are synchronized or new versions are saved to the cloud from other devices, adopting the NSFilePresenter protocol will enable you to receive timely information about those changes and to coordinate your access to the item with the system's automatic synchronization system.

The main source of APIs for dealing with ubiquitous items is NSFileManager. It is from here that you'll obtain the URL for your store, and place items into the store or take them out. NSFileManager has a number of methods you'll use, outlined in Table 5-10.

Table 5-10. NSFileManager's Ubiquitous Item APIs

Method	Description
`-(NSURL*)URLForUbiquityContainerIdentifier:(NSURL*)identifier`	Retrieves a URL for the root of the iCloud data store for your application's container identifier.
`- (BOOL)setUbiquitous:(BOOL)flag itemAtURL:(NSURL*)url destinationURL:(NSURL*)destinationURL error:(NSError**)error`	Adds an item to or removes it from your iCloud storage container. When adding, the destination URL must be prefixed with the result of `URLForUbiquityContainerIdentifier`.
`-(BOOL)isUbiquitousItemAtURL:(NSURL*)url`	Determines whether the item at the given URL is synchronized with other devices via iCloud.
`-(BOOL)startDownloadingUbiquitousItemAtURL:(NSURL*)url error:(NSError**)error`	If the specified item is not yet stored locally, this begins downloading it.
`-(BOOL)evictUbiquitousItemAtURL:(NSURL*)url error:(NSError**)error`	Removes the local copy of the item at the given URL. Does not remove it from the iCloud store.
`-(NSURL*)URLForPublishingUbiquitousItemAtURL:(NSURL*)url expirationDate:(NSDate**)expirationDate error:(NSError**)error`	Returns a URL suitable for sharing the specified item with other users. Also returns by reference the date at which the shareable URL will become invalid.

The NSURL class also defines some resource keys used to access information about ubiquitous items, shown in Table 5-11.

Table 5-11. NSURL Ubiquitous Item Resource Keys

Resource Key	Description
`NSURLIsUbiquitousItemKey`	Whether the URL refers to a ubiquitous item.
`NSURLUbiquitousItemHasUnresovedConflictsKey`	Whether the item at the URL has conflicts against the cloud store's version that are yet to be resolved.
`NSURLUbiquitousItemIsDownloadedKey, NSURLUbiquitousItemIsDownloadingKey`	Whether the given item has been downloaded to local storage or exists only in the cloud, or whether it is currently in the process of being downloaded.
`NSURLUbiquitousItemIsUploadedKey, NSURLUbiquitousItemIsUploadingKey`	Whether the given item has been uploaded to cloud storage, or whether it is currently being uploaded.

Using these APIs and NSURL resource keys is the primary means of placing items into cloud storage or removing them and keeping track of their status. All other operations happen in exactly the same manner as for local items—you read and write to the files using NSURL instances to specify their location, and the system handles the rest. Listing 5-38 shows an example of an item being moved into the cloud and modified, then removed from the cloud.

Listing 5-38. Adding, Updating, and Removing Ubiquitous Items

```
NSURL * localURL = ...

// save to iCloud
// get a ubiquitous item URL
NSURL * ubiquitousURL = [[NSFileManager defaultManager]
                                URLForUbiquityContainerIdentifier: myIdentifer];
ubiquitousURL = [ubiquitousURL URLByAppendingPathComponents:
                                @[ @"Documents", [localURL lastPathComponent] ]];

[[NSFileManager defaultManager] setUbiquitous:YES itemAtURL:myURL
                                destinationURL:ubiquitousURL error:NULL];

...

// write some new data
NSData * myData = ...
NSFileCoordinator *c = [[NSFileCoordinator alloc] initWithFilePresenter:self];
[c coordinateWritingItemAtURL:ubiquitousURL options:0 error:NULL byAccessor:^(NSURL*url)
{
    [myData writeToURL:url options:0 error:NULL];
}];

...

// remove the item from iCloud
[[NSFileManager defaultManager] setUbiquitous:NO itemAtURL:ubiquitousURL
                                destinationURL:localURL error:NULL];
```

Uploading of items to the iCloud store happens automatically without any programmer input. Downloading is started on-demand through NSFileManager's -startDownloadingUbiquitous ItemAtURL:error: method. The progresses of uploads and downloads, however, are handled using a live-updating NSMetadataQuery. There are actually a number of metadata keys for ubiquitous items, most of which mirror those supported by NSURL's resource API, but starting with NSMetadata rather than NSURL. For instance, NSURLUbiquitousItemIsDownloadedKey matches NSMetadataUbiquitousItemIsDownloadedKey. Two additional keys supported by the metadata APIs, however, are NSMetadataUbiquitousItemPercentDownloadedKey and NSMetadataUbiquitousItemPercentUploadedKey. Dynamic notification of upload and download progress happens by monitoring a query for these keys. Listing 5-39 gives an example of how this could be implemented.

Listing 5-39. Monitoring Download Progress

```
- (BOOL) startDownloadingUbiquitousItem: (NSURL *) url error: (NSError **) error
{
    BOOL ok = [[NSFileManager defaultManager] startDownloadingUbiquitousItemAtURL:url
                                                        error: error];
    if ( !ok )
        return ( NO );

    NSDictionary * attrs = [url resourceValuesForKeys:
                                @[NSURLUbiquitousItemIsDownloadedKey] error: error];
```

```objc
    if ( attrs == nil )
        return ( NO );

    if ( [[attrs objectForKey: NSURLUbiquitousItemIsDownloadedKey] boolValue] )
        return ( YES );     // already downloaded

    // metadata query time
    NSMetadataQuery * query = [[NSMetadataQuery alloc] init];
    [query setPredicate: [NSPredicate predicateWithFormat: @"%K > 0",
                                        NSMetadataUbiquitousItemPercentDownloadedKey]];

    // limit search to only this item
    [query setSearchScopes: @[url]];

    // fetch the percent-downloaded key when updating results
    [query setValueListAttributes: @[NSMetadataUbiquitousItemPercentDownloadedKey,
                                        NSMetadataUbiquitousItemIsDownloadedKey]];

    // save the query (no use having ARC deallocate it while we're waiting for results)
    _query = query;

    // register for live updates
    [[NSNotificationCenter defaultCenter] addObserver: self
                            selector: @selector(liveUpdate:)
                                name: NSMetadataQueryDidUpdateNotification
                              object: query];

    // start it running
    [query startQuery];
}

- (void) liveUpdate: (NSNotification *) note
{
    NSMetadataQuery * query = [note object];
    if ( [query resultCount] == 0 )
        return;

    NSMetadataItem * item = [query resultAtIndex: 0];
    double progress = [[item valueForAttribute:
                            NSMetadataUbiquitousItemPercentDownloadedKey] doubleValue];
    [self setDownloadProgress: progress];

    if ( [[item valueForAttribute: NSMetadataUbiquitousItemIsDownloadedKey] boolValue] )
    {
        // finished downloading, stop the query
        [query stopQuery];
        _query = nil;
        [self downloadComplete];
    }
}
```

I'm sorry to say that, as interesting a topic as it is, this is as far as I'll go with iCloud right now. You'll see some real-life use of it in a later chapter, however, when you put together a complete application.

Summary

This chapter has been quite a long one, hasn't it? So, what have you learned here?

- You've learned the details of files and folders and their attributes.

- You've learned the basics of file and folder permissions, and access control lists.

- You've met NSURL and explored its resource access and caching mechanisms.

- You now know the methods of implementing proper synchronous and asynchronous file access, including coordinating access with other processes via NSFileCoordinator and NSFilePresenter.

- You've explored the Spotlight metadata APIs and learned about live queries and predicates.

- Lastly, you learned how to place items into an iCloud ubiquitous store and how to work with them once they're there.

That's a lot of information, but it's not letting up. In the next chapter, I'll show you the fundamentals of working with networked resources and how to handle common data types used to transmit data across a network.

Chapter 6

Networking: Connections, Data, and the Cloud

In today's world of ubiquitous mobile devices and always-on connections to the Internet, the topic of networking is of great importance. On iOS alone, a great quantity of applications make use of the network in one way or the other, whether using built-in systems like iCloud synchronization or GameKit's communication framework, or by communicating directly with servers over the Internet. Moreover, the expectations of consumers often clashes with the capabilities and limitations of wide-area mobile networks such as EDGE, 3G, and HDPSA+, leaving you, the application programmer, to make the best of a high-latency, low-throughput network channel.

Well, luckily for you, I have a positive ocean of information and experience to share on this front. In this chapter you'll learn about the URL loading system, and asynchronous, synchronous, and synthetic-synchronous network access. You'll learn the best ways to handle common types of data passed across the network and how to correctly handle binary data in a system-agnostic fashion. You'll also see how to locate services on the network plus how you can create your own and make their information available in the same manner.

Perhaps most importantly, though, you'll learn the rationale behind the following core tenets of network-centric programming on the Mac and iOS:

  - Never access the network from the main thread.
  - Use asynchronous network primitives wherever possible.
  - Use streams for all data handling.
  - Keep data handling and transport handling unaware of one another.

Stick to these four rules and you'll not go far wrong. In fact, you'll be in a much better position to handle anything the network can throw at you—because it will throw everything it can, sooner or later.

Basic Principles

You've already learned a lot about the local filesystem (yes, you're allowed to exclaim something about "understatement" at this point), and while the data access APIs on the Mac and iOS are frequently storage-agnostic, there can be a world of difference between loading a file from disk and loading it from the network. To underline the lessons of this chapter, I'm going to take a few minutes to explain these differences and give you a good grounding point for anything you might learn about networking in future.

With both network and local-file access there are a certain set of problems that might impact your application's performance. These fall into two broad groups:

- *Latency* refers to the amount of time it takes to reach the resource you want to access. In terms of local disks, this usually refers to the seek-time of the underlying storage medium. In network terms, this refers to the round-trip time of a command packet.

- *Throughput* refers to the speed at which data can be sent to or retrieved from the resource. Local disks usually have very high throughput and are able to move hundreds of megabytes in a second. On a network this could be anywhere from tens of megabytes per second to a few kilobytes per second.

Also associated with these two types is the available bandwidth. For local storage, the reads and writes typically travel through a hardware bus, which has much higher throughput than the hard disks themselves. So unless a lot of disks are being used at the same time, the overall throughput is likely to match that of the physical media in use by a particular operation. This means that if you read or write to multiple devices at the same time you will likely not see any appreciable change in the throughput from each device compared to handling that device alone.

On the network, however, the available bandwidth is usually much more restrictive, and each single operation can easily saturate the connection, eating up all the available bandwidth. As a result, performing more operations in parallel will likely result in all the operations slowing down as the available bandwidth is apportioned between them. In addition, there are more nodes on the journey between your device and the actual resource, such as wireless access points and routers. Any of these might have their own bandwidth concerns and any number of other clients, and they might have specific rules that they enforce to prevent any single client from using up too much bandwidth. For an example, many common access points and routers will allow only four concurrent requests using the HTTP protocol to go from a single client to a single destination resource; all others are blocked until some of the first four are done. As a result, it is often useful for HTTP client software to implement the same limit internally to avoid having many concurrent operations spinning their wheels and using up local resources like memory, CPU, and battery power.

On the flip side, there is frequently little difference in requesting a number of different resources from the same location via the network, while doing so with files on the same local disk can cause a lot of slow-down. The reason is down to the cause of latency on disk-based storage: the seek time. When a single large file is being read, the disk will seek to the file once and then read a (largely) contiguous stream of data. When multiple files are being read and written in parallel, the disk's read head needs to move back and forth across the magnetic platter to switch between the files frequently, leading to that phenomenon known as *disk thrashing*—the clunking and clicking sounds that you can hear coming from your computer during periods of high activity. Recent advances in solid-state storage mean that a lot of people now use solid state drives (SSDs) rather than platter-based magnetic hard disk drives, so the latency issue is much less of a problem on systems equipped with such storage. The iPhone, of course, uses solid-state storage.

Network Latency

Latency on network transmissions is most frequently caused by either congestion of the network (which can occur at any stop on the journey, remember) or by inefficiency of the underlying transmission protocol. Wired network connections and Wi-Fi wireless connections use versions of the Ethernet protocol. This protocol is responsible for locating other devices on the local network and ferrying data between them in an ordered fashion. Mobile devices using the cellular network, however, use a protocol such as GSM or HSDPA, which is working in a much more error-prone environment and needs to maintain data throughput even when devices are moving at high speed between endpoints such as cell towers. As a result, those protocols have significant overhead when compared to Ethernet. This isn't helped when you consider that most Ethernet or Wi-Fi devices have throughputs in the tens or hundreds of megabits per second while cellular networks are only just beginning to reach past the 15 Mbit boundary with HSDPA+ and "4G"[1]. As a result, it is common to see a latency of up to a full second (even two!) when making a connection over a cellular network, particularly over the slower protocols like GSM or 3G.

If your application is making a lot of connections, for instance when fetching data from a server over the HTTP protocol, then latency can really cause you problems. Imagine you need to make about 20 separate calls to pull down a full list of 200 comments (the server returns 10 per page). Every call will by default make a new connection, and each connection will encounter a long delay due to latency. If the latency is quite bad, then regardless of the actual throughput speed you're guaranteed to see this take somewhere between 10 and 40 seconds, which isn't a very good experience. If the throughput is also slow, it becomes even worse. I've seen an implementation of syncing data from such an API take over an *hour* when there are a lot of calls to be made, and almost half of that time was due to network latency.

Asynchronicity

With all these potential pitfalls waiting to trip you up, it becomes *vitally important* that you interact with network resources in a fully asynchronous manner. I can't state this strongly enough: it *must always be asynchronous, no matter what.*

---

[1] I put this in quotes because the 4G standard actually specifies that there should be one *gigabit* per second of bandwidth to attain that label

It's easy to fall into the trap of convincing yourself that something doesn't need to be done in an asynchronous manner. Perhaps you're only using the network occasionally; perhaps you're only sending or receiving very small amounts of data. Perhaps you only send data, but don't wait for a reply, or you only perform network operations in response to user input. We've heard all these excuses, and I have some news for you: *the network will still get you*. For example:

- *I only use the network occasionally.*
  If you're doing it occasionally, the user likely isn't expecting it. If your occasional activity causes the application to become unresponsive, your user is likely to be more upset than if it were a regular occurrence, because they're unable to predict when it will happen.

- *I only send very small packets of data.*
  Small packets might move quite quickly even on networks with low throughput, but network latency doesn't care about the packet size. The action of making the connection could take long enough that the application becomes unresponsive, even for a short time, and that's a Bad Thing.

- *I only send; I never wait for a reply.*
  You might not be waiting for a reply, but your send operation won't complete until the network stack receives a confirmation that the data was received correctly. You could use a protocol with non-guaranteed transfer of data, but for sending user data somewhere that's a bad idea—you *want* to know the data got there safely.

- *It's always caused by user input, so they're conditioned to expect some small delay.*
  The user might change their mind. If you're doing everything synchronously, you don't have any way to asynchronously cancel the operation if the user decides it's taking too long.

If you have another reason to stick with synchronous networking, please let me know what it is—I'll be only too happy to shoot it down.

Sockets, Ports, Streams, and Datagrams

The networking system on OS X and iOS uses the BSD sockets system. This essentially makes a network connection appear similar to a file: data is sent and received by writing to or reading from a standard file handle, and the kernel takes care of the rest. There are some extra capabilities, but for your purposes you're unlikely to need to look at them here. The main difference when dealing with network connections is that data isn't available on-demand, nor is the space in which to write. Incoming data is available only once it arrives through the transport medium, and outgoing data is stored temporarily in a system buffer until the system is able to send it across the wire. When you looked at NSStream in the previous chapter, you saw events and methods based around these concepts: data available to read and space available to write.

A network connection's file handle is called a *socket*. Once created, these can be used almost like regular file handles, right up to the point of wrapping it with an NSFileHandle instance. The chief difference is the inability to seek to a location in the data stream—it's strictly an ordered-access system.

There are two primary types of sockets:

- *Stream sockets* are designed to send large collections of ordered data from one end of a connection to the other. The underlying transport typically provides guaranteed delivery of content—and in the correct order.

- *Datagram sockets*, on the other hand, do not provide any guarantees of either delivery or ordering. Each parcel of data is considered a separate stand-alone element, and no attempt is made to ensure that the datagrams follow the same route through the network. Each datagram could follow a different route, depending on the conditions at each node on the journey.

Datagram sockets, normally using the Unified Datagram Protocol (UDP) over the Internet Protocol (IP), are typically used for things like streaming media, where a datagram from a certain location in the underlying data stream is expected to arrive at a certain time, but the data is of a type that can be reassembled reasonably well without receiving every byte in order. For example, if you've ever watched a live webcast you've probably seen the speaker's image replaced at some point by various pieces of some earlier frame in the video, seemingly warped and wrapped to match the speaker's movements. This is an example of missing datagrams. The video data provides a full frame only every now and then, and in between these the data consists only of modifications to apply to that frame to shape it into the current frame. When a full frame is missed, this results in the strange effect of warping the wrong frame image to create a new one, causing the visual effect described above.

Most network communication, however, uses streaming sockets, typically using the Transmission Control Protocol (TCP) over IP. TCP provides guaranteed delivery at the expense of guaranteed time-to-destination. If something goes wrong partway through the transfer, the receiving endpoint is able to check that it received the packet correctly and request a resend if it didn't arrive properly. The TCP protocol also ensures that ordering is maintained, even when some packets arrive correctly and some do not; if packet A fails and packet B succeeds, the contents of packet B will be kept around until the content of A can be delivered successfully.

TCP also implements *transmission windows*. These allow each endpoint to communicate to the other some details on the amount of data it can successfully handle. As a result, unlike UDP (Unified Datagram Protocol), one endpoint never sends any data that the receiver cannot currently handle. Datagram protocols, on the other hand, are designed to pump data out as fast as possible (or at least at a continuous rate), allowing the receiver to just skip any packets that arrive before it can handle them.

In all the examples that follow, I will be using TCP/IP, rather than datagrams. Datagram protocols typically require more work at the application level to correctly handle errors such as missing packets, which is *very definitely* beyond the scope of this book.

Underneath the TCP and UDP protocols lies the Internet Protocol. This is the source of many things you may recognize already: IP addresses as dotted octets such as 192.168.23.5, and stem from version 4 of the IP protocol. An IP address references a single host on the network; each connection endpoint is made available through a *port* on that address, which is a 16-bit number identifying a particular endpoint. There are a number of standard port assignments registered with the relevant authorities, so certain services are usually accessible through a known port number. HTTP, for example, uses port 80, while secure HTTP uses port 443. The Apple Filing Protocol, when served over TCP/IP, uses port 548, and there are many, many more standard assignments in use—a fair chunk of the available 65535 ports supported by the protocol.

> **Note** The term "dotted octet" refers to the textual representation of what is actually just a 32-bit number. Each of the four segments of an IP address represents a single byte, and the word "octet" is another word for "byte"—a byte contains eight bits. Once upon a time different systems used different sizes of bytes, hence the remaining use of the word "octet" here.

The 32-bit addressing scheme used by IPv4 (read: Internet Protocol, version four) only allows for around 4.3 billion unique addresses. Add to that the fact that large ranges of these addresses are off-limits for general use—for use only as local-network private addresses, or for different types of communication, such as multicast IP—then it's hardly surprising to discover that we've actually run out. Service providers snapped up the last available IPv4 addresses in early 2012. The solution to this is the current rollout of IPv6, the latest version of the standard. This update uses a 128-bit addressing system, which is expected to last far beyond the lifetimes of anyone alive today. From the software's point of view, however, the only difference is in how an address is specified. As you'll see later in this chapter, this is frequently obviated by service discovery systems, which remove the need for handling addresses directly. For those occasions when you do need to work with them, the same POSIX routines that work with IPv4 addresses also handle IPv6 out of the box.

The Cocoa URL Loading System

The highest-level API for accessing network resources on OS X and iOS revolves around the judicious use of NSURLs. There is a large framework behind these objects, which is invoked either automatically by object methods such as -initWithContentsOfURL: or explicitly through the NSURLRequest or NSURLConnection classes. A graphical overview of the URL system can be seen in Figure 6-1.

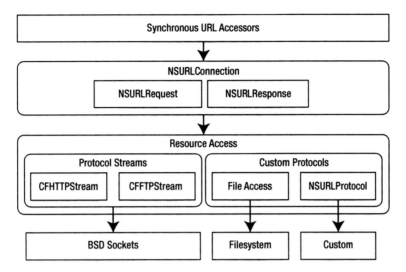

Figure 6-1. *Components of the Cocoa URL loading system*

The URL loading system itself provides out-of-the-box support for a number of commonly used protocols:

- File Transfer Protocol (FTP), using `ftp://server.com/path/to/item`.

- Hypertext Transfer Protocol (HTTP), using `http://server.com/path/to/item`.

- Secure Hypertext Transfer Protocol (HTTPS), using `https://server.com/path/to/item`.

- Local files, using `file:///path/to/item` or `file://localhost/path/to/item`.

It also provides the means for you to implement your own URL-based protocol handling via the `NSURLProtocol` class. This is beyond the scope of this book, but it's worth looking at the headers and documentation if you'd like to provide URL-based access to the interior of a container file such as a zip or xar archive or implement URL support for your own custom protocol.

The URL loading system also has support for handling authentication on any of the above protocols using a challenge-response format. Making use of this requires you to use the `NSURLConnection` class directly to manage your resource access, however, as you'll need to provide a delegate object to respond to any authentication challenges which arise. You will see this later.

All URL loads are performed using asynchronous methods. Whether created by you or created by a system framework on your behalf, an `NSURLConnection` lies at the heart of all URL access operations. The difference is that when using one-shot synchronous methods to load data from a URL, you are in fact using a *synthetic synchronous* method. This is because the method itself is using an asynchronous API based on callbacks and delegation to implement the data access, but is silently waiting for it to complete before returning. This is better than a plain synchronous approach (at least this way the waiting is done in a manner that allows other processing to occur) but still not as good as programming directly against the asynchronous API. For instance, if a synthetic synchronous method waits by spinning the current run-loop in the default mode, then it would be bad for it to do so while the current run-loop is actually in an event-tracking mode. And if it simply ran the current run-loop in its current mode, the same thing might happen if the event-tracking sequence ends: this thing is still running a non-default run-loop while it waits for an indeterminate amount of time.

The actual transfer of data is typically implemented using streams. The core implementations of URL connections, requests, and responses (in CFNetwork, a CoreFoundation-based framework) have custom stream classes to perform the work of communicating using a particular protocol. Your NSURLProtocol-based accessors may or may not use streams internally, though the NSStream APIs do provide perhaps the most cooperative set of methods to implement a properly asynchronous protocol handler. Note that the stream classes used to implement the built-in protocol support are usually entirely private, conforming only to the public interfaces defined by NSInputStream or NSOutputStream. In fact, if you're using NSURLConnection you'll typically never see the streams themselves as the connection object hides the underlying objects and hands its delegate already-accumulated data packages and high-level events.

Using NSURLConnection

Loading data from a remote resource (or sending data to it) begins with a request, encapsulated by the NSURLRequest object. At its simplest, a URL request contains a URL, a timeout (the default is 60 seconds), and a specification of some caching behavior. Each protocol defines its own default caching behavior, but you can choose to override this by requesting that only cached data is returned, or that the cache should be ignored and the remote resource always refetched. There is also an NSMutableURLRequest class that allows you to modify any of these attributes and supply some additional metadata, such as an associated base document URL or whether to allow the request to utilize an available cellular network.

For HTTP requests, there are some additional methods available to set some of the attributes of the request, specific to the HTTP protocol. These allow you to set the method and any header values, as well as supply body data for the request either as an NSData object or an NSInputStream instance. It is usually *much* better to provide an input stream if at all possible, especially if you're doing something like uploading a file. To do so, you could just create a new input stream using the local file's URL and provide that to the NSURLRequest object. You can also tell the URL request to attempt to use HTTP pipelining to send multiple requests in sequence without waiting for replies for each one. Note that whether this actually happens is up to the server, which may not support pipelining.

Listing 6-1 shows an example of creating a URL request to fetch the contents of Apple's home page.

Listing 6-1. Fetching Apple's Home Page using a HTTP Request

```
NSURL *url = [NSURL URLWithString: @"http://www.apple.com/"];
NSMutableURLRequest *request = [NSMutableURLRequest requestWithURL: url];
[request setHTTPMethod: @"GET"];
[request setHTTPShouldUsePipelining: YES];
```

Once you have your request, you use it to initialize an NSURLConnection instance. This object will then take on the handling of the actual transmission of the request and the receipt and parsing of its response. By default a new NSURLConnection instance will schedule itself with the current run-loop's default mode and immediately send its request and begin processing, although you can override this behavior if you wish and use the -start method to kick off the process, as seen in Listing 6-2.

Listing 6-2. Initializing an NSURLConnection

```
NSURLConnection *connection = [[NSURLConnection alloc] initWithRequest:request
                                   delegate:delegate startImmediately:NO];

// you can either schedule the connection on a run loop or an operation queue
if ( [self shouldUseRunLoop] )
    [connection scheduleInRunLoop:[NSRunLoop currentRunLoop] mode:NSDefaultRunLoopMode];
else
    [connection setDelegateQueue: [self operationQueue]];

// fire up the connection, sending the request
[connection start];
```

NSURLConnection uses a delegation system to handle the events that occur, providing the delegate with any returned data (for HTTP, this refers to *body* data; the headers are parsed into a response object automatically), reporting any errors, and requesting confirmation or input for any authentication challenges or redirection it might encounter.

The delegate methods for NSURLConnection are split into three separate protocols:

- NSURLConnectionDelegate declares methods that allow the delegate to handle errors and authentication challenges.

- NSURLConnectionDataDelegate adds methods that notify the delegate of the receipt of responses and data, and allow the delegate to modify outgoing requests due to redirection and to monitor the transfer of sent data. In the case where a stream was provided for body data, the delegate will also be asked to provide a new stream should the request need to be restarted.

- NSURLConnectionDownloadDelegate adds methods that notify the delegate of the process of downloading a file to local storage. This functionality is only available on iOS within Newsstand applications, however, so I will not cover it in this chapter.

Both NSURLConnectionDataDelegate and NSURLConnectionDownloadDelegate incorporate the methods declared by the NSURLConnectionDelegate protocol. You can think of them as being members of a class hierarchy.

Let's break down the delegate methods into groups. First you'll look at authentication, which is implemented using the `NSURLAuthenticationChallenge` and `NSURLCredential` classes.

Authentication

The URL connection notifies its delegate of an authentication challenge using two methods. Firstly it will check whether it ought to use the built-in credential store to look up authentication information automatically by calling `-connectionShouldUseCredentialStorage:` when the connection is started. If the delegate does not implement this method, the connection will assume that the answer is YES.

When an authentication challenge is received from the remote service, this value will be used to construct a default challenge response. If the credential store was consulted, this response may already contain valid credentials. Either way, if implemented the delegate's `-connection:willSendRequestForAuthenticationChallenge:` method, providing details on the challenge and any applicable saved credential that the system would attempt to use to meet the challenge. Usually you will want to implement this method because doing so is likely the primary means by which credentials will be added to the store for later use.

The second parameter is an instance of `NSURLAuthenticationChallenge`, which encapsulates all available information about the challenge itself. Through this object you can determine the authentication method, the proposed credential (if one was available from the store, or if a protocol implements a common "anonymous" credential), the number of previous failed attempts, and more.

For example, you can access an `NSURLProtectionSpace` object that describes the domain against which the credential would be applied; this normally refers to the host, port, and protocol used, and may (depending on the protocol) specify a realm to further narrow down the authentication's applied scope. For example, a standard HTTP connection might specify a protocol of HTTP, a host of `www.apple.com`, and a port of 80 (the default port for HTTP services). An example realm for HTTP might be a subfolder: perhaps most of the host is accessible, but getting to `www.apple.com/secure/` requires a credential, so the realm would be "secure" since the credential would only provide access to items within that folder resource. The protection space also provides information on whether the credential will be transmitted securely, along with the details of things like the certificate trust chain for a secure connection. You can use any of this to make a decision on whether to return a valid credential back to the server.

The core of the matter revolves around the creation of an `NSURLCredential` object. In order to authenticate against a service you need to create a credential and provide that to the sender of the authentication challenge, accessed via the authentication challenge's `-sender` method. The authentication challenge sender itself is any object that corresponds to the `NSAuthenticationChallengeSender` protocol, which declares the methods shown in Table 6-1. You use those methods to inform the challenge sender of your decision regarding the current authentication attempt: you can provide a credential, cancel the authentication, and more.

Table 6-1. *Authentication Challenge Sender Methods*

Method	Description
- (void)useCredential:(NSURLCredential *) credential forAuthenticationChallenge: (NSURLAuthenticationChallenge *)challenge	Call this method to provide a credential used to attempt authentication.
- (void)continueWithoutCredentialFor AuthenticationChallenge: (NSURLAuthenticationChallenge *)challenge	Attempts to continue access without providing a credential. Typically this will result in some alternative result; for instance an HTTP server might return a HTML page containing a descriptive error and further instructions.
- (void)cancelAuthenticationChallenge: (NSURLAuthenticationChallenge *)challenge	Cancels the authentication attempt, which typically causes the connection to abort with an error.
- (void) performDefaultHandlingForAuthenticationChallenge: (NSURLAuthenticationChallenge *)challenge	Instructs the sender to fall back on default behavior, as if the URL connection's delegate did not implement the authentication delegation methods. Optional.
- (void)rejectProtectionSpaceAndContinueWithChallenge: (NSURLAuthenticationChallenge *)challenge	Rejects the authentication protection space and continues trying to access. In some protocols this may result in a different form of authentication being attempted. Optional.

It's worth noting that by declaring this interface as an Objective-C protocol, it is possible to create authentication challenges for your own custom URL protocol handlers. The NSURLAuthenticationChallenge method takes a reference to a sender object in its constructor, and (unlike some classes in the URL loading system[2]) its creation API is publicly available to use.

You most likely implementation, however, is going to involve simply asking the user to provide logon credentials at some point. You could then keep these in the credential store or place them manually in the user's keychain for later secure access. The latter is beyond the scope of this book, so for an example of proper handling of the former look no further than Listing 6-3. Note that it is *absolutely required* that you call one of the methods from Table 6-1 in response to a -connection:willSendAuthenticationChallenge: message, as the connection attempt will not proceed until you have done so.

---

[2]NSHTTPURLResponse, we're looking at you. Yes, you with the initializer that was only introduced in iOS 5 and OS X 10.7, despite the class existing all the way back to OS X 10.0.

Listing 6-3. Implementing Authentication in an NSURLConnectionDelegate

```
- (BOOL) connectionShouldUseCredentialStorage:(NSURLConnection*)connection
{
    return ( YES );
}

- (void) connection:(NSURLConnection*)connection
        willSendAuthenticationChallenge:(NSURLAuthenticationChallenge*)challenge
{
    // look at the challenge-- does it have a proposed credential?
    if ( [challenge proposedCredential] != nil )
    {
        // has it failed already? If not, try it
        if ( [challenge previousFailureCount] == 0 )
        {
            // use the proposed credential and return
            [[challenge sender] useCredential: [challenge proposedCredential]
                    forAuthenticationChallenge: challenge];
            return;
        }
    }

    // if we get here, then either there's no proposed credential or it failed
    // that means we need to ask for one
    NSString *user = nil, *pass = nil;
    if ( [self promptForAuthenticationForChallenge:challenge
                                     returningUser: &user pass: &pass] == NO )
    {
        // the user cancelled the dialog, so cancel authentication
        [[challenge sender] cancelAuthenticationChallenge: challenge];
        return;
    }

    // if there was no username, try the default handling
    if ( [user length] == 0 )
    {
        // this method is optional, so check for it
        if ( [[challenge sender] respondsToSelector:
                        @selector(performDefaultHandlingForAuthenticationChallenge:)] )
        {
            [[challenge sender] performDefaultHandlingForAuthenticationChallenge:
                                                                        challenge];
        }
        else
        {
            [[challenge sender] continueWithoutCredentialForAuthenticationChallenge:
                                                                        challenge];
        }

        // we've made a decision, so return now
        return;
    }
```

```
    // Note that it's perfectly valid to send an empty password. It's up to the server
    // to decide whether that's allowed upon receipt.
    NSURLCredential * credential = [NSURLCredential credentialWithUser:user
                                    password:pass
                                    persistence:NSURLCredentialPersistenceForSession];
    [[challenge sender] useCredential: credential
            forAuthenticationChallenge: challenge];
}
```

In cases where authentication is based upon server-side and client-side certificates, it is possible to initialize an NSURLCredential instance with a certificate chain and identity or by indicating that you have chosen to trust a secure identity provided by the server. In some cases, both of these may be required in separate steps: first you choose whether to trust the server, then you provide a secure identity so the server can decide if it trusts you.

URL Connection Data Handling

When you implement an object confirming to the NSURLConnectionDataDelegate protocol, you can monitor or affect four areas of the transaction:

- You can allow, deny, or modify any requests sent as a result of receiving a redirection request (only appropriate for certain protocols).

- You can observe and store the parsed URL response (an instance of NSURLResponse or its subclass NSHTTPURLResponse), handle packets of data as they arrive, and be notified when the connection has completed all its work.

- You can monitor the flow of data sent in the body of a request and provide a new copy if required to resend.

- You can affect the storage of a URL response in the URL system's response cache by allowing or denying it or by modifying or replacing a proposed NSCachedURLResponse object.

All of these methods are optional. In most cases, you'll likely only implement -connection:didReceiveData: and -connectionDidFinishLoading:. Among the common reasons for implementing the confirmation methods, however, is to implement some basic security checking. For example, Listing 6-4 shows implementations of the redirection handler and caching handler, which think about security considerations.

Listing 6-4. Security Considerations in NSURLConnectionDataDelegate

```
- (NSURLRequest*)connection:(NSURLConnection*)connection
            willSendRequest:(NSURLRequest*)request
            redirectResponse:(NSURLResponse*)response
{
    // we know the server we're talking to, and it will never send us elsewhere
    // therefore, we do NOT accept redirects to a different host
    NSString *responseHost = [[response URL] host];
    NSString *newRequestHost = [[request URL] host];
    if ( [responseHost isEqualToString: newRequestHost] == NO )
```

```objc
    {
        // this is unexpected behaviour from a secure server: don't follow
        // return nil to reject the request
        return ( nil );
    }

    // we're going to allow the redirect
    // if we wanted to ensure certain headers are set (i.e. a content hash)
    //  we would create a mutable copy of the request and modify and return it

    // for now, let's just return the proposed request to use that, unchanged
    return ( request );
}

- (NSCachedURLResponse*)connection:(NSURLConnection*)connection
               willCacheResponse:(NSCachedURLResponse*)cachedResponse
{
    // don't cache anything from within our secure realm
    // our secure realm is inside '/secure' on the server, so any URLs whose
    //  paths begin with that component should not be cached, ever
    NSArray *components = [[[cachedResponse response] URL] pathComponents];
    if ( [components count] > 0 &&
        [[components objectAtIndex: 0] isEqualToString: @"secure"] )
    {
        // the response is from the secure domain, so don't cache it
        return ( nil );
    }

    // non-sensitive data can be cached as-is
    return ( cachedResponse );
}
```

Handling responses and data is as simple as implementing the appropriate methods and inspecting the values passed in: -connection:didReceiveResponse: and -connection:didReceiveData: respectively. Handling of both of these types is simple enough that I won't provide explicit examples here (in 99% of cases, the response and data are just put into local variables), but I would like to make one rather important suggestion: *don't accumulate response data in memory.*

Well, ok, small amounts are safe enough, but if you're talking to an API that might return kilobytes of data, it is *much* better to drop it all into a temporary file somewhere. Once all the data has been downloaded you can either read it from the file in a stream or you can use memory-mapping (via NSData's -initWithContentsOfURL:options:error:) to get a regular data object without allocating potentially large amounts of memory. This is more important for iOS, of course, but it's a good idea and a good habit to form. Listing 6-5 shows how you might handle this.

Listing 6-5. Accumulating Returned Data in a Temporary File

```
- (id)init
{
    self = [super init];
    ...

    self.tmpFilePath = [NSString pathWithComponents: @[NSTemporaryDirectory(), ...]];
    self.tmpFile = [NSFileHandle fileHandleForWritingAtPath: path];
    ...

    return ( self );
}

- (void)dealloc
{
    // delete the temporary file, we don't need it any more
    [[NSFileManager defaultManager] removeItemAtPath:self.tmpFilePath error:NULL];
}

...

- (void)connection:(NSURLConnection*)connection didReceiveData:(NSData*)data
{
    // push it out to the temp file
    [self.tmpFile writeData: data];
}

...

- (void) connectionDidFinishLoading:(NSURLConnection*)connection
{
    // close the file, we don't need to access it any more
    [self.tmpFile closeFile];

    // get a cheap NSData object by memory-mapping the file
    // we also specify uncached reads to avoid building up kernel
    // memory buffers for data we'll only read once
    self.data = [NSData dataWithContentsOfFile:self.tmpFilePath
                           options:NSDataReadingMappedAlways|NSDataReadingUncached
                           error:NULL];
}
```

Using this approach you can successfully receive and handle a large amount of data while keeping your application's memory footprint low, which in this time of ubiquitous mobile computing is a very useful trait indeed.

Network Streams

You might be thinking to yourself, "Why would I accrue all this data immediately? What about the stream APIs I worked with in Chapter 5? Didn't you say they were especially useful for network programming?"

Well, you're absolutely right. You've already seen that an NSURLRequest can take an NSInputStream from which to read any body data associated with the request. What you haven't seen yet is how to provide the incoming data as a stream; the data only arrives through the NSURLConnectionDataDelegate methods, which makes them of lesser utility when compared to pure streams. After all, none of the standard system classes have methods that take arbitrary partial data packages, but a number do have stream support:

- NSPropertyListSerialization supports reading data from a stream to create property list types (dictionaries or arrays containing strings, numbers, dates or raw data) and writing serialized data to an output stream.

- NSXMLParser can parse data received from an input stream as well as the contents of a URL or a provided data blob.

- NSJSONSerialization will both read from and write to stream classes to parse and create JSON (JavaScript Object Notation) data.

I'm sure you noticed the common theme amongst the three classes listed above: they all deal with serializing or parsing structured data, and two of them deal with types that are widely used for sending data across networks. Property lists might sound like an odd choice, but at WWDC 2010, David den Boer (hi Dave!), manager of the team that created the Apple Store app for the iPhone, revealed that by using property lists for data transfer they saw a *massive* improvement in throughput and thus, by extension, application responsiveness[3].

Now, let's say you've requested some XML data from a HTTP server, and the data comes back in 800 16KB blocks passed to your -connection:didReceiveData: method. That's about 12MB of XML. That much data could take a while to download, depending on the network conditions at the time. If you download it to a file like I suggested, you're going to spend a fair amount of time fetching the data before you've even begun to think about parsing it. Additionally, if the network is quite slow then your application will actually spend most of its time idle, waiting for the next data packet. That there is *prime CPU real estate*, which could be put to better use by parsing and handling the data as it arrives. The way to do this is to use NSInputStream to fetch the data, but unless you dive down into the CoreFoundation-based CFNetwork API (which is all pure C), then you're stuck with NSURLConnection's data-received callbacks. Aren't you?

Luckily, it's relatively easy to create a simple stream class, as you saw in the previous chapter, and therefore it's possible to create an NSInputStream subclass that serves up the data provided by an NSURLConnection. In fact, one of your authors has already done so[4]. The basic principle works like this:

- Initialize your input stream subclass using an NSURLRequest. Create an NSURLConnection here, but do not start it until the stream is opened.

---

[3]There's a video of this: WWDC 2010 in iTunes U, Session 117. Dave's section begins at the 27-minute mark.
[4]See http://github.com/AlanQuatermain/AQURLConnectionInputStream

- Make the request and response objects available via custom properties on the stream (accessible via NSStream's -propertyForKey: API).

- Don't send NSStreamEventOpenCompleted to the stream's delegate until either -connection:didReceiveResponse: or -connection:didReceiveData: has been called for the first time.

- Send any data received in -connection:didReceiveData: straight to the input stream's delegate by sending NSStreamEventHasBytesAvailable. Continue sending that event until the entire data packet has been consumed, or until the delegate chooses not to read any data (i.e., it's waiting for a larger packet).

- When data arrives, place it into an instance variable (or copy it into a special buffer) so it's accessible from -read:maxLength: and -getBuffer:length:.

- Since NSURLConnection has its own methods to be scheduled with an NSRunLoop, your implementation of the schedule/remove methods will just call straight through to your connection's implementation.

- Since the URL connection's delegation methods have already been dispatched to the run-loop and mode selected by the stream's client, you can just call the delegate's -stream:handleEvent: method directly, so no messing about with run-loop sources.

Most of this is fairly straightforward, but for illustration Listing 6-6 shows the implementation of data handling in such a stream.

Listing 6-6. Farming out NSURLConnection Data as an NSInputStream

```
- (void) connection: (NSURLConnection *) connection didReceiveData: (NSData *) data
{
    if ( _streamStatus == NSStreamStatusOpening )
    {
        _streamStatus = NSStreamStatusOpen;
        [_delegate stream: self handleEvent: NSStreamEventOpenCompleted];
    }

    [_buffer appendData: data];
    NSUInteger bufLen = 0;

    // we break when we run out of data, are closed, or when the delegate
    // doesn't read any bytes
    do
    {
        bufLen = [_buffer length];
        [_delegate stream: self handleEvent: NSStreamEventHasBytesAvailable];

    } while ( (bufLen != [_buffer length]) &&
            (_streamStatus == NSStreamStatusOpen) &&
            ([_buffer length] > 0) );
}
```

Network Data

Data sent across the network can be anything, but the most common formats currently used are JSON (JavaScript Object Notation) and XML (eXtensible Markup Language). The Foundation framework on OS X and iOS provides facilities for the handling of both types of data.

Reading and Writing JSON

The Foundation framework provides the NSJSONSerialization class for working with JSON. This class converts between JSON string data and property list types such as dictionaries, arrays, strings, and numbers. Figure 6-2 shows how the data is mapped to different types.

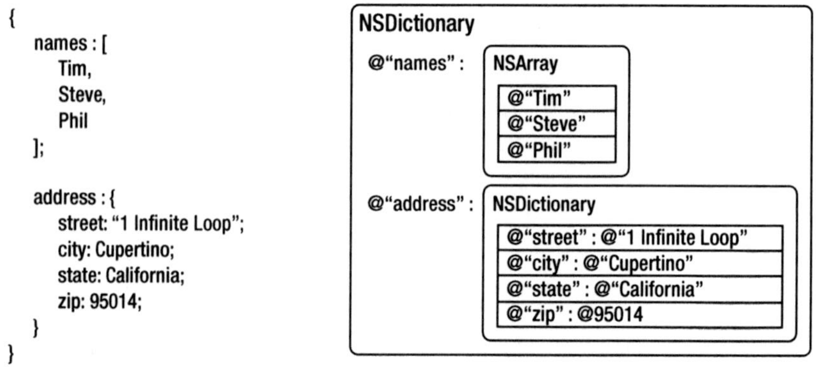

Figure 6-2. *An example of equivalent JSON and property list types*

When reading JSON data, all keyed lists (elements between { and } characters) are turned into NSDictionary instances, and all flat arrays (elements between [and] characters) are turned into NSArray instances. Any strings encountered along with the names of named items in keyed lists are turned into NSStrings, and all purely numeric strings (except for keys) are represented as NSNumbers. Lastly, any values of null are represented using NSNull.

The same thing applies if you're going the other way, of course: any array or dictionary can be transformed into JSON data, provided it only contains the objects specified above. The jsonize sample project (available in its entirety online) converts between property list and JSON formats. Its core conversion method is shown in Listing 6-7.

Listing 6-7. Converting Between JSON and Property List Formats

```
NSData * converted = nil;
if ( inputIsJSON )
{
    id obj = [NSJSONSerialization JSONObjectWithData: inputData options: 0
                                              error: &error];
    if ( obj != nil )
    {
        converted = [NSPropertyListSerialization dataWithPropertyList: obj
                        format: NSPropertyListXMLFormat_v1_0 options: 0 error: &error];
    }
}
else
{
    id obj = [NSPropertyListSerialization propertyListWithData: inputData
                                          options: 0 format: NULL error: &error];
    if ( obj != nil )
    {
        if ( [NSJSONSerialization isValidJSONObject: obj] == NO )
        {
            ...
        }

        converted = [NSJSONSerialization dataWithJSONObject: obj
                                options: NSJSONWritingPrettyPrinted error: &error];
    }
}
```

> **Tip** To quickly find a built application in Xcode, pop open the Products group in the Project Navigator, right-click (or Control-click) the built application in there, and choose "Show in Finder" (the topmost option) in the pop-up menu. Then you can open the Terminal application, type cd and a space, and drag the containing folder (in this case Debug) from the Finder onto the Terminal window to have its path entered for you. Press Enter and you'll be ready to run the application.

It's also possible to both read and write JSON data (and property list data) to or from a stream. This means that you can create an NSInputStream wrapping your connection as I showed earlier and hand that directly to the NSJSONSerialization API to have it handled. Of course, the API in question is a synchronous call, which means it's not exactly perfect, but it at least solves the "download all before parsing" issue discussed above.

Working with XML

On OS X there are two APIs available to work with generic XML data. There's a tree-based parser, which creates a hierarchical structure matching that of the XML document; this is rooted in the NSXMLDocument class. There's also an event-based parser, implemented by the NSXMLParser class. On iOS, you only have the event-based parser, and with a little profiling it's not difficult to see why that decision was made. For example, using NSXMLParser's stream API to parse a 23MB XML file on OS X, the system allocated an additional 70-80MB of memory while parsing, and working based on a single data object used an extra 130MB of memory. NSXMLDocument, on the other hand, allocated a whopping *370MB* of memory!

The result for the streaming parser seems quite high here, but it's ultimately affected by the memory available in the system; on a laptop there's plenty of room to expand and consume the data as fast as possible, while on a mobile device such as an iPhone there's much less room and the data will be handled in smaller chunks as a result. In Jim's parser, the data is always handled in 4KB chunks, with the result that it uses a grand total of 68 *kilobytes* of data while running[5]. It takes a bit longer though, so be aware of the trade-off.

The following examples use the XML document from Listing 6-8 to illustrate the various concepts.

Listing 6-8. A Sample XML Document

```
<?xml version="1.0"?>
<CATALOG>
      <PLANT>
              <COMMON LANG="EN">Bloodroot</COMMON>
              <BOTANICAL>Sanguinaria canadensis</BOTANICAL>
              <ZONE>4</ZONE>
              <LIGHT>Mostly Shady</LIGHT>
              <PRICE>2.44</PRICE>
              <AVAILABILITY>031599</AVAILABILITY>
      </PLANT>
      <PLANT>
              <COMMON LANG="EN">Columbine</COMMON>
              <BOTANICAL>Aquilegia canadensis</BOTANICAL>
              <ZONE>3</ZONE>
              <LIGHT>Mostly Shady</LIGHT>
              <PRICE>9.37</PRICE>
              <AVAILABILITY>030699</AVAILABILITY>
      </PLANT>
      <PLANT>
              <COMMON LANG="EN">Marsh Marigold</COMMON>
              <BOTANICAL>Caltha palustris</BOTANICAL>
              <ZONE>4</ZONE>
              <LIGHT>Mostly Sunny</LIGHT>
              <PRICE>6.81</PRICE>
              <AVAILABILITY>051799</AVAILABILITY>
      </PLANT>
</CATALOG>
```

---

[5]More information can be found online here:
http://alanquatermain.me/post/93664991/aqxmlparser-test-redux

XML Trees

An XML tree is composed of *nodes*, represented on OS X by the NSXMLNode class. Any piece of data within an XML document is a node, including the tags, any text, processing instructions, and the document itself. A tag pair and its contents is an *element*, represented by NSXMLElement, and only elements can contain other nodes. In Listing 6-8, for example, the root node is a CATALOG element, and this contains three PLANT elements and some text nodes. Don't see the text nodes? Oh, they're there all right—all that whitespace used to make the source look pleasant is still included in the document. For example, the first text node within the CATALOG element consists of two characters: a newline and a tab character. Following that is the first PLANT element followed by another newline/tab pair, and so on. As a result, it is often much better to serve up XML data in as compressed a format as possible, to avoid having your tree (and thus your memory!) cluttered up with text node objects for data in which you're not at all interested.

Another approach is to take advantage of the fact that whitespace within an XML tag itself is ignored by placing the newlines and tabs within the tags themselves. This produces XML similar to that seen in Listing 6-9. Since there is no space between the closing and opening braces used to delimit the tags, there are no extra text nodes in the XML tree. It looks a little strange, perhaps , but it's both structured and clean.

Listing 6-9. A Nicely Formatted XML Document with a Compact Tree Structure

```
<CATALOG
    ><PLANT
        ><COMMON LANG="EN">Bloodroot</COMMON
        ><BOTANICAL>Sanguinaria canadensis</BOTANICAL
        ><ZONE>4</ZONE
        ><LIGHT>Mostly Shady</LIGHT
        ><PRICE>2.44</PRICE
        ><AVAILABILITY>031599</AVAILABILITY
    ></PLANT
></CATALOG>
```

XPath and XQuery

The primary advantage of tree-based parsers is that the generated structure is easy to work with programmatically. The most common way to work with structured XML documents is to use XPath or XQuery expressions. These provide a way to simply access groups of data within a larger XML document and are used by calling the NSXMLNode instance methods -nodesForXPath:error:, -objectsForXQuery:error: or -objectsForXQuery:constants:error:.

XPaths, as their name suggests, are based around the same concept as filesystem paths. The same as filesystem paths, *absolute* XPaths begin with a forward-slash character — /. Relative XPaths omit this leading character.

An XPath expression is applied to a particular node in the XML tree. When searching a document you will often supply an absolute XPath or perform the search based on the root node or the NSXMLDocument itself. The XPath specification does also supply a number of functions and special selectors to assist in tree traversal. You can see a few examples of XPaths in Listing 6-10 designed to work on the XML from Listing 6-8. Can you determine what they're selecting just by reading them?

Listing 6-10. Some Example XPaths

```
/CATALOG/PLANT/COMMON

/CATALOG/PLANT/BOTANICAL/text()

/CATALOG/PLANT[ZONE>3]/COMMON

//COMMON[@LANG='EN']
```

The first example selects every COMMON element in the document that is a child of a PLANT element, which is a child of a CATALOG element, which is the root of the document. The second locates every BOTANICAL element in the same position, but returns the text content of that element (not the text *node* within the element, but the actual raw, unprocessed characters that fall between the element's opening and closing tags).

The third example specifies that it should only match PLANT elements that have a ZONE sub-element, and further that only those whose ZONE element contains a numeric value greater than 3. It will then select and return the COMMON elements within those matched PLANT elements.

The last example has two differences: first of all, it begins with two path delimiters, which means that the parser can match the first element specified anywhere in the element tree, regardless of its parents. The statement in the square brackets is similar to that in the third example, but by placing an ampersat (@) at the start of the name you state that you're comparing not a sub-element's value but the value of one of this element's attributes. Since you're comparing the value against a string, the value is enclosed in single quotes to indicate that.

XQuery builds a scripting language on top of the XPath syntax; it essentially enables you to query the contents of an XML document in the way you would query an SQL database. It's quite powerful and wider in scope than I can devote time to here, but Listing 6-11 contains a short example query to whet your appetite. The query itself finds all PLANT elements whose PRICE sub-element's value is greater than five and returns the COMMON sub-elements, sorted into ascending order based on the COMMON sub-element's value. If you're familiar with the capabilities of SQL queries, then you have an idea as to how this could be used to interact with quite complex XML documents.

Listing 6-11. A Sample XQuery Expression

```
For $x in /CATALOG/PLANT
Where $x/PRICE > 5
Order by $x/COMMON
Return $x/COMMON
```

Event-Based XML Handling

Handling XML with the NSXMLParser class is based entirely on event messages sent to the parser's delegate. The parser reads and interprets the XML document in a linear fashion and notifies its delegate of each type of content it encounters, whether opening tags, closing tags, characters, CDATA (raw Character Data, not parsed or interpreted), entities, processing instructions, or others. There are quite a few. Most of the time, however, you'll be interested in only a few of them:

- Opening tags and their attributes, provided through the `-parser:didStartElement:namespaceURI:qualifiedName:attributes:` method.

- Closing tags, provided through `-parser:didEndElement:namespaceURI:qualifiedName:`.

- Text, provided through `-parser:foundCharacters:`; and raw CDATA blocks, provided through `-parser:foundCDATA:`.

The delegate can also be given details of any fatal parsing or validation errors encountered, but since these errors are returned through NSXMLParser's -parserError method, it's not common to implement the delegation methods for them.

Now, these are long method names, and if you're inspecting a large document with many different tags, each of which has its own handling, you're looking at a lot of if statements inside your element handlers, which isn't ideal. Rather than do that, I suggest an alternative approach that makes use of Objective-C's dynamic type system and message dispatch.

The aim is to create delegate classes that implement some simple methods to handle start and/or end tags, named according to some predetermined rules. Since opening tags contain an element's attributes, you'll define your handler for those as '-start<Element>WithAttributes:(NSDictionary*)attributes', where <Element> will be replaced with the real element's name, with its first character uppercased. Thus you will have methods like -startTitleWithAttributes: for <title> tags, and -startPLANTWithAttributes: for <PLANT> tags (remember that XML is case-sensitive). For ending tags you'll simply use -end<Element>, thus -endTitle or -endPLANT.

The magic behind this will be a shared superclass, one that will conform to the NSXMLParserDelegate protocol. In its start and end element handlers it will build a selector name as a string and check with the runtime to see if it implements that method. If so, it calls the method (passing attributes to start tag handlers). This superclass will also handle text and CDATA by accumulating it within an NSString instance variable, which will be cleared each time a new start or end tag for an element is encountered. This will be made available to subclasses via a property. The handlers for text and CDATA blocks can be seen in Listing 6-12.

Listing 6-12. Handling Text and CDATA

```
- (void)parser:(NSXMLParser*)parser foundCharacters:(NSString*)string
{
    if ( [string length] == 0 )
        return;

    @autoreleasepool {
        if ( self.characters != nil )
            self.characters = [self.characters stringByAppendingString:string];
        else
            self.characters = string;
    }
}
```

```objc
- (void)parser:(NSXMLParser*)parser foundCDATA:(NSData*)CDATABlock
{
    if ( [CDATABlock length] == 0 )
        return;

    NSString *str = [[NSString alloc] initWithData:CDATABlock
                                          encoding:NSUTF8StringEncoding];
    [self parser:parser foundCharacters:str];
}
```

The handling of elements' start and end tags is a little more involved, but ultimately still fairly simple to understand. An important consideration is that any element names that contain hyphens will not be usable as-is; you could replace hyphens with underscores, but I have chosen to convert them to CamelCase to match the rest of the method definition. You can see an implementation of this in Listing 6-13.

Listing 6-13. Handling Element Start and End Tags

```objc
- (NSString*)selectorCleanNameForElementName:(NSString*)elementName
{
    NSMutableString *selStr = [NSMutableString new];

    @autoreleasepool {
        // ensure the first character of the element name is uppercased
        [selStr appendString: [[elementName substringToIndex:1] uppercaseString]];

        // append the rest of the string (provided it's not 1-character long)
        if ( [elementName length] > 1 )
            [selStr appendString: [elementName substringFromIndex:1]];

        // handle hyphens properly
        NSRange range = [selStr rangeOfString:@"-"];
        for ( ; range.location != NSNotFound; range = [selStr rangeOfString:@"-"] )
        {
            NSString *cap = [[selStr substringWithRange:NSMakeRange(range.location+1,1)]
                                    uppercaseString];
            range.length += 1;
            [selStr replaceCharactersInRange:range withString:cap];
        }
    }

    return ( selStr );
}

- (void)parser:(NSXMLParser*)parser didStartElement:(NSString*)elementName
        namespaceURI:(NSString*)namespaceURI qualifiedName:(NSString*)qName
        attributes:(NSDictionary*)attributes
{
    @autoreleasepool {
        NSString *cleanName = [self selectorCleanNameForElementName:elementName];
        NSString *selStr = [NSString stringWithFormat:@"start%@WithAttributes:",
                                                      cleanName];
```

```
        SEL selector = NSSelectorFromString(selStr);
        if ( [self respondsToSelector:selector] )
            [self performSelector:selector withObject:attributes];

        self.characters = nil;
    }
}

- (void)parser:(NSXMLParser*)parser didEndElement:(NSString*)elementName
      namespaceURI:(NSString*)namespaceURI qualifiedName:(NSString*)qName
{
    @autoreleasepool {
        NSString *cleanName = [self selectorCleanNameForElementName:elementName];
        NSString *selStr = [NSString stringWithFormat:@"end%@", cleanName];

        SEL selector = NSSelectorFromString(selStr);
        if ( [self respondsToSelector:selector] )
            [self performSelector:selector];

        self.characters = nil;
    }
}
```

Network Service Location

Back in the days of yore (a.k.a. the 1990s) Apple computers used a suite of protocols called AppleTalk to communicate on a local network (or even further!). While the main networking protocol hasn't aged well and is very rarely used today, the suite had some very useful features, not the least of which was the Name Binding Protocol (NBP), which had the capability to advertise the availability of services across the network. In the world of the Internet Protocol and Ethernet, however, nothing similar existed. To connect to a web server, you needed to know its address and you would connect to port 80. If there was another web server running on a different port, someone would have to tell you about it explicitly so that you might connect. The Domain Name System (DNS) offers a means of obtaining an IP address based on a name such as www.apple.com. This normally requires a dedicated server and manual configuration, however, which makes it a poor solution for non-technical users.

In 2002, Apple engineer Stuart Cheshire designed and published a new standard through the Internet Engineering Task Force entitled *DNS Service Discovery*. This standard described various updates to the DNS system and protocol, adding support for the resolution of information on individual services on a system to their individual port numbers. It also added a protocol through which a query to a DNS service could remain active, receiving updates whenever changes occurred without needing to reconnect and poll the server continually. This was then married to the *multicast DNS* (mDNS) system built into OS X 10.2 to allow all hosts on a local area network to provide information on any services available on that host. The result was named Rendezvous, although its name was sadly changed to the less appropriate Bonjour[6] two years and one trademark lawsuit later.

The Bonjour service is available in both OS X and iOS, implemented at a very low level. Luckily for you, it has a series of higher-level APIs available right up to the Cocoa layer, allowing you to

---

[6]Oh yes, I went there.

not only find services on the local network but also advertise your own in only a few easy steps.

Service Resolution

You can search the network for services of a given type using an instance of the NSNetServiceBrowser class. The service browser object operates asynchronously and sends messages to a delegate object on a given run loop as it encounters various events. A browser can be used to search for available domains either for browsing or registering new services (a domain may be browsable but not support dynamic addition of new items), or it can search a domain for services. The browser's delegate can implement a number of different methods to receive updates during the search process, which are outlined in Table 6-2.

Table 6-2. NSNetServiceBrowser Delegate Methods

Message	Description
- (void) netServiceBrowserWillSearch: (NSNetServiceBrowser*)browser	The browser sends this message to its delegate before it begins any form of search operation. If the search cannot start, the delegate will instead receive a -netService Browser:didNotSearch: message.
- (void) netServiceBrowserDidStopSearch: (NSNetServiceBrowser*)browser	Sent to the browser's delegate whenever a search stops running, whether because all results have been received or because the browser was explicitly stopped.
- (void) netServiceBrowser:(NSNetServiceBrowser*)browser didNotSearch:(NSDictionary*)errorDict	When the browser is unable to begin a search for some reason, it will send this message to its delegate. The supplied dictionary contains two key/value pairs describing the error domain and code.

- (void)
netServiceBrowser:(NSNetServiceBrowser*)browser
    didFindDomain:(NSString*)domain
        moreComing:(BOOL)moreComing
	Each domain discovered during a search for browse or register domains will be reported to this method. If the passed domain is the last one, moreComing will be NO.

- (void)
netServiceBrowser:(NSNetServiceBrowser*)browser
    didFindService:(NSNetService*)service
        moreComing:(BOOL)moreComing
	Each service of the requested type found by the browser is reported to this method. When moreComing is NO, all results have been processed.

- (void)
netServiceBrowser:(NSNetServiceBrowser*)browser
    didRemoveDomain:(NSString*)domain
        moreComing:(BOOL)moreComing
	When a domain becomes unavailable, your delegate object will be notified through this method.

- (void)
netServiceBrowser:(NSNetServiceBrowser*)browser
    didRemoveService:(NSNetService*)service
        moreComing:(BOOL)moreComing
	When a service becomes unavailable, this method will be called to notify your delegate object of the change.

The NSNetServiceBrowser class needs to have a delegate set and be scheduled in a run-loop before you can receive these methods. Use -setDelegate: and -scheduleInRunLoop:forMode: to make this happen.

Once you've attached your browser to a run-loop, you can search for domains using either -searchForBrowsableDomains or -searchForRegistrationDomains. You can search for services by specifying a type and domain to -searchForServicesOfType:inDomain:. For most purposes, however, you won't need to search for domains yourself; when you search for a service, simply pass an empty string as the domain parameter and the browser will automatically search all appropriate domains. This typically includes the local domain, which refers to the link-local network (everything on the same side of a network router), but may also include an iCloud domain (for example, nnnnnn.members.btmm.icloud.com) if the user has an iCloud account. This is how features such as Back To My Mac are able to display your home computer in the Finder while at work—because it's registered with your account's corresponding iCloud domain, which is searched by default by NSNetServiceBrowser.

Service types are designed to work along with the host and domain components of the DNS standard and are thus nested with their transport types. The idea is that a host is given the address host.domain.com and services on that host are given the address service.transport. host.domain.com. By convention all address components that refer to items within a single host use names that begin with underscore characters. The services themselves are named based on their corresponding registered names as recorded in your computers services file (located at /etc/services), and they ordinarily use the transports mentioned in that file. Transports are again prefixed with an underscore character. Some examples of common service types can be seen in Table 6-3.

Table 6-3. Common DNS Service Types

Service Type	Description
_http._tcp	Web servers, which operate using the HyperText Transfer Protocol over TCP.
_ftp._tcp	File Transfer Protocol servers.
_afpovertcp._tcp	The AppleShare Filing Protocol (the standard means of accessing another computer's files on the Mac), in its TCP/IP implementation.
_daap._tcp	iTunes libraries, shared on the network using the Digital Audio Access Protocol.

So, to search for available web servers, you would specify a service type of _http._tcp and an empty domain. Listing 6-14 shows how you might go about doing this.

Listing 6-14. Searching for Web Servers

```
NSNetServiceBrowser *browser = [NSNetServiceBrowser new];
[browser setDelegate:self];
[browser scheduleInRunLoop:[NSRunLoop mainRunLoop] forMode:NSRunLoopCommonModes];
[browser searchForServicesOfType:@"_http._tcp" inDomain:@""];
```

When the browser returns services to you, those services have a name and type but any other details have not yet been resolved. To do so, you need to provide a delegate to the given

NSNetService instance and implement the -netServiceDidResolveAddress: method in that delegate to find out when the information becomes available. You then ask the service to resolve by sending it the -resolveWithTimeout: method, as shown in Listing 6-15.

Listing 6-15.   Resolving an NSNetService

```
- (void)netServiceBrowser:(NSNetServiceBrowser*)browser
          didFindService:(NSNetService*)service
              moreComing:(BOOL)moreComing
{
    [service setDelegate:self];
    [service scheduleInRunLoop:[NSRunLoop mainRunLoop] forMode:NSRunLoopCommonModes];
    [service resolveWithTimeout:5.0];
}

- (void)netServiceDidResolveAddress:(NSNetService*)sender
{
    NSLog(@"Service %@ resolved", [sender name]);
    NSLog(@"  - host name: %@", [sender hostName]);
    NSLog(@"  - port: %ld", [sender port]);
    NSLog(@"  - IP v4 Address: %@", [self IP4Address:[sender addresses]]);
    NSLog(@"  - IP v6 Address: %@", [self IP6Address:[sender addresses]]);
}
```

The -addresses method of NSNetService will return an array of data objects encapsulating low-level socket addresses, which you can use to create connected sockets using C-based methods from either the POSIX or CoreFoundation layers. If you'd like to stay at the Foundation layer, you can call -getInputStream:outputStream: to receive by reference a pair of streams ready to open and communicate with the service.

Publishing a Service

Service publishing is done directly through the NSNetService class itself. Having created a service and made it available for incoming connections, the details you want to provide are you service's type, name, and the port on which you are listening for new connections. You provide this to a new instance of NSNetService in its registration initializer, -initWithDomain:type:name:port:. As when browsing services, passing an empty string in the domain parameter will register your service in all available domains. You then publish service's information for others to find by sending the -publish or -publishWithOptions: message to your NSNetService instance. When you're done, you notify the rest of the network that your service is no longer available by sending -stop.

In order to receive information about the status of your service's DNS record publication, you can provide a delegate object. When publishing a service record, the messages from Table 6-4 are sent to the delegate.

Table 6-4. NSNetService Publication Delegate Messages

Message	Description
- (void)netServiceWillPublish:(NSNetService*)service	Sent to the delegate before the publish operation is due to start.
- (void)netServiceDidPublish:(NSNetService*)service	Notifies the delegate that the service was successfully published.
- (void) netService:(NSNetService*)service didNotPublish:(NSDictionary*)errorInfo	Provides error information if a publish operation failed for any reason.

The provided sample projects NSServiceBrowser and NSServiceVendor show some more in-depth examples of the use of services. As an example, you can use the VendService command-line application to vend a service with a given name and type, and then use the NSServiceBrowser graphical application to look for it on the network. You can then shut down and start up more services of the same type and see them appear and disappear in the browser.

Summary

I hope this chapter was a lot simpler to digest than earlier chapters; part of this is because of the groundwork you've done leading up to this point—on the shoulders of giants you stand. The main lesson from this chapter is the correct use of the available asynchronous networking APIs in the Foundation framework. Here's a summary of the key points:

- Always use asynchronous methods. I am *so* not kidding on this one.

- Handle network URLs properly through the judicious use of NSURLRequest and NSURLConnection.

- Authenticate access to network resources in a protocol-agnostic manner through NSURLConnection's authentication delegation.

- Process network data in JSON and XML formats. Now you know why iOS doesn't include any tree-based XML parsers by default.

- Parse network data as it arrives.

- Use XPath and XQuery on those tree-based XML parsers.

- Discover network services using NSNetServiceBrowser and vending your own with NSNetService.

It is my hope that the core lessons here will remain firmly entrenched in your mind for the remainder of your career.

Chapter 7

User Interfaces:
The Application Kit

On Mac OS X, the Application Kit (`AppKit.framework`) contains all the primary elements you'll need to create a feature-rich graphical application. There are others, of course, but everything has its roots in the AppKit. It's here the concepts of windows, views, controls, and input events are defined, along with the core Objective-C APIs for dealing with rendering of graphics and text.

This chapter will give you a thorough grounding in the concepts embodied within the Application Kit and its companion tool, Interface Builder. As a result, this chapter will not deal with any iOS or UIKit topics except noting contrasts between the two platforms' respective approaches. The information here will still be useful to iOS developers, however, as iOS uses the same core concepts listed above; it just differs in its implementation. You'll have enough knowledge of the components of graphical interfaces that you should be able to pick up iOS user interface programming with little difficulty.

I would also like to point out that this chapter is going to be predominantly based on the theory behind user interfaces. The practical part will arrive in Chapter 9 where I will guide you through the creation of a full application using the techniques you've learned in the book so far.

Coding Practices: Model-View-Controller

Deeply enshrined in all of Apple's user interface code is the use of the *model-view-controller* programming paradigm. This defines a means by which classes that manage *data* are encapsulated separately from those that manage the *presentation* of that data, with a *controller* object acting as an intermediary between the two.

The idea is to enforce a strong and rigid boundary between a data's form and its representation to the user; either ought to be able to change relatively independently of the other. Under *no circumstances* should any user interface code need to know about the structure or storage of data in order to present it to the user, and likewise data should not need to be aware of its presentation context. It is the job of the controller object to deal with both of these classes: when the presentation object needs some data, it requests it from the controller. The controller knows about the data object's format, so it can fetch it and massage it into the format required by the presentation object. Similarly, if the data object is modified and the user interface needs to be updated, it is the controller that observes the change and informs the presentation object in an appropriate manner.

An example of this abstraction can be seen in the NSWindow and NSWindowController classes. NSWindow defines an interface with an actual window, along with all the means of setting its attributes and content as well as receiving information about changes to that window. The window does not, however, have any intrinsic methods for interacting with any form of data whatsoever; something has to manually tell the window what it needs to do in order to represent that data. As a result, NSWindow is completely data-agnostic and can effectively be used for anything you might desire.

The NSWindowController object is a companion class that provides you with much of the structure required to load an initialize a window. It understands interface builder design documents and can create a window from the instructions therein. It also keeps track of the window for you, and it is this class that you would extend to implement the specifics of your application.

Thus it is that, while some libraries[1] would have you subclass a Window object to create a PreferenceWindow object that would lay itself out and handle user input and such, when using the AppKit you'll virtually never need to subclass the NSWindow object yourself. You'll instead subclass NSWindowController to manage the window and any associated labels, text fields, buttons, and more. This paradigm exists all through the AppKit classes, even in data-specific views such as tables or lists. The view objects typically know about some types of atomic data (numbers, strings); how to lay out subviews particular to their use case; and how to request the actual data objects from an associated controller (or *data source*) object. You will see this later when you learn about table views, for example.

Windows, Panels, and Views

On OS X, a window, as represented by the NSWindow class, refers to a single window onscreen. Specifically, a window is the top-level graphical element within an application, which contains various other elements. Figure 7-1 shows a window from the Finder application. All a window's contents will move with it, but separate windows can be manipulated individually.

---

[1]I'm thinking primarily of the C++ Microsoft Foundation Classes and the original Java Foundation Classes when I say this.

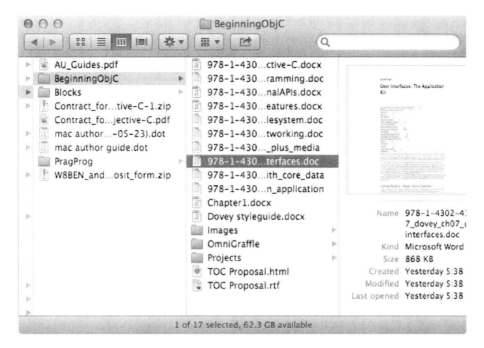

Figure 7-1. *A typical Finder window*

Windows typically have a trio of buttons in the top-left corner that provide the ability to *close*, *minimize*, or *zoom* the window. Closing a window takes it off the screen (and usually causes the associated application to discard any unsaved content associated with it); minimizing a window will shrink it down to a tile within the user's Dock, ready to be brought back later; zooming the window will make it expand to make the best use of the available screen space. One important fact about zooming, which often catches new Mac users off-guard, is that the Zoom button does not *maximize* the window like it does on Windows and other operating systems. If you're reading a document that is 400 points wide and 700 points tall, then making the window grow to 1440 points wide and 760 points tall isn't going to be terribly useful—you're covering up a lot of screen real estate with blank space. In other words, the Zoom button simply expands the window in each dimension to the point where that dimension is as wide as it needs to be. In the above example, the window might grow to the maximum possible height (the space available between the menu bar and the Dock), but will likely only grow a little wider than the 400 point width of the document. Clicking the Zoom button again will typically restore the window to its prior size and location (something that is handled for you by the NSWindow class itself).

GETTING TO THE POINT

When talking about screen coordinates, you'll note that I almost exclusively use *points* rather than *pixels* to describe the location and size of an item. The drawing APIs in Cocoa all exclusively work in a system of points, although typically these two terms refer to the same number of units. However, with the release of the Retina Display on the iPhone in 2010 and the MacBook Pro in 2012, this is no longer strictly true: outside of certain low-level APIs (hello, OpenGL!) a 10x10 point square will be drawn using a 20x20 pixel grid, and 12 point text will in fact be 24 pixels in height.

All this means that you should be thinking in terms of units that may not actually match up to the dots on a screen, but of relative sizes. This is all the more important when you start to deal with lower-level routines that *do* actually work in terms of pixels, as the core graphics routines will unless you specify a scaling factor other than 1-to-1 (the Retina Display devices use a scaling factor of 1-to-2 to use two pixels for each single drawing unit).

Another type of window you'll see a lot in OS X is a *panel*, represented by the NSPanel class, a subclass of NSWindow. The panel itself is only slightly different from a window, but it defines a few extra visual features that aren't commonly available to regular windows, such as the *utility window* appearance, where the title bar and Close/Minimize/Zoom buttons (commonly called *traffic lights* due to their red-amber-green coloring) are smaller than usual, and the window will always "float" above any other windows, staying accessible. Another key[2] feature of panels is that they can offer a fully interactive user interface without actually becoming focused; in Cocoa parlance, they can work without becoming the *key window*[3]. Figure 7-2 shows an example of a floating utility window. You can see that its own traffic-light buttons are transparent, indicating that it's not the key window, while those of the document window behind it are colored.

Figure 7-2. A floating utility panel

One further type of window you'll see is a *document-modal* window, commonly referred to as a *sheet* due to its appearance. While an *application-modal* window will appear as normal but will prevent interaction with any other part of the application, a sheet is attached to another window and only prevents interaction with that single window or document. In most applications, the Save panel is presented as a sheet attached to the window of the document being saved. In Xcode, when you create a new project, the application creates a new project window and then displays the project creation interface using a sheet attached to that window. Figure 7-3 shows a sheet window from the Finder application.

---

[2]This is a pun. You'll get it in a minute.
[3]See? I didn't say it was a *good* pun . . .

Figure 7-3. *A sheet window*

The contents of a window are exclusively represented using *views*, represented by the NSView class. Views provide handling of four primary factors: a hierarchy where one view will contain others; the location of a view within its superview, the input responder status of that view (is it currently the item receiving direct user input?), and the ability to draw its contents. Views also support some intricate built-in handling for the relative placement of their subviews using *constraints*, as you'll see when you start to assemble them using Interface Builder. This means that, much of the time, you won't need to manually adjust the positions of subviews when your view changes its size; the system uses some rules that you provide to determine the new placement of subviews, even during live resize. The NSView class also provides for the transformation of coordinates and rectangles between the local coordinate systems of multiple views and implements the basic routines used for handling drag-and-drop operations, tool-tip display, and tracking the location of the mouse cursor. Virtually everything else you encounter in this chapter is built on top of the extensive range of methods provided by NSView.

Controls

A view that provides some form of user input is called a *control* and is represented by the NSControl class and its subclasses. Examples of controls include buttons, text fields, scrollbars, pop-up menus, sliders, and so on. Each of these types is encapsulated in an appropriate subclass of NSControl; the class itself provides the core mechanisms for triggering actions and managing the target of that action, plus hooks for setting a control's value using a wide range of basic data types.

The implementation of controls in AppKit is a bone of contention for many Cocoa programmers, being based on the concept of *cells*. An NSCell is analogous to an NSControl, but NSControl is a subclass of NSView and thus includes all the mechanics of views, including backing stores, buffers, and various other graphical state data. An NSCell, however, is a subclass of NSObject and contains just the information necessary to manage a control's state, its data, and how to draw it onscreen. As such, most controls (if not all—certainly all the standard AppKit controls) are actually just regular NSViews with methods that pass through directly to their respective cells.

So when setting a button's appearance or key-equivalent, it's actually an NSButtonCell that implements this logic, not the NSButton class itself.

The reason for this separation is largely down to history. When the Application Kit was first designed in the late 1980s, computers typically had up to 1MB of video memory and less than 4MB of RAM. Views, with all their associated graphical state information both within the application and within the system's window manager, required a lot of resources. Thus when a table or a grid (represented by the NSMatrix class) was placed onscreen, it was highly uneconomical to represent each of these items using a separate view; the memory requirements would be massive for the time. As a result, many of these "view collection" classes actually utilized a single view, which would use a single NSCell object to represent different pieces of content. As each control was rendered, the cell would be updated with that control's data and told to draw itself at a particular location within the view. This is how tables were implemented prior to OS X 10.7; each table contained a view for each of its columns, and each column used a single cell to draw its content on each row within that column. When the column contained text on each row, an NSTextFieldCell would be used to draw the text; if a button was required, an NSButtonCell would be used, and so on. Additionally, only the visible rows would ever be drawn, saving a lot of time. This meant that a table with five columns and 2,000 rows would not have to manage 10,000 subviews (plus headers!), but would instead have five subviews, each of which would "stamp" the content for its corresponding row into place using its cell. It also meant that the NSTableColumnView class was implemented in a data-agnostic fashion, as discussed in the Model-View-Controller section above: it could be initialized with any subclass of NSCell and would use regular NSCell methods to set its content and draw it at a specified location within the column's view. Any additional handling required by a specific type of cell would be handled by the table view's controller via a delegate method, which would pass the cell along with its row and column location before the cell would be drawn.

The upside to this pattern is that it's a very efficient way to work with large collections of controls. The downside is that any custom control would need to follow this pattern, creating a cell for itself that would do most of the work and a control class that would simply re-export the cell's interface. It also makes it difficult to implement things like providing, since view that would span multiple columns in a table, or have different sections of a table display data in a different manner from one another. This paradigm is still true for NSControl instances today, but at least table views have another option, as in OS X 10.7 it was made possible to build tables using a view for each cell, with no limitations as to the classes of those views. This essentially matches the behavior of the UITableView class on iOS, which uses a view for each of its cells. On OS X, however, a view-based table can still have multiple columns. In this book, you will use the newer view-based Table API whenever you need to interact with or define a table's contents.

Buttons

Buttons are the simplest form of control within AppKit. A button is simply an item that performs an action when it is clicked and that changes its state whenever it captures a mouse-click until the mouse button is released. Typically buttons will darken slightly when clicked and will revert to their original visual state when the mouse button is released. It performs this handling using the event-tracking facilities of the NSControl class, telling its cell to become highlighted on mouse-down and to unhighlight on mouse-up or when the mouse is moved outside the bounds of the control. As noted, the control simply manages some higher-level abstract concepts while its cell determines what it means to be highlighted, selected, bordered, and more.

A button is given an action to perform in a relatively simple manner: first its target object (an id) is set by calling the NSControl method -setTarget:, then its action (a message selector) is set using NSControl's -setAction: method. When the button receives a mouse click (the mouse button is pressed and released within the bounds of the view), it sends the action message to its target. The code in Listing 7-1 shows how this works in practice. Note that you will rarely need to do this using code as most user interfaces are set up and connected together using the Interface Builder tool within Xcode, which handles all this on your behalf.

Listing 7-1. Setting a Button's Target and Action

```
- (id)initWithFrame:(NSRect)frameRect
{
    ...

    myButton.target = self;
    myButton.action = @selector(closeButtonClicked:);

    ...
}

- (void)closeButtonClicked:(id)sender
{
    // close the window containing this view
    [[self window] performClose: sender];
}
```

The action of an NSControl is expected to return void, and optionally takes a single argument of type id. This argument is the control, which triggered the action. This enables you to potentially handle events from multiple sources with a single action method, or to modify the sender somehow without needing to keep it stored in an instance variable.

Text Input

The standard text input control in the Application Kit is the text field, represented by the NSTextField class. There is also an NSTextView class, which implements support for editing long-form text with rich attributes and attachments within a scrolling view; look no further than the TextEdit application to see this in action.

The text field control has a number of different states: it can be used to display non-editable, non-selectable labels with a transparent background; it can also be used to implement editable text input fields, such as those you used in the first chapter of this book. As a result, there are a number of special state flags appropriate for a text field:

- *Enabled*: An enabled text field has its text rendered in black (by default), while a disabled field is rendered in grey and is never editable.

- *Selectable*: A text field can be selectable (and thus copyable) by the user separately from whether it is editable. A label might show feedback that you'd like the user to be able to copy, but a title label is unlikely to need selectability.

▓ *Editable*: When a text field is editable, it typically gains a bezeled border and a white background. The control can still be set as disabled, preventing editing while keeping the border and background in place.

There are some interesting nuances to the actual text input, however. It might interest you to know that the text field control doesn't actually work with character input itself; instead it delegates this to an NSText object owned by the window. This is the window's *field editor*, which is cached by the window and used by any text control that needs to provide live-editing capabilities. The control requests the field editor from its window and places, and styles it such that it remains within the control's "editable" area. Thus when you click on an editable text field, the field itself remains unchanged and a new view is placed over top of it, matching exactly the region within the bounds of the field's bezel or outline.

The NSText object is the highest-level member of the Cocoa text rendering API. It is used not only as a field editor but also as the content of an NSTextView itself and supports working with raw strings as well as RTF (Rich Text Format) and RTFD (Rich Text Format Directory, or Rich Text Format with Attachments). It has full handling for tab stops and rulers, plus it handles different writing directions and any rich-text attributes you could name.

Interface Builder

The NeXT Interface Builder was the first commercial development environment to enabled programmers to visually place UI elements using the mouse rather than by typing it all as code. While Java programmers were wrestling with GridBagLayouts, NeXTstep programmers were finding that they could build more and more of their application solely using the Interface Builder, hooking up objects to their code with a drag of the mouse. By the mid-1990s release of the NeXTstep 3.0 operating system, frameworks such as the Database Kit enabled the creation of quite sophisticated data-driven applications without a single line of code[4].

In Xcode version 4, the functionality of the Interface Builder application has been built directly into the Xcode IDE as the editor for any user interface resources. It is here that you'll build almost all of your Mac OS X user interfaces, and possibly those for iOS as well.

> **Note**   Although Interface Builder supports the creation of iOS user interfaces, the fact is that iOS' UIKit framework was originally designed without this in mind. As a result, creating user interfaces purely with code is substantially easier using UIKit, and a lot of developers find themselves relying substantially less on Interface Builder for iOS programming than they do for OS X, as AppKit was designed with Interface Builder in mind.

---

[4]You can see this in action in a video of Steve Jobs introducing the new system on YouTube at www.youtube.com/watch?v=j02b8Fuz73A (or search for "steve jobs nextstep 3 demo").

On OS X, Interface Builder will be your primary means of designing user interfaces and configuring common user elements. These typically include

■ Menus and menu items

■ Windows and utility panels

■ Data views such as tables, grids, and images

■ Controls, including buttons, labels, and editable text fields

■ Controller objects used to arrange data for ready display

Interface Builder works on resources stored in XIB (Xcode Interface Builder) files. Figure 7-4 shows a sample of an Interface Builder document being edited.

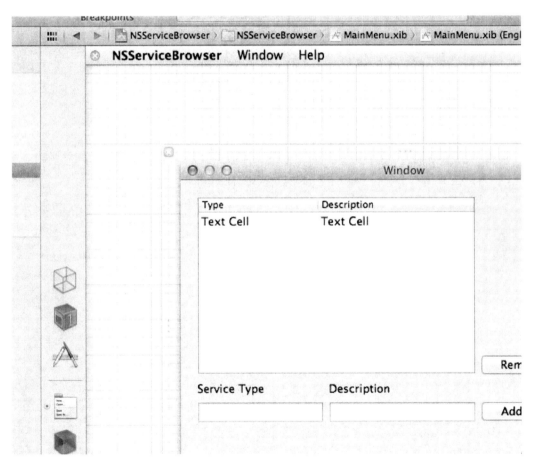

Figure 7-4. Editing a user interface in Xcode's Interface Builder pane

Interface Builder connects your interface to your code using a system of *outlets* and *actions*. An outlet is a variable on an object that is connected to a user interface item when an interface is loaded into memory. For example, if your window controller class wants to have a reference to a table view you created using Interface Builder, you create a property with the IBOutlet keyword in your class and you connect the table view to that outlet. Then when the interface is loaded, the value of that property is set using the appropriate NSTableView instance.

An action works the opposite way where outlets let your code link to items in the interface and an action is a method that the interface will call in response to some form of user input. Common action sources are button clicks or typing a value into a text field. You define an action in your source code by adding a method with a return type of IBAction (a special synonym for void) that optionally takes a single parameter of type id. This parameter is the user interface object that is sending this action message and is typically called sender. Listing 7-2 shows an example class with an outlet and an action.

Listing 7-2. Outlet Properties and Action Methods

```
@interface MyController : NSWindowController
@property (weak) IBOutlet NSTableView *myTableView;
- (IBAction) selectAll: (id) sender;
@end
```

> **Note**   In iOS, there are some slight differences in the handling of outlets and actions. Where Mac OS X will retain any top-level objects (such as the objects seen in the lower-left of Figure 7-2), iOS does not, so you *must* retain all your outlets on iOS using strong references, where on OS X you could use a weak reference to have the property set to nil when the interface is unloaded. As for actions, iOS adds a second optional parameter to action methods, that of the UIEvent that triggered the action, allowing you to obtain the number and locations of any touches, for example. The method declaration in this case is
>
> - (IBAction) performAction: (id) sender forEvent: (UIEvent *) event;

Outlets and actions are linked together in Interface Builder very, very simply: you hold down the Control key and drag from one object to another. When you release the mouse button, a menu pops up with the available options: any available actions on the second object that the first could invoke and any outlets on the first that could point to the second. You can also open the Outlets Inspector directly (see Figure 7-5) and drag from one of the circles to the right of an item onto its target to make the connection.

Figure 7-5. The Outlets Inspector

User Interface Creation

As you saw when designing your first small application in Chapter 1, controls are added to your interface by dragging them from the Object Library, located in the lower half of the Utilities pane to the right of your Xcode window. From here you can add virtually any type of button, label, or input control, along with a number of data display and layout views. Their properties can be edited using the upper part of Xcode's Utilities pane; the third-to-rightmost of the tabs provide facilities for editing just about every property you could want.

- The Identity Inspector allows you to modify the most basic information about an onscreen element, such as giving it an identifier, a tooltip, applying some help, and/or a description of the item for accessibility interfaces (such as screen readers) and the like. The editable attributes here are typically the same for all views.

- The Attributes Inspector lets you work with the attributes of the specific object in hand. Here you'll see different attributes for buttons or for labels, for data views, for image views, and so on. For image views you can specify an image for them to display here. You can adjust views' background colors; for table views you can choose their content style (use cells or complete views for each row/column) and how they resize. Button styles and states, text styles, window styles, and more. This is where you'll perform most of the edits to your controls and views.

- The Size Inspector lets you adjust the size and placement of an item and provides some very basic adjustments to auto-layout constraints in the shape of minimum and maximum sizes. If you're using the older springs-and-struts model of layout, this is where you'll choose which edges of your view are anchored to its parent and which dimensions are automatically resizable. Constraint-based auto-layout is done elsewhere, as you will see shortly.

- The Outlets Inspector lets you inspect all incoming and outgoing *outlet connections* associated with the selected item. These vary depending on the item; for example, an `NSTableView` has outlets available for its `delegate` and `dataSource` members, so you could connect these to your window controller so it could provide data to the table. All views have a `nextKeyView` outlet so you can choose the order in which the tab key will move focus between items. The outlets inspector also shows you the actions sent by an object; a button's Sent Action is visible here as well. You can see some connected outlets in Figure 7-5.

▨ The Bindings Inspector allows you to work with the Cocoa Bindings mechanism, which enables you to bind user interface state directly to the state of other objects via key-value coding and key-value observation. This allows certain properties of your interface to automatically adjust based on changes in your data object hierarchy. You can see an example of this in Figure 7-6.

Figure 7-6. The Bindings Inspector

▨ The View Effects Inspector lets you apply CoreAnimation filters and compositing effects directly to the views in your interface. Sadly, this area is very large in scope and thus beyond the bounds of what I can discuss in this book. There is however a wealth of information on this topic Out There, as they say.

Layout Constraints

New in OS X 10.7 Lion and iOS 6.0 is the Cocoa Auto Layout system, which is based on a system of constraints and a linear equation solver that transforms these into layout frames dynamically as items are adjusted. You saw in Chapter 1 how Interface Builder provides some layout guides as you moved your controls towards the edge of a window or close to other controls. The constraints system is based upon storing those guides instead of storing the frame coordinates for each view. As a result, it is easy to define a row of controls where each is laid out a fixed distance from the one to its left. When you further add a constraint saying that the rightmost is to sit a fixed distance from the right edge of its superview, the constraint solver will adjust the widths of the controls such that they all fit correctly.

To see this in action, create a simple AppKit application: launch Xcode and choose "Create a new Xcode Project" from the Welcome to Xcode window (or select File ➤ New ➤ Project from the menu bar). From the OS X section of the New Project sheet, select Application and then Cocoa Application. Press Next and give your application a name. Ensure that "Create Document-Based Application," "Use Core Data," and "Include Unit Tests" are NOT checked because you won't require any of the boilerplate code those options generate. Click Next again to save your project. Select MainMenu.xib in the Project Navigator to the left, and you should see something similar to Figure 7-7. You might need to select the window in the Document Outline on the left edge of the editor to make the window appear.

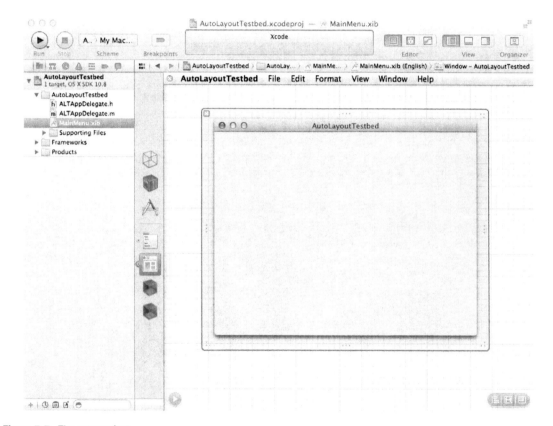

Figure 7-7. The new project

> **Tip**   If you're using a version of Xcode older than 4.4, you might need to open the Utilities panel here, select the Document Inspector, and enable the "Use Auto Layout" checkbox.

Some Simple Buttons

Let's start out by adding a few buttons. From the lower part of the Utilities pane, select the Object Library and drag a button from here to the lower-left part of the window, aligning it using the automatic guides that appear. Do the same thing to place a button in the lower-right part of the window. You'll notice each time that a pair of struts appears to connect the buttons to the closest edges of the window; these are the constraints that the auto layout system uses to position these buttons correctly.

Now drag out a third button and place it just to the right of the button in the lower-left part of the window. A guide will pop up to help snap it into place at the correct distance from its sibling. This button has two constraints: as before, there is one linking it to the bottom of the window, but there's one more attaching it to the button to its left. This tells the system that this third button must always be placed a set distance to the right of the other.

Next, add a fourth button along the bottom edge of the window, but this time drop it in the center; again, you'll be aided in this by a pop-up guide to help you get it aligned properly at the bottom-center. Now set some titles for the buttons: from left to right, use Add, Remove, Export, and Close.

Lastly, drag in a Table View from the Object Palette and position it filling the window area above the buttons. Use the guides to fix it the right distance from the edges of the window and from the buttons below. Your window should now look something like Figure 7-8.

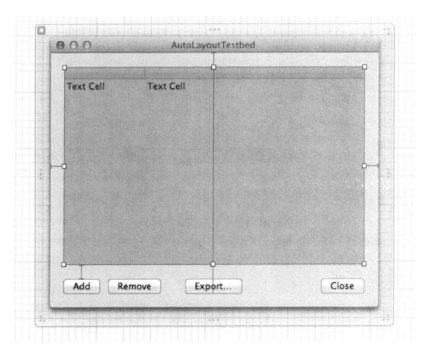

Figure 7-8. The initial window layout

Now launch your application and try resizing the window. Notice how everything stays in the right place? The buttons to the left stay there, the button to the right stays at the bottom right, the table grows and shrinks with the window, and the Export button stays centered. Good, huh? Not quite; try shrinking the window's width a bit more and you'll see the Export and Remove buttons begin to overlap. Well, this isn't ideal. What's happening?

The answer to that question is that it's precisely what the constraints allowed. The two buttons on the left will never overlap one another, but there is no constraint specifying that same thing for the others. The Export button simply stays dead center all the time as a result. What you'd really like, however, is for that button to stop moving once it comes too close to those buttons on the left. For this to happen, you'll need to provide some additional constraints of your own.

In the lower-right corner of the document editor you will see the little pill-shaped button shown in Figure 7-9. This is actually a set of three buttons, each of which provides quick access to the facilities available in Cocoa Auto Layout. Select the Remove and Export buttons (hold the Command key while clicking to select multiple obejcts), then click on the middlemost of the three buttons (the one with the constraint strut that looks rather like a capital "H"). Select Horizontal Spacing from the pop-up menu that appears and you'll see a new constraint appear between the two buttons.

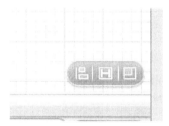

Figure 7-9. *The Auto Layout controls*

If you run the application now, you'll see something strange happening when you enlarge the window: the Remove button stays a fixed distance from the Export button, which itself stays in the center of the window. The Add button will expand and contract automatically to fill the available space. However, if you *shrink* the window, you'll see that it will stop shrinking quite quickly. This is because the constraint you added says that the Export button should be both centered and a fixed distance from the Remove button, and that this is more important than the window's size being adjustable. As a result, if a given window size cannot satisfy the constraints around these buttons, the window cannot become any smaller.

Sadly, this doesn't quite have the behavior you want. Ideally the space between the Remove and Export buttons should be flexible; it just shouldn't go below a particular value. Luckily, this is an easy thing to rectify.

In Interface Builder, select the constraint between those two buttons and open the Attributes Inspector. You'll see details somewhat like those in Figure 7-10.

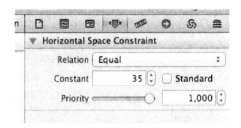

Figure 7-10. The inflexible constraint's attributes

You can see that it's set to enforce a horizontal spacing equal to 35 points, with a high priority (actually, priority 1000 means "required"). Pull open the pop-up menu for the Relation property and you'll see that there are also greater-than-or-equal-to and less-than-or-equal-to values. You want to set a minimum spacing, so select "Greater Than Or Equal." Additionally, you want the minimum distance to match the distance between the Add and Remove buttons, which is the system's built-in spacing rule. Select the Standard checkbox to set that as the distance that the rule applies.

Run your application again and you'll see that the window can be shrunk until the Export button reaches the edge of the Remove button, but no further. You can even see this happening in Interface Builder itself if you try to resize the window there.

Next, look at the Add and Remove buttons. Given that they are a matched pair, they would look nicer if they were the same width. This is easy to set up, and it will even remain in force if the titles of the buttons themselves change at any time, even at runtime. Select the two buttons in Interface Builder; from the constraint options in the lower right of the editor, select the middlemost button again. This pops up the Pin menu once again, but this time you'll select the "Widths Equally" item. This adds a constraint saying that the two buttons must be the same width, thus whichever needs to be the largest will define the width for both buttons. Right now the Add button has been stretched to match the Remove button's width, but try changing Add to Add Another and see what happens: the Remove button expands to match the new size of the Add Another button, and likely the whole window will grow to prevent it from overlapping the centered Export button. Change the name back to Add for now, though.

The last change you'll make concerns the button to the right of the window. At present, when the window stops shrinking, there is a large space between the Export and Close buttons. It would be ideal if the window shrunk until the Export button ran into the Remove button and then continued shrinking until the Close button hit the edge of the Export button too. This requires breaking the center-alignment constraint on the Export button, however, which is where the constraint's *priority* comes into play.

You've already seen the priority field in the Attributes Inspector in Figure 7-7. You've also seen that its default priority of 1000 (i.e., "required") means that the window will not shrink beyond a certain amount. This is because the window's size constraints (the ones automatically created to reflect the user resizing the window) have a lower priority and are thus broken in favor of keeping this button centered. This priority is one of a number defined in AppKit/NSLayoutConstraint.h, shown in Table 7-1.

Table 7-1. *Predefined Layout Priorities*

Name	Description
NSLayoutPriorityRequired = 1000	A required constraint. Do not exceed this value.
NSLayoutPriorityDefaultHigh = 750	The priority level at which a button resists compressing its content. Note that it is higher than NSLayoutPriorityWindowSizeStayPut. Thus dragging to resize a window will not make buttons clip; rather the window frame is constrained.
NSLayoutPriorityDragThatCanResizeWindow = 510	This is the appropriate priority level for a drag that may end up resizing the window. This needn't be a drag whose explicit purpose is to resize the window. The user might be dragging around window contents, and it might be desirable that the window become bigger to accommodate.
NSLayoutPriorityWindowSizeStayPut = 500	This is the priority level at which the window prefers to stay the same size. It's generally not appropriate to make a constraint at exactly this priority. You want it to be higher or lower.
NSLayoutPriorityDragThatCannotResizeWindow = 490	This is the priority level at which a split view divider, say, is dragged. It won't resize the window.
NSLayoutPriorityDefaultLow = 250	This is the priority level at which a button hugs its contents horizontally.
NSLayoutPriorityFittingSizeCompression = 50	When you issue -[NSView fittingSize], the smallest size that is large enough for the view's contents is computed. This is the priority level that the view wants to be as small as possible in that computation. It's quite low. It is generally not appropriate to make a constraint at exactly this priority. You want it to be higher or lower.

As you can see, any priority below 500 will not affect a window's ability to resize. Thus you need only reduce the priority of the horizontal-center constraint to, for example, 400 in order to let a window's resizing break that constraint when it is necessary to become smaller. To do this, select the Export button in Interface Builder and then select the vertical blue line going through the center of the window. In the Attributes Inspector, set the Priority of this constraint to 400. You'll see that the constraint line is now dotted, indicating that it is optional. The layout system will do its best to enforce this constraint, but other things may now take priority.

One other thing needed now is to create a minimum-space constraint between the Export and Close buttons so they won't also overlap. Select them, choose Horizontal Spacing from the menu (as before), edit its attributes to be "Greater Than Or Equal," and use the standard spacing.

Now when you run your application, the Export button will stay centered until it hits the edge of the Remove button, but the window will still shrink (breaking the horizontal-center constraint) until the Close button is up against the edge of the Export button. This is much better; it does exactly what you want[5] in any situation and it didn't require a single line of code.

Yes, a high-five would indeed be appropriate right about now.

Layout and Animation

The Cocoa layout and rendering system was designed quite a long time ago (about 25 years ago, to be precise). As a result, it uses primarily CPU-based drawing and rendering of content. In recent times, however, the rise of programmable GPUs (graphics programming units) means that a lot of this work can be done more effectively (and in parallel) using the graphics processor itself. Apple has not been resting on its laurels and has implemented a number of new technologies designed to make better use of the hardware available.

The first such technology Apple unveiled was a graphics filtering and processing system called Core Image. It provides a programmable hardware-agnostic graphics-processing pipeline using a language similar to the OpenGL Shading Language (GLSL). It uses the LLVM compiler suite to compile this code into a mid-level format, which is then compiled directly to GLSL or to the current CPU, whether PowerPC (32- or 64-bit), 32-bit i386, 64-bit X86-64, and now even 32-bit ARMv7 code, since Core Image was brought into iOS 5. The runtime determines the available resources and dynamically compiles the Core Image code for the appropriate processor based on hardware availability and its current load. Additionally, since it compiles these filters into a single pipeline, a number of different filters can be combined into a single operation, resulting in one calculation per pixel as opposed to one operation per pixel per filter. This makes it much faster than other filtering systems that apply filters iteratively, and thus means that it is very much suitable for use in a live-updating user interface.

Along with Core Image, Apple introduced another technology called Core Video. This provides a form of direct video input/output manipulation that pairs with the filter pipeline in Core Image to provide fast processing and display of frame-by-frame animated content, even when fairly complex filters such as Gaussian blurs or colorization are being performed. Core Video works through the use of a separate, high-priority thread known as the display link. This provides access to a frame buffer used for directly compositing output onto the screen and handling issues of latency and differing display refresh rates. The display link is in charge of the entire pipeline, requesting processing of individual frames of video or animation based on the hardware's capability to output these frames. It also manages an internal frame buffer and a list of ready-to-render frames. If you're familiar with the close-to-hardware model of Microsoft's Direct2D or Direct3D, then the CoreVideo display link is quite similar; it is used these days as the basis for (and the driver of) a lot of the things happening on screen in both OS X and iOS.

Building on both of these high-performance graphics processing pipelines, Apple released Core Animation in OS X 10.5 and iOS. Formerly called the Layer Kit, this API provides a new,

---

[5]Actually, not quite: you can shrink the window vertically to a point where the table view disappears completely. Can you add a constraint to the table view to prevent it from getting smaller than 80 points in height?

completely modern approach to the ideas encapsulated by view hierarchies. However, instead of manually building views by drawing everything directly to a single window, a Core Animation *layer* is used for each discrete object, and each layer manages its own backing store. When the time comes to update a window, therefore, only those particular layers that actually contain changes need to be updated, regardless of whether they overlap with or contain other layers. Once the layers themselves are all rendered, their backing stores are then *composited* using a high-performance display-link–driven compositor into a window's content. For example, given the view hierarchy outlined in Figure 7-11, the original Cocoa renderer and Core Animation's layer-based approach will undertake two entirely different operations to redraw the window's contents when View 2 changes.

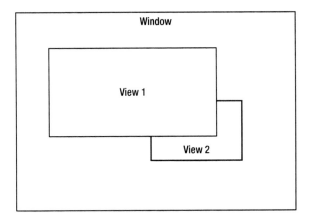

Figure 7-11. Overlapping views in a window

- Cocoa computes the area within the window taken up by View 2 and figures out which views intersect that area. It then instructs each of those views to draw into the window's backing store, starting with the rearmost view and ending with the frontmost. Thus it causes View 2 to draw first, and then View 1 is drawn (or rather, the part of View 1 that intersected with View 2 is drawn). This is done using the "painter's model," where each pixel is simply set to its new value, like a new paint stroke over an older one. Additionally, this is all done almost entirely on the CPU, apart from (perhaps) a few particular graphics commands being handled on the GPU. The rendering pipeline itself is running code written by the developer on every redraw, thus running on the CPU.

- Core Animation, on the other hand, simply tells View 2 to redraw itself once. The view's rendering is managed by a Core Animation layer and draws directly into the layer's own backing store, which again is performed on the CPU. As a result, it does not matter that it overlaps with any other views; only this single view will redraw. Once that drawing is complete, the window's backing store is updated by Core Animation, taking the backing stores of both View 1 and View 2, which are cached (ideally in the GPU's own memory), and it will *composite* those together, potentially applying Core Image filters as part of the compositing operation. Thus what you learned about the Core Image pipeline will also apply here: the compositing pipeline will combine all filters and backing store composite operations into a single operation per destination pixel, resulting in an optimized, high-throughput mechanism to update the window. Additionally, the compositing will run on the GPU, gaining not only greater performance through the GPU's specialty processing core, but freeing the CPU for the more important work of handling user input and processing user data.

Core Animation was originally designed for iOS; as a totally new system and application framework, it made sense to avoid porting across a rendering pipeline originally designed for 20-year-old computers. Instead, something much closer to the way OpenGL handles individual textures was devised. This actually happened around the time of OS X 10.4, albeit in absolute secrecy until the first version of the iPhone was released. When iOS 2.0 was published, the API was made public (and adopted the "Core" naming convention). It was also brought into OS X to provide the same benefits to the desktop operating system.

In OS X, however, the legacy API and system still needed to exist to support many years' worth of applications. As a result, Core Animation is an opt-in mechanism on OS X. To opt in, you tell your NSView instances to use a Core Animation layer as their backing store using the -setWantsLayer: method or -setLayer: methods, the former of which is available as a simple checkbox in Interface Builder. Once a view is set to use a layer, all its subviews are automatically set to use layers as well, all the way down the view hierarchy. The AppKit drawing system then does all the work of managing that layer, and your own rendering code likely never needs to change; you will simply notice that your view's -drawRect: method is called much less and only upon certain occasions.

There is one distinction to be made here: when you use -setWantsLayer: or the Interface Builder "wants layer" checkbox, you are asking the App Kit to create and manage a layer for this view on your behalf. The layer is available to you, but most of the interaction is handled for you by the App Kit; frame rectangles and borders are automatically translated into similar calls that operate directly on the view's layer. This gives you what is termed a *layer-backed* view. If, on the other hand, you create a Core Animation CALayer object yourself and pass that to your view's -setLayer: method, App Kit will back off and will expect you to handle that work yourself. Thus any borders set using the NSView API will render using the CPU-based pipeline into the layer's backing store; if you set a border color and width on your layer, however, that border will be applied at composition time on the GPU instead.

Animating

What about animation, you ask? Well, Core Animation gets its name from the fact that its layer-backed implementation makes it ideal for performing animations. A layer can have its frame set once to its final value and be drawn once. Then its backing store will be resized and repositioned back to its original position, and that *image* is moved from the view's original position to its new one. All this work is done during the compositing phase and thus makes best use of the GPU.

The plain Cocoa animation system, on the other hand, performs animation by updating the frame of the view itself in an iterative manner, usually meaning that the frame must be redrawn (using the slower CPU-based path outlined above) for each stage of the animation. As a result, with Core Animation your view's frame when animating from 10,10 to 100,100 will be *either* 10,10 or 100,100. With Cocoa animation, the frame could be anything between those values depending on the current point within the animation.

Implement animations can be a fairly complex topic worthy of a book in itself, but luckily App Kit provides a simple cover for most of your needs: the *animator proxy* object. If there is a setting on a view that you'd like to change in an animated fashion, then instead of calling -[myView setSomething: value], you can ask the view for its animator proxy object and call the same method on that instead, as -[[myView animator] setSomething: value]. This works appropriately for layer-backed or plain views, such that it will use the Cocoa animation system for a plain view and will defer everything to Core Animation in the case of a view with an associated layer.

To adjust the properties of your animation, you can use the current NSAnimationContext object. You obtain this by calling [NSAnimationContext currentContext]. You can then give it a *timing function* to define the timing curve of the animation (such as ease in, ease out, linear, etc.). You can also set its duration and supply a block to be called when it completes. The NSAnimationContext class also provides a simple one-shot animation method, which takes two blocks: the first defines the changes to animate either using animator proxies or direct property modification, and the second is called when the animation finishes running. In OS X 10.8, layer-backed views will by default *not* implicitly animate changes to properties unless you set the allowsImplicitAnimation property on the current animation context to YES. If you use an animation proxy object, however, this is automatically set to YES on your behalf. You can see an example of the blocks-based method in use in Listing 7-3.

Listing 7-3. NSAnimationContext in Action

```
[NSAnimationContext runAnimationGroup: ^(NSAnimationContext *context) {
    context.duration = 0.66;
    context.timingFunction = [CAMediaTimingFunction functionWithName:
        kCAMediaTimingFunctionEaseOut];
    [[myView animator] setFrame: NSMakeRect(10.0,10.0,250.0,180.0)];
} completionHandler: ^{
    [myLabel setStringValue: @"Animation complete!"];
}];
```

EXPLICIT VS. IMPLICIT ANIMATION

In Cocoa parlance, an *explicit* animation is one where the property change has been explicitly requested via an animation method, such as those provided by an animation proxy. An *implicit* animation is when a value is simply changed directly, but due to surrounding circumstances the system will actually apply an animation to that change.

An example is when you change the frame of a view that contains other views. Using your view's animator proxy, you *explicitly* animate the change to your view's frame. As a result, your view might adjust the frames of its own subviews, for which it will *not* use an animator proxy. By default, those changes will be animated for you, as *implicit* animations will have been enabled automatically through the use of an animator proxy. If they are not implicitly animated, they will snap to their new locations immediately while their parent view gradually grows or shrinks to encompass them. When using constraints, the same applies to any sibling views that have constraints based on the layout of the animating view.

Layout and Render Flow

Cocoa uses a deferred update mechanism for the graphics system. This means that, rather than you explicitly redrawing your views each time you make a change, you simply mark the view as "needs display;" when it's appropriate to redraw, the system will ask your view to draw itself. The new auto-layout mechanism also operates in this manner. Where displaying uses the -setNeedsDisplay: and -setNeedsDisplayInRect: methods of NSView, updating the layout of items using constraint-based calculations is based on -setNeedsLayout: and -setNeedsUpdateConstraints:. This means that, where non-auto-layout code performs a single display pass when updating the window, auto-layout code actually performs three passes through the view hierarchy, as shown in Figure 7-12.

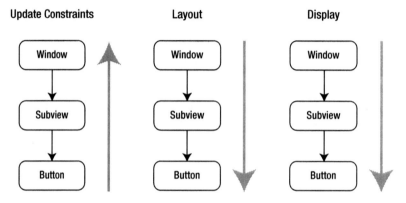

Figure 7-12. *The three-pass Cocoa window update flow*

First, the system updates the constraints on each view, starting with the lowest child in the hierarchy (i.e., the topmost views first). It does this by calling -updateConstraints on each view that implements this method, allowing that view to make adjustments to any attached constraints (such as those affecting only its subviews) that might be necessary, such as if a long row of items needs to wrap due to the size of the view changing. It makes this pass, ending at the topmost view (the window's contentView), such that each view's children have already been adjusted by the time their parent needs to adjust any constraints that apply to those views themselves.

The second pass is top-down. Starting with the window's content view it calls -layout on each view encountered so it can actually put its subviews in the right place and at the right size by adjusting the frames of its subviews. Those subviews are then tasked with doing the same, which they will do based on their new size.

The last pass then takes effect, again running top-down. In the standard Cocoa model, the rearmost view is drawn and others are drawn on top of it. In the layer-backed model, each view that needs to be redrawn is redrawn into its layer's backing store; when all layers are updated, they are composited together into the window's backing store to update the UI.

Drawing Your Interface

When you create a custom NSView subclass, you do all your drawing inside the -drawRect: method. This is called by the system when it needs to redraw your window's contents, and the system sets up a graphics context for you and tells you which area of your view's bounds need to be redrawn through the method's single parameter. This is called and implemented in the same fashion whether you're using regular Cocoa rendering or the CoreAnimation layer-backed pipeline; the system sets up everything for you automatically.

There are two levels of APIs available for performing your drawing. The real work is done using the primitives described in the Core Graphics framework, which is the set with which Core Animation operates. For Cocoa applications, however, there is an Objective-C API built on top of this, consisting of a few key classes and some helper functions.

The act of drawing itself is accomplished with the aid of a *graphics context*, represented by the NSGraphicsContext class (which itself wraps the CGContextRef C type). This object encapsulates information about the backing store in which all drawing will occur and also manages things like per-view coordinate transformations (used to implement rotation, scaling, and to offset a view's drawing so each view can use its own internal coordinates). It also keeps track of the *clipping region* for the current operation; this defines the area in which drawing can occur, such that any operations that draw outside that region are ignored (the output is *clipped* to just the allowed region).

You can create your own NSGraphicsContext objects, primarily so that you can draw into images either in memory on disk, but within your view's -drawRect: method you will usually only need to interact with the currently-defined graphics context, accessible by calling [NSGraphicsContext currentContext]. Once you have this, there are a few settings that you can change, seen in Table 7-2.

Table 7-2. NSGraphicsContext State Modifications

Method	Description
`-(BOOL)shouldAntialias;` `-(void)setShouldAntialias:(BOOL)flag;`	Enables or disables anti-aliasing while drawing graphics primitives. Anti-aliasing is a technique that interpolates the color values of adjacent pictures to give curves a smoother appearance by removing the jagged steps of the colored pixels known as *aliasing*.

`-(NSImageInterpolation)setImageInterpolation;`
`-(void)setImageInterpolation:`
`        (NSImageInterpolation)value;`
	When resizing bitmapped images, the pixels are interpolated to prevent visual artifacts. The greater the interpolation, the slower the drawing (although "slow" is a fairly relative term these days).

`-(NSPoint)patternPhase;` `-(void)setPatternPhase:(NSPoint)phase;`	Determines a pixel offset for the lower-left corner of a pattern image being tiled onto the screen. This can be used to ensure that it lines up correctly with the content of a superview. If the same 5x5 pattern is in a superview and your frame starts at 8x8, then you want to phase your pattern by an extra 2 pixels in each dimension to ensure they align correctly.

`-(NSCompositingOperation)compositingOperation;`
`-(void)setCompositingOperation:`
`        (NSCompositingOperation)operation;`
	Defines the algorithm used to composite different pixel values on top of one another; the new value overwrites old, or one of a number of mathematical expressions used to modify the current pixel value with the new one.

`-(NSColorRenderingIntent)colorRenderingIntent;`
`-(void)setColorRenderingIntent:`
`        (NSColorRenderingIntent)intent;`
	Specifies how a color should be drawn when it isn't available in the current color space. NSGraphicsContext understands different levels of either perceptual or colormetric output or can opt for saturation.

Most frequently, however, you'll likely only want to save and restore the current graphics state using -saveGraphicsState and -restoreGraphicsState. This will allow you to make changes (most of which will happen behind the scenes when using other graphics objects) to the context and revert those changes so they don't affect other views.

There are a few functions, documented in <AppKit/NSGraphics.h>, that are used as simple one-shot methods to either draw something or to modify the graphics context. These are mostly limited to methods to draw and fill rectangles or to draw standard system bezels and frames such as the blue focus glow. In Listing 7-4 you can see how to fill a view with white pixels and draw the default focus glow.

Listing 7-4. Drawing Rectangles

```
// fill a rectangle using the current fill color
NSRectFill([self bounds]);
// frame the rectangle using the current line color
NSFrameRect([self bounds]);
```

```
// draw the focus ring
NSSetFocusRingStyle(NSFocusRingOnly);
NSFrameRect([self bounds]);
```

This doesn't work properly when using CoreAnimation, however; the focus glow is clipped by the layer's contents rectangle. Happily, there is a new API in OS X 10.7 that you can use to get focus rings. If your view is currently the first responder, the system will call your view's -focusRingMaskBounds method. Here you will typically return the rectangle that bounds your content or whatever content is "visible," such as the rectangle taken up by a button image within a larger button view. You will then be asked to draw the mask for the focus ring through your -drawFocusRingMask method. In here you simply draw anything that fills the same area as your content. You might draw your content in the same manner as -drawRect: or you might just fill your bounds with a rectangle, as shown in Listing 7-5.

Listing 7-5. *Drawing a Focus Ring in a Layer-Backed View*

```
- (NSRect)focusRingMaskBounds
{
    return [self bounds];
}

- (void)drawFocusRingMask
{
    // we fill our bounds, so that's the mask for our focus rect
    [[NSColor blackColor] setFill];
    NSRectFill([self bounds]);
}
```

Cocoa Graphics Primitives

There are a few primitive classes provided by the App Kit. These encapsulate fundamentals like colors and color spaces (such as 32-bit RGB, printers' CMYK, floating-point OpenGL, and so on) along with graphics primitives such as gradients, lines, and images. In the interest of brevity, I will skip over the color space issues (your NSGraphicsContext will already know about its target color space) and go straight on to colors, courtesy of the NSColor class.

Colors

NSColor provides a number of factory methods that return common colors in the standard 32-bit RGBA color space, along with methods to create one from given components in either RGBA, CMYK, or grayscale formats. Since different color spaces use values of different sizes and types to represent each color (8-bits per component in 32-bit RGBA, 1 32-bit float per component in OpenGL floating-point), NSColor uses single-precision floating-point values for its internal representations, with each component having a value between 0.0 (no color) to 1.0 (full saturation). Thus, a red color could be obtained using [NSColor colorWithCalibratedRed: 1.0 green: 0.0 blue: 0.0 alpha: 1.0] and a yellow color using [NSColor colorWithCalibratedRed: 0.0 green: 1.0 blue: 1.0 alpha: 1.0]. Most of the time you will find yourself either using the built-in factory methods to locate common colors (or system-defined colors, such as the default text color or the disabled control background, etc.).

Once you have a color, you use it by calling -setStroke, -setFill, or -set to set the current context's stroke color, fill color, or both. Listing 7-6 shows a pair of simple colors being used to fill and outline a rectangle.

Listing 7-6. Filling and Stroking a Rectangle

```
NSRect r = NSMakeRect(0.0, 0.0, 100.0, 100.0);
[[NSColor darkGrayColor] setStroke];
[[NSColor lightGrayColor] setFill];
NSFillRect(r);
NSFrameRect(r);
```

Gradients

Gradients are implemented using the NSGradient class. A gradient consists of a number of colors laid out along a range of 0.0 to 1.0 in a virtual coordinate space owned by the gradient itself. Gradients can then be drawn in either a linear or radial fashion; a linear gradient fills an area by stretching itself to fill the area's height and varying the color along the area's width. A radial gradient draws its starting color at the center of a circle and varies the color of each pixel based on its distance from that center point. You can see an example of both in Figure 7-13.

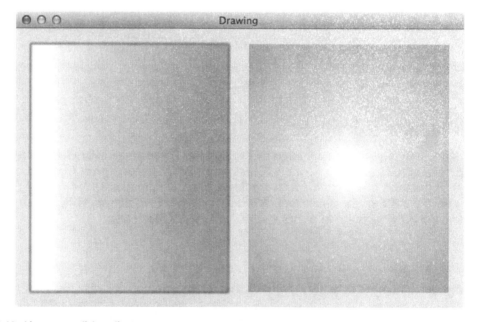

Figure 7-13. Linear vs. radial gradients

Drawing these gradients is simplicity itself; the gradients in Figure 7-13 has a pair of colors (a starting and ending color) and is drawn directly using either the linear or radial style. You can see the relevant code in Listing 7-7.

Listing 7-7. Drawing Gradients

```
// Create a gradient and use it to fill our bounds
NSGradient * gradient = [[NSGradient alloc] initWithStartingColor: [NSColor whiteColor]
                                            endingColor: [NSColor lightGrayColor]];

if ( self.linear )
    [gradient drawInRect: [self bounds] angle: 0.0];
else
    [gradient drawInRect: [self bounds] relativeCenterPosition: NSMakePoint(0, 0)];
```

With a little persistence and a few coordinates, it's possible to create even more interesting gradients. You can supply an array of colors that will be spaced out evenly for you or an array of colors with one-dimensional coordinates for each in order to space them out for you. One useful example of this is to easily draw a drop shadow below something like a title bar, as shown in Listing 7-8; this produces the gradient seen in Figure 7-14.

Listing 7-8. A Shadow Gradient

```
NSRect r = [self bounds];

// fill the background
[[NSColor whiteColor] setFill];
NSRectFill([self bounds]);

// the top 40 pixels will be a bar: no border, just a drop shadow in the 40 pixels below it
r.origin.y = NSMaxY(r) - 80.0;
r.size.height = 40.0;

// the nice shadow gradient—this is grayscale, so use a grayscale color space
NSArray * colors = @[
    [NSColor colorWithCalibratedWhite:0.0 alpha:0.0],
    [NSColor colorWithCalibratedWhite:0.0 alpha:0.1],
    [NSColor colorWithCalibratedWhite:0.0 alpha:0.3]
];
const CGFloat locations[3] = {
    0.0, 0.8, 1.0
};

gradient = [[NSGradient alloc] initWithColors: colors atLocations: locations colorSpace:
[NSColorSpace genericGrayColorSpace]];

// now draw it flowing bottom to top (clear to dark)
[gradient drawInRect: r angle: 90.0];
```

Figure 7-14. A simple shadow gradient

Note that the only drawing being done here is to place a gradient in the middle of a white rectangle; instantly the illusion of two separate views overlapping one another is created.

Images

Images are handled using the NSImage class. This is a reasonably complex class, as it handles not only bitmaps but also compressed images in a variety of formats. It also needs to manage bitmap output representations for a variety of targets: a screen at 72dpi (dots per inch) is the most common, but Retina Display Macs use double this resolution, and printers can use anywhere from 50 to many hundreds of dots per inch. NSImage handles this all for you in as transparent a manner as possible.

Ordinarily you include your own images within your application's bundle. For example, to load MyArtwork.png you simply call [NSImage imageNamed: @"MyArtwork"]. When loading images from elsewhere, you can use a similarly simple method: [[NSImage alloc] initByReferencingURL: aURL].

If you want to actually create an image using the other graphics primitives discussed in this chapter, you can create one by using [NSImage imageWithSize:aSize flipped:shouldBeFlipped drawingHandler: ^BOOL(NSRect rect){...}], which will create the image and call the provided block to draw its content for you. This method was added in OS X 10.8; previously you would have needed to create the image using [[NSImage alloc] initWithSize:aSize], then called [myImage lockFocus] (or -lockFocusFlipped), drawn into the active NSGraphicsContext, then called [myImage unlockFocus].

Listing 7-9 shows a simple example that illustrates both methods of creating an arbitrary image containing two rectangles.

Listing 7-9. Drawing into an NSImage

```
// On OS X 10.8:
NSImage * myImage = [NSImage imageWithSize:NSMakeSize(100,100) flipped:NO
                          drawingHandler: ^BOOL(NSRect rect) {
    [[NSColor whiteColor] setFill];
    NSRectFill(rect);

    NSRect square = NSMakeRect(0.0,0.0,50.0,50.0);

    // draw a square in the lower-left quadrant
    [[NSColor lightGrayColor] setFill];
    NSRectFill(square);

    // draw a square in the upper-right quadrant
    square.origin.x = square.origin.y = 50.0;
    [[NSColor darkGrayColor] setFill];
    NSRectFill(square);
}];
```

```
// On OS X 10.7 and earlier:
NSImage * myImage = [[NSImage alloc] initWithSize:NSMakeSize(100.0,100.0)];
[myImage lockFocus];

[[NSColor whiteColor] setFill];
NSRectFill(rect);

NSRect square = NSMakeRect(0.0,0.0,50.0,50.0);

// draw a square in the lower-left quadrant
[[NSColor lightGrayColor] setFill];
NSRectFill(square);

// draw a square in the upper-right quadrant
square.origin.x = square.origin.y = 50.0;
[[NSColor darkGrayColor] setFill];
NSRectFill(square);

[myImage unlockFocus];
```

> **Tip**   The coordinate system in Cocoa places its origin (the 0,0 coordinate) in the lower-left, like
> the strict Cartesian coordinate system. If you want to place it in the upper-left, as has become
> common in other operating systems, you can make use of the "flipped" attribute to do this for
> you. On custom NSView subclasses you can override -isFlipped to gain a top-left origin when
> drawing in that view. When drawing to an NSImage, you can pass YES to the flipped: parameter
> of -imageWithSize:flipped:displayHandler: or you can call -lockFocusFlipped: in
> lieu of -lockFocus.

Now that you have your image, you probably want to put it onscreen, right? Well, the *best* way to do this is to use NSImageView. This might sound strange; surely this is another level of abstraction and will thus result in slower throughput. Well, it happens that Apple's engineers have put a *vast* amount of time, effort, and ingenuity into optimizing their views, so using an image view (or a text field for text) actually gains you a whole lot of highly-optimized rendering code that you would otherwise have to write yourself.

But, for the sake of completeness, here's how a view gets placed on the screen: you either call -drawAtPoint:fromRect:operation:fraction: or -drawInRect:fromRect:operation:fraction:. As interesting as these methods are, however, I *strongly* advise you to use NSImageView instead, so I'll skip the details of these methods and let you figure them out yourself; if you genuinely need them, you'll understand the extensive documentation provided by Apple.

Lines and Curves

Lines and curves (together known as *paths*) are encapsulated using the NSBezierPath class. This provides a number of methods for accumulating a path from various line fragments. These fragments can be straight point-to-point lines or curves represented using Bezier control points. It also provides a number of simple primitives to easily obtain a path describing certain common geometric forms including rectangles, ovals, and rounded rectangles given a single bounding rectangle.

To build a path manually, you start out by calling -moveToPoint:, and then call either -lineToPoint: or -curveToPoint:controlPoint1:controlPoint2:. There are also some even simpler additive methods, such as -appendBezierPathWithArcWithCenter:radius:startAngle: endAngle:clockwise:. Listing 7-10 shows an example of how to draw a rectangle with a curved line on its right-hand edge.

Listing 7-10. Creating an NSBezierPath

```
NSBezierPath *path = [NSBezierPath bezierPath];
NSRect rect = NSMakeRect(20.0,20.0,140.0,80.0);

// start at bottom-right and go clockwise
[path moveToPoint: NSMakePoint(NSMaxX(rect),NSMinY(rect))];
[path lineToPoint: rect.origin];
[path lineToPoint: NSMakePoint(NSMinX(rect),NSMaxY(rect))];
[path lineToPoint: NSMakePoint(NSMaxX(rect),NSMaxY(rect))];

// three straight edges drawn, now do a sine-curve for the right edge
NSPoint leftControlPoint = NSMakePoint(NSMaxX(rect)-20.0,NSMidY(rect));
NSPoint rightControlPoint = NSMakePoint(NSMaxX(rect)+20.0,NSMidY(rect));
[path curveToPoint: NSMakePoint(NSMaxX(rect),NSMinY(rect))
    controlPoint1: leftControlPoint
    controlPoint2: rightControlPoint];

// close the path
[path closePath];
```

Once you have your path defined, it can be both filled and stroked, using the -fill and -stroke methods respectively. The width and (optional) dot pattern of the stroke can also be set using -setLineWidth: and -setLineDash:count:phase:, and there are other methods for defining how the corners are drawn and more. Figure 7-15 shows the result of stroking and filling the path above using a four-point line width.

Figure 7-15. The finished path, stroked and filled

It is also possible to fill a path using a gradient. To do this, you use one of NSGradient's -drawInBezierPath: methods. Figure 7-16 shows the result of using the same path with a radial gradient via -drawInBezierPath:relativeCenterPosition:.

Figure 7-16. *A gradient within a bezier path*

Video Playback

OS X provides many tools for working with media, primarily centered within the AVFoundation framework. It provides a quite intricate and slightly low-level approach to handling media, however, concentrating more on manipulation and the ability to handle lots of different events and status changes. When you want to just play a movie, Apple has you covered with the QTKit framework, which provides a high-level interface to the QuickTime media playback system.

In this section you'll create a simple document-based application for viewing movie files. To start, open Xcode and create a new Cocoa Application. Check the "Create Document-Based Application" checkbox and uncheck "Use Core Data" and "Include Unit Tests" because you won't need them. In fact, you'll need barely a dozen lines of code in total!

Defining Documents

Save the project and select the project in the Project Navigator (it's the item at the very top of the list). Then select the Summary pane in the editor.

If you have a Mac Developer account or a Developer ID with which to code-sign your applications, select the "Enable Entitlements" and "Enable App Sandboxing" checkboxes and select "Read Access" from the User Selected File Access pop-up.

Under the Linked Frameworks section, click the Add button and choose QTKit.framework from the chooser window that appears.

Now switch to the Info pane of the editor. In here, pop open the Document Types section and edit the information to appear similar to that shown in Figure 7-17. The primary information to enter is that in the Identifier field: the UTI (Uniform Type Identifier) of public.movie. This will ensure that all files that contain movie data (that is, contain both video and audio) are openable by this application. Also ensure that your application's Role value is Viewer because you don't want to think about editing these movies; you just want to display them.

Figure 7-17. The video document type

The User Interface

Open the document nib file that Xcode generated for you. It should be called `MyDocument.xib` or something similar—Xcode 4.4 and above take the class prefix you provide in the New Application dialog and use that to name the files. In the sample project, I used VP, so my class and nib are called `VPDocument`.

Now, it turns out that the built-in playback controls within the `QTMovieView` you're going to use aren't compatible with Cocoa Auto Layout. As a result, you must go into the File Inspector for your nib file and uncheck the "Use Auto Layout" checkbox. Yes, this made me sad too.

Select the window, and in the Attributes Inspector open the Full Screen pop-up menu and select the Primary Window option. This denotes that the window will have a Full Screen button at the right of its title bar and that the window's content view will fill the screen at that point.

Now you'll need to open up the Object Library. From the pop-up menu, select the QTKit section and you should see two objects available: QuickTime Capture View and QuickTime Movie View. The second item is the one you want, so drag it from the library onto the window in the interface editor. Position it so that it fills the entire content area of the window, and, keeping it selected, look in the Size Inspector.

Since you disabled the use of Cocoa Auto Layout, this inspector now shows the classic Cocoa springs-and-struts interface. By clicking on the red elements in the Autosizing image, you can adjust the behavior of the movie view's size and position as its superview grows and shrinks. The arrows in the center define whether it can grow in horizontal or vertical dimensions, and the struts around the outside define whether this edge remains a fixed distance from the same edge of its superview.

You want to have all of these options turned on, as shown in Figure 7-18. This tells the system that the view should grow in both dimensions and it should stick to the edges of its superview.

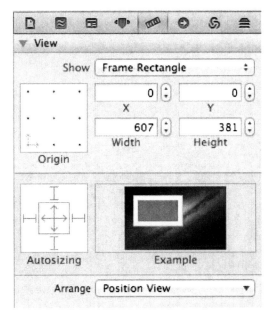

Figure 7-18. Autosizing with springs and struts

Now switch to the Attributes Inspector, and check the following checkboxes:

- Preserves Aspect Ratio

- Show Controller

- Volume

- Step

- Hot Spot

Leave all the others unchecked, and save the nib file; there's nothing more to change here, for the moment.

Document Code

There is very little left to do. Apple's application frameworks will take the document metadata you've entered to register your application with the system as a viewer for movies and will similarly adjust the contents of the standard Open dialog to open only documents that conform to the `public.movie` UTI. You've added a movie view to your document interface, so each movie you open will get its own window with its own document object. Now you need to hook the interface and the document object together, and load the movie from its file.

The default document object created for you by Xcode will contain stubs of two data-based methods: `-dataOfType:error:` and `-readFromData:ofType:error:`. Since this is a viewer app only, you can delete the first method. And since movie files are usually quite large, it makes more sense to initialize the movie from its URL rather than loading all the data into memory, so delete the second method and replace it with the stub code from Listing 7-11.

Listing 7-11. Initializing a Document's Contents from a URL

```
- (BOOL) readFromURL: (NSURL *) url
            ofType: (NSString *) typeName
             error: (NSError **) outError
{
    // code here
}
```

Before you load the data from the given URL, you'll want a property in which to store it. Since a QTMovieView is initialized using a QTMovie object, add the property (in bold text) from Listing 7-12 to your document class's header file. You must also add #import <QTKit/QTKit.h> to the top of the file.

Listing 7-12. The QTMovie Property

```
@interface VPDocument : NSDocument
@property (nonatomic, strong) QTMovie * movie;
@end
```

Now that you've added a property to store the loaded movie, you can fill out the function you defined earlier. The QTMovie class provides a simple class method to check whether a given URL can be used to initialize a movie, so use it to perform a quick sanity check on the input. If that fails, it'll return a nicely descriptive error. Then you simply initialize a new QTMovie instance using the URL and store it in your property. If the movie was created, return YES; otherwise return NO (the error will have been filled out for you by QTMovie's initializer). The full implementation can be seen in Listing 7-13.

Listing 7-13. Loading a QTMovie

```
- (BOOL) readFromURL: (NSURL *) url
            ofType: (NSString *) typeName
             error: (NSError **) outError
{
    if ( [QTMovie canInitWithURL: url] == NO )
    {
        if ( outError != NULL )
        {
            // going out of our way to provide a useful error
            NSMutableDictionary * info = [NSMutableDictionary new];
            info[NSLocalizedDescriptionKey] =
                    NSLocalizedString(@"Invalid Input", @"error description");
            info[NSLocalizedFailureReasonErrorKey] =
                    [NSString stringWithFormat:
                        NSLocalizedString(@"The file '%@' cannot be opened for playback"
                        @" by QuickTime.", @"error reason"), [url lastPathComponent]];
            info[NSLocalizedRecoverySuggestionErrorKey] =
                    NSLocalizedString(@"You can check that the file you selected "
                            @"is playable in the OS X QuickTime player, or "
                            @"using QuickLook in the Finder.", @"error suggestion");
```

```
            *outError = [NSError errorWithDomain: QTKitErrorDomain
                                            code: QTErrorIncompatibleInput
                                        userInfo: info];
    }

    return ( NO );
}

    self.movie = [[QTMovie alloc] initWithURL: url error: outError];
    return ( self.movie != nil );
}
```

Tying It Together

How do you get the movie shown in the view? Well, the simplest way is to use Cocoa Bindings. Open the nib file once more and select the movie view. From the Bindings Inspector, pop open the Movie item and bind it to the File's Owner object using the movie key (which references the property you just added). Save the file, then build and run the project.

The result will be an application with no windows. Press ⌘-O to open a new document and choose a movie file. You should see a new document window appear with a simple set of controls along the bottom. Click the Play button and the movie will play back in this window. Try out the rest of the UI; it should all work as expected, from resizing to full screen to multiple movie windows and more.

You can see an example of the finished product in Figure 7-19.

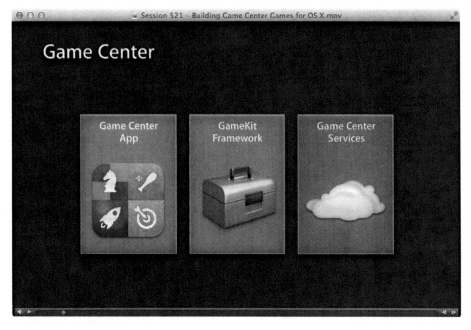

Figure 7-19. The finished application

Summary

This fairly complex chapter has dealt with some intricate topics that reach a fair ways further than this book can really encompass. You saw how the window and view hierarchy worked and how the Cocoa layout and rendering system put them onto the screen. You saw how Core Animation provides some useful modern graphics facilities and the sort of pitfalls it can have in some situations. You learned about the available drawing primitives and how to use them, and you can now display video content in an application.

While this chapter hasn't provided a large concrete example of creating a user interface, I hope that it has provided you with the knowledge to understand the possibilities and challenges that await you in the future—as near a future as the penultimate chapter of this book, no less!

Chapter 8

Data Management with Core Data

Working with structured data has long been a complex topic with many facets to consider, such as the structure of data in memory vs. its structure in permanent storage, the means to convert between the two, and the best way to deal with potentially infinite data sets without jeopardizing performance at any level. There are many different approaches to solving this problem; data formats such as XML and JSON play their part, as do large-scale storage engines such as SQL databases, key-value stores like Tokyo Cabinet, and document stores like CouchDB. All have their own representations, APIs, and their own sets of features and limitations. Choosing between them is often a decision that is hard to change later, once you've committed thousands of lines of code to a particular paradigm.

This is where Core Data comes in. It has its genus in two projects from the NeXTstep and OpenStep operating systems: first came the Database Kit, which provided a database-agnostic programming interface backed by drivers for the popular databases of the day. Out of this grew the Enterprise Objects Framework (EOF), a component of NeXT's WebObjects dynamic web site system. EOF was rebuilt using new paradigms to give it less of a database and more of a "queryable object store" feel. The WebObjects product and its frameworks were later ported to Java, and now exist only as a Java system distributed primarily with the OS X Server tools and running atop standard Java Server containers[1]. One of EOF's major advancements was its management of *relationships* between different entities using a system of *faulting* to fetch data from the backing store only when required for a given entity or one of its relationships.

In this chapter you'll learn to make use of Core Data, the object persistence framework built on the foundations of EOF. You'll learn about modeling your data, storing and retrieving it, how to integrate with iCloud, and how to bind a user interface to the contents of a Core Data store.

---

[1]WebObjects was a huge paradigm shift in its day (even with its $50,000 price tag), powering web sites for Disney and the original Dell online store. These days it's less visible but is still used by Toyota Canada and, of course, Apple, where it powers a lot of internal systems as well as the Apple Store.

Introducing Core Data

The Core Data framework introduced by Apple in OS X 10.4 (and ported to iOS in iOS 3.0) is a direct descendant of EOF. Its focus is different, however, in that where EOF is designed to work with separate database servers, Core Data's aim is to work with local data stores as an *object persistence* mechanism, providing a world-class object modeling and lifecycle management system. It gives you an object-oriented system of entities and attributes used to model your data and marries that to two types of storage systems: an *atomic* store, so named because it loads all data into memory in a single operation and works with it purely in memory, and an *incremental* store that keeps data on-disk and loads data incrementally as needed. Married to this is a powerful caching and lookup system that provides a good balance between performance and memory footprint, and a storage management subsystem that enables you to have a single view of your data whether stored in a single file or many, and whether using one or a number of separate models. What's more, these three components are architecturally independent of one another's implementation—the context and caching system uses a single interface to talk to any data store, and the interface with the persistence layer is similarly defined.

The Core Data API is based around a few core types, which together implement the three interface layers described above and the object modeling functionality itself. The stack itself is conceptually laid out as shown in Figure 8-1.

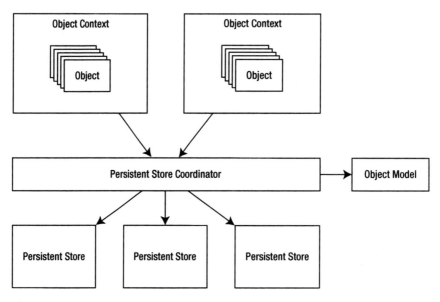

Figure 8-1. Elements of the Core Data stack

■ Object modeling is implemented using the NSManagedObjectModel class, which represents either a single entity graph loaded from one or more object-model definition files. The model's entities, properties, and relationships are defined by the NSEntityDescription and NSPropertyDescription classes, the latter with subclasses for attributes and relationships: NSAttributeDescription and NSRelationshipDescription.

At runtime, the entities themselves are represented by the NSManagedObject class or custom subclasses of this that you can create.

▨ Persistent storage is provided by the NSPersistentStore class, which encapsulates a single store on disk or in memory. Stores for a given model are managed by an NSPersistentStoreCoordinator instance, which determines which store to query for different entities. When you create your own atomic or incremental stores, you will subclass one of NSPersistentStore's two provided subclasses: NSAtomicStore or NSIncrementalStore. The persistent storage layer determines how managed objects are written out to permanent storage; as a result, some types of store might not implement all the features available in another; this only comes into play in fairly advanced cases, however, which you will not encounter during this book.

▨ Object lifecycle management is handled by the NSManagedObjectContext class, which implements the caching mechanism and the majority of Core Data's public interface. Virtually all the operations you perform will, at some level, make use of an object context. When you create a new managed object or query a store, you will be doing so by messaging an instance of NSManagedObjectContext. Every managed object is associated with a single context, and each context is associated with a persistent store coordinator, which in turn has an object model defining its entity set.

▨ Managed objects are instantiated by querying an object context; this query is an instance of NSFetchRequest. A fetch request will have a predicate (our old friend NSPredicate, whom you will remember from the Spotlight metadata section in Chapter 5), some sort descriptors used to sort the results, and various other attributes used to fine-tune the result set based on stores and the type of objects returned. You will explore NSFetchRequest in full a little later in this chapter.

Core Data provides four types of built-in storage (three on iOS), and allows you to create your own using either atomic (from OS X 10.5 and iOS 3.0) and incremental (from OS X 10.7 and iOS 5) storage paradigms. The three provided storage mechanisms are selected by specifying a constant to the NSPersistentStoreCoordinator when initializing a store.

▨ The *in-memory* store is an atomic store that does not write data back out to disk. If you are managing an object graph that does not need to persist across relaunches of the application, then this type is probably the one for you. You specify an in-memory store using the constant NSInMemoryStoreType.

▨ The *XML* store is another atomic store, meaning it is all loaded into memory once, and at the same time, but is written out to permanent storage using a plain-text XML format. This store is useful for debugging purposes, as you can easily open the persistent store in a text editor for manual inspection. You obtain an XML store using the constant NSXMLStoreType, but note that the XML store is *not* available on iOS.

▓ The *binary* store rounds out the collection of built-in atomic stores. This writes out all data in an optimized binary format for quick loads and saves of potentially large data sets, but its internals and output data format are a private implementation detail. You obtain a binary store using the NSBinaryStoreType constant.

▓ The most frequently used type of store is the *SQLite*[2] incremental store, which uses a SQLite database as its backing store. The SQLite database resides permanently on disk, and objects are loaded from it into object contexts' caches on demand; your NSFetchRequests and NSPredicates are effectively transformed into SQL expressions on the fly and sent straight to the SQLite engine for processing. As a result, there are a few small restrictions on the sort of predicates you can use with a SQLite store. You obtain a SQLite store using the NSSQLiteStoreType constant.

Components of an Object Model

An object graph, as represented by an NSManagedObjectModel instance, contains a number of different objects. First and foremost are *entities*. These are analogous to objects in your Objective-C programs, and they have both *properties* (actual named values stored as part of an entity instance) and *relationships* (links to instances of another entity within the model). Each property has an effectively scalar type: an integer of one size or another; a floating-point value; a fixed-precision decimal; and types such as strings, dates, and raw data blobs.

Relationships refer to one or more instances of a single entity type. Additionally, the objects on either side of a relationship are managed and updated for you—you won't need to fetch the objects associated through a relationship and keep updating that list manually. Instead, when you access a relationship, the system will return an automatically updating list of instances. This list can also be memory-managed, resulting in an entity's related objects being removed from memory when necessary; they are simply reloaded when the relationship property is next accessed. You can create one- or two-way, to-one or to-many relationships, and each relationship can (and should) have an *inverse relationship*. For example, if you had a Book entity and a Shelf entity, there might be a two-way relationship between them; the Book would have a to-one relationship to a single Shelf called shelf, while a Shelf would have a to-many relationship to multiple Books, called books. The Book's shelf relationship would have as its inverse the Shelf's books relationship. Because they are linked in this way, Core Data can update both sides of the relationship whenever changes are made to only one object—if a Book is deleted or connected to a different Shelf, it will be automatically removed from the current Shelf object's books relationship, and vice versa.

Entities also implement an inheritance model analogous to subclassing in object-oriented programming. There isn't anything quite the same as a protocol in an object model, but there are *abstract entities*. These, as you might realize if you're familiar with other object-oriented programming languages, are entities that define some properties and/or relationships but that

---

[2]Interesting side note: *SQLite* is not pronounced "sequel-ite" as most people imagine. Its creator calls it "*ess*-queue-el-ite," like a mineral or element name such as coprolite.

cannot be instantiated. Instead, they simply provide a root entity from which you can create specialized sub-entities. You will see abstract entities in a short while.

Entities can contain one more type of data: a *fetched property*. This is similar to a relationship in that it represents a list of objects of a single type (or subtypes). The difference is that fetched properties are represented internally using a fetch request, and the first time they're evaluated that fetch request is performed and the results are cached until the owning object goes away or is reset. As such, a fetched property can be used to obtain a more strictly defined set of related objects, but it won't be automatically updated as relationships are, and it won't be cleaned out automatically.

A managed object model can also contain two other types of object. One is a *configuration*, which groups sets of entities together. Having multiple configurations in a managed object model can, for instance, let you split the storage for the entities in that model across multiple on-disk files and thus different store types—each store can be given a configuration name as well as an object model. The other type is a *fetch request*, which is simply an instance of our friend NSFetchRequest defined at compile time and stored for quick and easy retrieval. This is loaded along with the model and can be duplicated very quickly, having its predicate already compiled into a form appropriate for its store. For complex, frequently used fetch requests this can be much faster than manually creating a new request each time you need to access some items from the store.

Whose Fault Is It Anyway?

Core Data manages the interface between in-memory object representation and on-disk persistent storage using a technique borrowed from virtual memory system programmers: *faulting*. The basic concept is that a managed object can be in one of two states: it can be a *fault*, meaning that while the object exists none of its actual data has yet been fetched from the persistent store. All it contains so far is its object ID, which identifies the persistent store with which it's associated along with some information used to locate the object's data within that store.

When an object's attributes are first accessed, this fires a *fault* in the memory-management sense, causing all the object's data to be read from the persistent store. At this point, the object is considered to be *fully faulted*. Later, in response to memory pressure (or an explicit request by the programmer) an object can be turned into a fault once more, dropping the data that was loaded from the store. Note that if modifications have taken place, the object *cannot* be turned into a fault again: those changes must be saved by sending the -save: message to the object's context.

Relationships are also implemented using the same faulting mechanism. An object with relationships to a group of other objects, even when it has itself been fully-faulted, does not load the contents of its relationship. Instead, a relationship to a single object is represented by a special type of fault; when fired, this fault will be replaced by the real object, loaded from the store.

Similarly, a to-many relationship exists as a special type of faulting NSSet. The set exists and its count is known, but its actual contents haven't been loaded into memory yet—even as faults. Instead, they are loaded in batches as the elements of the set are accessed. Similarly, part of a relationship set can be dumped out of memory as it brings more in. This makes it very easy to support relationships to a very large number of objects.

Creating an Object Model

Since Core Data is all about persistence of an object graph, it seems that a good place to start would be to define one. You'll create a simple Contacts model where you will be able to store people's names, phone numbers, e-mail addresses, and mailing addresses[3].

You'll start by creating a new Cocoa Application with Xcode. Ensure that "Use Core Data" is checked and "Document-Based Application" is *not* checked. Once the project has been created, select the data model file in the project navigator—it will be named `<ProjectName>.xcdatamodel`, where `<ProjectName>` is the name of your project, with any spaces replaced by underscores. You will be presented with an empty model editor in *table* mode. Here your entities are shown in a source list to the left, and the attributes, relationships, and fetched properties (more on these later) for the selected entity appear in a table filling the majority of the editor. Below this area, at the bottom of the window, are a few buttons. The leftmost toggles the Entity list between showing a flat list in alphabetical order and a hierarchical list showing the inheritance tree. Next is a button to add a new entity—if you click and hold here, you can also add new fetch requests and configurations.

To the right hand side of the editor, along the bottom, are two more buttons: a popup button that allows you to add new attributes, relationships, or fetched properties to a selected entity; and a toggle that will switch the editor's view between table and graph mode. *Graph* mode allows you to lay out your data model visually on simulated graph paper, with entities connected by different graph lines indicating inheritance and relationships, including the direction and type of each relationship (to-one or to-many).

How might you model this data? Well, clearly your central entity is a Person. A person has a first and last name, and has a variety of addresses, whether e-mail or surface mail. They also have one or more phone numbers. A phone number is a number (most likely formatted), and an e-mail address is similarly a string conforming to a certain format. A mailing address has several fields: one or two lines for the house and street, a city/town, county/state, a postal code, and a country.

You can model a person fairly simply by placing all these attributes into a single entity. In the editor for your data model, click the Add Entity button located toward the bottom of the window, and a new entity will be created for you, with its name highlighted ready to accept its new name. Type `Person` and press Enter.

> **Tip**   To easily change any entity name or attribute name, double-click on the name in the model editor. This works in both Table and Graph mode.

In the topmost table on the right side of the editor (the Attributes table), click the + button to add a new attribute and name it `firstName`. From the Type column, pull down the menu and select the `String` type.

---

[3]You will be expanding this model in the next chapter to encompass everything within the system Contacts application.

Look at the utilities pane on the right side of the window and select the third tab to show the Data Model inspector. Assuming the attribute is still highlighted, you will see its name and attributes here. Within this inspector you can choose whether to index the attribute's value in Spotlight and whether it should be stored in its own file (useful for large data objects such as images). You can also enter some validation criteria and adjust some of the attributes properties: whether it is *optional*, *transient* (computed at runtime rather than stored on disk), or *indexed* for fast search lookup. The default value is that *optional* is set and the others are unset. For the first name, you will want to index it and it is a required field, so uncheck the Optional box and check the Indexed box.

Now that you know how to create and adjust attributes, add the remaining values from Table 8-1. When you're done, switch to Graph mode and you should see something like Figure 8-2.

Table 8-1. *Basic Person Attributes*

Attribute Name	Type	Properties
firstName	String	Indexed, required
lastName	String	Indexed, required
phoneNumber	String	Indexed, optional
emailAddress	String	Indexed, optional
street1	String	Optional
street2	String	Optional
city	String	Optional
region	String	Optional
postalCode	String	Optional
country	String	Optional

Figure 8-2. *A simple Person entity*

A Better Model

This works, but it leaves a few things to be desired. For example, there is no obvious grouping for the mailing address: all the properties are equal, and there is nothing telling you that everything in Table 8-1 from street1 to country actually comprises a single mailing address. You can fix this by creating a second entity to model the mailing address and move those properties to this new entity. Create the new entity by clicking the Add Entity button and name it MailingAddress. Switch back to Table mode, then select the mailing address attributes from your Person entity and cut them out (using ⌘-X), then select the MailingAddress entity and paste them in using ⌘-V.

Next, create a relationship from the Person to the MailingAddress by selecting the Person entity and clicking the + button below the Relationships table. Name the new relationship mailingAddress and set its destination to be the MailingAddress entity. Now create the inverse relationship by selecting the MailingAddress entity and adding a new relationship called person. This will target the Person entity, and its inverse will be that entity's mailingAddress relationship. Additionally, the person relationship should be Required, so uncheck the Optional checkbox in the inspector.

Switch back to graph mode; your graph should now look something like Figure 8-3.

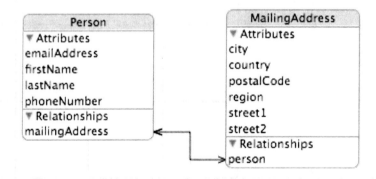

Figure 8-3. The new MailingAddress entity and relationship

Relationships and Abstract Entities

This still isn't ideal though. The mailing address is nicely encapsulated, but you still only have one e-mail, one phone, and one mailing address per person. To solve this, you need to extract them all into other entities and set up to-many relationships to each of them. Additionally, you need to refactor the idea of an address into an abstract entity, which you will subclass to create mailing addresses and suchlike.

The basic Address entity has a single property: a required String attribute called label. This allows you to label the different addresses as '"work," "home,"' and so on. The Address entity itself is *abstract*, because it doesn't provide anything useful in itself—only its concrete subclasses representing phone numbers, e-mail addresses, and mailing addresses will be of any real use. (Once you've created the Address entity, you can make it abstract by selecting the entity itself and checking the Abstract Entity checkbox in the inspector.)

Now select the MailingAddress entity once again and in the inspector pull down the Parent Entity checkbox; select the Address entity there.

Your next step is to create new Address sub-entities for phone numbers and e-mail addresses. These are simple: each is a single new entity with Address as its parent, and each contains a single attribute—a phoneNumber or an email. Make these attributes Required because an instance would not be very useful without them. Also add a person relationship targeting the Person entity.

Now you want to adjust your Person entity's relationships. You already have a relationship with the MailingAddress entity, but it is only a to-one relationship. Select it, and in the inspector check the To-Many Relationship checkbox. Now delete the emailAddress and phoneNumber attributes and add two more relationships, naming them phoneNumbers and emailAddresses. They should target the PhoneNumber and EmailAddress entities, respectively, and should both be Optional and To-Many.

There's one other step for these relationships here: if a Person were deleted, what would happen to all the addresses owned by that person? If you select the mailingAddresses, phoneNumbers, or emailAddresses relationship and look in the inspector, you can see the answer: there's a pull-down menu labeled Delete Rule, which is currently set to the value Nullify. This means that when a Person is deleted from the store, all its addresses stay around, and the content of their person relationship is nullified (set to point to nothing). That then leaves these Address objects floating around unconnected, or would if their person relationships were not marked Required. As it is, the store would not validate in this situation, and thus would not save.

The solution is to tell Core Data that when you remove a person, you want it to *cascade* that deletion to the objects on the other side of this relationship. Since each Address sub entity is only attached to a single Person, this is safe—it won't delete data relied upon by other objects. Click on the Delete Rule pull-down menu in the inspector and select Cascade. Note that the opposite is not true: when removing an Address, you do *not* want to delete its associated Person; you just want to disconnect the relationship, which is the purpose of the Nullify rule. Repeat this for all the relationships on the Person entity.

The resulting object graph is shown in Figure 8-4.

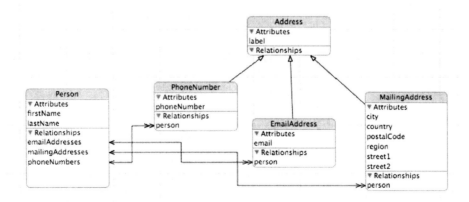

Figure 8-4. The completed model with all relationships

In the object graph, inheritance is represented with a hollow-headed arrow pointing from a sub-entity to its parent. Relationships are represented with open-headed arrows between the attributes themselves, with the arrowhead pointing in the direction of the relationship—a relationship from A to B points towards B. Where a relationship has an inverse, the arrow line has an arrowhead at both ends. A double-headed arrow indicates that there is a *to-many* relationship in that direction, while a single-headed arrow shows a *to-one* relationship. In Figure 8-3, the arrows pointing towards the Address sub-entities are double-headed representing the Person entity's to-many relationship to those addresses.

Custom Classes

The model is now complete, which is great, but the programming API for it is still not perfect. Right now, you will be dealing with instances of NSManagedObject for every entity instance and can only access values using the -valueForKey: and -setValue:forKey: KVO methods on those instances. You can do better than that, and so too can Core Data.

In the model editor, select all your entities, and from the *Editor* menu, select *Create Managed Object Subclass*. You will be presented with a dialog asking for a location for the generated files; leave it pointed at the project folder, but check the "*Use scalar properties for primitive types*" checkbox. This will generate properties that use actual Booleans, integers, or floating-point numbers for scalar values instead of wrapping everything in an NSNumber or other object type. Click *Create* (or press Enter) and classes for each of your entities will be generated for you and placed into the Project Navigator.

Each new class has the same name as its corresponding entity. If you return to the model editor and select one of your entities, you will now see in the inspector that its Class field has been filled out with the name of the new class, where before it was always NSManagedObject.

In the Project Navigator, select Person.h to open it in the editor. You should see code like that seen in Listing 8-1.

Listing 8-1. The Person Class Interface

```
@class EmailAddress, MailingAddress;

@interface Person : NSManagedObject

@property (nonatomic, retain) NSString * firstName;
@property (nonatomic, retain) NSString * lastName;
@property (nonatomic, retain) NSSet *emailAddresses;
@property (nonatomic, retain) NSSet *mailingAddresses;
@property (nonatomic, retain) NSSet *phoneNumbers;
@end

@interface Person (CoreDataGeneratedAccessors)

- (void)addEmailAddressesObject:(EmailAddress *)value;
- (void)removeEmailAddressesObject:(EmailAddress *)value;
- (void)addEmailAddresses:(NSSet *)values;
- (void)removeEmailAddresses:(NSSet *)values;

- (void)addMailingAddressesObject:(MailingAddress *)value;
- (void)removeMailingAddressesObject:(MailingAddress *)value;
```

```
- (void)addMailingAddresses:(NSSet *)values;
- (void)removeMailingAddresses:(NSSet *)values;
- (void)addPhoneNumbersObject:(NSManagedObject *)value;
- (void)removePhoneNumbersObject:(NSManagedObject *)value;
- (void)addPhoneNumbers:(NSSet *)values;
- (void)removePhoneNumbers:(NSSet *)values;

@end
```

The first thing you'll notice is that the new class is a subclass of NSManagedObject. It is thus subject to all the usual rules and serves as a point to override all of that class's validation methods and life-cycle methods—more on that shortly. The subclass's primary raison d'être is to provide the property-based accessors you can see within its @interface. The two attributes are represented using NSString instances, and the relationships are instances of NSSet. This last is an important distinction to note: the contents of a relationship are always unordered, and they are always *unique*, meaning that a single object cannot be added to a relationship twice. This does not mean to say that you cannot have two separate objects with identical data, however; by default this is not something handled by Core Data, although you might implement -isEqual: on your managed object subclass to prevent this.

It is possible to have an *ordered* list as a relationship destination, which would then use the NSOrderedSet class (available from OS X 10.7 and iOS 5.0 onwards). The downside to this is that ordering the results adds overhead, so it's better to use this feature only if it's really required that the data be ordered on-disk. Simply using it as a means of sorting by name isn't useful, since you can do that yourself with less overhead at display time.

Below the main @interface block is a category that defines some relationship-mutation methods. These provide simple means to add and remove single or multiple items to and from each relationship. By using these methods, Core Data can maintain the integrity of the object graph by ensuring the inverse relationships are kept up to date; adding an EmailAddress by calling [aPerson addMailingAddressesObject:address] will also set the address object's person relationship to point to aPerson. The reverse is, naturally, also true.

If you now open the implementation file for Person, you will see the very skeletal implementation shown in Listing 8-2.

Listing 8-2. The Person Class Implementation

```
@implementation Person

@dynamic firstName;
@dynamic lastName;
@dynamic emailAddresses;
@dynamic mailingAddresses;
@dynamic phoneNumbers;

@end
```

As you learned earlier in this book, the @dynamic property keyword tells the compiler that the methods for this property will be generated *at runtime*. This is part of the magic of Core Data: it generates all these methods for us dynamically and in a highly optimized fashion. Calling these accessors is thus noticeably faster than using either -valueForKey: or NSManagedObject's -primitiveValueForKey: method. In fact, these aren't the only methods generated by Core

Data: it also generates customized -primitiveValue... methods for each property, such as -primitiveValueForFirstName or -setPrimitiveValueForFirstName:. These are all created on-demand at runtime, as are the relationship mutation methods seen in the header file.

Now open EmailAddress.h and look at its properties, seen in Listing 8-3.

Listing 8-3. The EmailAddress Class Interface

```
@class Person;

@interface EmailAddress : NSManagedObject

@property (nonatomic, retain) NSString * email;
@property (nonatomic, retain) Person *person;

@end
```

Note that here the person relationship is not implemented using an NSSet, as it's a to-one relationship. Instead, it is simply a pointer to the relevant Person object. Once you have an EmailAddress, you can access its associated Person just by using that property as-is.

> **Note**   Your source code may declare the type of the person property as NSManagedObject. This seems to be a bug induced by the fact that the Person class had not been created when the code for this subclass was first generated (they are generated in alphabetical order). You can change your source to match that seen in Listing 8-3 with impunity: the returned object is guaranteed to be an instance of the Person class.

Transient Properties

In Core Data parlance, a *transient property* is one that is not kept in the persistent store but instead is generated at runtime, usually based on the values of some other properties. It is added to the model to correctly model the object graph, but Core Data makes no attempt to define or return its value—you will have to implement it yourself. Additionally, transient properties are by definition *read-only*. Its value will change in response to changes elsewhere within an entity's attributes.

Let's create a transient property that returns a person's full name. In the model editor, select the Person entity and add a new String attribute, naming it fullName. Select the attribute and set its type to Optional and check the *Transient* checkbox. Now you'll go back to the code to implement it.

In the Person header, add a new nonatomic, retain NSString property called fullName; it should match the other attribute properties. Now go to the implementation file and add the code from Listing 8-4 within the class's @implementation block.

Listing 8-4. The fullName Transient Property Implementation

```
- (NSString *) fullName
{
    if ( self.firstName !=nil && self.lastName !=nil )
        return ( [NSString stringWithFormat: @"%@ %@", self.firstName, self.lastName] );
```

```
    if ( self.firstName != nil )
        return ( self.firstName );
    else
        return ( self.lastName );
}
```

The idea here is that if both a first and last name are set, then the method will return those items separated by a space character. Otherwise, if the lastName property is nil, it will return the firstName, and vice versa. So, if firstName is "Jane" and lastName is "Doe," the fullName property will return "Jane Doe."

> **Caution**   Since they are not persistent, transient properties cannot be used within predicates or sort descriptors when querying an incremental store such as the SQLite store. Instead you can filter or sort the values returned as a result of running your fetch request after the fact.

You will also want a means of *setting* this property. Since it's transient, the value won't be stored in its own right; instead, changing the fullName will alter the firstName and lastName properties accordingly. The technique is simple: if there is no space in the name, the whole thing is set as the firstName property. If there is a space, then what comes before is the firstName and what follows is the lastName.

This could be implemented reasonably simply by using the NSString method -componentsSeparatedByString: to return an array of space-separated components. This, though, would create an array of potentially more than two strings, and if there were more than two components, you would have to build the lastName property by combining all but the first into yet another string. Instead, use the memory-friendly option: searching for whitespace in the string and fetching the strings before and after that point. NSString's -substringToIndex: works well enough for the prefix part, but for the suffix (to make the lastName property) you want to search past the whitespace to ensure you skip any concurrent spaces, tabs, or newlines. A simple -substringFromIndex: then fetches the last name.

Lastly, it would be useful to trim any whitespace from the start and end of the input string. This can be accomplished using -stringByTrimmingCharactersFromSet:. Listing 8-5 shows the completed setter method.

Listing 8-5. Setting the fullName Transient Property

```
- (void) setFullName: (NSString *) fullName
{
    NSCharacterSet * whitespace = [NSCharacterSet whitespaceAndNewlineCharacterSet];
    NSCharacterSet * nonWhitespace = [whitespace invertedSet];

    fullName = [fullName stringByTrimmingCharactersInSet: whitespace];
    NSRange r = [fullName rangeOfCharacterFromSet: whitespace];
    if ( r.location == NSNotFound )
    {
        // a single name
        self.firstName = fullName;
```

```
        self.lastName = nil;
        return;
    }

    self.firstName = [fullName substringToIndex: r.location];
    r = NSMakeRange(r.location, [fullName length]-r.location);
    r = [fullName rangeOfCharacterFromSet: nonWhitespace options: 0 range: r];
    self.lastName = [fullName substringFromIndex: r.location];
}
```

Now, if this new property were used through key-value observation, for instance in a UI binding, then there's currently nothing in here to tell the system that it's about to change. The regular methods to call on an object when one of its properties is changing are the -willChangeValueForKey: and -didChangeValueForKey: pair. However, the actual properties changing in this case are the firstName and lastName properties, which already post change notifications for their own keys; you don't want to reimplement these (losing the performance optimizations of the Core Data auto-generated code) just to post an extra set of notifications, do you?

Luckily, there's a set of class methods that can help you in this situation. The core method is +(NSSet*)keyPathsForValuesAffectingValueForKey:(NSString *)key, but there's more runtime fun in store! If a class has a value keyed to "name," then it will look for a key-specific version of this method named +(NSSet*)keyPathsForValuesAffectingName. The return value from this method is a set of all the keys that, should they be the focus of a KVO change notification, imply that "name" has also been changed. Since the property you're looking at here is fullName, and it depends upon the values of the firstName and lastName properties, you will want to implement the method as seen in Listing 8-6.

Listing 8-6. Implementing a KVO Dependency for the fullName Property

```
+ (NSSet *) keyPathsForValuesAffectingFullName
{
    return ( [NSSet setWithObjects: @"firstName", @"lastName", nil] );
}
```

With that done, any changes to either the firstName or lastName properties will trigger similar change notifications for the fullName property, thus keeping any bound values current automatically.

Validation

One of Core Data's powerful built-in features is that of validation. Part of this is implemented on a per-property basis and can be set (to a certain degree) in the model editor. Part is implemented in code by creating a custom subclass and implementing per-property KVC validation methods such as -validateValue:forKey:error:. Lastly, NSManagedObject provides some of its own validation methods, seen in Table 8-2.

Table 8-2. *Managed Object Validation Methods*

Method	Description
`-(BOOL)validateForDelete:(NSError**)error`	Determines whether the receiver can be deleted from the object store in its current state. The default implementation performs basic checking based on the presence or absence of values.
`-(BOOL)validateForInsert:(NSError**)error`	Determines whether a new object can be inserted into a data store for the first time.
`-(BOOL)validateForUpdate:(NSError**)error`	Determines whether some changes made to an object are valid. This is called when the object is to be written out to persistent storage.

Most of the time your validation logic will be based on particular values, and thus will be part of the data model. For example, for numeric values you can specify a minimum and maximum allowed value. If you want only multiples of 100, then you need to write your own validation methods in a custom subclass. For strings, you can provide minimum and maximum length predicates as well as a format predicate in the form of a regular expression. For all (or almost all) properties you can also provide a default value, which will be used if no other is supplied when the object is first inserted into a managed object context.

Update the model to add some validation and some default values. Firstly, in the model editor, select the `label` attribute of the `Address` entity, and in the Core Data Inspector, set its default value to "Home." Since this is a required attribute, it is very useful to supply a default value— this way, when a new object is created so it can be displayed for editing, everything will work as expected. Without the default value, any automatic creation by an object controller for this purpose would fail with a validation error.

There are some other required attributes: the `email` property of `EmailAddress` and the `phoneNumber` property of the `PhoneNumber` entity. Give these default values of "johnnyappleseed@ me.com" and "(123) 555-1234," respectively. Also, the `Person` entity's `lastName` attribute is required: set a default value here, too (we used `firstName` = "John" and `lastName` = "Appleseed" because we're both huge Apple geeks and thus like to copy Apple's usual example).

You can implement validation on the e-mail address and phone number using regular expressions (often called *regex* for short). The full syntax of regular expressions is easily available online, and is also rather large and complex, so please forgive us as we gloss over them a little here. First, select the `email` attribute of the `EmailAddress` entity and set its regular expression (labeled "Reg. Ex." in the inspector) to the value in Listing 8-7.

Listing 8-7. An Email Validation Regular Expression

```
^[A-Za-z0-9._%+-]+@([A-Za-z0-9.-]+\.)+[A-Za-z]{2,4}$
```

Let's break this apart to learn a little about the syntax of regular expressions and to see how it is used to validate e-mail addresses.

■ ^

This character is used to denote the beginning of a line (or, in this case, a complete string). Its presence means that the items following it must match the first characters in the line. If the first characters do not match the following clause, then the expression will not match the string at all.

■ `[A-Za-z0-9._%+-]+`

Any text enclosed within square brackets is a character set. It can contain a list of any characters along with some special ranges—pairs of characters separated by a hyphen. A range encloses every ASCII or Unicode character value between the two used to delimit the range, along with the two typed. Thus `A-Z` refers to all uppercase Latin characters A through Z, `a-z` refers to their lowercase counterparts, and `0-9` refers to the full set of Arabic decimal digits. You can also see a period, underscore, percentage sign, plus, and minus, so these characters are also part of the set. Having defined that set, an *operator* follows it. This case uses the `+` operator, which in regex parlance means "one or more." Therefore the expression so far states that the string must begin with one or more of the characters within this set.

■ `@`

A single character on its own refers to itself. The ampersat here states that there must be an ampersat in the source string. Thus the expression so far says "One or more characters of a defined set starting the string, followed by an ampersat." Should a character occur that is neither a member of the set nor an ampersat, then the match would fail.

■ `([A-Za-z0-9.-]+\.)+`

Any expression within parentheses indicates a *group*. In this case you can see that the group contains another set of characters: A through Z, both upper- and lower-case, the ten Arabic decimal numerals, a period, and a hyphen. Then you see the `+` operator once more, meaning "one or more of." After this is a backslash and a period character. The period is a special character in regular expressions (although *no* character is special when placed within a character set), and means "any character." As a result, to match a single period character you must *escape* it by preceding it with a backslash, which you see here. The whole thing is surrounded by parentheses, meaning it can be captured and treated as a single unit. This group is then subject to our friend the `+` operator once more, meaning that it can match multiple times. The regular expression now matches everything up to the ampersat as described above, followed by multiple sequences of characters ending in a period character.

■ `[A-Za-z]{2,4}`

Again you have a character set, this time consisting of only the upper- and lower-case Latin alphabet. After this comes a special operator. A pair of curly braces containing a number (or two numbers separated by a comma, as you see here) gives a strict count for the number of characters that can be matched. Here it matches 2 to 4 characters, which must follow on from what you've already stated: Set A, ampersat, Set B and a period (at least once), then either two, three, or four characters from Set C.

▨ $

The last component is another special character; this one denotes the end of a line or string. Thus your input string cannot have any additional characters after the 2-4 characters matched by the previous rule: the string must end there.

Phew. That took some explaining, and you've really only scratched the surface of what's possible. Many resources exist to learn more about regular expressions, including Apple's own documentation, if you want to learn more.

For phone numbers, you need a very complicated regular expression to really catch everything. For now, assume an optional 1- to 3-digit country code preceded by a plus sign, some digits within optional braces, and a set of following digits interspersed with either spaces, periods, or hyphens. The number can optionally have an extension, specified using either xDDDD or ext DDDD. The resulting regex is shown in Listing 8-8.

Listing 8-8. A Phone Number Matching Regular Expression

```
(\+\d{1,3}\s?)?\(?\d{3,5}\)?[\s-.]?\d+[\s-.]\d+(\s?(x|ext)\s?\d+)?
```

The new items you see in here are \d, which means "any decimal digit," \s, which means "any whitespace character," and ?, which is an operator meaning "zero or one times." Note that the literal parentheses in the expression are escaped with backslash characters to prevent their being interpreted as group delimiters.

Due to experience, however, this will fail somewhere important, and a real validation expression would be very long indeed, so for now I recommend that you delete this from the model and allow any string value for a phone number.

Firing It Up

You can see the startup mechanism for a Core Data application by looking inside the application delegate generated for you by Xcode. Open APAppDelegate.m and have a look around. There are a few key methods in here that implement your Core Data startup mechanism. Just about the whole file, in fact.

The key tasks undertaken here are

▨ Locating a place to store your data. This is handled by -applicationFilesDirectory.

▨ Loading your object model, which occurs lazily in the managedObjectModel property accessor method.

▨ Creating a persistent store coordinator and attaching a managed object context; again these are lazily initialized in the persistentStoreCoordinator and managedObjectContext property accessors.

▨ Hooking into the system undo mechanism. Each window maintains an undo manager to handle all this for any and all content views in the window. In the

-windowWillReturnUndoManager: window delegate method, your application actually discards the window's undo manager and instead returns that of the managed object context.

- Saving data. This tells the managed object context to commit any pending edit actions to its in-memory state, then asks the context to save. Saving a managed object context writes any modifications back out to the persistent store (or stores).

- Termination handling. The application shouldn't quit while there are unsaved changes in the managed object context, so the application delegate method -applicationShouldTerminate: is called to verify that this action is appropriate. This then checks a few things: if the context hasn't yet been initialized, you quit. If it exists and you can't commit any in-process editing, you cancel the termination attempt. The same thing happens if you can't save the data, but with an added twist: it presents an error dialog first. If the error dialog offered a means of resolving the error and the user succeeded in doing so, you cancel termination. Otherwise, you put up a hand-crafted alert dialog asking the user to confirm whether they still want to quit, despite not being able to save their changes.

The main points of initializing a Core Data stack can be seen in Listing 8-9.

Listing 8-9. Initializing a Core Data Stack

```
// this is a Core Data stack, laid out bottom-to-top
NSManagedObjectModel * model = nil;
NSPersistentStore * store = nil;
NSPersistentStoreCoordinator * coordinator = nil;
NSManagedObjectContext * context = nil;

// first we load the model
NSURL *modelURL = [[NSBundle mainBundle] URLForResource:@"Core_Data_Contacts"
                                        withExtension:@"momd"];
model = [[NSManagedObjectModel alloc] initWithContentsOfURL:modelURL];
if (model == nil)
    return (NO);

// next comes the persistent store
// first ensure the folder exists, then create the store
// and add it to the coordinator (in one step)
NSURL *url = [applicationFilesDirectory URLByAppendingPathComponent:
                                        @"Core_Data_Contacts.storedata"];
coordinator = [[NSPersistentStoreCoordinator alloc] initWithManagedObjectModel:mom];
if (![coordinator addPersistentStoreWithType:NSXMLStoreType
                        configuration:nil
                                URL:url
                        options:nil error:&error]) {
    [[NSApplication sharedApplication] presentError:error];
    return (NO);
}
```

```
// now create the object context
context = [[NSManagedObjectContext alloc] init];
[context setPersistentStoreCoordinator:coordinator];

return (YES);
```

That's really all there is to it. Of course, the error reporting could be better (and in the example application, it is), but the crux of it boils down to get model, get coordinator and store, and create context on coordinator. Simple.

Persistent Store Options

There are quite a few clever things you can do with a Core Data store these days. You've already seen that the system will automatically convert from scalar values to boxed types on your behalf. It can also use *external records*. This means taking some data that would ordinarily be in an attribute value and placing it in an external file. This is very useful for storing large items such as images, which aren't really appropriate to be stored in something like an SQL database or an XML file.

The relevant option is available as a checkbox in the Core Data inspector when you have any attribute selected and is accessible at runtime through NSAttributeDescription's setAllowsExternalBinaryStorage: method. Note the wording on that method, though: "*allows* external binary storage." This means that Core Data will decide for you, on a case-by-case basis, whether it is more efficient to store the data inside the persistent store or in an external file; it's not a guarantee that the data will always live in a separate file of its own.

Core Data also has full built-in support for iCloud. This means that it is automatically able to synchronize content access using the methods discussed in Chapter 5. It also means that if you use an incremental store type such as the SQLite store, changes can be synchronized with a user's iCloud account in a much more fine-grained fashion.

To enable iCloud synchronization on your Core Data store, you need to provide one or two specific items in the options dictionary passed to NSPersistentStoreCoordinator's -addPersistentStoreWithType:configuration:URL:options:error: method. The first, and required, option is the name of the store, used so that multiple devices can refer to the same store. This is specified using the key NSPersistentStoreUbiquitousContentNameKey. The second item is optional and is used to specify the location of the database within the application's ubiquity container. If you don't specify one of these manually (using NSPersistentStoreUbiquitousContentURLKey), an appropriate value will be generated for you based on the NSFileManager API URLForUbiquityContainerIdentifier: instead.

When you want to delete an iCloud-based store (or just to remove it from iCloud), you need to remove the directory identified by the NSPersistentStoreUbiquitousContentURLKey or the appropriate item from within your ubiquity container (as returned from NSFileManager). This process needs to take place using the file coordination APIs.

Storage for Ubiquitous Core Data

For SQLite stores, you must also be sure to place your store inside your application's sandbox and *not* within the ubiquity container. The changes for SQLite stores aren't propagated based on the file's modification, they're handled internally by Core Data; putting your store in an auto-synchronizing location would only cause confusion.

For atomic stores, there is no special per-change synchronization taking place: the store file is placed into the ubiquity container as normal, and Core Data will monitor the synchronization state of that file as a whole on your behalf.

There are some further restrictions in the functionality of SQLite stores in iCloud:

- You cannot use ordered relationships.

- You shouldn't seed initial content using a pre-packaged store file copied into place. Instead, either generate the entities in code and insert them or use NSPersistentStoreCoordinator's migratePersistentStore:toURL:options: withType:error: to migrate the contents of your pre-packaged store into the iCloud-synchronized one.

- You can only use lightweight (automatic) migration between model versions—custom migrations with developer-defined mapping models are not supported.

A further note regarding model versions: when multiple versions of the app work with a single data store, the iCloud version uses the most current model. This means that older versions of the application will not sync. However, when those apps are upgraded to the new model version, they will again be able to sync, and they will send any unsent changes up to iCloud to be synchronized with more recent versions of the app.

Setting up iCloud requires some information from a paid Mac Developer account; don't worry, that will be covered in the next chapter where you'll add iCloud support to this application.

Multithreading and Core Data

Correctly managing your Core Data store across multiple threads is a thorny issue. A lot of its speed comes from the fact that it makes various assertions about its threading use:

- An NSManagedObject instance will only be used on a single thread.

- An NSManagedObjectContext expects to be queried by only one thread at a time—and ideally only one thread *ever*.

This means that, for example, you can't fetch some objects from an object context and enumerate them using a concurrent enumeration method—unexpected things might happen. Nor can you pass these objects between threads. This is very much to be explicitly avoided.

Confinement

Up until OS X 10.7 and iOS 5.0, Core Data supported only one form of multithreading support: *thread confinement*. This describes the situation where every thread has its own NSManagedObjectContext instance, all of which refer to the same NSPersistentStoreCoordinator (which *is* multithread-safe). This means that you would always query your thread's own context to fetch objects and make changes.

As a result, it's important to remember that managed objects are tied to a single context, and thus if you need to store them in an instance somewhere, you should likely instead store their object ID, represented by the NSManagedObjectID class and obtained by sending -objectID to a managed object.

You can reverse the process by handing your NSManagedObjectID into NSManagedObjectContext's objectWithID: or existingObjectWithID:error: methods. The difference between the two is important: the first method may return a fault, meaning that the data isn't guaranteed to exist when the time comes to access it (trust me, I've run into this situation in numerous places). The second, however, will always return a fully faulted object or nil. Thus if the current thread's context hasn't yet learned of a change on-disk that removed this object, it will discover this when it attempts to load its data. If you fetch a fault referring to a deleted object, any attempt to access its values will result in Core Data throwing an exception.

Listing 8-10 shows some useful utility code I've used in a few shipping applications to help with thread confinement. It provides a means to fetch (or create, if necessary) a managed object context specific to the calling thread.

Listing 8-10. Per-Thread NSManagedObjectContexts

```
static NSString * const AQPerThreadManagedObjectContext =
                                    @"AQPerThreadManagedObjectContext";

void StoreManagedObjectContextForCurrentThread(NSManagedObjectContext * context)
{
    [[[NSThread currentThread] threadDictionary] setObject: context
                                    forKey: AQPerThreadManagedObjectContext];
}

NSManagedObjectContext * PerThreadManagedObjectContext(void)
{
    NSManagedObjectContext * result=[[[NSThread currentThread] threadDictionary]
                                objectForKey: AQPerThreadManagedObjectContext];
    if ( result !=nil )
        return ( result );

    NSManagedObjectContext * moc=[[NSManagedObjectContext alloc] init];
    [moc setMergePolicy: NSMergeByPropertyObjectTrumpMergePolicy];
    [moc setPersistentStoreCoordinator: GetPersistentStoreCoordinator()];
    StoreManagedObjectContextForCurrentThread(moc);
    [moc release];      // now owned by the thread dictionary

    return ( moc );
}
```

To use this, you first create your regular managed object context during application startup *on the main thread*. This is important: instances of NSManagedObjectContext behave differently if created on the main thread. Having created it, pass it to StoreManagedObjectContextForCurrentThread(). Once this is done, simply call PerThreadManagedObjectContext() any time you need to access your data store.

Private Queueing

The first of two new Core Data threading policies introduced with OS X 10.7 and iOS 5.0 is that of giving each context its own private dispatch queue upon which to perform its operations. The queue is created by the object context itself, and all internal operations take place by synchronously or asynchronously running blocks of code on that queue. From the outside, you as the programmer need to make use of a new `NSManagedObjectContext` API to synchronize your own fetches and saves using that queue.

The two new methods are `-performBlock:` and `-performBlockAndWait:`, which map logically to `dispatch_async()` and `dispatch_sync()`. They each have their uses. For example, if you want to save the data in the context, you might want to call both `-commitEditing` and `-save:`. Using the new API, you wrap this code inside a block passed to `-performBlock:`. If you are running a fetch request or refreshing an object with the latest data from the store, however, then you likely want to have that take effect synchronously, so you wrap that call in a block passed to `-performBlockAndWait:` instead.

Main-Thread Queueing

The third and last threading mechanism makes your context use a shared queue targeting the application's main queue. This means that, so long as you remember to use `-performBlock:` and `-performBlockAndWait:` properly, *every* Core Data operation will be performed on the main thread. This makes a lot of things potentially safer—you can pull data and update your UI inside a `-performBlock:` call without worrying about touching the UI from a background thread. On the downside, it means that any Core Data operations that take a long time will effectively hang your application, since the main thread can't process anything else while Core Data is busy. On the other hand, when your user interface is driven by a managed object context, it is much better to have that context be bound to the main thread explicitly, since the user interface might need to be updated, and such updates *must* take place on the main thread.

Hierarchical Contexts

One last change introduced to assist with multi-threading issues is that of *parent* and *child* contexts, available to any contexts that implement one of the queue-based threading policies. The idea is that you can create a new managed object context and set another context as its parent. Any operations on this child context no longer talk directly to the persistent store—instead the request is sent to the parent context. If you fetch some objects from a child, then those objects will be returned from the parent context, potentially without even performing any I/O to talk to the persistent store. Saving your child context likewise just pushes its changes up to its parent—nothing gets written out to disk until the topmost parent is told to save.

There's a common pattern with detail editors in Core Data applications: when you go into edit mode, you create a new managed object context referring to the same data. This is then used as the source context for the editor user interface. When the editor is saved, the context is sent a `-save:` message and the data is written to the persistent store. The main context then intercepts a notification that another context saved and updates itself by refreshing any cached or live objects from the persistent store to ensure it has the latest values.

On the other hand, if the user cancels their edits, the context is sent a -reset message instead to discard all unsaved changes and is ultimately itself discarded as the editor closes.

Under the new hierarchical system, this becomes both simpler and faster. When you create your editor's object context, you simply set the main context as its parent. Then you make changes as before and send either -reset or -save: to the context when the user cancels or confirms the changes. If you save the changes, however, those changes are just pushed directly into the main context in a thread-safe manner (based on the two contexts' respective threading policies). Nothing is written to persistent storage (yet), and the main context doesn't need to perform a potentially expensive fetch operation to get the latest data—it's all happened in memory, where it's nice and fast.

Of course, your next step is likely to send -save: to the main context to get the changes written out, too. But if you were looking at a deeply nested editing flow, where for example multiple screens might slide in on an iPhone, then you could give each new editor (or subeditor, if you prefer) its own context with its parent set to the previous screen's context. Then as you save your changes in the last editor, they get pushed upwards to the next editor, and those to the next editor, and so on until you reach the top of the stack and save the completed item to the persistent store.

Or, if you like, you could make lots of edits and decide at the last minute to cancel everything. Because each editor screen has its own context and is simply saving its own context into its parent, even after a few saves from subeditors nothing has yet reached the main store, and it can all still be discarded easily. If you were doing this the older way, writing each one out to disk and having the main context update itself each time a save occurred, then you would have to resort to using a lot of undo-management to revert all your changes back to their initial state. This way, nothing on-disk is changed until *everything* has been accepted.

Implementing Thread-Safe Contexts

To cement all this, tweak your application delegate's methods to create the main context using the main-queue threading policy and to work with it in an appropriate manner. Go to APAppDelegate.m in the Project Navigator and open it. Find the managedObjectContext method, and replace the NSManagedObject creation with the bolded line from Listing 8-11.

Listing 8-11. Setting a Context's Threading Policy

```
_managedObjectContext=[[NSManagedObjectContext alloc] initWithConcurrencyType:
NSMainQueueConcurrencyType];
 [_managedObjectContext setPersistentStoreCoordinator:coordinator];
```

Next, take a look at the save and terminate handlers. The saveAction: method is easy to change; add the bolded lines from Listing 8-12.

Listing 8-12. Saving a Context Through a Private Queue

```
- (IBAction)saveAction:(id)sender
{
    [[self managedObjectContext] performBlock:^{
        NSError *error=nil;
```

```
        if (![[self managedObjectContext] commitEditing]) {
            NSLog(@"%@:%@ unable to commit editing before saving",
                [self class], NSStringFromSelector(_cmd));
        }

        if (![[self managedObjectContext] save:&error]) {
            dispatch_async(dispatch_get_main_queue(), ^{
                [[NSApplication sharedApplication] presentError:error];
            });
        }
    }];
}
```

Notice that the error presentation call to NSApplication was dispatched to the main queue since it's ultimately a UI call and should always take place on the main thread. You told your context to use the main queue, which runs on the main thread, but sometimes the system optimizes things by simply synchronizing against the main thread but running the code on the current thread. You'll likely see this if you call dispatch_sync() passing a queue that currently has no work scheduled—the block just executes immediately and on the current thread. As such, it is a very good idea to *always* wrap UI work within a block in a dispatch_async() to the main queue.

The terminate method is a little more involved. You're not just dispatching some operation; you're checking the result each time and potentially returning from the function itself. This means you need to use -performBlockAndWait:, as shown in Listing 8-13. Again, the new lines are bolded.

Listing 8-13. Handling Termination with a Queue-Based Context, Part 1

```
- (NSApplicationTerminateReply)applicationShouldTerminate:(NSApplication *)sender
{
    // Save changes in the application's managed object context before the
    // application terminates.

    if (!_managedObjectContext) {
        return NSTerminateNow;
    }

    __block NSApplicationTerminateReply reply=NSTerminateLater;
    [[self managedObjectContext] performBlockAndWait: ^{
        if (![[self managedObjectContext] commitEditing]) {
            NSLog(@"%@:%@ unable to commit editing to terminate", [self class],
                NSStringFromSelector(_cmd));
            reply=NSTerminateCancel;
        }
    }];

    if ( reply !=NSTerminateLater )
        return reply;

    [[self managedObjectContext] performBlockAndWait: ^{
        if (![[self managedObjectContext] hasChanges]) {
            reply=NSTerminateNow;
        }
    }];
```

```
if ( reply !=NSTerminateLater )
    return reply;
```

The second part of the method is a little more involved. If the save fails, then the error is presented synchronously. You need to perform this routine on the main thread, but here you run into a problem: you're already blocking the main thread, waiting for *this* block to return.

Luckily, the NSApplication class is ready for applications that need to determine whether termination should be permitted in an asynchronous fashion. In these cases, the return value from -applicationShouldTerminate: would be NSTerminateLater, which you've already seen in Listing 8-12. Then, when a decision has been made, you send -replyToApplicationShouldTerminate: passing a BOOL indicating that either YES it should terminate or NO it should not.

So this gives you a fairly simple procedure: you enqueue the save call using the normal -performBlock: method, which will return immediately. You then return NSTerminateLater. When the block runs, it will attempt to save. As each circumstance comes to pass, you reach a decision on whether to allow the application to terminate, and call -replyToApplicationShouldTerminate: with an appropriate argument. Listing 8-14 shows how this turns out.

Listing 8-14. Handling Termination with a Queue-Based Context, Part 2

```
[[self managedObjectContext] performBlock: ^{
    NSError *error=nil;
    if (![[self managedObjectContext] save:&error]) {
        // failed to save the context-- jump back to the main thread
        // to perform UI work to make the decision. This can be either sync
        // or async, but async is generally a better idea.
        dispatch_async(dispatch_get_main_queue(), ^{
            // Customize this code block to include application-specific
            // recovery steps.
            BOOL result=[sender presentError:error];
            if (result) {
                // cancel termination, as before
                [sender replyToApplicationShouldTerminate: NO];
                return;
            }

            // Present a confirmation dialog to the user, and let them
            // make the decision for us.
            NSString *question=NSLocalizedString(
                @"Could not save changes while quitting. Quit anyway?",
                @"Quit without saves error question message");
            NSString *info=NSLocalizedString(
                @"Quitting now will lose any changes you have made since the last"
                @" successful save", @"Quit without saves error question info");
            NSString *quitButton=NSLocalizedString(@"Quit anyway",
                                          @"Quit anyway button title");
            NSString *cancelButton=NSLocalizedString(@"Cancel",
                                          @"Cancel button title");
            NSAlert *alert=[[NSAlert alloc] init];
            [alert setMessageText:question];
```

```
                    [alert setInformativeText:info];
                    [alert addButtonWithTitle:quitButton];
                    [alert addButtonWithTitle:cancelButton];

                    NSInteger answer=[alert runModal];

                    // if the answer is NSAlertDefaultReturn then they clicked
                    // the Quit button.
                    [sender replyToApplicationShouldTerminate:
                                                    (answer == NSAlertDefaultReturn)];
                });
            } else {
                // the context saved successfully, so we can terminate
                [sender replyToApplicationShouldTerminate: YES];
            }
        }];

        // we've dispatched an async save operation-- we'll decide if we can terminate
        // once we know how that turns out.
        return NSTerminateLater;
```

There you are—your application delegate is now fully enrolled in the private queue threading policy!

Populating Your Store

You need some data in your data store, and we haven't yet covered the general use of managed objects yet—creation, deletion, and so on. So let's cover that before you start working with user interfaces.

Address Book Data

This is an address book application, so it seems appropriate to load it with data from your own address books, doesn't it? That should make for a suitable set of test data. The way to read the data from the Contacts application (or Address Book to those of you not yet running OS X 10.8) is to use the API published within AddressBook.framework. This provides a nice Objective-C API for enumerating people and their associated data. There's a lot more in the Address Book system than you currently have in your data model, but that needn't stop you—you can be selective about what you import.

Start off simply: you only want to import this data once, so in your application launch routine, simply check to see if there are any Person objects in your data store. If there are, then you're good. If not, create an importer object to get it filled out. Find applicationDidFinishLaunching: in APAppDelegate.m and replace its contents with the code from Listing 8-15.

Listing 8-15. Checking Whether an Initial Data Import Is Required

```
- (void)applicationDidFinishLaunching:(NSNotification *)aNotification
{
    NSFetchRequest *request=[[NSFetchRequest alloc] initWithEntityName:@"Person"];
    // simple request: we just want all Person objects, so no predicates
```

```
    // we actually only want to know how many there are, so we use this special
    // method on NSManagedObjectContext:
    NSManagedObjectContext * context=[self managedObjectContext];
    [context performBlock: ^{
        // we don't care about the error-- if something goes wrong, we still
        // need to pull in some data
        NSUInteger count=[context countForFetchRequest: request error: NULL];
        if ( count == 0 )
        {
            // back out to the main thread-- don't hog the context's queue
            dispatch_async(dispatch_get_main_queue(), ^{
                [self importAddressBookData];
            });
        }
    }];
}
```

The -importAddressBookData method referenced here will be written soon; first though, you need something to do the importing itself. Right-click (or Control-click, or two-finger-click) on APApplicationDelegate.m in the Project Navigator and from the pop-up menu choose *New File* to create a new file.

In the sheet that appears, ensure that the Cocoa section in the OS X group is selected in the panel on the left, and select Objective-C class from the document list on the right. Click *Next* and type a name for this class: APAddressBookImporter. In the pop-up list, choose NSObject as its superclass. Click *Next*, and click *Choose* to select the default location to place the new files. Now select APAddressBookImporter.h in the Project Navigator to open the header file.

You're going to use hierarchical contexts to manage these imports. As a result, when you create an importer, you need to hand it a parent context. Then the only other public interface you need is a form of "go do it" method, ideally one that runs asynchronously and takes a block as an argument through which it can report completion (whether success or failure). The interface for the class can be seen in Listing 8-16.

Listing 8-16. The Address Book Importer Interface

```
#import < Foundation/Foundation.h>
#import < CoreData/CoreData.h>

@interface APAddressBookImporter : NSObject
- (id)initWithParentObjectContext:(NSManagedObjectContext *)parent;
- (void)beginImportingWithCompletion:(void (^)(NSError *error)) completion;
@end
```

Now select APAddressBookImporter.m in the Project Navigator to open the implementation file. The first order of business here is to implement the initializer; it will need to create a new managed object context with the private queue thread policy and assign its parent context. Along with that, place the instance variables inside the @implementation block since they're not exposed through any public API. You also want to be sure to import the < AddressBook/AddressBook.h> header and those for your model classes at the top of the file. Your implementation should now look something like Listing 8-17.

Listing 8-17. Initializing the Importer

```objc
#import "APAddressBookImporter.h"
#import <AddressBook/AddressBook.h>

#import "Person.h"
#import "MailingAddress.h"
#import "EmailAddress.h"
#import "PhoneNumber.h"

@implementation APAddressBookImporter
{
    NSManagedObjectContext * _context;
}

- (id) initWithParentObjectContext: (NSManagedObjectContext *) parent
{
    self = [super init];
    if ( self == nil )
        return ( nil );

    _context = [[NSManagedObjectContext alloc] initWithConcurrencyType:
                                            NSPrivateQueueConcurrencyType];
    [_context setParentContext: parent];
    // because it has a parent, it doesn't need a persistentStoreCoordinator

    return ( self );
}

@end
```

You also want to keep hold of the completion block passed into the
beginImportingWithCompletion: method. The best way to handle this is to define a property with
a storage type of copy and to use that to store and access the block. This isn't part of the public
API, and properties can only be declared in the public interface or a class extension, so it looks
like you must use the latter. Place the code from Listing 8-18 above your @implementation block.

Listing 8-18. The Completion Handler Property

```objc
@interface APAddressBookImporter ()
@property (nonatomic, copy) void (^completionHandler)(NSError *);
@end
```

The syntax may look a little weird, but if you go back to the early chapters and look at the
sections on function-pointer and block syntax, you'll see that it's actually correct: the type is
void, and everything that follows it is the name. The braces in there simply denote that it's a
callable block of code.

The actual work of importing is done in the background; you accomplish this using dispatch_
async(), and everything else you do will take place within that single block. Unfortunately, the
Address Book API expects that anything loaded from a single ABAddressBook instance will be
used on the same thread (hm, that sounds… familiar…) so you won't parallelize this further.

In APAddressBookImporter.m, place the code from Listing 8-19 just below your initializer.

Listing 8-19. The Start of the Importer Method

```
- (void) beginImportingWithCompletion: (void (^)(NSError *)) completion
{
    self.completionHandler = completion;

    dispatch_async(dispatch_get_global_queue(DISPATCH_QUEUE_PRIORITY_DEFAULT, 0), ^{
        ABAddressBook * addressBook = [ABAddressBook addressBook];
    });
}
```

You can see that the first thing you do here is store the completion block in your corresponding property. Since the property was declared using the copy keyword, this will send a -copy message to the block, ensuring that it now lives on the heap. You dispatch your work to a background queue and then return immediately.

Within the work block, you have only one statement so far: you fetch an address book reference from the AddressBook API.

You'll be creating lots of objects from your own model in this block, and creating new managed object instances requires a reference to the NSEntityDescription of the corresponding model entity. This is quite a long line of code, so it's useful to get this out of the way early on and pack the entities into local variables; this helps keep your logic code cleaner and free of potentially space-consuming boilerplate as you enumerate ABPerson objects, creating your own to match.

Enter the code from Listing 8-20 into the work block.

Listing 8-20. Enumerating ABPerson Records

```
// get our entity descriptions ready to use to create objects
NSEntityDescription *entity = [NSEntityDescription entityForName: @"Person"
                                      inManagedObjectContext: _context];

for ( ABPerson * abPerson in [addressBook people] )
{
    // Create a new Person object in our own database
    Person * myPerson = [[Person alloc] initWithEntity: entity
                        insertIntoManagedObjectContext: _context];

    // now fetch some values from the Address Book for this person
    myPerson.firstName = [abPerson valueForProperty: kABFirstNameProperty];
    myPerson.lastName = [abPerson valueForProperty: kABLastNameProperty];
}
```

You've now begun enumerating all the people in the system address book and have copied their first and last names into a new instance of your Person managed object class. Next you need to copy across any e-mail addresses, phone numbers, and mailing addresses, creating the appropriate managed objects for each. Once that's done, you can save the context, pushing this person into the main context, where it will show up in the user interface (this is coming, we promise!). This save operation is, naturally, going to be performed within a -performBlockAndWait: call to keep it nicely synchronized.

Add the code from Listing 8-21 to the bottom of the for loop. You'll add the methods used in this snippet very shortly.

Listing 18-21. Importing Other Attributes and Saving the Context

```
// email addresses
[self importEmailsFromABPerson: abPerson toMine: myPerson];

// phone numbers
[self importPhonesFromABPerson: abPerson toMine: myPerson];

// mailing addresses
[self importAddressesFromABPerson: abPerson toMine: myPerson];

// now save the contents of the context and/or clean up, in a
// synchronized fashion
[_context performBlockAndWait: ^{
    // if the person is valid, save it. Otherwise, reset the context.
    if ( [myPerson validateForUpdate: NULL] == NO )
    {
        [_context reset];
    }
    else
    {
        NSError * error = nil;
        if ( [_context save: &error] == NO )
        {
            // zap this record and its related objects
            [_context deleteObject: myPerson];
        }
    }
}];
```

You're being especially proactive here. You send a -validateForUpdate: message to the person object before attempting to save to break out validation errors from anything else that might prevent a successful save. Partly this is for reasons of *intense paranoi—*er, *safety*. Partly it's because, since this data has been copied directly from an external source that doesn't necessarily have the same validation criteria, it's useful to personally make sure everything checks out nicely in that regard.

If the validation fails, you will discard all unsaved changes by sending the -reset message to your managed object context. This will dump anything it has in its caches and make it refer back to the persistent store (or in this case its parent context) for any and all data.

Now for your address entities—these are broken out into their own importer functions. In the interest of brevity, we'll show one in Listing 8-22, which should provide enough information for you to write the others on your own. If you get stuck, the full implementation is in the Core Data Contacts sample project.

Listing 8-22. Importing E-mail Addresses

```
- (void)importEmailsFromABPerson:(ABPerson *)abPerson toMine:(Person *)myPerson
{
    NSEntityDescription *entity = [NSEntityDescription entityForName:@"EmailAddress"
                                              inManagedObjectContext: _context];
    ABMultiValue * abEmails = [abPerson valueForProperty: kABEmailProperty];
```

```
for ( NSUInteger i=0, max=[abEmails count]; i<max; i++ )
{
    NSString * label=[abEmails labelAtIndex: i];
    NSString * email=[abEmails valueAtIndex: i];

    // skip any weird entries which won't fit with our model validation
    if ( label == nil || email == nil )
        continue;
    EmailAddress * e=[[EmailAddress alloc] initWithEntity: entity
                            insertIntoManagedObjectContext: _context];
    e.label=ABLocalizedPropertyOrLabel(label);
    e.email=email;

    // rather than call the 'add to relationship' methods on myPerson,
    // we'll just set the to-one relationship on the email, which
    // does the same thing
    e.person=myPerson;

    // ensure it's valid -- if not, delete it
    if ( [e validateForUpdate: NULL] == NO )
    {
        [_context performBlockAndWait: ^{
            [_context deleteObject: e];
        }];
        continue;
    }
}
}
```

Lastly, return to APAppDelegate.m and create the -importAddressBookData method referenced earlier. You need to create a new APAddressBookImporter object and call its -beginImportingWithCompletion: method, handling any errors reported as appropriate. You also need to save the object context at this point—remember that the importer's child context only pushed data up to its parent when it saved; it didn't actually cause the data to be written out to persistent storage. The complete method can be seen in Listing 8-23.

Listing 8-23. Running the Importer

```
- (void)importAddressBookData
{
    APAddressBookImporter * importer=[[APAddressBookImporter alloc]
initWithParentObjectContext: self.managedObjectContext];
    [importer beginImportingWithCompletion: ^(NSError *error) {
        if ( error !=nil )
        {
            [NSApp presentError: error];
        }

        if ( [self.managedObjectContext hasChanges] )
        {
            [self.managedObjectContext performBlock: ^{
                NSError * saveError=nil;
```

```
                if ( [self.managedObjectContext save: &saveError] == NO )
                    [NSApp presentError: saveError];
            }];
        }
    }];
}
```

The User Interface

Next you want to be able to view, browse, and edit your contact data through a user interface. This begins with the file `MainMenu.xib`; select this in the Project Navigator to open the interface editor, where you will be presented with the default menu and window seen in Figure 8-5.

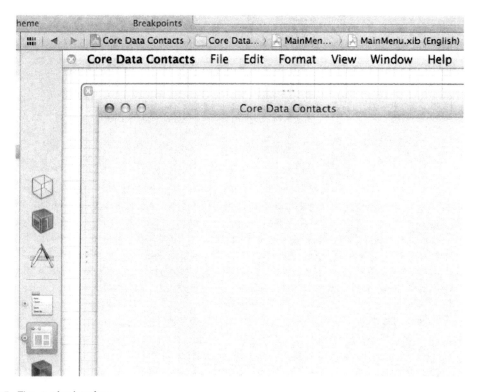

Figure 8-5. *The starting interface*

The user interface is split into three primary components: a list of people; a tabbed pane for browsing lists of a single person's phone numbers, e-mails, or addresses; and a search field across the top of the window for filtering the contents of the list of people.

The actual contents of these lists will be managed using *controller objects,* specifically an `NSArrayController` to manage the list of people and three more for each of the address types you'll display. These will all be hooked into the `NSManagedObjectContext` owned by the application delegate, which is visible in the interface editor as the topmost of the two blue cubes in the object list at the left of the editor.

To create these controllers, look to the Object Library and select "Objects and Controllers" from the pop-up menu. Scroll down a little to find the Array Controller object and drag four of these onto the object palette to the left of the editor, below the existing blue cubes representing other objects in the nib.

At the moment they all have identical names: Array Controller. This isn't very descriptive, so change them: at the bottom left of the interface editor is a button with what looks like a common Play symbol, shown in Figure 8-6. This replaces the simple palette on the left of the editor with a full document outline.

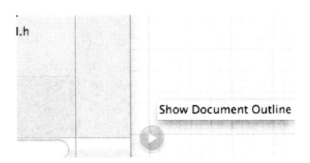

Figure 8-6. The Document Outline button

Now you can change the names of your array controllers. Simply select each one and then either click its name a second time (*not* a double-click) or press the Enter key. Name the four controllers People Controller, Phones Controller, Emails Controller, and Addresses Controller, respectively.

> **Note** Due to a bug in Xcode, the names will seem to revert back to their original state when you press Enter to complete your edit. This is just a visual flaw, however: close and reopen the Document Outline and you'll see that your names have indeed been applied.

Wire them up to the data from the managed object context, starting with the People Controller. Select that controller and in the Attributes Inspector change its mode to *Entity Name*. Below that, type Person as the entity name itself. Also check the *Prepares Content* and *Auto Rearrange Content* checkboxes, then switch to the Bindings Inspector.

You need to bind one thing: the Managed Object Context. The actual content of the array is fetched automatically from this context: it fetches all instances of the Person entity from the store, so you don't need to worry about the Content Set or Content Array bindings for this controller.

Bind the controller's Managed Object Context parameter to the app delegate's managedObjectContext property, and then repeat this step for the other three controllers. You're not done with those controllers yet, though: in their case, you want to bind their content to depend upon the currently selected Person object.

For each of the other three controllers, change their attributes in the Attribute Inspector. They should all be set up in the same way as the People Controller, but their entity names will be different: PhoneNumber, Email, and MailingAddress, respectively.

To hook up their content, go to the Bindings Inspector and find the Content Set binding. Bind it to the People Controller, with a *Controller Key* of selection and a *Model Key Path* of phoneNumbers, emailAddressess, or mailingAddresses as appropriate. The inspector should offer to automatically complete these keys for you. Also ensure that the *"Deletes Objects On Remove"* checkbox is checked—you want the controller to actually remove items from the context, not just remove their references within the array controller.

Sort Ordering

You now need to ensure that the contents of these array controllers are sorted properly, and that can also be handled using bindings: specifically, each controller's Sort Descriptors binding. You need something to bind them to, however, so you need to add some more properties to the APAppDelegate object. The list of people will be sorted using lastName then firstName, and the addresses will be ordered based on their label. All comparisons will be case-insensitive.

Add the code from Listing 8-24 to APAppDelegate.h.

Listing 8-24. The Sort Descriptor Properties

```
@property (readonly, strong, nonatomic) NSArray * personSortDescriptors;
@property (readonly, strong, nonatomic) NSArray * labelSortDescriptors;
```

The implementation goes into the -awakeFromNib method of APAppDelegate.m. This method, if it exists, is called on every object that is referenced somehow in a nib file once the nib has been completely loaded and all connections and bindings are set up. Since the App Delegate itself is created within MainMenu.xib, this object is no exception. However, at this point the UI has already been bound to any properties, so changing their values alone won't do anything. You could define the properties as settable and use the default setters, true, but for the sake of instruction you're going to manually fire the key-value observation methods for the properties as you create the backing variables, which will let the bound elements in the UI know to update their values. The code can be seen in Listing 8-25; the lines in bold are the KVO notifications.

Listing 8-25. Creating the Sort Descriptors

```
- (void) awakeFromNib
{
    SEL compareSelector = @selector(caseInsensitiveCompare:);
    if ( _personSortDescriptors == nil )
    {
        NSSortDescriptor * sortLast = nil, * sortFirst = nil;
        sortLast = [NSSortDescriptor sortDescriptorWithKey: @"lastName"
                                                 ascending: YES
                                                  selector: compareSelector];
        sortFirst = [NSSortDescriptor sortDescriptorWithKey: @"firstName"
                                                  ascending: YES
                                                   selector: compareSelector];
```

```
        [self willChangeValueForKey: @"personSortDescriptors"];
        _personSortDescriptors=@[sortLast, sortFirst];
        [self didChangeValueForKey: @"personSortDescriptors"];
    }
    if ( _labelSortDescriptors == nil )
    {
        NSSortDescriptor * sortLabel=nil;
        sortLabel=[NSSortDescriptor sortDescriptorWithKey: @"label"
                                           ascending: YES
                                            selector: compareSelector];
        [self willChangeValueForKey: @"labelSortDescriptors"];
        _labelSortDescriptors=@[sortLabel];
        [self didChangeValueForKey: @"labelSortDescriptors"];
    }
}
```

Now that these properties are set up correctly, return to MainMenu.xib and select the People Controller. Open the Bindings Inspector and bind its *sort descriptors* to the App Delegate object, with a Model Key Path of personSortDescriptors; this value should auto-complete for you if everything has been done properly. Repeat this for each of the other three controllers, but in their case you will want to bind to the App Delegate's labelSortDescriptors property instead.

Laying It Out

Your next task is to lay out your interface within the window. As mentioned, there will be a list of people to the left, a context-sensitive tabbed pane for browsing addresses to the right, with a search field above. Start by placing the search field across the top: in the Object Library, choose *Controls* from the pop-up menu, then scroll down the list of objects until you find the Search Field object. Drag that from the library onto the top of the window, letting it snap into place with the guidelines at the top left of the window, as seen in Figure 8-7.

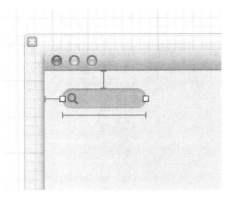

Figure 8-7. Positioning the search field

Click and drag on the rightmost handle (the small square) to stretch the field such that it snaps into place on the opposite side of the window. If you resize the window in the interface editor now, the search field should resize with it.

To make this take effect, bind it to the People Controller using a neat feature of the NSSearchField class: it generates a complete NSPredicate from its contents, and that can be bound directly to the filterPredicate property of an array controller. So, with the search field still selected, open the Bindings Inspector and pop open the Predicate setting. Bind it to the People Controller, with a controller key of filterPredicate (this should be set automatically). Scroll down slightly, and change the Predicate Format value to 'fullName contains[c] $value'.

It would also be nice if the table would change while you are typing, not just when you press the Enter key. To enable this, open the Attributes Inspector and check the *"Searches Immediately"* option.

The other two components of the interface will be placed within a *split view*. This type of view implements the frequently-seen behavior of placing a drag handle between two views that allows you to resize one at the expense of the other. Examples include the sidebar in the Finder application or the source lists in iTunes or Mail.

The split view can be found within the *Layout Views* section of the Object Library; you're looking for the Vertical Split View object. Drag that onto the window, snapping it into place below the search field and then resizing it so that it snaps to the guides just inside the window's edges. Click to select the handle in the middle of the view and drag it over to the left a little, so the leftmost view occupies about • of the total area. Next, open the Attributes Inspector and change the view's style to *Thick Divider*. The results should look something like that seen in Figure 8-8.

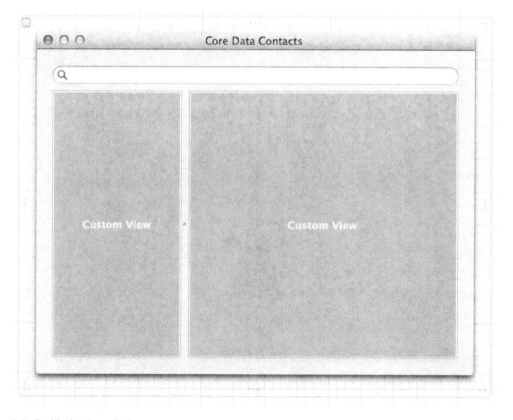

Figure 8-8. Positioning the split view

The left pane will contain a table view, and the right pane a tab view. To set up the leftmost, switch to the *Data Views* section of the Object Library and drag a Table View object onto the Custom View on the left of the splitter. Position and resize it such that it completely covers its parent view—don't snap to the guides a little inside; snap to the absolute edges, so none of the Custom View object can be seen. You may find that you need to adjust the split view's splitter a little to be able to reach all the resize handles on the table view.

> **Note**   While the interface editor ordinarily obeys auto-layout constraints while resizing items, this doesn't appear to hold true for the subviews of a split view—moving the splitter doesn't cause the contents of its subviews to resize automatically, which can be quite annoying. If you choose Simulate *Document* from the *Editor* menu, however, you'll see that your table view does indeed behave as expected.

Now that the table view is in place, there are a few changes to make. Select the table view by clicking it twice (the first click will select the enclosing scroll view). You can verify what you've selected by looking at the top of the Attributes Inspector: if it says scroll view, you need to select again.

There are quite a few attributes to change here. First of all, you only want one column. You also want to uncheck the *Headers* and *Reordering* checkboxes. In the next section, change the highlight mode to *Source List*, and in the section below that, only the *Type Select* option should be checked. Figure 8-9 shows how this should appear.

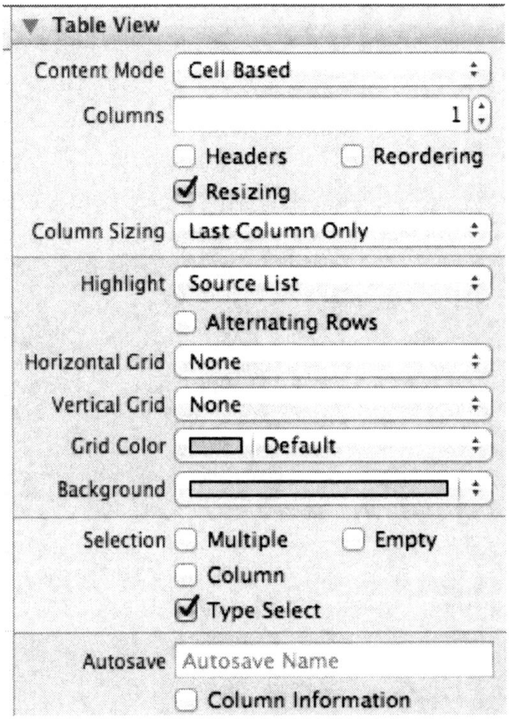

Figure 8-9. Table view attributes

Now, with the table view still selected, switch to the Bindings Inspector. There are two items you want to bind here: the table's content and its selection indices, both of which will be bound to properties of the `People Controller`. Pop open the Content binding and select the `People Controller`, clicking the checkbox to bind it. The default controller key of `arrangedObjects` is what you want, so you don't need to make any more changes.

To bind the selection indices, pop open Selection Indexes[4] and again choose the `People Controller`, but this time enter `selectionIndexes` as the controller key. Setting this binding means that the array controller's `selection` property (used as the source of your other array controllers' content) correctly reflects the item selected within the table. You've already disabled multiple selection on the table itself in the Attributes Inspector, so the table view will ensure that only one item at a time is selected, and that one item is always selected.

The last task on this table view is to bind the cells' values. Since this is a cell-based table view, this is done through the `table` column. Click once on the table view again to select the table column view (again, check with the Attributes Inspector that you're looking at the Table Column object).

First of all, ensure that the column is as wide as the table view by dragging its resize-handle to the right. In the Attributes Inspector, ensure that the *Editable* checkbox is set—this will allow your users to edit their contacts' names by directly editing the values within the table view. In the Bindings Inspector, open up the Value setting and bind it to the `People Controller`. The controller key of `arrangedObjects` is again correct, but this time enter a model key path of `fullName`.

The people list is now set up. If you launch the application, you should see all your contacts listed there, and you should be able to select and edit each person's name and dynamically filter the list.

Adding and Removing People

Now you can see and edit people's names, but you can't add new ones or remove any existing entries. To do that, you need to add a couple of buttons that will target the `People Controller`'s `-add:` and `-remove:` action methods. To do *that*, you must make some room below the split view: select it and drag its bottom resize handle upwards—its content will be resized automatically for you.

In the Object Library, from the *Controls* section, drag a Gradient Button into the bottom-left corner of the window. In the Attributes Inspector, delete the button's Title and enter `NSAddTemplate` into the Image field (it should auto-complete this name for you). Now drag the right resize handle to make it an appropriate size—22 points should look about right. With the button still selected, press ⌘-D to duplicate it. Place the duplicate to the right of the first button. It will snap into place the standard distance away, but let's change that. Open the Size inspector and scroll down to see the new button's constraints. Click on the cog icon to the right of the *"Leading Space to:"* constraint and choose *Select and Edit*. Uncheck the *Standard*

---

[4]Apple frequently uses "indexes" in their method names. The writer in me refuses to accept that, however, so I always use the *correct* word—indices (grumble-grumble-mutter).

checkbox and enter a value of 0. This actually doesn't look very nice—there appears to be a thick line between the two buttons, caused by the two borders lying adjacent to one another. To fix this, set the constraint's value to −1 instead to make them overlap by the width of that border, resulting in a much cleaner appearance.

> **Note**   Your humble author encountered a rather annoying bug when adjusting constraints manually within the interface editor: every time I changed something, the constraint would be de-selected, meaning I would have to go and manually select it again to make a further change. If this happens to you, I'd advise not using the stepper control to bring the value down from 8 to −1, as it will de-select it once on every click. I sincerely hope that this bug is fixed by the time you read this.

This second button will be used to remove items, so open the Attributes Editor and change the image value to NSRemoveTemplate, which again should be auto-completed for you.

To hook up the buttons to their actions, hold down the Control key and drag from each button onto the People Controller in the document outline. A menu will pop up at the destination of the drag, allowing you to select an action: for the Add button, choose -add:, and for the Remove button, choose -remove:. Lastly, pull the bottom of the split view down until it snaps into place just above the buttons.

Run your application again, and you should be able to add and delete people with impunity. Note that new people will start out with the default names you specified for the firstName and lastName attributes of the Person entity within the object model.

Viewing Addresses

You've already set up bindings to enable interaction with people's addresses, e-mails, and phone numbers—now you're going to add the user interface for those items.

Find the Tab View object in the Object Library's *Layout Views* section and drag one into the right-hand pane of the split view. Like the table view, resize it to completely fill its parent view. In the interface editor, it will look as though it's being clipped, but if you launch the application or simulate the interface you'll see that it actually draws nicely.

In the Attributes Inspector, set the number of tabs to three. To change the title of each tab, double-click on it in the interface editor to edit it in-place. Name your tabs, from left to right, "Phones," "Emails," and "Addresses."

You switch between tabs in the editor by selecting the tab view and then clicking once on a tab. Do this now to select the Phones tab. In each tab, add a table view displaying all the addresses of a particular type, bound to the appropriate array controller. You also want to be able to add and remove addresses, so you need to add the same Add and Remove buttons within each tab, too.

Start by adding these buttons in the simplest way possible: select the ones at the bottom-left of the window and duplicate them by pressing ⌘-D. Then, with the two duplicates still selected, drag them inside the tab view and snap them into place at the bottom-left of the subview. Set their actions by dragging from them to the appropriate array controller and connecting them to the `-add:` and `-remove:` actions on that controller. Repeat these steps to add buttons to the Emails and Addresses tabs.

Next come the table views: drag one into each tab, filling the area above the Add/Remove buttons, snapping into place on the inner guides for the tab view's edges. For each table view, open the Attributes Inspector and set its content mode to *View Based*. Give them all two columns, and uncheck the *Headers* and *Reordering* checkboxes. Also ensure that multiple-selection and column-selection are disabled. As with the People table, bind their Content and Selection Indexes to the appropriate controllers' `arrangedObjects` and `selectionIndexes` properties.

Your interface should now look something like that in Figure 8-10.

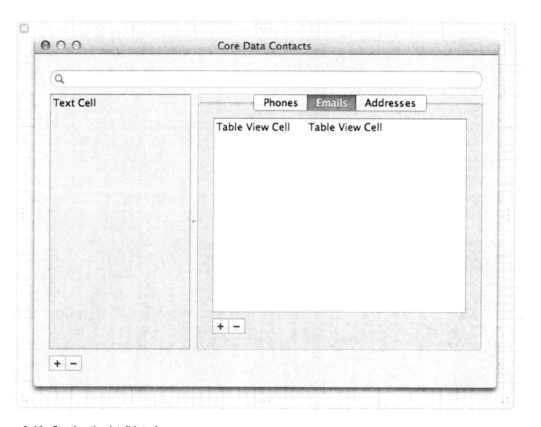

Figure 8-10. Starting the detail interface

As these tables are view-based, their setup is a little different than the one you made earlier. Each cell is actually a view in its own right, and the table has given each cell an `objectValue` corresponding to the contents of its array controller's `arrangedObjects` property. Each cell then contains views whose contents you can bind based on their cell view's `objectValue` property, which will in this case be an instance of the `PhoneNumber`, `EmailAddress`, or `MailingAddress` classes.

The first column, to the left, will contain the labels for these addresses. To de-emphasize these a little, change the size of the provided text fields from Regular to Small. Select the text field (you need to either click on it a few times or drill down directly using the Document Outline) and open the Size Inspector. Pull down the *Size* menu in the *Control* section and choose *Small*. Now switch to the Attributes Inspector to alter the nature of this field a little.

The label will work best if it's aligned to the right, placing the label text up against the value. The buttons next to the *Alignment* option here will let you make that change. Additionally, rather than give every new field a default value of Table View Cell, delete its *Title* property and type "Label" into its *Placeholder* property.

You also want to be able to edit labels in-place in a manner similar to the `people` table. To do this, you need to change the behavior of the text field: further down the Attributes Inspector, pull down the Behavior menu and choose Editable. This will give it the exact same behavior as the user names you were able to edit earlier.

The final step is to bind the value of the text field to the appropriate value from the data store: in the Bindings Inspector, bind the Value property to Table Cell View, with a Model Key Path of `objectValue.label`. The editor will likely claim that it can't find any completions and place an exclamation mark in the Model Key Path's field, but you can safely ignore that.

You might notice that the label is now positioned a little higher within its cell than would be ideal—its baseline doesn't align nicely with the baseline of the larger text in the next column. Fortunately, Cocoa Autolayout makes this nice and easy to deal with. *Unfortunately*, this can't be done in the interface editor. You can select both text fields easily enough, but the editor doesn't seem to recognize that it can create constraints between these two items. For now, take the easy route and just move the label field down a little until it looks better: with the field selected, use the cursor keys on your keyboard to move it down a point at a time until you like the look of it. I found that two points lower did the trick. Cocoa Autolayout will see that it stays in that vertical position as the parent views resize. Again, repeat this for all three tables.

On to the value columns: you'll be doing things one way for the Phone and Email tabs, and something a little more complicated for the Addresses tab.

For Phones and Emails, you won't have to change much, as the control size and layout are already how you want them. Replace their titles with placeholders of "Phone Number" and "Email," respectively, and set their behavior to *Editable* as before. Then bind their values to their Table Cell Views' `objectValue.phoneNumber` or `objectValue.email` as appropriate. You're now done with the first two types of address information. If you run the application, you should be able to browse that information properly, similar to that shown in Figure 8-11.

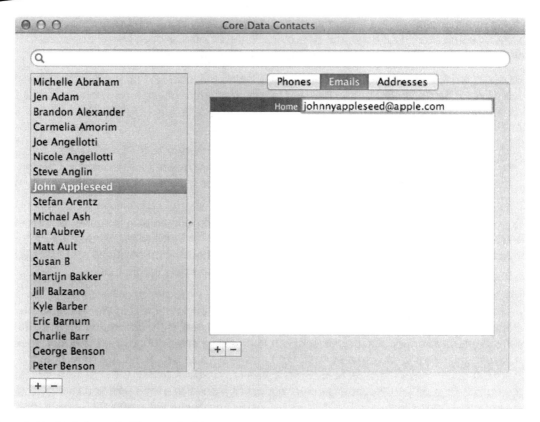

Figure 8-11. Displaying and editing e-mail addresses

A More Complex Cell View

The cell view for the MailingAddress type is a little more complicated because there are plenty of different properties to display and edit. This means that you need a significantly larger cell with lots of text fields, each bound to a different key path below its table view cell's `objectValue` property.

First things first: select the address value cell and drag its bottom resize handle downwards to make some room. I found 97 points to be the sweet spot. You then need to move the text field upwards again, since it's centered vertically and horizontally within the cell view—align it with the baseline of the label field as before.

This will serve to display the `street` property from the address, but since streets sometimes contain two lines, make it a little taller. Set the placeholder for the field to a two-line value to help determine the correct size. To enter multiple lines, press the Option key while pressing Enter.

For the other components, simply duplicate this one and resize it back to its default height of 17 points. Create three duplicates, one below the other, for the `city`, `region`, and `country` properties. Use the Constraint controls to pin the vertical spacing between each field to be two points in height.

The city and country fields will stretch to fill the width of their cells, but make the region field a little narrower and place another text field (another duplicate will do) to its right to display the postalCode property. Make this about 70 points wide and position it aligned to the right edge of the cell. Drag the region field's right edge until it snaps into place next to the postal code field. Also ensure that the baselines of the two cells are correctly aligned.

When resizing the interface, the postal code field should be able to grow, but it's more important that the region field grow. To implement this, select the region field and open the Size Inspector. There are two items you will want to change there: the Content Hugging Priority and the Content Compression Resistance Priority. The former defines how important it is that the view's size remains tightly fixed around its contents' size, while the latter defines how important it is that the view resists being made smaller than its content. For your purposes, you want the region field's content hugging priority to be a little lower than normal. This means that when the layout engine calculates the positioning of items based on their constraints, it will be less important that the region field should cling to its content size—it will be more acceptable to expand that field than any others, such as the postal code field.

Set the region field's content hugging priority to 200, down from the default of 250. Now select the two-line Street field and pin its height; this will prevent it from shrinking down to a single line in height when being displayed, potentially throwing out the layout of the other fields.

Ensure that all these fields' behaviors are set to Editable, and bind their values appropriately: to their Table Cell View's objectValue.street, objectValue.city, objectValue.region, objectValue.postalCode, and objectValue.country.

If you launch the application now, you should be able to browse, add, remove, and edit addresses. The interface should look like Figure 8-12. Your application is complete!

Figure 8-12. The Address viewer in action

Summary

In this chapter I've covered the basics of what Core Data is and how it works, along with some of the techniques for managing different types of relational data models. You should now have a good idea how to go about implementing your data storage using Core Data, and really you should—it's fantastic, and it scales very very well.

You also learned about the potential pitfalls of using Core Data in a highly multithreaded environment, how Core Data can help you out, and what you need to do to keep things running smoothly. You also created a complete editor for your data store, driven almost entirely using Cocoa Bindings and laid out using Cocoa Autolayout.

In short, you should now have everything you need in order to go forth and learn more. Good luck and remember that it's (usually) easier than you think!

The next chapter will tie together everything I've shown you so far into a concrete project by adding iCloud, Bonjour, Core Data, and networking components to this application, along with the use of the Application Sandbox and proper process-separation using XPC.

Chapter 9

Writing an Application

It's taken a long time to get here, but now you're going to put everything we've taught you so far into use in a real, tangible application. The app itself will build on the foundation created in the previous chapter and will add a number of new features, such as:

- Synchronization of data across users' devices using Core Data's iCloud integration.

- Sandboxing because all Mac App Store apps need to be sandboxed. So you'll enable that while still keeping access to the things you need, like iCloud and the system Address Book.

- A network service to browse and vend data from instances of this application, all encapsulated in a properly sandboxed XPC service for better security.

The finished project is available online at this book's web site[1] and on my personal GitHub site,[2] where any future updates will be made. In the course of this chapter you will be guided through the details of implementing each of the above steps and taught the reasoning behind some of the decisions made during that implementation.

Enabling iCloud[3]

The first and easiest step is to enable the use of *entitlements* for your application and to supply unique identifiers for the iCloud key-value store and ubiquity containers. To do this, select the project file in the Project Navigator and then select the application target in the project

---

[1]www.apress.com/9781430243687
[2]http://github.com/AlanQuatermain/Beginning-ObjC-Project
[3]Note that you need to be a Mac Developer Program member to be able to support iCloud in your application. If you aren't one, simply skip the iCloud-specific steps in this chapter.

editor. Across the top are a number of tabs; switch to the **Summary** tab and scroll down to see the Entitlements section. Check the **"Use Entitlements File"** checkbox, then look to the bottom of the pane to find the iCloud section. Check the **"Enable iCloud"** and **"Use store with identifier"** checkboxes, and enter the application's bindle identifier in the **Key-Value Store** field. Press the Add button in the **Ubiquity Containers** section and add the bundle identifier there as well. The result should look something like Figure 9-1.

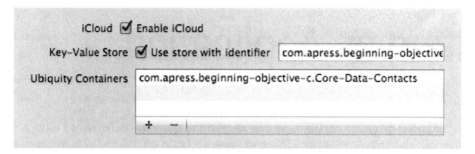

Figure 9-1. Setting up iCloud

Enabling the App Sandbox

Scrolling a little further down, you'll see a checkbox to **enable app sandboxing**: check it, and from the list of items below it, select only the **"Allow Address Book Data Access"** checkbox. This means that your application is tightly sandboxed and cannot make use of any system resources other than the contents of its personal sandbox and the Address Book—the latter of which needs to be confirmed by the user. This means that, whatever might happen to this application, it cannot be used by a hacker to gain access to a user's personal data except the data of this application. It won't be able to read or write any other files, it won't be allowed to make or receive network connections, and more. Look at the other checkboxes to see the type of actions this application now *cannot* perform.

Since the user will be prompted to allow access to the system Address Book, it would be nice to provide an explanation of why this is being requested. This is simple enough to do by switching to the **Info** tab of the project editor. Here is where you can edit the contents of your application's `Info.plist` file. This file provides the system with lots of useful information about your application: name, bundle identifier, version number, and any copyright information. You can localize these values by placing similar key-value pairs into the `InfoPlist.strings` file; there is a version of this file for each language your application supports. Right now there's only an English version, but if you should add a new language, all localized English resources will be copied into that new language's files, ready for translation.

Select the bottom-most item in the info list and a couple of buttons will appear to the right of the title. Click the add (+) button to add a new item, and from the pop-up menu, select "Privacy – Contacts Usage Description." Then in the rightmost column enter the text from Listing 9-1.

Listing 9-1. The Contacts Usage Description

```
This application can populate its initial data using the contents of your Contacts application.
```

Because this is going to be presented to the user in an alert, it is a good idea to localize it. To do so, select `InfoPlist.strings` in the Project Navigator and type the code from Listing 9-2.

Listing 9-2. Localizing the Contacts Usage Description

```
"NSContactsUsageDescription" = " This application can populate its initial data using the contents of your Address Book.";
```

The format of Strings files is just a list of strings in pairs, terminated by semicolons. When the system looks up the `NSContactsUsageDescription` key in the `Info.plist` file (that's the real name underlying the "Privacy – Contacts Usage Description" title you selected), it will also look in the language-specific `InfoPlist.strings` file for a value for that same key. If it finds a localized version, that's what will be displayed; otherwise, the version from the `Info.plist` is displayed as-is.

Launch your application now— everything should work just as before.

Core Data and iCloud

To get iCloud synchronization working with Core Data, there are a few things you need to take into account. You need to check, first of all, whether the user has enabled iCloud at all. You then need to obtain the URL of a *ubiquity container* for your application. This second step must be done on a background thread to avoid blocking the user interface. If that succeeds, then you can open the Core Data store with the correct iCloud options.

However, since you have to do some of this work in the background, you will still need to open your data store in a local-only fashion first. This gives the user the best experience, as the application still launches immediately and gives fast access to their data. Once you've obtained the relevant iCloud option values, you can close and re-open the persistent store without needing to re-create the entire Core Data stack. Having done so, you would then ideally store the iCloud options in your application preferences so you can use them again immediately on the next launch.

The first thing to do is to load any options from your application preferences. With those in hand, you create the store in the usual fashion. Listing 9-3 shows the additions to the existing `-persistentStoreCoordinator` method in in `APAppDeledate.m`; the new code is bolded.

Listing 9-3.   Fetching Ubiquity Options Before Initializing the Data Store

```
NSURL *url = [applicationFilesDirectory
URLByAppendingPathComponent:@"Core_Data_Contacts.storedata"];
NSPersistentStoreCoordinator *coordinator = [[NSPersistentStoreCoordinator alloc]
                                          initWithManagedObjectModel:mom];

// see if we've successfully opened the store using ubiquity options before,
// and if so, use them.
NSDictionary * options = [[NSUserDefaults standardUserDefaults] dictionaryForKey:
                                          @"DataStoreUbiquityOptions"];
NSPersistentStore * store = nil;
store = [coordinator addPersistentStoreWithType: NSSQLiteStoreType
                                  configuration: nil
                                            URL: url
                                        options: options
                                          error: &error];
```

At this point, your application could be in any of three "success" states:

- Data store opened with iCloud enabled.

- Data store opened without trying iCloud.

- Data store failed to open with iCloud options.

Listing 9-4 deals with these consequences. The first thing to do is check if the store variable is nil. If so, you want to see if the loaded options were nil. If they were, then you've hit the single total-failure issue: no iCloud, and the store won't open. If there are some iCloud options, your next step is to open the store again without passing those options. If that works, then your iCloud sync is somewhat broken, at least for now, and you should clear out the transaction log folder used by Core Data—this turns off iCloud synchronization for this Core Data store.

Listing 9-4.   Gracefully Handling Core Data iCloud Store Initialization

```
if ( store == nil )
{
    NSLog(@"Unable to initialize data store: %@", error);

    // if we passed in some iCloud options, try again without them
    if ( options != nil )
    {
        store = [coordinator addPersistentStoreWithType: NSSQLiteStoreType
                                          configuration: nil
                                                    URL: url
                                                options: nil
                                                  error: &error];
```

```
        if ( store != nil )
        {
            // it worked, so zap the log directory for the Core Data sync
            // and we'll retry it with a different version later
            NSString * name = options[NSPersistentStoreUbiquitousContentNameKey];
            NSURL * containerURL = options[NSPersistentStoreUbiquitousContentURLKey];
            containerURL = [containerURL URLByAppendingPathComponent: name
                                                         isDirectory: YES];

            // delete this folder in a coordinated fashion
            NSFileCoordinator * coordinator = [[NSFileCoordinator alloc]
                                                    initWithFilePresenter: nil];
            [coordinator coordinateWritingItemAtURL: containerURL
                                            options: NSFileCoordinatorWritingForDeleting
                                              error: &error
                                         byAccessor:^(NSURL *newURL) {
                NSError * fileError = nil;
                if ( [[NSFileManager defaultManager] removeItemAtURL: newURL
                                                               error: &fileError] == NO )
                {
                    NSLog(@"Failed to remove transaction log folder: %@", fileError);
                }
            }];

            // set this to nil to trigger a retry
            options = nil;
        }
    }

    if ( store == nil )
    {
        // it still didn't work!
        [[NSApplication sharedApplication] presentError:error];
        return nil;
    }
}
```

Note that when falling back to a non-iCloud store, the `options` dictionary variable is explicitly set to `nil`. This is to trigger the iCloud setup clause at the end of the method, shown in Listing 9-5.

Listing 9-5. Attempting iCloud Setup

```
// perhaps we can setup iCloud support now?
if ( options == nil && [[NSFileManager defaultManager] ubiquityIdentityToken] != nil )
{
    [self initializeUbiquityForStore: store];
}

_persistentStoreCoordinator = coordinator;

return _persistentStoreCoordinator;
```

The real work of upgrading this store to use iCloud is in the new -initializeUbiquityForStore: method. In it you'll asynchronously fetch the URL for your ubiquity container and create a unique name for your store. This name will be stored in the app preferences for easy retrieval should iCloud availability drop sometimes; this way the name is guaranteed to stay constant in the face of such events. Create a new method in your app delegate using the code from Listing 9-6.

Listing 9-6. Core Data Ubiquity Options

```
- (void) initializeUbiquityForStore: (NSPersistentStore *) store
{
    // fetching a ubiquity container URL from NSFileManager should not be
    // performed on the main thread, or so the documentation tells us
    // let's do this on a low-priority queue, then
    dispatch_async(dispatch_get_global_queue(DISPATCH_QUEUE_PRIORITY_LOW, 0), ^{
        // passing 'nil' uses the first item in your app's container list
        NSURL * url = [[NSFileManager defaultManager]
                                      URLForUbiquityContainerIdentifier: nil];
        if ( url == nil )
            return;      // no ubiquity container

        NSURL * storeURL = [store URL];

        // see if we stored a ubiquity name already
        NSString * name = [[NSUserDefaults standardUserDefaults]
                                      stringForKey: @"UbiquitousContentName"];
        if ( name == nil )
        {
            // a unique name
            name = [[NSUUID UUID] UUIDString];
            // store it for later use
            [[NSUserDefaults standardUserDefaults] setObject: name
                                      forKey: @"UbiquitousContentName"];
        }

        // ...
    });
}
```

An important facet here is to do the work on a background queue, here enabled using dispatch_async(). Since this is not necessary for the general function of the application, and since it also relies on some network data transfer, it's a good idea to perform it on the *low-priority queue*, as seen here. The content's name is required to be unique, so a new name is generated using the NSUUID class; this is stored in the local preferences for later reference. If an iCloud store is being re-initialized, the existing name is used again.

Once this is done, you have everything you need to initialize the options dictionary, ready to close and reopen the store with iCloud support enabled. Everything from this point on will happen inside a -performBlock: invocation on the main object context; this will ensure everything remains synchronized nicely. Listing 9-7 shows this setup phase and goes inside the dispatch_async() call from Listing 9-6.

Listing 9-7. Getting Ready to Reinitialize the Store

```
// the options dictionary itself:
NSDictionary * options = @{
    NSPersistentStoreUbiquitousContentNameKey : name,
    NSPersistentStoreUbiquitousContentURLKey : url
};

// remove the current store & re-add it with the new options
// do all this in a context perform block to ensure nothing else
// is modifying the store's contents during the swap
NSManagedObjectContext * moc = self.managedObjectContext;
[moc performBlock:^{
    // ...
}];
```

Before reopening the store with the new options, you need to ensure any current changes are saved to disk—just in case. Calling -hasChanges on the context will tell you whether that's necessary. If the save fails, log the error but don't cancel the operation, because the context still has cached copies of all the changes, and that *shouldn't* be affected by pulling out this store. The store's identifier will stay the same (it's part of the store metadata on disk) so the objects in the cache will remain associated with it across a reload.

Once the context has been saved, you're free to remove the existing store and re-add it, this time specifying the iCloud options. Should that fail, your fallback is the same as before: open the store in local-only mode. If it succeeds, record the options dictionary in the application preferences for quick retrieval upon next launch. Listing 9-8 contains the code from within the -performBlock: call, rounding out the entire method.

Listing 9-8. Reopening the Store with Ubiquity Information

```
if ( [moc hasChanges] )
{
    NSError * saveError = nil;
    if ( [moc save: &saveError] == NO )
        NSLog(@"Failed to save before upgrading store to iCloud: %@", saveError);
}

// remove the store while we're synchronized with the context
NSError *storeError = nil;
if ( [[moc persistentStoreCoordinator] removePersistentStore: store
                                              error: &storeError] == NO )
{
    // if we fail to remove, we can't re-add with iCloud options
    NSLog(@"Failed to remove local store: %@", storeError);
    return;
}
```

```
NSPersistentStore * newStore = nil;
newStore = [[moc persistentStoreCoordinator] addPersistentStoreWithType: NSSQLiteStoreType
                                                  configuration: nil
                                                            URL: storeURL
                                                        options: options
                                                          error: &storeError];

if ( newStore == nil )
{
    NSLog(@"Failed to add iCloud to store: %@", storeError);

    // re-open without iCloud -- we know this works
    [[moc persistentStoreCoordinator] addPersistentStoreWithType: NSSQLiteStoreType
                                            configuration: nil
                                                      URL: storeURL
                                                  options: nil
                                                    error: NULL];

    return;
}

// it opened successfully, so store the options dictionary for quick
// retrieval upon next launch
[[NSUserDefaults standardUserDefaults] setObject: options
                                  forKey: @"DataStoreUbiquityOptions"];
```

Sharing Your Data

Your application now has a highly limited surface area exposed to attacks thanks to the use of the App Sandbox and is also keeping users' data synchronized across multiple devices using iCloud. The only piece of functionality remaining to be implemented is to make the data browsable by other instances of the application on the local network. This is no small task, however; you will not only need to define an application-level protocol (stipulating the commands and data used to communicate with other instances) but also a transport protocol to send these commands across the network. Over and above even that, however, is the sandboxing issue: you've severely limited the vulnerability of your application by prohibiting all use of networking APIs. How, then, to add such capabilities without reintroducing those attack vectors?

The answer lies with another key component of the OS X sandboxing system—XPC (Cross Process Communication). You can create and bundle an XPC *service* to provide all the networking code, which would then run as a separate process in its own sandbox. In addition, the interface between the XPC service and the main application will be tightly controlled to the point where only predefined data types may be used in communications.

Usefully, OS X 10.8 includes an entirely Objective-C based API for implementing and communicating with XPC services, which allows you to send cross-process messages as plain Objective-C messages. This means that your first task will be to create a new target for the project defining this service.

Creating an XPC Service

In Xcode select **File ➤ New ➤ Target** and from the **Framework & Library** section choose the XPC Service type, then press Next. Name the target Networker and click Finish to create the new target. Before starting to work with the code though, you need to ensure that the service is built and included when building the main application. Select the project file in the Project Explorer and click on the main application's target. Switch to the **Build Phases** tab and pop open the **Target Dependencies** section. Click the Add button and select the Networker target. This will make Xcode require that the Networker XPC service be built correctly any time you request that the main app be built.

Next you need to tell Xcode to bundle the XPC service into the main application. Click the **Add Build Phase** button in the lower right of the editor and select **Add Copy Files** from the pop-up menu. In the new Copy Files build phase, set the **Destination** to Wrapper and the **Subpath** to Contents/XPCServices. In the Project Navigator, open the Products group (it's right at the very bottom of the navigator) and drag the com.yourcompany.Networker item onto the table in your Copy Files build phase. Your main app's build phases editor should look like that in Figure 9-2.

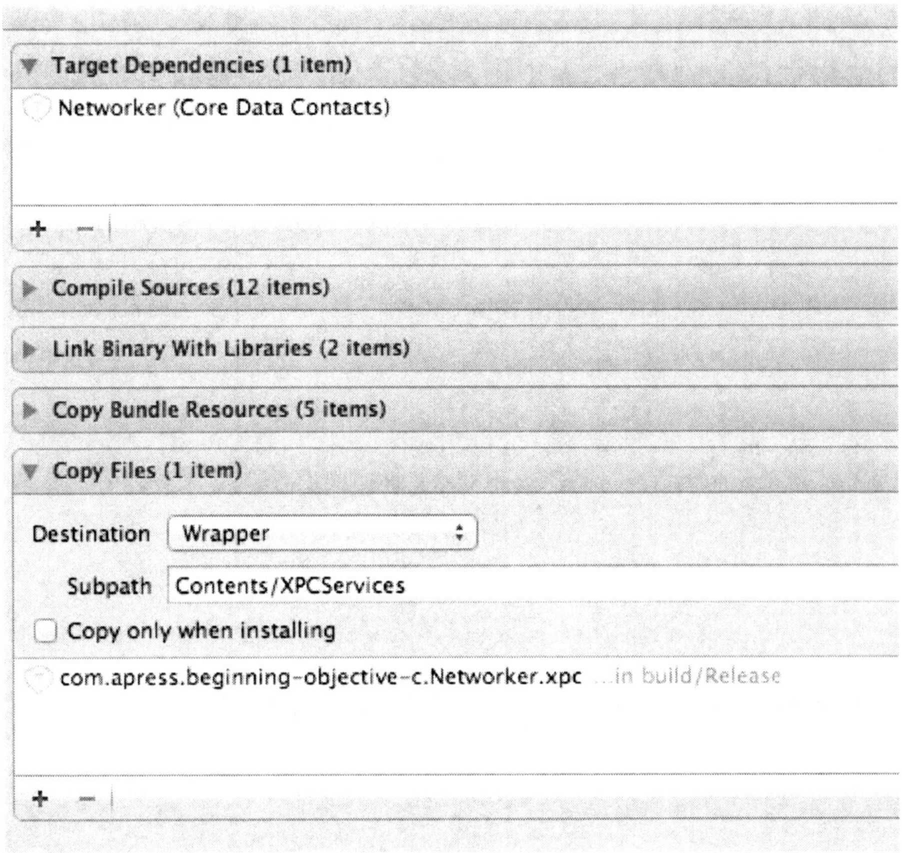

Figure 9-2. The Target Dependencies and Copy Files build phases

Next you need to set up the entitlements for the XPC service. Select the Networker target and switch to the Info tab. At the bottom of the property list is the XPCService dictionary. Open that and change its ServiceType value to `Application` and its RunLoopType to `NSRunLoop`. This sets it up to run as requested by an application (rather than as an always on system- or user-level service) and tells it to use a Cocoa run loop to run rather than the BSD-level `dispatch_main()` method favored by the original C XPC API. This last is a crucial part of the setup for a Cocoa XPC service, as the Cocoa APIs are primarily designed to work in concert with a `run` loop, and your service won't have one unless you set this value properly in the `Info.plist` file.

The last piece of housekeeping is to set up the appropriate sandbox entitlements; the service should be able to both make and receive network connections, but otherwise it should have *no* access to any system resources. Unfortunately Xcode doesn't provide a nice graphical editor for entitlements on XPC Service targets, so you must create the file manually.

In the Project Navigator, open the `Networker` group and its `Supporting Files` subgroup. Add a new file here by right-clicking on one of the existing members of the group (the `Info.plist` file, for example) and choosing **New File** from the pop-up menu. From the Resources section, choose the Property List template and name the file `Networker.entitlements`. Ensure that *no target* is selected, however: this file isn't added to the product as a resource, the compiler uses it as input while code-signing the application.

Select the new file in the Project Navigator to open it in the editor. You need to add three keys to the root of the property list, using the information in Table 9-1.

Table 9-1. Networker.entitlements Property List Keys and Values

Key	Type	Value
com.apple.security.app-sandbox	Boolean	YES
com.apple.security.network.client	Boolean	YES
com.apple.security.network.server	Boolean	YES

To ensure the compiler applies these entitlements, open the Networker target again and switch to the **Build Settings** tab. Find the **Code Signing Entitlements** setting within the **Code Signing** section and give it a value of `Networker/Networker.entitlements`. Your value should look like that in Figure 9-3.

Figure 9-3. Code signing settings

Objective-C XPC Service Setup

Now that all the compilation setup is out of the way, you can start on the code itself. Open `main.m` from the Networker group in the Project Navigator; you'll see a lot of boilerplate code using C functions like `xpc_connection_create()` and `xpc_connection_set_event_hander()`. You're going to use none of this, so delete the contents of the `main()` function and any other functions or declarations in the file.

Setting up a new XPC service using the Objective-C API is much shorter than the process used by plain C applications. It comprises a simple three-step process:

- Initializes an instance of the `XPCServiceListener` class.

- Creates an object that conforms to the `XPCServiceListenerDelegate` protocol and sets it as the listener's delegate.

- Sends a `-resume` message to the listener. This will then run the service indefinitely.

That basically amounts to four lines of code for `main()`, not including the mandatory `return` statement. You also need the delegate object, however, so let's create that first. Above the `main()` method definition, enter the code from Listing 9-9.

Listing 9-9.   The XPC Listener Delegate

```
@interface APXPCRemoteAddressBookBrowser : NSObject <NSXPCListenerDelegate>
@end

#pragma mark -

@implementation APXPCRemoteAddressBookBrowser

- (BOOL) listener: (NSXPCListener *) listener shouldAcceptNewConnection: (NSXPCConnection *)
newConnection
{
    // ...
    return ( YES );
}

@end
```

The `main()` method would then be written to use this object, as shown in Listing 9-10.

Listing 9-10.   XPC Service Startup

```
int main(int argc, const char *argv[])
{
    APXPCRemoteAddressBookBrowser * xpcDelegate = [APXPCRemoteAddressBookBrowser new];

    NSXPCListener * listener = [NSXPCListener serviceListener];
    listener.delegate = xpcDelegate;
```

```
    // this runs essentially forever
    [listener resume];

    return 0;
}
```

That's not *quite* everything, though; the listener delegate needs to define the Objective-C interface exported by the service, along with an object that implements that interface. When the main application connects to the service it will receive an object that to all intents and purposes is that very object. Any messages sent to this will be packaged up and sent to the *real* receiver in the XPC service. In addition, since XPC mandates that all transactions must take place in an asynchronous manner, the calling application supplies a block to receive the reply. Thanks to some very clever people at Apple, an identical block is passed to the receiver within the XPC service, and when that block is called there, its counterpart will receive its arguments in the other application.

That's not all, however—since XPC is implemented as a peer-to-peer system, it's entirely possible for the service to issue calls to the main application in exactly the same way. In fact, this is precisely how the application will respond to requests from its clients across the network.

Remote Access Protocols

The data model you'll be exporting is actually fairly simple, which means that you won't need to define a complicated interface for accessing that data. In fact, it all boils down to a total of four methods:

- Obtain a list of users.
- Fetch a single user's phone numbers.
- Fetch a single user's e-mail addresses.
- Fetch a single user's mailing addresses.

The data itself can be easily packaged up using an NSDictionary instance, recording values as plain strings. Any error conditions can also be easily returned; you break the error into string and numeral types and place those into the dictionary. This can then be quickly converted into JSON format using the NSJSONSerialization class for transport. By using JSON instead of a binary data blob created by an NSCoder, you gain two benefits: your network traffic is easy to read, being a simple string, and the data is not tied to any one platform's serialization capabilities, meaning you are free to investigate implementations on other platforms in the future.

Now, since your networking code is going to be 100% asynchronous, each of the methods in the remote address book interface is going to have a void return type. The actual result of the invocation will be passed to a caller-provided reply block; this actually matches the way in which the Cocoa XPC API is implemented, too. Create a new header file in the Networker target named APRemoteAddressBookInterface.h and add the protocol from Listing 9-11.

Listing 9-11.   The Address Book Interface

```
#import <Foundation/Foundation.h>

@protocol APAddressBook <NSObject>
- (void) allPeople: (void (^)(NSArray *, NSError *)) reply;
- (void) mailingAddressesForPersonWithIdentifier: (NSString *) identifier
                                    reply: (void (^)(NSArray *, NSError *)) reply;
- (void) emailAddressesForPersonWithIdentifier: (NSString *) identifier
                                    reply: (void (^)(NSArray *, NSError *)) reply;
- (void) phoneNumbersForPersonWithIdentifier: (NSString *) identifier
                                    reply: (void (^)(NSArray *, NSError *)) reply;
@end
```

As discussed earlier, this interface will be used both for communicating with remote address books and for vending information from the local application. For remote address books, the local app must also be able to disconnect, so remote address books confirm to a sub-protocol described in Listing 9-12. This protocol will also go inside APRemoteAddressBookInterface.h.

Listing 9-12.   The Remote Address Book Protocol

```
// A remote address book instance needs an additional command to shut down its network
// connection and reclaim any resources on both client and server sides.
@protocol APRemoteAddressBook <APAddressBook>
- (void) disconnect;
@end
```

The last element is the interface by which the main app will communicate with its XPC service. This needs to define methods to vend the local address book on the network and to obtain a list of other address books. It will also need a method through which the application can gain access to the remote address books themselves. This protocol is shown in Listing 9-13.

Listing 9-13.   The Primary XPC Service Interface

```
@protocol APRemoteAddressBookBrowser <NSObject>
- (void) vendAddressBook: (id<APAddressBook>) addressBook
          errorHandler: (void (^)(NSError *)) errorHandler;
- (void) availableServiceNames: (void (^)(NSArray *, NSError *)) reply;
- (void) connectToServiceWithName: (NSString *) name
              replyHandler: (void (^)(id<APRemoteAddressBook>, NSError *)) replyHandler;
@end
```

In this protocol, you can see that the application vends its own data by providing an APAddressBook interface. The XPC service will then set up the network server and will forward any received commands directly to the supplied APAddressBook across the XPC connection for processing.

Initializing The Connection

Now that the relevant protocols have been defined, you can implement your XPCListenerDelegate's -listener:shouldAcceptConnection: message. The main purpose of this method is to configure the provided NSXPCConnection object by specifying its exported interface and the object implementing that interface that it will vend to the associated client. Once this is done, the listener delegate will then start the processing loop for the connection by sending it a -resume message.

Interfaces are specified using instances of the NSXPCInterface class, which are initialized with an Objective-C protocol describing its methods. This is set as the connection's exportedInterface property while an instance of the implementing class is set as its exportedObject property.

Open the main.m file within the Networker target and add #import "APRemoteAddressBook.h" just below the Foundation import statement. Next, place the code from Listing 9-14 into the listener delegate method you created earlier.

Listing 9-14.   Configuring an Incoming XPC Connection

```
NSXPCInterface * myInterface = [NSXPCInterface interfaceWithProtocol:
                                     @protocol(APRemoteAddressBookBrowser)];

newConnection.exportedInterface = myInterface;
newConnection.exportedObject = self;
[newConnection resume];

return ( YES );
```

Ordinarily, this is the only configuration a new connection would need. In this instance, however, there are a couple more steps required due to the custom objects and protocols involved.

Vending Custom Objects With XPC

The transmission system used to send Objective-C messages and objects over an XPC connection is implemented using objects that implement the NSSecureCoding protocol. This protocol differs from NSCoding by using a whitelist of allowed classes that may be encoded and decoded. The whitelist automatically includes any object that implements the NSSecureCoding protocol for sending objects by value, and so all the basic Objective-C data types and containers provided by Apple are included. For your own classes, you need only conform to this protocol, with two exceptions:

- Your custom object will be passed within a container class such as an NSArray or NSDictionary.

- Your custom object will be vended *by reference* as a proxy, rather than by copy.

In both cases, the connection needs to be told to expect these new object types; otherwise it will deem it a potential security error and refuse to use them. The NSXPCInterface class is again the means for accomplishing this.

To handle custom objects within a collection, you would provide some additions to the class whitelist for the NSXPCInterface defining the receiver of the relevant message. The same applies if the collection is being provided to a caller-passed reply block. The code excerpted in Listing 9-15 shows how this would normally be achieved.

Listing 9-15. Passing Custom Objects in an XPC Collection

```
@interface MyCustomObject
...
@end

@protocol MyFilter <NSObject>
- (void) filterObjects: (NSArray *) objects
                 reply: (void (^)(NSArray * filtered)) reply;
@end

...

- (void) listener: (NSXPCListener *) listener
    shouldAcceptConnection: (NSXPCConnection *) connection
{
    NSXPCInterface * myInterface =
        [NSXPCInterface interfaceWithProtocol: @protocol(MyFilter)];

    // define the class whitelist
    NSSet * expectedClasses = [NSSet setWithObject: [MyCustomObject class]];

    // set this list for the input collection...
    [myInterface setClasses: expectedClasses
               forSelector: @selector(filterObjects:reply:)
             argumentIndex: 0 // the first parameter
                   ofReply: NO];  // an argument of the method itself

    // ...and also on the collection passed to the reply block
    [myInterface setClasses: expectedClasses
               forSelector: @selector(filterObjects:reply:)
             argumentIndex: 0 // the first parameter
                   ofReply: YES];

    connection.exportedInterface = myInterface;
    ...
}
```

In your application, you won't be sending custom objects across the XPC connection. You will, however, be vending objects by proxy. This has a slightly different implementation—rather than specifying a class whitelist for a message parameter, you specify an NSXPCInterface describing the object to be proxied. Once you have the interface defined, you inform your main interface by calling a method very similar to the one used to update the class whitelist.

In the primary interface defined by the APRemoteAddressBookBrowser protocol there are two such objects. The first is the APAddressBook-conforming object passed into -vendAddressBook:

errorHandler:. Here the real object resides within the main application and a proxy is given to the XPC service. When the service sends messages to the proxy, they are encoded and routed across the XPC connection to the real object in the main application.

The second proxied object is the remote address book instance conforming to the APRemoteAddressBook protocol, which is passed into the reply block for the -connectToServic eWithName:replyHandler: method. In this case, the real object resides within the XPC service, performing the various network calls required to communicate with the remote application, while the main app receives the proxy. The peer-based design of the XPC system makes these types of exchanges very simple to implement since there is no inherent request/response pairing, just a bidirectional messaging channel.

With the correct setup for the custom objects, then, the final implementation of your XPC listener delegate method is as shown in Listing 9-16.

Listing 9-16.   Vending Proxied Objects Over XPC

```
NSXPCInterface * myInterface = [NSXPCInterface interfaceWithProtocol:
                                        @protocol(APRemoteAddressBookBrowser)];

// add proxy details for the return value of -connectToServiceWithName:
NSXPCInterface * bookInterface = [NSXPCInterface interfaceWithProtocol:
                                            @protocol(APRemoteAddressBook)];
// first argument of the reply block is to be sent as a proxy
[myInterface setInterface: bookInterface
            forSelector: @selector(connectToServiceWithName:replyHandler:)
          argumentIndex: 0
                ofReply: YES];

// proxy details for the object sent to -vendAddressBook:errorHandler:
NSXPCInterface * addressBookInterface = [NSXPCInterface interfaceWithProtocol:
                                            @protocol(APAddressBook)];
// first argument to the function is a proxy object
[myInterface setInterface: addressBookInterface
            forSelector: @selector(vendAddressBook:errorHandler:)
          argumentIndex: 0
                ofReply: NO];

newConnection.exportedInterface = myInterface;
newConnection.exportedObject = self;
[newConnection resume];
return ( YES );
```

Implementing the Browser

The object that the service is going to vend will be the single object that's currently serving as the listener delegate. This is because the browser is conceptually a single object managing a list of available services. To keep things clean, however, you're going to implement the browser as a new class and make your listener delegate a subclass of that.

Create a new Objective-C class within the Networker group and name it
APRemoteAddressBookBrowser. Ensure that it's only included in the Networker target, not the
main application. Open the header file and add the APRemoteAddressBookBrowser protocol to
the class declaration—you need to import APRemoteAddressBookInterface.h for this to work.
Since this object will also be managing NSNetService and NSNetServiceBrowser instances, add
the NSNetServiceDelegate and NSNetServiceBrowserDelegate protocols there too. The resulting
class interface will look like Listing 9-17.

Listing 9-17. The Remote Address Book Browser Class

```
@interface APRemoteAddressBookBrowser : NSObject <APRemoteAddressBookBrowser,
    NSNetServiceDelegate, NSNetServiceBrowserDelegate>
@end
```

This object has a number of responsibilities. First and foremost, as its name implies, is browsing
for the location of other address book services on the network. As it locates them, it will need to
keep hold of their information ready to hand that information out.

It will additionally vend a local address book instance on the network. This involves creating the
server communications socket and listening for incoming connections, and also publishing an
NSNetService so it can be discovered by other applications. In addition, it will need to keep hold
of the objects that handle the receipt and handling of messages from remote apps—if it doesn't,
ARC will clean them up before they're even used.

Along with this, it needs to be able to make connections to remote address book applications
and farm out commands. Again, there will be discrete objects to handle such connections, but
those objects must be packed away somewhere to keep them around.

The last piece of the puzzle concerns the asynchronous nature of the NSNetService class. When
a service is resolved, everything happens asynchronously and the results are passed to the
service's delegate. To pass that information back into the context that requested the resolution,
you store a handler block that the resolution callbacks will call, passing in any error that might
have occurred (the service will already be captured by the block). The obvious candidate for a
container here would be an NSMutableDictionary to key the blocks to their services' names;
however, this won't work since the dictionaries only copy their *keys*, not their *values*. To get
copy-in semantics for the values and to ensure that the blocks are placed on the heap, you can
instead use the NSMapTable class, which acts similarly to a dictionary but allows you to specify
the types and memory semantics for its keys and values.

This, then, gives the implementation and initialization/deallocation routines seen in Listing 9-18.

Listing 9-18. Browser Initialization

```
@implementation APRemoteAddressBookBrowser
{
    NSNetServiceBrowser *        _browser;
    NSMutableDictionary *        _servicesByDomain;

    id<APAddressBook>            _localAddressBook;
    APServerSocket *             _serverSocket;
```

```
    NSMutableSet *              _clients;

    NSMutableSet *              _remoteAddressBooks;

    // NSNetService name string to handler blocks
    // this uses a map table so we can specify copy semantics for values
    NSMapTable *                _serviceResolutionHandlers;
}

- (id) init
{
    self = [super init];
    if ( self == nil )
        return ( nil );

    _servicesByDomain = [NSMutableDictionary new];
    _serviceResolutionHandlers = [[NSMapTable alloc]
        initWithKeyOptions: NSPointerFunctionsObjectPersonality|NSPointerFunctionsCopyIn
              valueOptions: NSPointerFunctionsObjectPersonality|NSPointerFunctionsCopyIn
                  capacity: 0];
    _clients = [NSMutableSet new];
    _remoteAddressBooks = [NSMutableSet new];

    _browser = [NSNetServiceBrowser new];
    [_browser setDelegate: self];
    [_browser searchForServicesOfType: @"_apad._tcp" inDomain: @""];

    return ( self );
}

- (void) dealloc
{
    [_serverSocket close];
    [_browser stop];
    [_servicesByDomain enumerateKeysAndObjectsUsingBlock: ^(id key, id obj, BOOL *stop){
        [obj makeObjectsPerformSelector: @selector(stop)];
    }];
}

...

@end
```

There's plenty to see here. First of all you've attached the member variables to the @implementation statement to keep them private. Right there you see the net service browser object and the storage for the located services. The services are broken up by domain since iCloud Back To My Mac users will see services advertised both on the local network and via the Back To My Mac service. Breaking them up by service will allow you to prefer the local instance rather than funneling everything through Apple's address translation servers.

Next are the variables used for vending the local address book: the proxy object used to obtain data, the communications socket, and the NSNetService through which the service is published.

Following this is the list of client connection handlers, which is literally just a set used to keep a reference to those objects. Below that is a similar set, this time keeping track of the address book objects being vended to your main app and the previously discussed NSMapTable of service resolution handlers.

The initializer is fairly straightforward, creating the collection objects ahead of time, and initializing the NSNetServiceBrowser and telling it to search for services in the default domains of your type: _apad._tcp.

Since this is ARC, you wouldn't normally need to implement -dealloc, but when using the NSNetService API it's very important to stop any and all services you've resolved, as well as stopping any browsers. If you don't do this, then system resources will remain tied up dealing with these services, even though the application that requested them is no longer running.

Service Discovery

The initializer method fired off the browser by calling NSNetServiceBrowser's -searchForServ icesOfType:inDomain: method. The results are returned through a pair of delegate methods implemented by this object. In these the browser returns any discovered or removed services one by one. Each time a service is delivered, the browser also provides information on whether more services remain to be delivered or whether this is the last service that has been discovered presently. This allows delegates to, for example, accumulate the entire list of services before processing.

In this application, you simply keep track of these services in arrays keyed to their domains, adding them in one method and removing them in the other, shown in Listing 9-19.

Listing 9-19. Handling Service Discovery

```
- (void) netServiceBrowser: (NSNetServiceBrowser *) aNetServiceBrowser
           didFindService: (NSNetService *) aNetService
              moreComing: (BOOL) moreComing
{
    NSMutableArray * servicesInDomain = _servicesByDomain[aNetService.domain];
    if ( servicesInDomain == nil )
    {
        servicesInDomain = [NSMutableArray new];
        _servicesByDomain[aNetService.domain] = servicesInDomain;
    }

    [servicesInDomain addObject: aNetService];
}

- (void) netServiceBrowser: (NSNetServiceBrowser *) aNetServiceBrowser
           didRemoveService: (NSNetService *) aNetService
              moreComing: (BOOL) moreComing
{
    [aNetService stop];
    NSMutableArray * servicesInDomain = _servicesByDomain[aNetService.domain];
    [servicesInDomain removeObject: aNetService];
}
```

Note that the first action taken when a service is removed is to tell that service to stop resolution by sending it a -stop message. You don't know for certain that the provided service is being resolved, but it's generally a good idea to be clear about your intent, and sending -stop to a non-resolving service has no side effects.

When the main application wants to display a list of services to which it can connect, the XPC service's browser object will skim through the list of objects and collate them into an NSSet of names. These will then be sorted into an array and sent back to the caller through the provided reply block.

To quickly and easily extract the names from all the services, you send -valueForKey: to each array of services. When sent to an array or set, this method will return a similar object (i.e., arrays return arrays, sets return sets) containing the result of sending the same -valueForKey: message to each contained object. So by sending -valueForKey: to your array of NSNetService objects you can easily obtain an array of service names.

If any object should return a nil value, that value will be represented in the returned array/set with an NSNull instance. As a result, it is prudent to filter the list using a simple NSPredicate to remove any such items before sending it on.

Place the code from Listing 9-20 into your APRemoteAddressBookBrowser implementation file to implement the first of the three methods it will export across the XPC connection.

Listing 9-20. Returning Service Names

```
- (void) availableServiceNames: (void (^)(NSArray *, NSError *)) reply
{
    // using a set ensures that no name appears more than once
    NSMutableSet * allNames = [NSMutableSet new];

    // A simple predicate to ensure no NSNulls are left in the list
    NSPredicate * nullFilter = [NSPredicate predicateWithBlock:
                                    ^BOOL(id evaluatedObject, NSDictionary *bindings) {
        if ( [evaluatedObject isKindOfClass: [NSNull class]] )
            return ( NO );
        return ( YES );
    }];

    // Fetch all the names from each domain and add them to the set
    [_servicesByDomain enumerateKeysAndObjectsUsingBlock: ^(id key, id obj, BOOL *stop){
        NSArray * names = [obj valueForKey: @"name"];
        [allNames addObjectsFromArray: [names filteredArrayUsingPredicate: nullFilter]];
    }];

    // sort it alphabetically, ignoring case
    // -[NSSet allObjects] returns an ordered NSArray of the set's contents
    NSArray * sorted = [[allNames allObjects] sortedArrayUsingSelector:
                                        @selector(caseInsensitiveCompare:)];

    // post it back
    reply(sorted, nil);
}
```

Vending Your Data

There are two more key functions provided by the `APRemoteAddressBookBrowser` class: connecting to remote address book applications and vending the local address book to others. The first option involves everything from connection management up to the user interface, so you'll tackle that last. Here you're going to manage the vendor side of the equation.

As seen earlier, the application vends its address book data by handing a proxy to the XPC service using the `-vendAddressBook:errorHandler:` message. This then seems like a good time to implement the application side of the XPC equation.

Since the application delegate is currently in charge of the global object context, it's fairly logical to put it in charge of the global XPC connection and its vended proxy object. To back this up, you need to add some instance variables to your app delegate. Open its implementation file and add a variable block following the `@implementation` statement; add the variables seen in Listing 9-21. Also add an import statement for `APRemoteAddressBookInterface.h` to make its protocols available.

Listing 9-21. XPC-Related App Delegate Instance Variables

```
@implementation APAppDelegate
{
    NSXPCConnection *                  _xpcConnection;
    id<APRemoteAddressBookBrowser>  _browser;
}
```

You have two top-level interface actions associated with networking functions: one will advertise this application's data and the other will fetch a list of available services ready to display a chooser interface to the user. When either of these actions is performed for the first time, the XPC connection will be initialized. In other words, the connection will be initialized *on demand*.

You create a connection here by initializing an instance of `NSXPCConnection` with the name of the service to which you want it to connect. This name is the bundle identifier of the XPC service bundle you created earlier; in the sample project it's `com.apress.beginning-objective-c.Networker`. You then need to set the interface of this connection in the same manner as the service itself (shown in Listing 9-16 earlier). From this side of the connection, however, you set the *remote object interface* through the `remoteObjectInterface` property rather than the `exportedInterface` property. The browser object is obtained by sending `-remoteObjectProxyWithErrorHandler:` (or just plain `-remoteObjectProxy`) message to the connection. Passing an error handler block is naturally the preferred way to do this, as not only is it invoked if the connection could not be established, it will be called any time the connection cannot send a message, for instance if the XPC service process were to crash.

In your application delegate, add the new method shown in Listing 9-22.

Listing 9-22. Connecting to an XPC Service

```
- (void) _initializeNetworker
{
    NSXPCInterface * interface = [NSXPCInterface interfaceWithProtocol:
                                    @protocol(APRemoteAddressBookBrowser)];
```

```
    // add proxy details for the return value of -connectToServiceWithName:
    NSXPCInterface * remoteBookInterface = [NSXPCInterface interfaceWithProtocol:
                                                    @protocol(APRemoteAddressBook)];
    // first argument of the reply block is to be sent as a proxy
    [interface setInterface: remoteBookInterface
              forSelector: @selector(connectToServiceWithName:replyHandler:)
            argumentIndex: 0
                  ofReply: YES];

    // proxy details for the commandHandler object sent to -setCommandHandler:
    NSXPCInterface * localBookInterface = [NSXPCInterface interfaceWithProtocol:
                                                    @protocol(APAddressBook)];
    // first argument to the function is a proxy object
    [interface setInterface: localBookInterface
              forSelector: @selector(setCommandHandler:errorHandler:)
            argumentIndex: 0
                  ofReply: NO];

    _xpcConnection = [[NSXPCConnection alloc] initWithServiceName:
                                        @"com.apress.beginning-objective-c.Networker"];
    _xpcConnection.remoteObjectInterface = interface;
    [_xpcConnection resume];
    _browser = [_xpcConnection remoteObjectProxyWithErrorHandler: ^(NSError * error) {
        _browser = nil;
        [NSApp presentError: error];
    }];
}
```

The underscore at the start of this method's name is a commonly accepted way of denoting that a method is intended for internal use only, usually only by other methods in the same class. Both of your action methods will call this if the _browser member variable has not yet been initialized.

Becoming a Vendor

Since the app delegate contains the object context, it makes a suitable implementer of the APAddressBook protocol. Therefore, when vending the app's data, it will pass itself as the address book object to the XPC service. The first step, then, is to declare this intent by adding the APAddressBook protocol to the class's interface. While you're there, you can also add the action method that will trigger the data vending to start. Open your app delegate's header file and add the bolded code from Listing 9-23.

Listing 9-23.   Declaring Support for the APAddressBook Protocol

```
#import "APRemoteAddressBookInterface.h"

@interface APAppDelegate : NSObject <NSApplicationDelegate, APAddressBook>

...
```

```
- (IBAction)vendAddressBook:(id)sender;
```

...

@end

Before you implement the code, let's update the interface. Open MainMenu.xib and open the Window menu from the menubar in the editor. From the **Windows & Menus** section of the Object Palette, drag a new **Separator menu item** onto the menu, just below the existing **Zoom** item. Below that add a new **menu item**. These items can be seen in Figure 9-4.

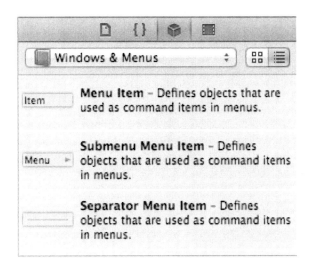

Figure 9-4. Menu item objects

Double-click the new menu item to edit its title— name it "Publish…" (Press ⌥-; to enter the ellipsis character). Now hold down the Control key and drag from the new menu item onto the App Delegate object in the outline. In the actions pop-up that appears, select the -vendAddressBook: action you created a moment ago, and save your work.

Almost all of the action is done now; the only remaining step is to implement the action method itself. Open the app delegate's implementation file and add the code from Listing 9-24.

Listing 9-24. The Vend Address Book Action

```
- (IBAction)vendAddressBook:(id)sender
{
    if ( _browser == nil )
        [self _initializeNetworker];

    // this will vend us on the network
    [_browser vendAddressBook: self errorHandler: ^(NSError *error) {
        if ( error != nil )
```

```
        {
            dispatch_async(dispatch_get_main_queue(), ^{
                [NSApp presentError: error];
            });
        }
    }];
}
```

As you can see, the first action is to ensure that the XPC connection has been initialized and a browser object obtained. The -vendAddressBook:errorHandler: is then called, passing the app delegate as the address book proxy object. If an error occurs, the supplied error handler block will be called, affording the delegate an opportunity to present an alert dialog to the user with the pertinent details.

Providing Data

The app delegate provides access to its data by implementing the methods of the APAddressBook protocol, described in APAddressBookInterface.h. Also in this file are the declarations for the keys used in the command dictionary. While you won't need to create those dictionaries here, you'll want to use one of the keys to add an identifier object to the details of each person. At the top of your app delegate's implementation file, add the code from Listing 9-25.

Listing 9-25. The Person Identifier Key

```
NSString * const APRemoteAddressBookCommandPersonIDKey = @"personID";
```

With this symbol properly defined, you can start implementing the data methods themselves, starting with -allPeople:. This will send back a simple NSArray instance containing an NSDictionary instance describing each Person object in the data store. The dictionaries will contain every attribute from the Person objects along with a unique identifier in the form of an NSString. This identifier will be passed into the other three methods of the APAddressBook protocol to identify the object from which further details are requested.

Since you're using Core Data, you have a handy unique identifier all ready and waiting: each object comes with an NSManagedObjectID that identifies its persistent store and any information necessary to locate the object within it. What's more, managed object IDs have a handy means of externalizing their data by producing a uniform resource identifier (URI) representation of their data. For items in an SQLite store, this is commonly of the form cdata://StoreUUID/EntityName/RowNumber. The URI is an instance of NSURL and provides a string representation of itself through its -absoluteString method. This also provides an easy way to get an NSManagedObjectID back again: a new NSURL can be created using the string, and an NSPersistentStoreCoordinator can use that URL to generate a proper NSManagedObjectID instance.

This can be encapsulated into the methods from Listing 9-26, which you can add to your app delegate implementation. Note that the -identifierForObject:error: method also attempts to ensure that no temporary object IDs are used; if an object has a temporary ID (because it hasn't yet been written to a persistent store), then the context is asked to assign it to one and generate a permanent object ID.

Listing 9-26.   *Handling Identifier Strings*

```
- (NSString *) identifierForObject: (NSManagedObject *) object
                             error: (NSError **) error
{
    NSManagedObjectID * objectID = [object objectID];
    if ( [objectID isTemporaryID] )
    {
        // this might actually change, so request a permanent one
        if ( [self.managedObjectContext obtainPermanentIDsForObjects: @[object]
                                                               error: error] == NO )
        {
            // can't get a permanent ID, so return nil and the error
            return ( nil );
        }

        // get the new permanent objectID
        objectID = [object objectID];
    }

    return ( [[objectID URIRepresentation] absoluteString] );
}

- (NSManagedObjectID *) objectIDFromIdentifier: (NSString *) identifier
                                         error: (NSError **) error
{
    NSURL * objectURI = [[NSURL alloc] initWithString: identifier];
    if ( objectURI == nil )
    {
        // URL data isn't valid
        if ( error != nil )
        {
            *error = [NSError errorWithDomain: NSURLErrorDomain
                                         code: NSURLErrorBadURL
                                     userInfo: nil];
        }

        return ( nil );
    }

    NSManagedObjectID * objectID = [self.persistentStoreCoordinator
                                    managedObjectIDForURIRepresentation: objectURI];
    if ( objectID == nil )
    {
        // Not a valid Object ID URI
        if ( error != nil )
        {
            *error = [NSError errorWithDomain: NSCocoaErrorDomain
                                         code: NSManagedObjectReferentialIntegrityError
                                     userInfo: nil];
        }
```

```
        return ( nil );
    }

    return ( objectID );
}
```

With these details out of the way, it's relatively simple to obtain the necessary data. For each method, you create an `NSFetchRequest` for the appropriate entity. When fetching all people, that's all the information you need— no predicate is necessary. For addresses of different kinds, you supply a predicate ensuring that each object returned has a particular object ID as the target of its `person` relationship. Additionally, since you won't need object IDs for the addresses, you can ask Core Data to return the relevant data to you already formatted within an `NSDictionary`, more on which shortly.

> **Note**   When constructing predicates where a value is a managed object, the `NSManagedObject` instance and its associated `NSManagedObjectID` are interchangeable.

Obtaining the list of people is now relatively straightforward. A single fetch request will turn them all up, although you batch the results to ensure that they're not *all* resident in memory at once. Then, for each `Person` object returned, you determine a unique identifier and pack that into a dictionary along with the values of the `firstName` and `lastName` attributes, which will then go into an array to be returned. The reply block is then called from outside the object context's queue by dispatching it to a global queue, ensuring that any XPC transmission processing can't interfere with any other Core Data processing.

First add import statements at the top of the file for `Person.h`, `MailingAddress.h`, `PhoneNumber.h`, and `EmailAddress.h`. The complete method are in Listing 9-27.

Listing 9-27. Vending All Person Objects

```
- (void) allPeople: (void (^)(NSArray *, NSError *)) reply
{
    NSFetchRequest * req = [NSFetchRequest fetchRequestWithEntityName: @"Person"];
    [req setFetchBatchSize: 25];

    // ensure the reply block is on the heap
    reply = [reply copy];

    // no ordering, etc.-- just fetch every Person instance
    [[self managedObjectContext] performBlock: ^{
        NSMutableArray * result = [NSMutableArray new];
        NSError * error = nil;
        NSArray * people = [[self managedObjectContext] executeFetchRequest: req
                                                                      error: &error];
        for ( Person * person in people )
        {
            NSString * identifier = [self identifierForObject: person error: NULL];
```

```
        if ( identifier == nil )
            continue;

        NSMutableDictionary * personInfo = [NSMutableDictionary new];
        personInfo[APRemoteAddressBookCommandPersonIDKey] = identifier;
        if ( person.firstName != nil )
            personInfo[@"firstName"] = person.firstName;
        if ( person.lastName != nil )
            personInfo[@"lastName"] = person.lastName;
        [result addObject: personInfo];
    }

    if ( [result count] == 0 )
        result = nil;

    dispatch_async(dispatch_get_global_queue(DISPATCH_QUEUE_PRIORITY_DEFAULT, 0), ^{
        reply(result, error);
    });
    }];
}
```

Address Data

Your address objects are all vended through similar methods: -<addressType>ForPersonWith
Identifier:reply:. These all return every attribute of their respective entities and all are fetched
based on their relationship with a single Person entity. This makes them a perfect target for some
generalization. You define a single method taking an entity name, an identifier string, and an
XPC reply block. This method will then unpack the object ID from the identifier, sending an error
to the reply block upon failure. Then an NSEntityDescription is obtained using the entity name
provided, and an NSFetchRequest made using that, its predicate set to limit the results to only
those objects whose person relationship refers to the Person identified by the object ID.

The request itself is set to return results in the form of an NSDictionary per object, rather than
the usual NSManagedObject or NSManagedObjectID instances. These dictionaries contain the
values for each attribute specified through the fetch request. Since you want to return all
attributes, you can ask the entity itself for a list of their names to pass to the fetch request's
-setPropertiesToFetch: method. This is accomplished by asking it to return a dictionary of
all attribute descriptions indexed by their names, and asking that dictionary for all its keys—
[[entity attributesByName] allKeys].

The results of the fetch request are already in the exact format you want to send back to the
reply block: an array of dictionaries. Having performed the fetch request, the results and error
can be passed to the reply immediately without any further work. Having implemented this
method, each of the three address-vending methods can be implemented in a single line; the
only difference between them is the name of the entity passed into the generic method.

The complete code for this method, along with one of the address methods, is shown in
Listing 9-28.

Listing 9-28. *Vending Address Data*

```objc
- (void) sendAttributesOfAddressEntityNamed: (NSString *) entityName
          associatedWithPersonIdentifiedBy: (NSString *) personID
                                    toBlock: (void (^)(NSArray *, NSError *)) reply
{
    NSError * error = nil;
    NSManagedObjectID * objectID = [self objectIDFromIdentifier: personID
                                                          error: &error];
    if ( objectID == nil )
    {
        reply(nil, error);
        return;
    }

    NSEntityDescription * entity = [NSEntityDescription entityForName: entityName
                                  inManagedObjectContext: self.managedObjectContext];

    NSFetchRequest * req = [NSFetchRequest new];
    [req setEntity: entity];
    [req setResultType: NSDictionaryResultType];
    [req setPropertiesToFetch: [[entity attributesByName] allKeys]];
    [req setPredicate: [NSPredicate predicateWithFormat: @"person == %@", objectID]];

    // ensure the reply block is on the heap
    reply = [reply copy];

    [self.managedObjectContext performBlock: ^{
        // the fetch request will return an array of dictionaries for us, all ready
        // to send to our caller
        NSError * error = nil;
        NSArray * result = [self.managedObjectContext executeFetchRequest: req
                                                                    error: &error];

        // let the object context carry on while doing XPC transfers
        dispatch_async(dispatch_get_global_queue(DISPATCH_QUEUE_PRIORITY_DEFAULT, 0), ^{
            reply(result, error);
        });
    }];
}

- (void) mailingAddressesForPersonWithIdentifier: (NSString *) identifier
                                           reply: (void (^)(NSArray *, NSError *)) reply
{
    [self sendAttributesOfAddressEntityNamed: @"MailingAddress"
                  associatedWithPersonIdentifiedBy: identifier
                                            toBlock: reply];
}
```

With this complete, the only remaining step is to implement the XPC service code to set up and tear down network connections and to send data between computers.

Server-Side Networking

Before you can send or receive data, you need to set up a *listening socket* to which other applications can connect. This is a special form of network channel: rather than reading data from it directly, when data arrives you pass the socket back to the IP networking stack to *accept* a new connection. Doing so will give you a new socket which you'll use to exchange data with the single client which connected. This process is repeated with each new connection that arrives.

Sadly, there is no friendly Cocoa API for initializing a server-side listening port. For that you need to drop down to the Core Foundation level, specifically the CFSocket APIs. To make this a little easier, I wrote a class that used this API to provide a Cocoa-style interface for creating your listening socket. It's named APServerSocket, and you should create it by adding a new Objective-C class to the Networker target, a subclass of NSObject. Its interface can be seen in Listing 9-29.

Listing 9-29.   The APServerSocket Class Interface

```
@interface APServerSocket : NSObject <NSNetServiceDelegate>

- (id) initWithConnectionHandler: (void (^)(int newSocket)) handler;
- (void) close;

@property (readonly) NSNetService * netService;

@end
```

The new object provides a very simple API. It doesn't need any connection details since it will be initialized using the local device's address, which is readily available. It creates and manages an NSNetService instance for vending the details on the network and can be shut down on command. Its only required parameter is a handler block, which will be called each time a new connection arrives and is passed the socket representing that connection.

The source file is, for the most part, quite simple. The socket itself is handled using an instance of CFSocketRef; this also handles the arrival of new connections and notifies its owner of the new socket values. The network service is advertised using the automatically selected port number once the socket has been set up. In the implementation file, add the code from Listing 9-30 to handle the basic operations.

Listing 9-30.   APServerSocket Initialization

```
#import <sys/socket.h>
#import <netinet/in.h>

@interface APServerSocket ()
- (void) handleNewSocket: (int) newSocket;
@end
```

```objc
@implementation APServerSocket
{
    CFSocketRef     _serverSocket;
    NSNetService *  _netService;
    void            (^_connectionHandler)(int);
}

@synthesize netService=_netService;

- (id) initWithConnectionHandler: (void (^)(int)) handler
{
    NSParameterAssert(handler != nil);
    self = [super init];
    if ( self == nil )
        return ( nil );

    _connectionHandler = [handler copy];
    if ( [self initializeConnection] == NO )
        return ( nil );

    return ( self );
}

- (void) dealloc
{
    [self close];
}

- (void) close
{
    [_netService stop];

    if ( _serverSocket != NULL )
    {
        CFRelease(_serverSocket);
        _serverSocket = NULL;
    }
}

- (void) handleNewSocket: (int) newSocket
{
    _connectionHandler(newSocket);
}
```

This part in itself isn't very complicated. The real work of initializing the connection happens in the initializeConnection method called from the class's initializer, shown in Listing 9-31.

Listing 9-31. Setting up a Server Socket

```objc
- (BOOL) initializeConnection
{
    // tell the new socket to pass the receiver as a parameter to its callbacks
```

```objc
CFSocketContext ctx = {
    .version = 0,
    .info = (__bridge void *)self,
    .retain = NULL,
    .release = NULL,
    .copyDescription = CFCopyDescription
};

_serverSocket = CFSocketCreate(kCFAllocatorDefault, AF_INET6, SOCK_STREAM,
                               IPPROTO_TCP, 0, _ServerSocketCallback, &ctx);
if ( _serverSocket == NULL )
{
    NSLog(@"Failed to create listening socket");
    return ( NO );
}

int val = 1;  // reuse the same port/address if claimed but not in active use
int socketFD = CFSocketGetNative(_serverSocket);
if ( setsockopt(socketFD, SOL_SOCKET, SO_REUSEADDR, &val, sizeof(int)) != 0 )
{
    NSLog(@"Failed to set socket options");
    return ( NO );
}

struct sockaddr_in6 address = {0};  // we're using IPv6. It's the future, people
address.sin6_len = sizeof(address);
address.sin6_family = AF_INET6;
address.sin6_addr = in6addr_any;  // any address for the local machine
address.sin6_port = 0;            // have the system choose an available port
NSData * addressData = [[NSData alloc] initWithBytesNoCopy: &address
                                                    length: sizeof(address)
                                               freeWhenDone: NO];

if ( CFSocketSetAddress(_serverSocket, (__bridge CFDataRef)addressData) !=
                                                            kCFSocketSuccess )
{
    NSLog(@"Failed to set server socket address");
    return ( NO );
}

// enable the accept callback and set it to automatically re-enable after each event
CFSocketSetSocketFlags(_serverSocket, kCFSocketAutomaticallyReenableAcceptCallBack);
CFSocketEnableCallBacks(_serverSocket, kCFSocketAcceptCallBack);

// find out what port we were assigned
socklen_t slen = sizeof(address);
getsockname(socketFD, (struct sockaddr *)&address, &slen);

UInt16 port = ntohs(address.sin6_port);
_netService = [[NSNetService alloc] initWithDomain: @"" // default domain
                                              type: @"_apad._tcp"
                                              name: @"" // default name
                                              port: port];
```

```
    [_netService scheduleInRunLoop: [NSRunLoop mainRunLoop]
                          forMode: NSDefaultRunLoopMode];
    [_netService setDelegate: self];
    [_netService publishWithOptions: 0];

    return ( YES );
}
```

There are a few steps here:

- A context is created, providing a non-retained reference to the receiver. This reference is then passed (as a void * type) to the callback function provided to the new CFSocketRef.

- The socket itself is created using a TCP, IPv6 stream socket (as opposed to datagrams— see Chapter 6 for more information). A C function, _ServerSocketCallback, is provided for the socket to call when events occur. The source for this callback is very simple and can be seen in Listing 9-32.

- Once the socket is created, a BSD-level API is used to mark its address as *reusable*. This means that the address can be reclaimed by the system for another socket should this one not be shut down cleanly, as might happen if the XPC service were to crash.

- Next an IPv6 address structure is created. The address and port are both set to wildcard values; the system will determine the appropriate addresses itself. By using an address of in6addr_any, the socket can be advertised on all available interfaces, each with its own IP address. A port number of zero likewise means that the system is free to select a port number itself. Since this will be advertised using an NSNetService, a well-known port isn't required for others to connect.

- Calling CFSocketSetAddress() binds the socket to a local address and configures it to listen for incoming connections. Once that is done, its *accept* callback is enabled and set to automatically re-enable after each event. This callback will call the function from Listing 9-32 each time a new incoming connection is accepted.

- To advertise the service on the network you need the system-assigned port number; this is obtained by fetching the address structure from the now-connected socket through the BSD-level getsockname() function. The data in the address is stored in *network byte order*, with the most-significant bytes in the lowest memory address. To ensure you read it correctly, the ntohs() macro (Network To Host Short) is used to perform a byte-swap if required. On both Intel and ARM processors, a swap takes place. On CPUs like the PowerPC used by earlier Macs, no change is made.

- The port number is then used to initialize an NSNetService instance, ready for publishing. The receiver is set as its delegate purely to log success or failure, and it is scheduled on the main run loop since all other threads are dispatch work queues, and thus are not running a run loop.

Listing 9-32. The CFSocket Callback Function

```
static void _ServerSocketCallback(CFSocketRef s, CFSocketCallBackType type,
                                  CFDataRef address, const void *data, void *info)
{
    APServerSocket * obj = (__bridge APServerSocket *)info;
    switch ( type )
    {
        case kCFSocketAcceptCallBack:
        {
            // pull out the new socket and pass it on
            int * socketPtr = (int *)data;
            [obj handleNewSocket: *socketPtr];
            break;
        }

        default:
            break;
    }
}
```

With this class implemented, you now have almost all the tools required to vend an address book; open APRemoteAddressBookBrowser.m and add #import "APServerSocket.h" with the other import statements. The -vendAddressBook:errorHandler: method can now be implemented: it will create the server socket if it hasn't already done so and will store the supplied APAddressBook proxy ready to fetch data requested by clients. The connection handler block supplied to the socket will be quite simple, too: the new socket will be handed to a new object to manage, and that object will be packed into the _clients set to keep it around until it's no longer needed. The code can be seen in Listing 9-33; the APAddressBookClient object will be described later, after we've gone over the data transfer protocol and encodings with which it must work.

Listing 9-33. Vending an Address Book

```
- (void) vendAddressBook: (id<APAddressBook>) addressBook
             errorHandler: (void (^)(NSError *)) errorHandler
{
    if ( _serverSocket == nil )
    {
        // listen for incoming connections
        // fire up a new listening socket object with a new-connection handler block
        _serverSocket = [[APServerSocket alloc] initWithConnectionHandler: ^(int newSocket) {
            NSLog(@"Accepted new connection");

            APAddressBookClient * client = nil;
            client = [[APAddressBookClient alloc] initWithSocket: newSocket
                                                        delegate: self];
            [_clients addObject: client];
        }];
```

```
        if ( _serverSocket == nil )
        {
            errorHandler([NSError errorWithDomain: NSPOSIXErrorDomain
                                              code: errno
                                          userInfo: nil]);
            return;
        }
    }

    _localAddressBook = addressBook;
}
```

Data Encoding

You're going to use JSON as your data transfer format. This is lightweight and easy to read, and it supports all the data types used in your object model out of the box. Additionally, the Cocoa frameworks provide an API to transform array and dictionaries of these types to and from JSON data in UTF-8 string format. The one potential hiccup is the NSError object: this is not a valid JSON data type, so it needs to be massaged into a dictionary format.

Translating error objects isn't a terribly difficult task on the face of it. The error code is an integer, the domain is a string, and the userInfo dictionary commonly contains message strings. This can be quite easily generated. Inside the Networker group, create a new file: choose the Objective-C Category template, and make a category on NSError called APDictionaryRepresentation. Open the resulting header file, NSError+APDictionaryRepresentation.h, and add the pair of methods shown in Listing 9-34.

Listing 9-34. NSError Transformation Methods

```
@interface NSError (APDictionaryRepresentation)
+ (NSError *) errorWithJSONDictionaryRepresentation: (NSDictionary *) dictionary;
- (NSDictionary *) jsonDictionaryRepresentation;
@end
```

The initial implementation of these methods is quite simple: the error's code, domain, and userInfo properties are dropped straight into a new dictionary using some predefined keys. The code for this can be seen in Listing 9-35.

Listing 9-35. NSError to JSON Dictionary Conversion

```
static NSString * APErrorDictionaryCodeKey = @"Code";
static NSString * APErrorDictionaryDomainKey = @"Domain";
static NSString * APErrorDictionaryUserInfoKey = @"UserInfo";

@implementation NSError (APDictionaryRepresentation)

+ (NSError *) errorWithJSONDictionaryRepresentation: (NSDictionary *) dictionary
{
    return ( [NSError errorWithDomain: dictionary[APErrorDictionaryDomainKey]
                                 code: [dictionary[APErrorDictionaryCodeKey] integerValue]
                             userInfo: dictionary[APErrorDictionaryUserInfoKey]] );
}
```

```
- (NSDictionary *) jsonDictionaryRepresentation
{
    NSMutableDictionary * dict = [NSMutableDictionary new];
    dict[APErrorDictionaryCodeKey] = @([self code]);
    dict[APErrorDictionaryDomainKey] = [self domain];
    if ( [self userInfo] != nil )
        dict[APErrorDictionaryUserInfoKey] = [self userInfo];

    return ( [dict copy] );
}

@end
```

Encoding Other Data

The current implementation might fail, however, if one of the values within the dictionary is not a valid JSON type. To counter this, you can resort to a double-fallback mechanism. First of all, if the value can be encoded using an NSCoder, you can take that data and base-64 encode it, adding the resulting string to the dictionary. This can then be unpacked at the other end of the connection. If coding isn't possible for any reason, you can fall back on using the string returned from the object's -description method, which is guaranteed to return something, even if not something terribly useful. It will, at the very least, let you see what type of object was there.

The first step is accomplished using the NSKeyedArchiver and NSKeyedUnarchiver classes. These take any objects conforming to the NSCoding protocol and use the methods of that protocol to create an encoded binary data representation of those objects. For simplicity, you can use +NSKeyedArchiver archivedDataWithRootObject:] to encode and +[NSKeyedUnarchiver unarchiveObjectWithData:] to decode. Sadly NSJSONSerialization doesn't handle NSData objects, so an additional step is required to encode this binary data into a valid UTF-8 string for transfer.

Base-64 encoding on OS X is available through the Security framework. Specifically, through the Security Transforms API. This API provides a means of defining transform objects that take data in at one end and produce something different at the other end. Example transforms provided by the system include encrypt and decrypt along with sign and verify, and there are also some encode/decode transforms for encodings such as GZip, Base-32, and Base-64. What's more, these transforms can be chained together so that you can take some data from a file and in one pass send it through a GZip decoder, a Base64 decoder, and finally a decryptor using the cryptographic algorithm and keys of your choice.

In your application, you only need to encode or decode base-64, so you won't need to chain anything together. Your encode and decode routines will therefore involve three steps for encoding, which are then mirrored for decoding:

  ▓ Encode the object into binary data using NSKeyedArchiver.

  ▓ Pass the data through a base-64 transform.

  ▓ Create an NSString object using the UTF-8 data output from the transform.

This gives you the encoder and decoder methods in Listing 9-36.

> **Note**   You will need to add `Security.framework` to your Networker target to use the Security
> Transforms API.

Listing 9-36.   Base-64 Transformations

```
#import <Security/SecEncodeTransform.h>
#import <Security/SecDecodeTransform.h>

static NSString * Base64String(id<NSCoding> object)
{
    NSData * coded = [NSKeyedArchiver archivedDataWithRootObject: object];
    if ( coded == nil )
        return ( nil );

    SecTransformRef tx = SecEncodeTransformCreate(kSecBase64Encoding, NULL);
    SecTransformSetAttribute(tx, kSecEncodeLineLengthAttribute, kSecLineLength64, NULL);
    SecTransformSetAttribute(tx, kSecTransformInputAttributeName,
                                   (__bridge CFDataRef)coded, NULL);

    CFErrorRef err = NULL;
    NSData * data = CFBridgingRelease(SecTransformExecute(tx, &err));
    CFRelease(tx);
    if ( data == nil )
    {
        NSLog(@"Base64 Encode Error: %@. Object = %@", err, object);
        return ( nil );
    }

    // render the data as a string
    return ( [[NSString alloc] initWithData: data encoding: NSUTF8StringEncoding] );
}

static id Base64Decode(NSString * string)
{
    NSData * data = [string dataUsingEncoding: NSUTF8StringEncoding];
    SecTransformRef tx = SecDecodeTransformCreate(kSecBase64Encoding, NULL);
    SecTransformSetAttribute(tx, kSecTransformInputAttributeName,
                                   (__bridge CFDataRef)data, NULL);

    CFErrorRef err = NULL;
    NSData * decoded = CFBridgingRelease(SecTransformExecute(tx, &err));
    CFRelease(tx);
    if ( data == nil )
    {
        NSLog(@"Base64 Encode Error: %@. Data = %@", err, data);
        return ( nil );
    }

    return ( [NSKeyedUnarchiver unarchiveObjectWithData: decoded] );
}
```

The error's userInfo could be passed directly into these methods, but if something within it doesn't implement the NSCoder protocol, the entire dictionary will fail to encode. As a result, it is better to encode each item individually, replacing it with the base-64 encoded string and modifying its key with a special prefix. The code in Listing 9-37 shows a method that implements this behavior: given a dictionary, it will check each key/value pair for JSON compatibility and any incompatible values will be either encoded as described above or will be replaced with the result of sending them the -description message.

Listing 9-37. Encoding a Dictionary

```
static NSString * APErrorEncodedKeyPrefix = @"com.apress.beginning-objective-c.base64.";

NSDictionary * EncodedDictionary(NSDictionary * source)
{
    NSMutableDictionary * result = [NSMutableDictionary new];
    [source enumerateKeysAndObjectsUsingBlock: ^(id key, id obj, BOOL *stop) {
        if ( [NSJSONSerialization isValidJSONObject: obj] == NO )
        {
            if ( [obj conformsToProtocol: @protocol(NSCoding)] == NO )
            {
                // use the description instead
                obj = [obj description];
            }
            else
            {
                // encode the object if possible
                NSString * str = Base64String(obj);
                if ( str == nil )
                {
                    // error encoding somewhere further down the chain
                    // use the description again
                    obj = [obj description];
                }
                else
                {
                    // it encoded nicely
                    obj = str;

                    // modify the key to denote that this value is encoded
                    key = [APErrorEncodedKeyPrefix stringByAppendingString: key];
                }
            }
        }

        // place the key & value into the dictionary
        result[key] = obj;
    }];
}
```

With this done, the final NSError category methods are those shown in Listing 9-38.

Listing 9-38.   Guaranteeably JSON-Encoding an NSError Object

```objc
+ (NSError *) errorWithJSONDictionaryRepresentation: (NSDictionary *) dictionary
{
    NSMutableDictionary * userInfo = [dictionary[APErrorDictionaryUserInfoKey] mutableCopy];
    if ( userInfo != nil )
    {
        NSArray * keys = [[userInfo allKeys] filteredArrayUsingPredicate:
    [NSPredicate predicateWithBlock: ^BOOL(id evaluatedObject, NSDictionary *bindings) {
            return ( [evaluatedObject hasPrefix: APErrorEncodedKeyPrefix] );
        }]];

        // declared __strong so we can modify key in ARC code
        for ( __strong NSString * key in keys )
        {
            NSString * encoded = userInfo[key];
            [userInfo removeObjectForKey: key];

            // get the original key...
            key = [key substringFromIndex: [APErrorEncodedKeyPrefix length]];
            // ... and the original value
            userInfo[key] = Base64Decode(encoded);
        }
    }

    return ( [NSError errorWithDomain: dictionary[APErrorDictionaryDomainKey]
                                  code: [dictionary[APErrorDictionaryCodeKey] integerValue]
                              userInfo: userInfo] );
}

- (NSDictionary *) jsonDictionaryRepresentation
{
    NSMutableDictionary * dict = [NSMutableDictionary new];
    dict[APErrorDictionaryCodeKey] = @([self code]);
    dict[APErrorDictionaryDomainKey] = [self domain];
    if ( [self userInfo] != nil )
    {
        dict[APErrorDictionaryUserInfoKey] = [self userInfo];

        if ( [NSJSONSerialization isValidJSONObject: dict] == NO )
            dict[APErrorDictionaryUserInfoKey] = EncodedDictionary([self userInfo]);
    }

    return ( [dict copy] );
}
```

Encoding Commands

The commands sent across the network correspond directly to the four methods of the
APAddressBook protocol: fetch all users; fetch addresses; fetch e-mails; and fetch phone
numbers. These methods all return arrays, which can be easily encoded into JSON data.

The commands take at most a single parameter: a person identifier. Their parameterized nature means that an NSDictionary would be the logical container for a command. When encoding the commands for transfer, however, there are some other concerns to address.

The first is a means of identifying the command being requested. This can be easily addressed using some constant values denoting the command itself. In more complex protocols these *command codes* are usually integers; this makes it cheap both to transfer (a few bytes at most) and to decipher. The receiver can use a compiler-optimized switch statement to inspect the command code and determine the appropriate action to take, and comparing integers is much easier than comparing a multi-byte structure such as a string.

For your purposes, however, you will use a string value to identify each command. Since there are few commands, the amount of time spent comparing them is of little concern, and by using strings you are able to visually verify the JSON data.

The command constants are declared in APRemoteAddressBookInterface.h and include a fifth command used to identify a reply message. The codes are shown in Listing 9-39.

Listing 9-39.   Command Codes

```
// command names
extern NSString * const APRemoteAddressBookCommandAllPeople;
extern NSString * const APRemoteAddressBookCommandGetMailingAddresses;
extern NSString * const APRemoteAddressBookCommandGetEmailAddresses;
extern NSString * const APRemoteAddressBookCommandGetPhoneNumbers;
extern NSString * const APRemoteAddressBookCommandReply;
```

Within each command message are the parameters. The command name is one, and (where appropriate) the person identifier is another. Replies can also include the result value and any error that might have occurred. That brings the parameter tally to four.

Since XPC messages are asynchronous, with commands and their replies being transferred in fundamentally any order, the network code must support the same approach. That means that a reply cannot be paired with its command by transmission order alone. To facilitate this, you're going to include an extra parameter in all commands: a UUID, which will be copied into the reply message and used to pair it with the relevant command. This, then, gives the parameter constants in Listing 9-40. The declarations are placed into APRemoteAddressBookInterface.h, while the definitions in Listing 9-41 will go into a source file. In the provided sample project, the definitions live in APRemoteAddressBook.m, which you haven't yet reached; you can place them in any implementation file, however, as long as they only appear in one of them.

Listing 9-40.   Command Parameter Keys

```
// command keys
extern NSString * const APRemoteAddressBookCommandNameKey;
extern NSString * const APRemoteAddressBookCommandUUIDKey;
extern NSString * const APRemoteAddressBookCommandPersonIDKey;
extern NSString * const APRemoteAddressBookCommandValueKey;
extern NSString * const APRemoteAddressBookCommandErrorKey;
```

Listing 9-41. Command Name and Parameter Definitions

```
// command parameters
NSString * const APRemoteAddressBookCommandNameKey = @"command";
NSString * const APRemoteAddressBookCommandUUIDKey = @"uuid";
NSString * const APRemoteAddressBookCommandPersonIDKey = @"personID";
NSString * const APRemoteAddressBookCommandValueKey = @"value";
NSString * const APRemoteAddressBookCommandErrorKey = @"error";


// command names
NSString * const APRemoteAddressBookCommandAllPeople = @"allPeople";
NSString * const APRemoteAddressBookCommandGetMailingAddresses = @"getAddresses";
NSString * const APRemoteAddressBookCommandGetEmailAddresses = @"getEmails";
NSString * const APRemoteAddressBookCommandGetPhoneNumbers = @"getPhoneNumbers";
NSString * const APRemoteAddressBookCommandReply = @"reply";
```

With the dictionary keys nailed down, you can envision how the JSON command messages will appear. Listing 9-42 shows a few different samples.

Listing 9-42. Sample Commands and Replies

```
// Requesting all people
{
    "command" : "allPeople",
    "uuid" : "CE36850C-6276-45FD-84C9-432D01F4877F"
}


// Requesting email addresses
{
    "command" : "getEmails",
    "uuid" : "B590CCE2-D7C7-485B-80F3-36B4BB0B0130",
    "personID" : "coredata://1A88B03A-FE45-4E69-8D85-1179B5A1898E/Person/z109"
}


// Successful emails result
{
    "command" : "reply",
    "uuid" : "B590CCE2-D7C7-485B-80F3-36B4BB0B0130",
    "value" : [
        {
            "email" : "somebody@example.com"
        },
        {
            "email" : "somebody@elsewhere.com"
        }
    ]
}


// Failing emails result
{
    "command" : "reply",
    "uuid" : "B590CCE2-D7C7-485B-80F3-36B4BB0B0130",
```

```
    "error" : {
        "Code" : 133000,
        "Domain" : "NSCocoaErrorDomain",
        "UserInfo" : {
            "LocalizedDescription" : "No object found with identifier 'coredata://1A88B03A-FE45-
4E69-8D85-1179B5A1898E/Person/z109'",
            "Affected Stores" : "<NSSQLCore 0x0000048f3cd894a0>"
        }
    }
}
```

Clients and Commands

As connections arrive from client applications, the XPC service is going to create instances of a new class, APAddressBookClient, to manage the connection and handle data transfer. This class's responsibilities include

- ▨ Ownership of the client connection's socket, including detecting when it has been disconnected and releasing resources.
- ▨ Reading data as it arrives and accumulating into single commands.
- ▨ Passing commands on for processing.
- ▨ Sending data to the client.

To post commands out for processing, it will specify a delegate protocol; this will define methods to handle incoming commands and to be notified of a client's disconnection. The object itself will only provide two methods: an initializer, which requires a delegate object, and a method to send a chunk of data.

Create a new Objective-C class in the Networker target, an NSObject subclass, and name it APAddressBookClient. Enter the code from Listing 9-43.

Listing 9-43. The APAddressBookClient Interface

```
@class APAddressBookClient;
@protocol APAddressBookClientDelegate <NSObject>
- (void) client: (APAddressBookClient *) client
  handleMessage: (NSDictionary *) message;
- (void) clientDisconnected: (APAddressBookClient *) client
                  withError: (NSError *) error;
@end

@interface APAddressBookClient : NSObject
- (id) initWithSocket: (CFSocketNativeHandle) sock
             delegate: (id<APAddressBookClientDelegate>) delegate;
- (void) sendData: (NSData *) data;
@end
```

The data transfer here is going to be implemented in a simple asynchronous manner using the dispatch_io API. You could absolutely use NSStream to do the same thing, but despite using a higher-level language, NSStream actually implements a lower-level API than dispatch_io. This is because, with NSStream, you still need to manually handle the space-available and data-available events to accumulate incoming data and send data out. The dispatch_io API, on the other hand, takes care of that for you, notifying you when the full amount has been read or written via callback, relieving you of this rather tiresome (not to mention verbose) task.

To get started, open APAddressBookClient.m and enter the code from Listing 9-44.

Listing 9-44.   Initializing the Client Data Handler

```
@implementation APAddressBookClient
{
    id<APAddressBookClientDelegate> _delegate __weak;
    dispatch_io_t                   _io;

    NSUInteger                      _inputSize;
    dispatch_data_t                 _inputData;
}

- (id) initWithSocket: (CFSocketNativeHandle) sock
            delegate: (id<APAddressBookClientDelegate>) delegate
{
    self = [super init];
    if ( self == nil )
        return ( nil );

    NSLog(@"Client attached");

    _io = dispatch_io_create(DISPATCH_IO_STREAM, sock,
                        dispatch_get_global_queue(DISPATCH_QUEUE_PRIORITY_DEFAULT, 0),
                        ^(int error) { close(sock); });
    [self initializeReader];

    _delegate = delegate;

    _inputSize = NSNotFound;       // 'not currently reading a message'
    _inputData = dispatch_data_empty;

    return ( self );
}

// ...

@end
```

Incoming Command Data

Incoming data is handled using the dispatch_io_read() method. In your case, you tell the IO channel to read data continually, passing back each chunk to a block that you provide. This will ultimately be called with each discrete piece of data that arrives on the channel and is guaranteed to happen in a nicely synchronized fashion.

Each command will be a blob of JSON data preceded by a four-byte length in network byte-order. As you receive data, you will accumulate it and read off the size. Once you have a size, you look to see if you've received all that data yet. When you have, you separate it out and pass it to the delegate object for processing.

This is all implemented beginning with the code in Listing 9-45, which sets up the read operation on the channel.

Listing 9-45.   Handling Incoming Commands

```
- (void) initializeReader
{
    dispatch_queue_t q = dispatch_get_global_queue(DISPATCH_QUEUE_PRIORITY_DEFAULT, 0);
    APAddressBookClient * weakSelf = self;
    dispatch_io_read(_io, 0, SIZE_MAX, q, ^(bool done, dispatch_data_t data, int err) {
        APAddressBookClient * client = weakSelf;
        if ( done )
        {
            id<APAddressBookClientDelegate> delegate = client->_delegate;
            NSError * error = nil;
            if ( err != 0 )
            {
                error = [NSError errorWithDomain: NSPOSIXErrorDomain
                                            code: err
                                        userInfo: nil];
            }

            [delegate clientDisconnected: client withError: error];
            return;
        }

        if ( data != nil )
        {
            // append the data & trigger processing
            _inputData = dispatch_data_create_concat(_inputData, data);
            [self tryToProcessData];
        }
    });
}
```

When data arrives, you append it to your data buffer, which is implemented using a dispatch_data object. This type keeps discrete blocks separate rather than copying ranges of bytes around and implements a wrapper that keeps track of the various separate blocks making up the whole. This makes it very useful for cases such as this where data is received in piecemeal fashion—it reduces the load on the memory-handling systems considerably by ultimately minimizing the allocation and copying performed to only that which is absolutely necessary. Thus the concatenation performed by dispatch_data_create_concat() actually only attaches the new block to the end of a list rather than resizing any memory buffers.

When data is received, some of it will be consumed. The first time this happens is when the four-byte length is read; subsequent operations will consume the JSON data for a complete command, then another length, and so on. This consumption is accomplished using the code in Listing 9-46

Listing 9-46.   Consuming Data from a dispatch_data Object

```
- (BOOL) consumeInputOfLength: (size_t) length intoBuffer: (uint8_t *) buf
{
    NSParameterAssert(length != 0);
    NSParameterAssert(buf != NULL);

    size_t avail = dispatch_data_get_size(_inputData);
    if ( avail < length )
        return ( NO );

    __block size_t off = 0;
    dispatch_data_apply(_inputData, ^bool(dispatch_data_t region, size_t offset,
                                          const void *buffer, size_t size) {
        size_t left = length - off;
        memcpy(buf + off, buffer, left);
        off += left;
        return ( off < length );
    });

    size_t newLen = avail - length;
    if ( newLen == 0 )
        _inputData = dispatch_data_empty;
    else
        _inputData = dispatch_data_create_subrange(_inputData, length, newLen);

    return ( YES );
}
```

After calling dispatch_data_get_size() to ensure enough data is available to satisfy the request, you step through all the separate buffers within the data object using the dispatch_data_apply() function, copying data out into the caller-provided memory buffer, stopping when the required amount has been copied by returning false from the block. If all the data has been consumed, the accumulation object is replaced with an empty one. If some remains, however, a new data object is created using a subset of the original—namely, only those bytes not copied out will remain. Again, the dispatch API performs this without allocating, copying, or moving any blocks of data around: the subrange object just references a (potentially) smaller number of discrete buffer objects internally, discarding any outside the requested subrange.

Processing the data is performed using the method in Listing 9-47.

Listing 9-47.   Processing Input Data

```
- (void) tryToProcessData
{
    if ( _inputSize == NSNotFound )
    {
        // need to read four bytes of size first
        union {
            uint32_t messageSize;
            uint8_t buf[4];
        } messageBuf;
```

```
        if ( [self consumeInputOfLength: 4 intoBuffer: messageBuf.buf] == NO )
            return;

        _inputSize = ntohl(messageBuf.messageSize);
    }

    // see if we already have enough data
    if ( dispatch_data_get_size(_inputData) < _inputSize )
        return;      // not enough there yet

    // otherwise, we can read the whole thing
    NSMutableData * data = [[NSMutableData alloc] initWithLength: _inputSize];
    [self consumeInputOfLength: _inputSize intoBuffer: [data mutableBytes]];

    // we've read everything, so dispatch the message and reset our ivars
    NSError * jsonError = nil;
    NSDictionary * message = [NSJSONSerialization JSONObjectWithData: data
                                                    options: 0
                                                      error: &jsonError];

    // set our size marker
    _inputSize = NSNotFound;

    if ( message == nil )
    {
        NSLog(@"Failed to decode message: %@", jsonError);
    }
    else
    {
        // dispatch the message
        [_delegate client: self handleMessage: message];
    }

    // is there more data? If so, recurse to handle it
    if ( dispatch_data_get_size(_inputData) > 0 )
        [self tryToProcessData];
}
```

This method performs three main steps:

- Firstly, if there is no command-length set yet in the _inputSize instance variable, that size is read from the start of the input buffer. Note that it is properly converted from network to host byte-order using ntohl().

- If a full command is not yet available, then the method returns early. Otherwise, it pulls out the full data block and parses it into Objective-C format using NSJSONSerialization. This object is then passed to the delegate for processing.

- If more data is available, then another command followed this one in close order; to handle it, the method calls itself again.

Sending Responses

Whew! That's all the nitty-gritty of handling incoming data. Thanks to your friend `dispatch_io`, however, sending a response is *much* simpler: a single call to `dispatch_io_write()` will do the trick, with the dispatch API taking care of all the waiting and buffer management for you, as seen in Listing 9-48.

Listing 9-48. Sending Data

```
- (void) sendData: (NSData *) data
{
    // the queue for all blocks here
    dispatch_queue_t q = dispatch_get_global_queue(DISPATCH_QUEUE_PRIORITY_DEFAULT, 0);

    // we want a dispatch_data_t referencing this NSData object
    // the logical thing is to have the dispatch cleanup block reference & release
    //  the NSData, except we can't call -release on it under ARC. The solution is to
    //  bridge-cast the NSData to a manually-counted CFDataRef, which we can release.
    CFDataRef cfData = CFBridgingRetain(data);
    dispatch_data_t ddata = dispatch_data_create(CFDataGetBytePtr(cfData),
                                        CFDataGetLength(cfData),
                                        q, ^{ CFRelease(cfData); });

    dispatch_io_write(_io, 0, ddata, q, ^(bool done, dispatch_data_t d, int err) {
        if ( err != 0 )
        {
            NSError * error = [NSError errorWithDomain: NSPOSIXErrorDomain
                                        code: err
                                    userInfo: nil];
            NSLog(@"Failed to send data: %@", error);
            return;
        }
        else if ( done )
        {
            NSLog(@"Sent %lu bytes of data", CFDataGetLength(cfData));
        }
    });
}
```

The only niggle here is the conversion of an NSData object to a `dispatch_data` object. You want the dispatch object to keep hold of the NSData instance and refer to its buffer directly, but there's no way under ARC to say "I'm done with this now." If you were using manual memory management, you could pass the dispatch object a cleanup block that would send a -release method to the underlying data. The block itself would actually retain and release the NSData object for you, which is great, except that the only thing you want to do is to release it, which ARC won't let you do yourselves. Since you can't do that, there's no reason for the block to reference the NSData object, so it won't be kept around.

The solution to this brain-twisting conundrum is to use *toll-free bridging* ton convert the NSData into a CFData object, which *is* manually managed. Even blocks won't manage the life cycle of a CoreFoundation object. So you take a copy of the input as a CoreFoundation type (remember that for immutable objects, *copy* actually only performs a *retain*) and you manually release it in the cleanup block of your new dispatch_data object.

The rest of the method is exceedingly simple: the data is passed into dispatch_io_write(), and the callback block is called when the write either succeeds or fails, giving the application a chance to react.

Command Processing

The commands decoded by instances of the APAddressBookClient object are passed on to their delegates; as you saw in Listing 9-33, that's the APAddressBookBrowser object. Before that can be implemented however, you need to inform the class of this fact: open APAddressBookBrowser.h and add the lines in bold from Listing 9-49.

Listing 9-49. Adopting the APAddressBookClient Protocol

```
#import "APRemoteAddressBookInterface.h"
#import "APAddressBookClient.h"

@interface APRemoteAddressBookBrowser : NSObject
    <APRemoteAddressBookBrowser, APAddressBookClientDelegate,
     NSNetServiceBrowserDelegate, NSNetServiceDelegate>
@end
```

The handling here is actually quite simple: the command's name and UUID are extracted and used to determine the message to send to the _localAddressBook instance (the proxy for the local application's address book, set in Listing 9-33). Each command has the same handler block, too—it receives an array of values and/or an error object, and it packs those up as JSON data, sending them back to the client that sent the command. The command dispatch method and the disconnection handler are shown in Listing 9-50.

Listing 9-50. Processing Incoming Commands

```
- (void) client: (APAddressBookClient *) client
  handleMessage: (NSDictionary *) command
{
    void (^dataHandler)(NSArray *, NSError *) = ^(NSArray * values, NSError * error) {
        // ...
    };

    NSString * name = command[APRemoteAddressBookCommandNameKey];
    NSString * identifier = command[APRemoteAddressBookCommandPersonIDKey];

    if ( [name isEqualToString: APRemoteAddressBookCommandAllPeople] )
    {
        [_localAddressBook allPeople: dataHandler];
    }
```

```objc
    else if ( [name isEqualToString: APRemoteAddressBookCommandGetMailingAddresses] )
    {
        [_localAddressBook mailingAddressesForPersonWithIdentifier: identifier
                                                        reply: dataHandler];
    }
    else if ( [name isEqualToString: APRemoteAddressBookCommandGetEmailAddresses] )
    {
        [_localAddressBook emailAddressesForPersonWithIdentifier: identifier
                                                      reply: dataHandler];
    }
    else if ( [name isEqualToString: APRemoteAddressBookCommandGetPhoneNumbers] )
    {
        [_localAddressBook phoneNumbersForPersonWithIdentifier: identifier
                                                    reply: dataHandler];
    }
    else
    {
        id userInfo = @{ NSLocalizedDescriptionKey : @"Unknown command" };
        NSError * error = [NSError errorWithDomain: APRemoteAddressBookErrorDomain
                                        code: 101
                                    userInfo: userInfo];
        dataHandler(nil, error);
    }
}

- (void) clientDisconnected: (APAddressBookClient *) client withError: (NSError *) error
{
    // not doing anything with the error, which has already been logged.
    [_clients removeObject: client];
}
```

The data handler is defined up front and passed to every address book proxy method to receive their replies. Place the code from Listing 9-51 inside the block.

Listing 9-51. Command Data Handler

```objc
NSMutableDictionary * result = [NSMutableDictionary new];
NSUUID * uuid = command[APRemoteAddressBookCommandUUIDKey];
result[APRemoteAddressBookCommandNameKey] = APRemoteAddressBookCommandReply;
result[APRemoteAddressBookCommandUUIDKey] = uuid;
if ( values != nil )
    result[APRemoteAddressBookCommandValueKey] = values;
if ( error != nil )
    result[APRemoteAddressBookCommandErrorKey] = [error jsonDictionaryRepresentation];

NSError * jsonError = nil;
NSData * jsonData = [NSJSONSerialization dataWithJSONObject: result
                                                options: 0
                                                  error: &jsonError];
if ( jsonData == nil )
{
    NSLog(@"Error building JSON reply: %@. Message = %@. Reply = %@",
        jsonError, command, result);
```

```
    return;
}
```

```
// send the data asynchronously
[client sendData: jsonData];
```

Accessing Remote Address Books

Now that everything is in place to make an address book available to other instances of the application on the network, you need a way to actually connect to them from your own instance. The application will perform this task in three steps:

- First, it will obtain a list of available services by sending the -availableServiceNames: message to its XPC service proxy object. This list will then be displayed to users in a window.

- When the user chooses a service, the application will ask its XPC proxy to make a connection by sending it the -attachToRemoteAddressBookWithName: handler: message.

- When the connection is made successfully, a new address book window will be presented and the list of people loaded asynchronously by sending -allPeople: to the XPC proxy. Similarly to the local address book, the address details will be obtained on demand as the user selects users from the master list.

We'll come back to the main application in a short while. For now, let's concentrate on the implementation inside the XPC service.

Reaching Out

You already saw how the XPC service handled the -availableServiceNames: message in Listing 9-20. Its counterpart, -connectToServiceWithName:replyHandler:, follows that in APAddressBookBrowser.m. Open that file and add the method stub seen in Listing 9-52.

Listing 9-52.   The Stub Connection Method

```
- (void) connectToServiceWithName: (NSString *) name
                    replyHandler: (void (^)(id<APRemoteAddressBook>, NSError *)) replyHandler
{
    NSLog(@"Connecting to service named '%@'", name);
    __block NSNetService * selected = nil;

    // search individual domains -- look in "local" domain first, then any others
    // ...

    // if no local services were found, look in the other domains
    // ...

    // if none were found at all, send back an error
    // ...
```

```
    // resolve if necessary then connect and send back a proxy
    if ( [selected hostName] == nil )
    {
        // resolve the service
        // ...
    }
    else
    {
        // it's already been resolved: just hook up a new connection
        // ...
    }
}
```

The complete method needs to perform the following steps:

- First, it looks for a service with the given name in the *local domain* (i.e. those with an address ending in ".local.").

- If no service matches, it goes on to search the other domains it has discovered so far. If no service can be located, it posts an error back to the calling application.

- Once a service has been selected, that service is resolved asynchronously. A handler block is stored to be run when the resolution completes.

- Upon successful resolution, a new APRemoteAddressBook instance is created to manage the connection and data transfer, and a proxy for that object is sent to the calling application.

The first step can be seen in Listing 9-53.

Listing 9-53.   Searching Services Found in the Local Domain

```
// search individual domains -- look in "local" domain first, then any others
NSMutableArray * localServices = _servicesByDomain[@"local."];
NSLog(@"Searching local services: %@", localServices);
for ( NSNetService * service in localServices )
{
    if ( [[service name] isEqualToString: name] )
    {
        NSLog(@"Found local service: %@", service);
        selected = service;
        break;
    }
}
```

This is a simple traversal of the already-located services with the provided name. If nothing is found, however, you need to look further, as shown in Listing 9-54.

Listing 9-54.   Searching Other Domains

```
// if no local services were found, look in the other domains
if ( selected == nil )
```

```
{
    [_servicesByDomain enumerateKeysAndObjectsUsingBlock: ^(id key, id obj, BOOL *stop) {
        if ( [key isEqualToString: @"local."] )
            return;     // skip local domain, we've already looked there

        NSLog(@"Searching services in domain '%@': %@", key, obj);
        for ( NSNetService * service in obj )
        {
            if ( [[service name] isEqualToString: name] )
            {
                NSLog(@"Found service: %@", service);
                selected = service;
                *stop = YES;
                break;
            }
        }
    }];
}
```

Here you use block-based enumeration to fetch the keys and values from the dictionary in a single step. When you see the local domain, you skip over it. Should the service remain unfound even now, an error is sent back to the caller, as in Listing 9-55.

Listing 9-55. Posting Back a Lookup Error

```
// if none were found at all, send back an error
if ( selected == nil )
{
    NSDictionary * info = @{ NSLocalizedDescriptionKey : NSLocalizedString(@"An address book
service with the provided name could not be found.", @"error") };
    NSError * error = [NSError errorWithDomain: APRemoteAddressBookErrorDomain
                                          code: APRemoteAddressBookErrorServiceNotFound
                                      userInfo: info];
    replyHandler(nil, error);
    return;
}
```

Once a service has been found, it needs to be resolved before you can connect to it. You can check whether it's ready to use by sending it a -hostName message; a nil result means it hasn't yet been resolved.

The resolution happens asynchronously by sending -resolveWithTimeout: to the service. When the service resolves or a timeout occurs, a delegate method is sent, using a preconfigured run loop. In this case, use the main run loop since the current thread isn't going to use one.

A block is placed into a dictionary, keyed by the service's name, to be run when the resolution completes. This block will send back either an error or a proxy for a new APRemoteAddressBook instance, as seen in Listing 9-56.

Listing 9-56. Resolving the Service

```
// resolve the service
// take a copy of the
```

```
void (^replyCopy)(id<APRemoteAddressBook>, NSError *) = [replyHandler copy];
// schedule it in the main run loop so the resolve success/failure will
// trigger there -- this method is returning shortly
[selected scheduleInRunLoop: [NSRunLoop mainRunLoop]
                    forMode: NSRunLoopCommonModes];

// ensure it's got a delegate set, so we know whether it resolved or not
[selected setDelegate: self];

// store a block to handle the result of the service resolution
__weak APRemoteAddressBookBrowser * weakSelf = self;
[_serviceResolutionHandlers setObject: ^(NSError * error) {
    if ( error != nil )
    {
        replyCopy(nil, error);
        return;
    }

    // it resolved successfully
    APRemoteAddressBookBrowser * browser = weakSelf;
    APRemoteAddressBook * book = [[APRemoteAddressBook alloc]
                                 initWithResolvedService: selected delegate: browser];
    [browser->_remoteAddressBooks addObject: book];  // keep it alive
    NSLog(@"Resolved successfully, book = %@", book);
    replyCopy(book, nil);
} forKey: [selected name]];

// start the lookup
[selected resolveWithTimeout: 10.0];
```

In the case where the service is already resolved, only the last step need be performed, as seen in Listing 9-57.

Listing 9-57.   Returning a New Address Book Proxy

```
// it's already been resolved: just hook up a new connection
APRemoteAddressBook * book = [[APRemoteAddressBook alloc]
                             initWithResolvedService: selected delegate: self];
[_remoteAddressBooks addObject: book];  // keep it alive
NSLog(@"Resolved successfully, book = %@", book);
replyHandler(book, nil);
```

As you just saw, when a service is asked to resolve, a block is placed in the _serviceResolutionHandlers dictionary, keyed by the service's name. The browser object then implements the two main service resolution delegate methods and uses them to call the stored block, passing in the result of the resolution attempt. If the service resolved successfully, the block is called with no parameters; should an error occur, that error is passed to the block so that it can be sent back to the calling application.

The delegate methods are implemented in Listing 9-58.

Listing 9-58.   Receiving Service Resolution Results

```
- (void) netServiceDidResolveAddress: (NSNetService *) sender
{
    void (^handler)(NSError *) = [_serviceResolutionHandlers objectForKey: [sender name]];
    if ( handler == nil )
        return;

    handler(nil);
    [_serviceResolutionHandlers removeObjectForKey: [sender name]];
}

- (void) netService: (NSNetService *) sender
        didNotResolve: (NSDictionary *) errorDict
{
    void (^handler)(NSError *) = [_serviceResolutionHandlers objectForKey: [sender name]];

    if ( handler == nil )
        return;

    // create an error object from the dictionary
    NSError * error = [NSError errorWithDomain: errorDict[NSNetServicesErrorDomain]
                                    code: [errorDict[NSNetServicesErrorCode] intValue]
                                userInfo: nil];
    NSLog(@"Error resolving: %@", error);
    handler(error);

    [_serviceResolutionHandlers removeObjectForKey: [sender name]];
}
```

Implementing the Remote Address Book

The APRemoteAddressBook class's delegate protocol specifies only one method, used to note when a server becomes unavailable. The implementation uses this to remove it from the list of connections, thus allowing it to be released; see Listing 9-59.

Listing 9-59.   Handling Server Disconnection

```
- (void) addressBookDidDisconnect: (APRemoteAddressBook *) book
{
    [_remoteAddressBooks removeObject: book];   // let it be released
}
```

Along with implementing this method, you need to add the protocol to the class's interface declaration: in APRemoteAddressBookBrowser.h add the bold lines from Listing 9-60. You create the class and protocol themselves in just a moment.

Listing 9-60.   Adopting the APRemoteAddressBook Delegation Protocol

```
#import "APRemoteAddressBookInterface.h"
#import "APRemoteAddressBook.h"
#import "APAddressBookClient.h"

@interface APRemoteAddressBookBrowser : NSObject
    <APRemoteAddressBookBrowser, APAddressBookClientDelegate,
     APRemoteAddressBookDelegate, NSNetServiceBrowserDelegate, NSNetServiceDelegate>
@end
```

You won't be able to compile this as-is, however, as no class yet exists. Let's remedy that. Create a new class in the XPC service target named APRemoteAddressBook and enter the code from Listing 9-61 in its header file.

Listing 9-61.   The Remote Address Book Class

```
#import "APRemoteAddressBookInterface.h"

@class APRemoteAddressBook;

@protocol APRemoteAddressBookDelegate <NSObject>
- (void) addressBookDidDisconnect: (APRemoteAddressBook *) book;
@end

@interface APRemoteAddressBook : NSObject <APRemoteAddressBook, NSStreamDelegate>
- (id) initWithResolvedService: (NSNetService *) resolvedService
                      delegate: (id<APRemoteAddressBookDelegate>) delegate;
@end
```

The class itself has a very simple interface—it takes an NSNetService instance from which it will obtain its communication channels and a delegate. Beyond that, its only API is that defined by the APRemoteAddressBook protocol (and by extension the APAddressBook protocol), seen in Listings 9-11 and 9-12.

The implementation of this class can be very similar to that used for APAddressBookClient, using dispatch_io and friends to handle data transfer. However, since this is a tutorial, we had you use a different, pure Objective-C approach for this class. This means that you'll be using NSStream objects to transfer data, and you'll handle concurrency and queuing yourself with an NSOperationQueue and a custom NSOperation.

In the sample project, the definitions of the various command dictionary keys are stored in the implementation file for this class, APRemoteAddressBook.m. If you want to keep yours in the same place, you can move them from any other file you've used into here to match—the code is in Listing 9-41.

Class Structure

The instance variables for the class, declared as part of its @implementation block, can be seen in Listing 9-62.

Listing 9-62.   Remote Address Book Class Layout

```
@implementation APRemoteAddressBook
{
    NSInputStream *          _inputStream;
    NSOutputStream *         _outputStream;

    NSOperationQueue *       _networkQ;

    // NSUUID -> APRemoteXPCReply_t block
    NSMutableDictionary *    _replyHandlersByUUID;

    __weak id<APRemoteAddressBookDelegate> _delegate;

    NSUInteger               _inputSize;
    NSMutableData *          _inputMessageData;
}

// ...

@end
```

There are a few items you can see here, some familiar, some not:

- Up front you can see the input and output streams used to receive and send data, respectively. These are both bound to the same communications channel and are obtained directly from the NSNetService passed to the class's initializer.

- The NSOperationQueue is where you will enqueue operations to send each command in a synchronous, ordered fashion. Receipt of reply data will be handled by an NSInputStream delegate method, called on the main run loop.

- Since all your networking is going to be fully asynchronous, you need a way to associate handling of a reply with the correct reply block passed into each APAddressBook protocol method. This is handled by enqueuing the reply block into the _replyHandlersByUUID dictionary, keyed by the NSUUID assigned to the particular command message being sent. When a reply comes in, it'll be tagged with the same UUID, allowing you to look up and call the appropriate reply block.

- The delegate you know already—it will be notified if the connection is closed.

- Similar to APAddressBookClient, you'll accumulate incoming data in _inputMessageData, keeping track of the length of the current message in _inputSize.

Setup and Tear-Down

Initialization is fairly straightforward. The input and output streams are obtained directly from the NSNetService, and your member variables are initialized, including your synchronous

NSOperationQueue. The input stream is scheduled on the main run loop and the class is set as its delegate; the output stream is handled separately on a per-operation basis. Then the streams are opened to complete initialization. The code can be seen in Listing 9-63.

Listing 9-63.   Initializing the Remote Address Book

```
- (id) initWithResolvedService: (NSNetService *) resolvedService
                     delegate: (id<APRemoteAddressBookDelegate>) delegate
{
    self = [super init];
    if ( self == nil )
        return ( nil );

    if ( [resolvedService getInputStream: &_inputStream
                            outputStream: &_outputStream] == NO )
        return ( nil );

    _delegate = delegate;
    _inputSize = NSNotFound;
    _inputMessageData = [NSMutableData new];

    _networkQ = [NSOperationQueue new];
    [_networkQ setMaxConcurrentOperationCount: 1];

    [_inputStream setDelegate: self];

    [_inputStream scheduleInRunLoop: [NSRunLoop mainRunLoop] forMode: NSRunLoopCommonModes];

    // NOT scheduling the output stream here: it's going to be scheduled only upon
    //   need while a single operation is sending data and needs to wait for output
    //   buffer space to become available.

    [_inputStream open];
    [_outputStream open];

    _replyHandlersByUUID = [NSMutableDictionary new];

    return ( self );
}
```

When the address book is deallocated, the connections get torn down. When using ARC, the -dealloc method can usually be left out and everything will work, but we've chosen to use one here for illustrative purposes in Listing 9-64.

Listing 9-64.   Remote Address Book Deallocation

```
- (void) dealloc
{
    NSLog(@"Remote address book deallocating: %@", self);
    [_networkQ cancelAllOperations];
    if ( [_inputStream streamStatus] != NSStreamStatusClosed )
```

```
    {
        [_inputStream removeFromRunLoop: [NSRunLoop mainRunLoop]
                              forMode: NSRunLoopCommonModes];
        [_inputStream close];
    }
    if ( [_outputStream streamStatus] != NSStreamStatusClosed )
    {
        [_outputStream close];
    }
}
```

Sending Commands

Our chosen approach for sending messages to the remote application is to encapsulate the send operation within a block, which may be called multiple times. This block will return a BOOL value indicating whether there is more data left to send. Using a block in this fashion means that the data itself doesn't need to be passed around, nor will the actual transmission logic need to be separated from the command packetization[4] logic. The block will then be passed to a simple NSOperation subclass, which will act as the delegate for the output stream, calling the block as appropriate whenever there is space on the stream to do so, until the data has all been sent (or an error occurs).

The operation itself has a simple interface and structure, shown in Listing 9-65. This class can be placed entirely within APRemoteAddressBook.m since no other code needs to reference it.

Listing 9-65. The Data-Send Operation

```
@interface APSendCommandOperation : NSOperation <NSStreamDelegate>
- (id) initWithStream: (NSOutputStream *) stream
            timeout: (NSTimeInterval) timeout
             sender: (BOOL (^)(BOOL *success)) sender;
@property (nonatomic, readonly) BOOL successful;
@property (nonatomic, readonly) NSError * error;
@end

@implementation APSendCommandOperation
{
    NSOutputStream * _stream;
    BOOL (^_sendData)(BOOL *);
    BOOL _repeat, _success;
    NSTimeInterval _timeout;
    NSError * _error;
}

@synthesize successful=_success, error=_error;

// ...

@end
```

---

[4]*Packetization* is the process of turning some formatted data into a flat sequence of bytes, known as a *data packet*.

As you can see, it is initialized with a stream to monitor and a block to call when space is available on that stream, along with a time in seconds to wait for the entire command to be sent. It also keeps track of whether it should wait for enough room to send more data (the _repeat flag) and whether the send as a whole was successful (_success).

Its initializer is very simple, merely storing the provided values and initializing its variables, as seen in Listing 9-66. Note that it doesn't assume ownership of the output stream at this point: that should only happen when the operation runs since, as you learned in Chapter 6, networking can take a long time. The stream may be used by any number of other operations between the time this one is initialized and the time it is run.

Listing 9-66.   Initializing the Operation

```
- (id) initWithStream: (NSOutputStream *) stream
             timeout: (NSTimeInterval) timeout
              sender: (BOOL (^)(BOOL *)) sender
{
    self = [super init];
    if ( self == nil )
        return ( nil );

    _stream = stream;
    _sendData = [sender copy];
    _repeat = _success = YES;
    _timeout = (timeout == 0.0 ? 30.0 : timeout);

    return ( self );
}
```

The guts of the operation can be seen in Listing 9-67. The -main method checks whether space is available on the stream and calls the block if so. If all the data was sent in that one pass, the operation completes immediately. If not, the operation sets itself as the stream's delegate and spins a run loop, waiting for space to become available. Whenever there's room, it calls the block again, potentially completing the operation in the process. Similarly, if an error occurs on the stream, the operation completes. It additionally creates a specific timeout date based on the initializer parameter, and if that time elapses then it signals failure, records an error, and stops.

Listing 9-67.   Running the Operation

```
- (void) main
{
    if ( [_stream hasSpaceAvailable] )
    {
        if ( _sendData(&_success) == NO )
            return; // all done, whether due to error or completion
    }

    [_stream setDelegate: self];
    [_stream scheduleInRunLoop: [NSRunLoop currentRunLoop]
                    forMode: NSDefaultRunLoopMode];
```

```objc
    NSDate * timeoutDate = [NSDate dateWithTimeIntervalSinceNow: _timeout];

    do
    {
        @autoreleasepool
        {
            [[NSRunLoop currentRunLoop] runMode: NSDefaultRunLoopMode
                                     beforeDate: timeoutDate];
        }

        // see if the timeout elapsed
        if ( [timeoutDate earlierDate: [NSDate date]] == timeoutDate )
        {
            _error = [NSError errorWithDomain: NSURLErrorDomain
                                        code: NSURLErrorTimedOut
                                    userInfo: nil];
            _success = NO;
        }

    } while ( _repeat && _success && [self isCancelled] == NO );

    [_stream setDelegate: nil];
    [_stream removeFromRunLoop: [NSRunLoop currentRunLoop]
                       forMode: NSDefaultRunLoopMode];
}

- (void) stream: (NSStream *) aStream handleEvent: (NSStreamEvent) eventCode
{
    switch ( eventCode )
    {
        case NSStreamEventHasSpaceAvailable:
            _repeat = _sendData(&_success);
            break;

        case NSStreamEventErrorOccurred:
            _error = [aStream streamError];
            _success = NO;
            break;

        default:
            break;
    }
}
```

Now that the operation code is complete, you can look at sending commands. The first step is to implement the methods of the APAddressBook protocol, as seen in Listing 9-68. Each method builds a dictionary repre sentation of the command and hands it off to a central method for processing.

Listing 9-68. Command Methods

```
- (void) allPeople: (void (^)(NSArray *, NSError *)) reply
{
    NSDictionary * command = @{
        APRemoteAddressBookCommandNameKey : APRemoteAddressBookCommandAllPeople,
        APRemoteAddressBookCommandUUIDKey : [[NSUUID UUID] UUIDString]
    };
    [self postMessage: command replyingTo: reply];
}


- (void) mailingAddressesForPersonWithIdentifier: (NSString *) identifier
                                          reply: (void (^)(NSArray *, NSError *)) reply
{
    NSDictionary * command = @{
        APRemoteAddressBookCommandNameKey :
                                   APRemoteAddressBookCommandGetMailingAddresses,
        APRemoteAddressBookCommandUUIDKey : [[NSUUID UUID] UUIDString],
        APRemoteAddressBookCommandPersonIDKey : identifier
    };
    [self postMessage: command replyingTo: reply];
}


- (void) emailAddressesForPersonWithIdentifier: (NSString *) identifier
                                        reply: (void (^)(NSArray *, NSError *)) reply
{
    NSDictionary * command = @{
        APRemoteAddressBookCommandNameKey : APRemoteAddressBookCommandGetEmailAddresses,
        APRemoteAddressBookCommandUUIDKey : [[NSUUID UUID] UUIDString],
        APRemoteAddressBookCommandPersonIDKey : identifier
    };
    [self postMessage: command replyingTo: reply];
}


- (void) phoneNumbersForPersonWithIdentifier: (NSString *) identifier
                                       reply: (void (^)(NSArray *, NSError *)) reply
{
    NSDictionary * command = @{
        APRemoteAddressBookCommandNameKey : APRemoteAddressBookCommandGetPhoneNumbers,
        APRemoteAddressBookCommandUUIDKey : [[NSUUID UUID] UUIDString],
        APRemoteAddressBookCommandPersonIDKey : identifier
    };
    [self postMessage: command replyingTo: reply];
}
```

The next step, then, is to implement the core method, -postMessage:replyingTo:. This involves a few steps: packetizing the message, creating the send operation, and handling the reply. Start by adding the code from Listing 9-69.

Listing 9-69. Encoding the Command

```
- (void) postMessage: (NSDictionary *) message
         replyingTo: (void (^)(NSArray *, NSError *)) reply
{
    // ensure the reply block is copied to the heap
    reply = [reply copy];

    NSError * error = nil;
    NSData * jsonData = [NSJSONSerialization dataWithJSONObject: message
                                                       options: 0
                                                         error: &error];
    if ( jsonData == nil )
    {
        NSLog(@"Failed to encode message: %@. Message = %@", error, message);
        reply(nil, error);
        return;
    }

    NSMutableData * dataToSend = [jsonData mutableCopy];
    // ...
}
```

At this point you've encoded the command or sent back an error. Assuming everything worked as expected, you now want to create the send operation and enqueue it, which involves defining the data-send block passed in. Use the code from Listing 9-70 for this.

Listing 9-70. Writing Data

```
void (^replyCopy)(NSArray *, NSError *) = [reply copy];
APSendCommandOperation * operation = [[APSendCommandOperation alloc]
                                    initWithStream: _outputStream
                                           timeout: 30.0
                                            sender: ^BOOL(BOOL *success) {
    NSInteger sent = [_outputStream write: [dataToSend bytes]
                               maxLength: [dataToSend length]];

    if ( sent < 0 )
    {
        NSError * error = [_outputStream streamError];
        NSLog(@"Failed to send message data: %@. Message = %@", error, message);
        *success = NO;

        // post back the reply here, while we have hold of the error
        replyCopy(nil, error);
        return ( NO );
    }
```

```
    else if ( sent > 0 )
    {
        // remove the bytes we successfully sent
        [dataToSend replaceBytesInRange: NSMakeRange(0, sent)
                             withBytes: NULL
                                length: 0];
    }

    return ( [dataToSend length] > 0 );
}];
```

Note that the first action taken is to copy the reply block, ensuring it stays on the heap. Inside
the block, the entire data packet is written using NSOutputStream's -write:maxLength: method.
If an error is returned, the block sets the success value to NO and returns NO, telling the operation
to stop. Otherwise, the amount of data sent is removed from the front of the data object. The
block then returns YES if more data remains, or NO to stop the operation if everything was sent
successfully.

Now that the operation has been initialized, you want to know when it completes so you can
wait for a reply to arrive. Doing this asynchronously is most easily accomplished by adding a
completion block to the operation. As shown in Listing 9-71, this block first needs to determine
whether a reply should be expected at all, or whether an error needs to be reported. If an error
occurred while trying to write to the stream, it was already sent back to the client application,
otherwise you need to fetch it from the operation here and send it on.

Listing 9-71. Handling Operation Errors

```
__weak APRemoteAddressBook * weakSelf = self;
__weak APSendCommandOperation * weakOp = operation;
[operation setCompletionBlock: ^{
    APSendCommandOperation * strongOp = weakOp;
    if ( [strongOp isCancelled] )
    {
        // no reply will arrive, so send back an error dictionary
        NSDictionary * info = @{
            NSLocalizedDescriptionKey :
                NSLocalizedString(@"The request was cancelled.", @"error")
        };
        NSError * error = [NSError errorWithDomain: NSOSStatusErrorDomain
                                             code: userCanceledErr
                                         userInfo: info];
        replyCopy(nil, error);
        return;
    }

    if ( strongOp == nil )
        return;      // another error, which has already been sent
    if ( strongOp.successful == NO )
    {
        if ( strongOp.error != nil )
```

```
        {
            // need to send the error back
            replyCopy(nil, strongOp.error);
        }

        return;
    }

    // ...
}];
```

Note that, to avoid retain-loops, weak references to both the operation and the address book object are created up-front, and strong references are made when the block is called.

If no errors have occurred, the XPC reply block is packed into _replyHandlersByUUID using the code in Listing 9-72.

Listing 9-72. Storing the Reply Block

```
APRemoteAddressBook * strongSelf = weakSelf;
if ( strongSelf == nil )
    return;      // handler object has been shut down already

// store the reply block, referenced by the command's unique ID
NSUUID * uuid = [[NSUUID alloc] initWithUUIDString:
                                    message[APRemoteAddressBookCommandUUIDKey]];
strongSelf->_replyHandlersByUUID[uuid] = replyCopy;
```

Now that the reply block has been saved off for later access, you'll want to wait for the result to arrive. Since the address book object is receiving delegate messages from the input stream, any replies will be handled there. However, if the reply doesn't arrive within a reasonable time frame, you will want to send an error back to the client application. To implement this, you can use dispatch_after(), which runs a block on a given queue after a certain amount of time has elapsed. Listing 9-73 shows how to do this and completes the implementation of the operation's completion block.

Listing 9-73. Installing a Reply Timeout

```
// we want a reply to arrive within thirty seconds. If no reply arrives
// (or if it's garbled) then we'll eventually time out and reply to the
// client with an error message.
double delayInSeconds = 30.0;
dispatch_time_t popTime = dispatch_time(DISPATCH_TIME_NOW, delayInSeconds * NSEC_PER_SEC);
dispatch_after(popTime, dispatch_get_main_queue(), ^(void){
    APRemoteAddressBook * delayStrongSelf = weakSelf;
    void (^aReply)(NSArray *, NSError *) = delayStrongSelf->_replyHandlersByUUID[uuid];
```

```
    if ( aReply != nil )
    {
        // a real reply hasn't arrived yet -- send a timeout error
        aReply(nil, [NSError errorWithDomain: NSURLErrorDomain
                                         code: NSURLErrorTimedOut
                                     userInfo: nil]);
        [delayStrongSelf->_replyHandlersByUUID removeObjectForKey: uuid];
    }
});
```

Now the operation is completely set up: its worker block is defined, and a completion block has been added to handle errors and setup for receiving replies. The only remaining step in this method is to actually schedule the operation by adding it to the queue, as in Listing 9-74.

Listing 9-74. Scheduling the Operation

```
[_networkQ addOperation: operation];
```

Receiving Replies

Any incoming data is obtained and accumulated through an NSStream delegate method attached to the input stream. That data is accumulated in the _inputMessageData instance variable and processed in the same manner as the incoming data in the APAddressBookClient class, with the length of the accumulated data compared against a preceding size value. One difference here is that everything is done in a single method and that a regular NSMutableData object is used to store everything rather than the optimized dispatch_data type.

The basic structure of the stream delegate method is actually quite simple: only three events need to be handled, as shown in Listing 9-75.

Listing 9-75. Input Stream Delegation

```
- (void) stream: (NSStream *) aStream handleEvent: (NSStreamEvent) eventCode
{
    if ( aStream != _inputStream )
        return;

    switch ( eventCode )
    {
        case NSStreamEventHasBytesAvailable:
        {
            // ...
            break;
        }

        case NSStreamEventErrorOccurred:
        {
            NSLog(@"Remote address book input stream error: %@", [aStream streamError]);
            // fall through to close/disconnect the stream
        }
```

```
        case NSStreamEventEndEncountered:
        {
            NSLog(@"No more data on remote address book input stream-- disconnecting");
            [self disconnect];
            break;
        }

        default:
            break;
    }
}
```

In both the error and end-of-file cases the -disconnect message is sent to terminate the connection. The error case actually falls through to the end-of-file case once it has logged the stream error, keeping the code nice and neat.

The first case, NSStreamEventHasBytesAvailable, is rather more complicated. Its first task is to determine whether it needs to read a four-byte size value or some data for a command. Listing 9-76 shows how to implement that first step.

Listing 9-76. Checking for an Incoming Size Value

```
// read everything -- accumulate it in our data ivar
if ( _inputSize == NSNotFound )
{
    // need to read four bytes of size first
    uint32_t messageSize = 0;
    NSInteger sizeRead = [_inputStream read: (uint8_t *)&messageSize maxLength: 4];
    if ( sizeRead < 4 )
    {
        // something horrible happened!
        NSLog(@"ARGH! Couldn't read message size from stream, only got %ld bytes!",
                sizeRead);
        return;
    }

    // byte-swap it properly
    _inputSize = ntohl(messageSize);
    NSLog(@"Incoming message is %lu bytes in size.", _inputSize);

    // clear out our mutable data, ready to accumulate a message blob
    [_inputMessageData setLength: 0];
}
```

Once a message length has been received, whether in this invocation or retained from earlier, you'll want to start pulling in the message data itself. You know how much you have and how much to expect, so you can easily work out how much to request from the stream. For the sake of your sanity, we recommend putting a limit on the amount of data loaded at any one time—we chose 16KB, but you are free to pick any size you like. Use -read:maxLength: to fetch bytes from the stream, and the result of that method will tell you how much was actually returned (it won't be more than you request, but it may be less). Listing 9-77 contains the relevant code, reading into a stock-based buffer.

Listing 9-77. Accumulating Message Data

```
// try to read some message data
// by definition we need some more data at this point
NSUInteger needed = _inputSize - [_inputMessageData length];

#define MAX_READ 1024*16
uint8_t readBytes[MAX_READ];
NSUInteger amountToRead = MIN(needed, MAX_READ);        // MAX 16KB at a time

NSInteger numRead = [_inputStream read: readBytes maxLength: amountToRead];
if ( numRead <= 0 )
    return;  // no data available

// append the input to our accumulator
[_inputMessageData appendBytes: readBytes length: numRead];
```

If this read loaded all the data you needed to complete the incoming message, you can now convert it into an NSDictionary using NSJSONSerialization in the usual fashion, as seen in Listing 9-78.

At this point you can look at the message's UUID and use that to pull the XPC reply block out of the _replyHandlersByUUID dictionary. If no block is available, then an error or timeout reply has already been sent, and the current message can be discarded. If the block is present, then it can be removed from the dictionary and called, passing it the result array and/or the error value from the message dictionary.

Listing 9-78. Processing Received Messages

```
// if we've read everything, we dispatch the message and reset our ivars
if ( numRead == needed )
{
    NSError * jsonError = nil;
    NSDictionary * message = [NSJSONSerialization JSONObjectWithData: _inputMessageData
                                                            options: 0
                                                              error: &jsonError];

    // set our size marker & empty the data accumulator
    _inputSize = NSNotFound;
    [_inputMessageData setLength: 0];

    if ( message == nil )
    {
        NSLog(@"Failed to decode message: %@", jsonError);
        return;
    }

    // dispatch the message
    NSUUID * uuid = [[NSUUID alloc] initWithUUIDString:
    message[APRemoteAddressBookCommandUUIDKey]];
    void (^reply)(NSArray *, NSError *) = _replyHandlersByUUID[uuid];
```

```
    // if the reply block has been consumed, a timeout occurred
    if ( reply == nil )
        break;

    // otherwise, we consume it
    [_replyHandlersByUUID removeObjectForKey: uuid];

    reply(message[APRemoteAddressBookCommandValueKey],
          message[APRemoteAddressBookCommandErrorKey]);
}
```

Now you have only one task left: the -disconnect method specified by the APRemoteAddressBook protocol. Its implementation, which closes down the streams and notifies the address book's delegate, can be seen in Listing 9-79.

Listing 9-79. Disconnecting from the Address Book

```
- (void) disconnect
{
    [_inputStream setDelegate: nil];
    [_outputStream setDelegate: nil];

    [_networkQ cancelAllOperations];

    [_inputStream removeFromRunLoop: [NSRunLoop mainRunLoop]
                            forMode: NSRunLoopCommonModes];
    [_outputStream removeFromRunLoop: [NSRunLoop mainRunLoop]
                             forMode: NSRunLoopCommonModes];

    [_inputStream close];
    [_outputStream close];

    [_delegate addressBookDidDisconnect: self];
}
```

Pat yourself on the back: your XPC service, and all your networking code, is complete.

Displaying Remote Address Books

It's now possible to attach your application to another instance on the network and to request its data, but so far there's no user interface to let the user actually look at the data. Neither is there any interface for browsing available stores. That's going to be remedied now.

The Browser UI

First of all, you need to update the interface so the user can request a list of address books to browse. Open MainMenu.xib and open the Window menu from the menubar in the editor. From the **Windows & Menus** section of the Object Palette, drag a new **Separator Menu item** onto the menu, just below the "**Publish...**" menu item you added earlier. Name it "**Browse...**" (including the ellipsis).

To use the menu item, you need an action method. Open APAppDelegate.h and add the code from Listing 9-80.

Listing 9-80. The Browse Action Method

```
- (IBAction)browseRemoteStores:(id)sender;
- (void)attachToRemoteAddressBookWithName:(NSString *)name
                           handler:(void (^)(id<APRemoteAddressBook>, NSError *)) handler;
```

You now have both the action for the menu item and one to use when the user has chosen a remote address book to which to connect. In the interface editor, Control-drag a connection from the new menu item to the App Delegate and choose the -browseRemoteStores: method as its action.

Open APAppDelegate.m and locate the -vendAddressBook: method. Type the code from Listing 9-81 below it to implement this action method.

Listing 9-81. Requesting a Service Browser

```
- (IBAction)browseRemoteStores:(id)sender
{
    if ( _browser == nil )
        [self _initializeNetworker];

    [_browser availableServiceNames: ^(id result, NSError *error) {
        dispatch_async(dispatch_get_main_queue(), ^{
            if ( error != nil )
            {
                [NSApp presentError: error];
            }
            else
            {
                _browserWindow = [[APRemoteBrowserWindowController alloc]
                                      initWithServiceNames: result delegate: self];
                [_browserWindow showWindow: self];
            }
        });
    }];
}
```

This code calls the XPC method -availableServiceNames:, and its reply block passes on the (successful) results to a new window controller object, APRemoteBrowserWindowController. Quickly skip to the top of the file and add an import statement for APRemoteBrowserWindowController.h.

There's also a new instance variable involved: _browserWindow, which holds a reference to the browser's window controller. Add that into the class's @implementation block. Now let's create that new class.

In Xcode, add a new file to the application target; make it a subclass of NSWindowController and give it the name just discussed. Also ensure that the "**With XIB for user interface**" button is checked. When the files have been created, open APRemoteBrowserWindowController.h.

Your task here is to declare some properties to be bound to the user interface and to define a delegation protocol used to provide information on the user's choice back to the application delegate. Enter the code from Listing 9-82.

Listing 9-82.   The Browser Interface

```
@class APRemoteBrowserWindowController;

@protocol APRemoteBrowserDelegate <NSObject>
- (void) remoteBrowser: (APRemoteBrowserWindowController *) browser
 connectToServiceNamed: (NSString *) serviceName;
@end

@interface APRemoteBrowserWindowController : NSWindowController

- (id) initWithServiceNames: (NSArray *) serviceNames
                   delegate: (id<APRemoteBrowserDelegate>) delegate;

@property (nonatomic, readonly) NSArray * serviceNames;
@property (nonatomic, assign) IBOutlet NSTableView * tableView;
@property (nonatomic, readonly, weak) id<APRemoteBrowserDelegate> delegate;

- (IBAction) connect: (id) sender;

@end
```

Now that the protocol is defined, switch to APAppDelegate.h and add APRemoteBrowserDelegate to that class's list of implemented protocols. You also need to import the new header file.

Now switch back to the browser's interface. From the Object Palette, drag a Push Button up to the lower right corner of the window and let the automatic guides snap it into place. Using the Attributes Inspector, change its title to Connect and set its key-equivalent to the Enter key (click in the Key Equivalent field and press Enter).

Now drag a Table View from the palette up to the very top edge of the window and resize it to meet the window's right and left edges. Now adjust its lower edge so that it snaps into place above the button. Using the Attributes Inspector, give it a single column that stretches across the table's entire width, and ensure it remains a cell-based table view, not view-based. Deselect the options to show the column headers and reordering; ensure that it is not multi-selectable and that it supports type-to-select. Click again in the table to select the column: ensure this is not editable.

Lastly, select the window again and give it a title of Address Books. If you simulate the interface now and try resizing it, you should see everything behave correctly, with the table filling the window's width and the button remaining at the bottom-right.

Control-drag from the Connect button to the File's Owner object and connect it to the -connect: action method. Control-drag from File's Owner to the table view to connect the tableView outlet, and from the table to the owner to connect the table's delegate and dataSource outlets—you're going to implement this table the old-fashioned way.

The finished article should look like that seen in Figure 9-5.

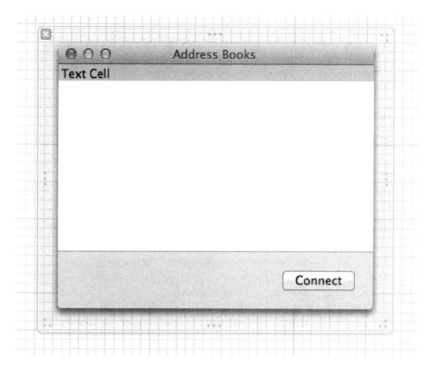

Figure 9-5. *The completed browser window*

The implementation of this class is actually very minimal. Its initialization, appearance, and action are shown in Listing 9-83.

Listing 9-83. *Browser Controller Implementation*

```
- (id) initWithServiceNames: (NSArray *) serviceNames
                  delegate: (id<APRemoteBrowserDelegate>) delegate
{
    self = [super initWithWindowNibName: [self className]];
    if ( self == nil )
        return ( nil );

    _serviceNames = [serviceNames sortedArrayUsingSelector: @selector(caseInsensitiveCompare:)];
    _delegate = delegate;

    return ( self );
}

- (void) windowDidLoad
{
    [super windowDidLoad];

    // Implement this method to handle any initialization after your window controller's window
has been loaded from its nib file.
```

```
    // make double-clicking a row the same as selecting it and clicking 'Connect'
    [self.tableView setTarget: self];
    [self.tableView setDoubleAction: @selector(connect:)];
}

- (IBAction) connect: (id) sender
{
    NSString * name = [_serviceNames objectAtIndex: [self.tableView selectedRow]];
    [_delegate remoteBrowser: self connectToServiceNamed: name];
}
```

Likewise, the setup for the table view is similarly simple: two methods with one line apiece, as in Listing 9-84.

Listing 9-84. Browser Controller Table Implementation

```
- (NSInteger) numberOfRowsInTableView: (NSTableView *) tableView
{
    return ( [_serviceNames count] );
}

- (id) tableView: (NSTableView *) tableView
        objectValueForTableColumn: (NSTableColumn *) tableColumn row: (NSInteger) row
{
    return ( [_serviceNames objectAtIndex: row] );
}
```

Making The Connection

Your next task is to implement the delegation method in the APAppDelegate.m. Open that file and just below the -browseRemoteStores: method add the code from Listing 9-85. This method is a small wrapper for the call to the XPC service, which your delegate method will use.

Listing 9-85. A Connection Wrapper Method

```
- (void)attachToRemoteAddressBookWithName:(NSString *)name
                         handler:(void (^)(id<APRemoteAddressBook>, NSError *)) handler;
{
    if ( _browser == nil )
        [self _initializeNetworker];

    [_browser connectToServiceWithName: name replyHandler: handler];
}
```

With that in place, you can start to work with the remote address book windows themselves.

The application delegate has some bookkeeping to do here. It will need to keep references to the new window controllers, and it will need to find out when the user closes the windows so it can release those references. The former requirement is fairly simple: an NSMutableSet seems like the logical choice since it prevents duplicate references and provides fast lookup.

When windows close, they post a notification. You could observe that notification in the usual way, but that would only tell you about the *window*, not the *controller*. A better way is to use the blocks-based notification system: this way you can reference the newly created controller directly from the block. You'll be handed an observer object, which you will keep hold of and release when you no longer wish to observe the notification. This object can't be referenced by the block, however, because that will lead to a retain cycle; instead you'll pack it into a dictionary, keyed by the name of the service to which you've connected. This way, the block can look it up to remove it when the notification is fired.

Your first task, then, is to add these two new variables to the app delegate class and initialize them properly in -awakeFromNib. Listing 9-86 shows this—the added lines are bolded.

Listing 9-86. Window Controller Bookkeeping

```
@implementation APAppDelegate
{
    NSXPCConnection *                   _xpcConnection;
    id<APRemoteAddressBookBrowser>  _browser;

    APRemoteBrowserWindowController * _browserWindow;
    NSMutableSet *                      _remoteBookWindows;
    NSMutableDictionary *               _remoteBookObservers;
}

@synthesize persistentStoreCoordinator = _persistentStoreCoordinator;
@synthesize managedObjectModel = _managedObjectModel;
@synthesize managedObjectContext = _managedObjectContext;

- (void) awakeFromNib
{
    _remoteBookWindows = [NSMutableSet new];
    _remoteBookObservers = [NSMutableDictionary new];

    SEL compareSelector = @selector(caseInsensitiveCompare:);
    // ...
}
```

With this complete, scroll down and create the browser delegate method beneath -attachToRemo teAddressBookWithName:handler:, using the code in Listing 9-87.

Listing 9-87. The Browser Delegate Method

```
- (void) remoteBrowser: (APRemoteBrowserWindowController *) browser
 connectToServiceNamed: (NSString *) serviceName
{
    [self attachToRemoteAddressBookWithName: serviceName
                            handler: ^(id<APRemoteAddressBook> book, NSError *error) {
        // we're modifying the UI, so do everything on the main thread
        dispatch_async(dispatch_get_main_queue(), ^{
            if ( error != nil )
```

```
        {
            [NSApp presentError: error];
            return;
        }
        // ...
    });
}];
}
```

Since the result of connecting will be to modify the UI, the handler method immediately dispatches its work onto the main queue. If error occurs, that error is immediately presented to the user and the block returns, leaving the browser window in place.

Viewing Remote Address Books

The remote address book window is allocated from its nib file in the same manner as the browser window. Provided it initializes successfully, the browser window is automatically closed, and its reference is removed from the app delegate, as shown in Listing 9-88.

Listing 9-88. Opening the Remote Address Book Window

```
APRemoteAddressBookWindowController * remote = nil;
remote = [[APRemoteAddressBookWindowController alloc] initWithRemoteAddressBook: book
                                                            name: serviceName];

// close the browser window once we connect
if ( remote != nil )
{
    [browser close];
    if ( _browserWindow == browser )
        _browserWindow = nil;
}

// show the remote window
[remote showWindow: self];

// ...
```

After this comes the notification-handling code. Since the block needs to reference the app delegate object in order to access the set and dictionary you created earlier, youl need to create a weak reference to the app delegate. Once the observer has been created, both it and the window controller are added to their respective containers. The remaining code from the method can be seen in Listing 9-89.

Listing 9-89. Monitoring Window-Close Notifications

```
__weak APAppDelegate * weakSelf = self;
id observer = [[NSNotificationCenter defaultCenter] addObserverForName:
NSWindowWillCloseNotification object: [remote window] queue: [NSOperationQueue mainQueue]
usingBlock: ^(NSNotification *note) {
    APAppDelegate * strongSelf = weakSelf;
```

```
    if ( strongSelf == nil )
        return;

    [strongSelf->_remoteBookObservers removeObjectForKey: serviceName];
    [_remoteBookWindows removeObject: remote];
}];

// keep these alive
[_remoteBookWindows addObject: remote];
_remoteBookObservers[serviceName] = observer;
```

The next big step is to define the new window controller itself. Since this isn't a document-based application, you have to do some of the heavy lifting yourself as regards things like loading the nib files and so on. Luckily, that's about all there really is to it; all the data handling is based on code you've already written. This chapter has been a long one, but don't worry— there are only about 200 lines of code left!

First, add a new Objective-C class to your application target. Make it a subclass of NSWindowController, name it APRemoteAddressBookWindowController, and give it a XIB file. Open the new class's header file and add the code from Listing 9-90.

Listing 9-90.   The Address Book Window Interface

```
#import "APRemoteAddressBookInterface.h"

@interface APRemoteAddressBookWindowController : NSWindowController <NSTableViewDelegate>

- (id) initWithRemoteAddressBook: (id<APRemoteAddressBook>) remoteAddressBook
                            name: (NSString *) serviceName;

@property (nonatomic, readonly) NSString * serviceName;
@property (nonatomic, assign) IBOutlet NSArrayController * peopleController;

@property (nonatomic, readonly) NSArray *personSortDescriptors;
@property (nonatomic, readonly) NSArray *labelSortDescriptors;

@property (nonatomic, readonly, getter=isLoadingPeople) BOOL loadingPeople;

@end
```

You can see here that it takes ownership of the APRemoteAddressBook proxy object provided by the XPC service, and it notes (and makes available for inspection) the associated service name. There are also some familiar looking properties here: an NSArrayController for the list of people is being connected from the nib, and the same sort descriptor arrays are being exported as used by the app delegate. The one new item is a BOOL property used to indicate whether the list of people is currently big loaded—an NSProgressIndicator will be bound to this property to indicate loading activity.

The initial implementation of the class, including its initializer, can be seen in Listing 9-91. Add this code to APRemoteAddressBookWindowController.m.

Listing 9-91.   The Remote Address Book Initialization and Layout

```objc
@interface APRemoteAddressBookWindowController () <NSWindowDelegate>
@property (nonatomic, readwrite, getter=isLoadingPeople) BOOL loadingPeople;
@end

@implementation APRemoteAddressBookWindowController
{
    id<APRemoteAddressBook>     _remoteAddressBook;
    NSOperationQueue *          _loaderQ;
}

- (id) initWithRemoteAddressBook: (id<APRemoteAddressBook>) remoteAddressBook
                            name: (NSString *) serviceName
{
    self = [super initWithWindowNibName: [self className]];
    if ( self == nil )
        return ( nil );

    _serviceName = [serviceName copy];
    _remoteAddressBook = remoteAddressBook;
    _loaderQ = [NSOperationQueue new];
    [_loaderQ setMaxConcurrentOperationCount: 1];

    return ( self );
}

- (BOOL) windowShouldClose: (id) sender
{
    // tell the network connection to disconnect now
    [_remoteAddressBook disconnect];
    return ( YES );
}

// ...

@end
```

Note that the `loadingPeople` property is redeclared in a class extension to be writable; this
gives you the ability to set the value using a property setter that sends all the relevant KVO
notifications needed to keep the UI bindings up to date automatically. Additionally, the controller
implements the `-windowShouldClose:` action method of its `NSWindow` to inform the remote
address book that it should disconnect.

When the window loads you need to set up your initial data, along with the sort descriptors to be
used by the UI bindings. The code in Listing 9-92 shows the start of that process.

Listing 9-92.   Setting up the Window

```objc
- (void) windowDidLoad
{
    [super windowDidLoad];

    [[self window] setDelegate: self];
```

```
    // setup the sort descriptors
    // remember to trigger KVO notifications so the relevant controllers can be
    //  updated-- they're already bound by this point
    if ( _personSortDescriptors == nil )
    {
        [self willChangeValueForKey: @"personSortDescriptors"];
        _personSortDescriptors = @[[NSSortDescriptor sortDescriptorWithKey: @"lastName"
                                                         ascending: YES]];
        [self didChangeValueForKey: @"personSortDescriptors"];
    }
    if ( _labelSortDescriptors == nil )
    {
        [self willChangeValueForKey: @"labelSortDescriptors"];
        _labelSortDescriptors = @[[NSSortDescriptor sortDescriptorWithKey: @"label"
                                                        ascending: YES]];
        [self didChangeValueForKey: @"labelSortDescriptors"];
    }

    // fetch all people (it's always an asynchronous call)
    [_remoteAddressBook allPeople: ^(id result, NSError *error) {
        if ( error != nil )
        {
            dispatch_async(dispatch_get_main_queue(), ^{
                [NSApp presentError: error];
            });
            return;
        }

        // ...
    }];
}
```

Data Management

The data obtained from the remote address book will be accessed using bindings—in fact, the UI and its bindings will be almost identical to that used by the local address book window. The difference here is that you'll need to manually pack the values into a tree structure using dictionaries to simulate the hierarchy of the Core Data store. This means that you will have an array of people, each of which is a dictionary. These dictionaries will contain values for each of the Person objects' attributes, accessed using the same keys. They will also contain arrays for each address type, whose elements are dictionaries matching the format of the Address subclasses.

When the list of people is returned successfully, you need to pull out the appropriate attributes and pack them into new, mutable, dictionaries. You also need to pre-compute the full-name attribute. To keep the bindings happy, you also need to add empty mutable arrays to be populated with the address details; these arrays will be filled in on demand as the user selects each individual user.

Additionally, you want to show loading activity for each address list as well as for the people list. In order to do so, add BOOL values to each person's dictionary to bind in the same manner as the loadingPeople property on the class. There will be one for each address type (i.e. one for each XPC method called).

Listing 9-93 shows the code used to populate this list. Once it's populated, the resulting array is set as the content of the connected NSArrayController; this task takes place on the main queue since it will prompt a UI update.

Listing 9-93. Populating the People List

```
NSArray * people = result;
NSMutableArray * contentArray = [[NSMutableArray alloc] initWithCapacity: [people count]];
for ( NSDictionary * person in people )
{
    NSMutableDictionary * mine = [person mutableCopy];

    // add the remaining pieces necessary for our UI etc.
    NSString * first = person[@"firstName"];
    NSString * last = person[@"lastName"];

    if ( first != nil && last != nil )
        mine[@"fullName"] = [NSString stringWithFormat: @"%@ %@", first, last];
    else if ( first != nil )
        mine[@"fullName"] = first;
    else if ( last != nil )
        mine[@"fullName"] = last;

    if ( first != nil )
        mine[@"firstName"] = first;
    if ( last != nil )
        mine[@"lastName"] = last;

    mine[@"loadingPhones"] = @NO;
    mine[@"loadingEmails"] = @NO;
    mine[@"loadingAddresses"] = @NO;

    mine[@"phoneNumbers"] = [NSMutableArray new];
    mine[@"emails"] = [NSMutableArray new];
    mine[@"addresses"] = [NSMutableArray new];

    // pack it into the output array
    [contentArray addObject: mine];
}

// now we want to update the UI by setting the content of our
//  peopleController outlet to this array
// this hits the UI though, so we do it on the main thread
dispatch_async(dispatch_get_main_queue(), ^{
    [self.peopleController setContent: contentArray];
});
```

Loading addresses, as mentioned above, is performed on demand as the user changes their selection in the list of people. To implement this, the controller implements an NSTableView delegate method: -tableViewSelectionDidChange:. When this method is called, it obtains the index of the current selection directly from the NSArrayController to which the table has been bound, using this to retrieve the appropriate dictionary from the content array. Start implementing this method with the code in Listing 9-94.

Listing 9-94. Responding to Selection Changes

```
- (void) tableViewSelectionDidChange: (NSNotification *) notification
{
    // find the Person's mutable dictionary
    if ( [self.peopleController selectionIndex] == NSNotFound )
        return;

    NSMutableDictionary * person = [self.peopleController selection];
    if ( person == nil )
        return;

    NSString * personID = [person valueForKey: APRemoteAddressBookCommandPersonIDKey];
    if ( personID == nil )
        return;       // can't do anything without the ID

    // kill any waiting load operations so this one can run quickly for the user
    [_loaderQ cancelAllOperations];

    // ...
}
```

The retrieval of addresses happens asynchronously using operations placed on the serial operation queue created in Listing 9-90. For each address type, the value of its loading indicator is read from the person's dictionary and inspected. If it's not already loading and no data is yet stored, then an operation is created to fetch it, using a block. The loading attribute is then set appropriately.

Since the reply will come back asynchronously, the loading attribute will stay on until either the data (or an error) comes back from the XPC service or until the operation terminates due to cancellation. The former is implemented in the XPC reply block, while the latter uses an operation completion block to check for cancellation.

The code for this can be seen in Listing 9-95. Note that each address type uses almost identical code: only the XPC method name and the two keys change each time.

Listing 9-95. Loading Addresses

```
if ( [[person valueForKey: @"loadingPhones"] isEqual: @NO] && [[person valueForKey:
@"phoneNumbers"] count] == 0 )
{
    [person setValue: @YES forKey: @"loadingPhones"];
    NSOperation * op = [NSBlockOperation blockOperationWithBlock: ^{
        [_remoteAddressBook phoneNumbersForPersonWithIdentifier: personID reply: ^(id result,
NSError *error) {
            // again, update the controller's content on the main queue, since it
            //  will update the UI in response.
```

```
                dispatch_async(dispatch_get_main_queue(), ^{
                    [person setValue: result forKey: @"phoneNumbers"];
                    [person setValue: @NO forKey: @"loadingPhones"];
                });
            }];
        }];

        // the completion block runs when the operation is complete or canceled
        __weak NSOperation * weakOp = op;
        [op setCompletionBlock: ^{
            // if cancelled, we're no longer loading
            if ( [weakOp isCancelled] )
                [person setValue: @NO forKey: @"loadingPhones"];
        }];
        [_loaderQ addOperation: op];
}
if ( [[person valueForKey: @"loadingEmails"] isEqual: @NO] && [[person valueForKey: @"emails"]
count] == 0 )
{
    [person setValue: @YES forKey: @"loadingEmails"];
    NSOperation * op = [NSBlockOperation blockOperationWithBlock: ^{
        [_remoteAddressBook emailAddressesForPersonWithIdentifier: personID reply: ^(id result,
NSError *error) {
            // again, update the controller's content on the main queue, since it
            //  will update the UI in response.
            dispatch_async(dispatch_get_main_queue(), ^{
                [person setValue: result forKey: @"emails"];
                [person setValue: @NO forKey: @"loadingEmails"];
            });
        }];
    }];

    // the completion block runs when the operation is complete or canceled
    __weak NSOperation * weakOp = op;
    [op setCompletionBlock: ^{
        if ( [weakOp isCancelled] )
            [person setValue: @NO forKey: @"loadingEmails"];
    }];
    [_loaderQ addOperation: op];
}
if ( [[person valueForKey: @"loadingAddresses"] isEqual: @NO] && [[person valueForKey:
@"addresses"] count] == 0 )
{
    [person setValue: @YES forKey: @"loadingAddresses"];
    NSOperation * op = [NSBlockOperation blockOperationWithBlock: ^{
        [_remoteAddressBook mailingAddressesForPersonWithIdentifier: personID reply: ^(id
result, NSError *error) {
            // again, update the controller's content on the main queue, since it
            //  will update the UI in response.
            dispatch_async(dispatch_get_main_queue(), ^{
```

```
                [person setValue: result forKey: @"addresses"];
                [person setValue: @NO forKey: @"loadingAddresses"];
            });
        }];
    }];

    // the completion block runs when the operation is complete or canceled
    __weak NSOperation * weakOp = op;
    [op setCompletionBlock: ^{
        if ( [weakOp isCancelled] )
            [person setValue: @NO forKey: @"loadingAddresses"];
    }];
    [_loaderQ addOperation: op];
}
```

…and just like that, you've finished all the code for this application!

Interfacing

Open `APRemoteAddressBookWindowController.xib` and delete its window. Now open `MainMenu.xib`, select the window, and copy it by pressing ⌘-C. Go back to `APRemoteAddressBookWindowController.xib` and paste it using ⌘-V. Your user interface is 90% complete. That was easy, wasn't it?

Mostly you need to hook up the relevant bindings to the user interface elements, but first you must resize things slightly to add some progress indicators. You place one at the bottom of the window below the People list, and one inside each pane of the tab view for their respective Address lists.

First, select the split view and drag its bottom edge upwards a little way—leave plenty of room at the bottom of the window. Open the Object Palette and locate the **Circular Progress Indicator**; drag one into the bottom-left corner of the window, letting the guides snap it into place relative to the window's bottom and left edges.

Now find a **Label** and drag it alongside the progress indicator. Its bottom edge should align with the progress indicator's bottom edge, and it should snap into place to the progress indicator's right. Set its text to "**Fetching People…**"—remember that you can type the ellipsis character using ⌥-; (Option-semicolon).

Select the progress indicator. In the Attributes Inspector, ensure the "**Display When Stopped**" checkbox is unchecked. Select the label and use the Attributes Inspector to set its **Text Color to Disabled Control Text Color**.

Now drag the bottom edge of the split view back down until it snaps into place above the progress indicator. The auto-layout struts should appear like those in Figure 9-6.

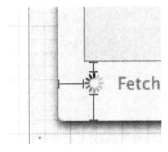

Figure 9-6. *Auto-layout guidelines*

Now select both the progress indicator and the label and copy them with -C. In each tab within the rightmost pane of the split view, drag the bottom of the table view up a little, click in the background of the tab pane, and paste with -V. Drag the two items together down to the bottom-left of the pane, then change the label to an appropriate variation of "Loading Addresses…" for the current tab. All cosmetic interface changes are now complete, and the result should look something like Figure 9-7.

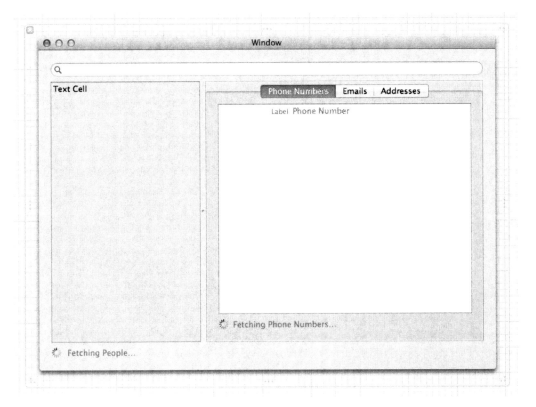

Figure 9-7. *The completed interface*

Bindings

The only remaining pieces of the puzzle are the bindings from the interface elements to their associated data. Drag out a new **Array Controller** from the Object Palette and name it People Controller. Drag a connection from the File's Owner object to this and set it to the peopleController outlet.

Select the new controller and look at the Attributes Inspector. Select all the checkboxes at the top, with the exception of "**Always Use Multi Values Marker.**" Set its mode to Class, with a value of NSDictionary, and uncheck the **Editable** checkbox (remote address books are only browseable, not editable). Lastly, add the keys from Listing 9-93 to the following key list: firstName, lastName, fullName, phoneNumbers, emails, addresses, loadingPhones, loadingEmails, and loadingAddresses.

Add three more array controllers with the same attributes: Phones Controller, Emails Controller, and Addresses Controller. For each one, add the appropriate keys to the key list.

Now you need to bind the UI to these controllers. The People Controller's content is set using the code from Listing 9-93, so that one is fine. Select the Phones Controller and bind its **Content Array** to the People Controller, with a **Controller Key** of Selection and a **Model Key Path** of phoneNumbers. Make similar bindings for the other two controllers, binding their Model Key Paths to emails and addresses as appropriate.

Now you need only do the same for the interface elements. Select the progress indicator at the bottom of the window and bind its **Animate** property to the File's Owner object with a key path of loadingPeople. Select the neighboring label and bind its Hidden property to the same value, with a **Value Transformer** of NSNegateBoolean. Repeat this process for each of the progress/label pairs inside the address tab panes, but bind them to the People Controller object with a **Controller Key** of selection and a **Model Key Path** of loadingPhones, loadingEmails, or loadingAddresses as appropriate.

Now to bind up the data in the tables, starting with the list of people. Select the table view in the left pane of the split view (click twice—you can look at the Attributes Inspector to ensure you have the right object selected) and bind its **Content** property to the People Controller's arrangedObjects controller key, with no key path. Also bind its **Selection Indexes** property to the People Controller's selectionIndexes controller key.

Click again on the table view to select the column; bind its Value property to the People Controller, with a **Controller Key** of selection and a **Model Key Path** of fullName. Select the Search Field at the top of the window and bind its **Predicate** property to the People Controller's filterPredicate controller key. The main list of people is now fully bound.

On each pane of the addresses tabbed view, select the table view and bind its **Content** property to the associated array controller's arrangedObjects controller key. Don't worry about the bindings for all the labels within the table: those are bound to their table cell's objectValue already, which is set by the **Content** binding you just added.

Now save your work and compile the app. You're done!

To test the remote address book, download the sample project and run the included abserversim command-line tool, which advertises an address book service vending the contents of the system address book. You should be able to connect to it and browse its contents from within your new application.

Summary

This has been a very long chapter, but boy, it was worth it.[5] You've built a complete, working application with the following features:

- A sandboxed main app with an XPC service for network communication.

- A sandboxed XPC service.

- Lots of data handling and network communication code using a couple of different approaches.

- Distributed Object proxying over XPC.

- Lots of new user interfaces using bindings and delegate/data-source methods.

There's only a little more to go now. In the next chapter, you'll see some ways in which iOS differs from OS X and you'll learn to publish an application on the App Store.

---

[5]No, seriously— if you thought it was long while *reading* it, imagine how long it took to *write* .

Chapter 10

Après Code: Distributing Your Application

This has been quite a journey, hasn't it? You've learned a lot in the pages of this book; enough, we hope, to give you the tools you need to become a great Objective-C programmer. Let's take a look back over everything you've seen so far.

- You were introduced to object-oriented programming following the Smalltalk model and how it differs from the Simula model adopted by languages such as C++ and Java.

- You saw the powerful and dynamic nature of messaging and learned to use blocks to pass around functions like first-class objects.

- You saw how blocks enable easy asynchronous programming techniques by capturing locally scoped variables on your behalf, saving you a lot of work maintaining state information.

- The flexible and powerful classes that make up the Foundation and Application kits were opened wide, bringing with them commonly used programming models such as delegation and dynamic programming.

- Many new language features were introduced, such as synthesized properties, collection subscripting, and object literals, along with more common elements like exceptions, synchronization, and interface protocols.

- You saw the many ways of working with the filesystem and you learned their relative strengths; you also learned to detect the common pitfalls of working with filesystem data and the facilities provided to best work around them, such as file coordination and bookmarks.

- You saw the many different ways of communicating across local- and wide-area networks, and you learned the properties and capabilities of the different protocols and transport media in use.

- The concepts of view hierarchies and window management have been laid out and described in detail, and you saw how to use Cocoa Auto Layout to build fluidly responsive user interfaces.

- You saw how the Cocoa drawing model works and how user input and layout events are passed through the view hierarchy.

- Core Data was brought into the picture in grand fashion, showing how you can define your data model in an object-oriented yet code-free fashion, with the framework providing lots of support for you.

- You saw how to use Cocoa Bindings to fit your data into a user interface in an almost entirely code-free fashion.

- You worked with the application sandbox and used XPC services to break the core functionality of an application into properly isolated components with secure, well-defined interfaces.

- You saw firsthand the benefits of dropping down a layer to the C-based Grand Dispatch APIs for their easy concurrency model and data- and throughput-handling facilities.

There are still a few steps between you and your first application, however. First of all, what about the iPhone and iPad? iOS uses the same Foundation framework as OS X, the same Grand Central Dispatch libraries, the same media libraries, and more. Then there's the issue of getting your application out there to the rest of the world, either through the iOS, the Mac App Store, or distributing it through your own web site. We'll give you an overview of all these topics.

Whither iOS?

Mac and iOS development is done using the same language: Objective-C. They even use a lot of the same frameworks and libraries under the hood. Almost all of the Foundation library can be used in either platform, including NSString, NSArray, NSDictionary, NSURLConnection, and so on. Even some platform-specific classes, like NSImage on OS X and UIImage on iOS, behave so similarly that it's common to find yourself typing the prefix of the wrong class when you're doing development on both platforms.

OS X developers have been using AppKit and Cocoa to write their apps for the Mac. In the time since these frameworks were written, they have accumulated cruft—same as any code. When Apple launched the iOS SDK in 2008, they took a fresh look at the user interface libraries and released the UIKit framework as part of Cocoa Touch.

The new frameworks benefit from the experience Apple gained writing AppKit and Cocoa. Apple used decades of writing, maintaining, and deprecating libraries to release UIKit and Cocoa Touch as very solid, mature frameworks, while leaving behind the mechanics dictated by two-decade-old technology.

While Cocoa has always used the Model-View-Controller paradigm, it's certainly possible to write apps on OS X without following the principles of MVC. When they released Cocoa Touch, Apple formalized the relationship between models, views, and controllers by providing a framework that works primarily with controllers, instead of views. In iOS 5, even the view hierarchy is explicitly mirrored by the controller hierarchy, passing through controller-specific events in the same manner used to propagate input events through a nested view hierarchy.

When an iOS app launches, the application delegate is responsible for setting the main view *controller*, not the main view. UIKit's containment-style view controllers (navigation controllers, tab bar controllers, split view controllers, and so on) all provide APIs to navigate through applications using view controllers, not views; to push a new view onto a navigation stack, you pass in a view controller, never a view itself—there's actually no API to work directly with views in this manner at all.

On OS X, an application may contain however many windows it likes, from one window to many to none at all. It's up to the developer to write an application that sits in the dock or the menu bar, or both, or neither. Applications can run in the background indefinitely until terminated by the user. There is a lot of flexibility when writing applications for OS X.

Contrast that to writing apps for iOS: windows in UIKit are actually *subclasses* of UIView and are managed directly by the UIApplication instance. There is usually a single UIWindow instance created by your application delegate, which has a single root view controller. The other windows you create are treated as the root of a full hierarchy, and their most common purpose is for the display of modal dialogs; these other windows serve primarily to capture events, preventing touches outside a modal view being handled by the application's main UI.

Developers also have no control over whether an application is listed in the user's home screen, dock, status bar, or otherwise; all applications have exactly one icon in one place. Applications on iOS can only exist in the background for a limited amount of time (and then only if they request it) unless they are implementing functionality of a specific type: Voice over IP connections, GPS tracking, or playback of audio.

Applications on iOS and OS X both use views of some kind to render their interfaces to the user. On iOS, developers use the UIView class; on OS X, the NSView class. On the surface, you would expect these views to be very similar. However, you do not need to look very far for striking differences.

On iOS, instances of UIView are always backed by CALayer objects. In fact, the UIView class is simply a lightweight wrapper around functionality provided by CALayer—in Core Animation terms, each UIView is a CALayer's delegate. This means that views on iOS already have a very powerful, built-in, transaction-based, and synchronized animation and transformation engine.

On OS X, NSView instances must explicitly request a backing CALayer. To access the transformations, you need to explicitly tell the view that it wants a layer. Animation on OS X is commonly performed by interacting directly with a view's CALayer or by interacting with a separate *animation proxy* object. The UIView class, on the other hand, has the concepts of transformations and animations built into its primary API.

Controls on iOS, such as buttons or switches, are really just a group of views provided by UIKit; their distinguishing feature is that they usually inherit from UIControl, a small UIView subclass that translates touch and gesture input into simpler action notifications to ease subclassing. On OS X, controls (typically subclasses of NSControl) use another class to do much of the heavy lifting. NSCell instances are used to render controls and maintain all the relevant state, though they aren't views themselves. By having the cell perform the rendering, the control is free to perform only the functions needed to fulfill the function of the control. Separating these concerns was important 15 to 20 years ago when a computer commonly had as much as 4 MB of RAM available to store large view objects. By using cells, views such as tables or matrices don't need tens of expensive subviews; they can just have a single cell instance that can be used to draw each control like a configurable rubber stamp.

Another difference between views on iOS and OS X is the geometric origin of a view. On iOS, the origin is always at the top left corner of a view, matching the value commonly used in other operating systems. On OS X (and in the CoreGraphics level on iOS), view origins are at the bottom left by default, matching both the Euclidean system of geometry and that commonly used in the printing system (yes, it came from the API's roots in Display PostScript). An individual NSView can override the -isFlipped method to return YES in order to vertically flip the view's coordinate system and have its origin become the top left corner.

All in all, iOS is similar enough to OS X that it's easy to pick up, and where there are differences, the APIs are clean and simple compared to their OS X counterparts. It's much easier to move from OS X to iOS programming than to go the other way as a result—and this is part of the reason we chose to concentrate primarily on OS X in this book. Having learned the hard way, the easy way should feel like second nature.

Distributing Your Application

By far the simplest way to distribute your application to millions of potential users worldwide is to use the App Store. For iOS, this is your only choice, but for OS X it's only one of many: you can also distribute your application any other way you desire, whether by direct download or in boxed physical media. In the latter case, you also have two routes you can take. If you choose to code-sign your application using an Apple Developer ID certificate, then computers running OS X 10.8 will (by default) happily launch your app. If you sign it with a different certificate or don't sign it at all, then the default reaction is for the operating system to warn the user and refuse to launch the app. They can disable this behavior or launch the app by choosing **Open** from the Finder's context menu to override it for a single app, however.

Unless you choose the last option (and you really shouldn't) you need to avail yourself of an Apple Developer account. These cost $99 per year in the US for either Mac or iOS accounts (so $198 total for both). Prices do vary by region, but they should be broadly comparable. This price also nets you free downloads from iTunes U of all sessions from WWDC (Apple's World-Wide Developer Conference) of your membership year.[1] You also have access to pre-release versions of new operating systems and development tools.

---

[1]Don't underestimate the value of WWDC videos. These are the single greatest learning resources for Mac and iOS programming available, taught by the same people who created the technology you're learning. Seasoned developers call WWDC "the fire hose" due to the immense amount of information conveyed during barely four days of talks.

Developer Certificate Utility

The Developer Certificate Utility, shown in Figure 10-1, is where you configure your application IDs and certificates.

Figure 10-1. *The Developer Certificate Center*

Your first step when registering a new application is to create a new App ID, as shown in Figure 10-2. This is where you associate your chosen bundle identifier with a single application in the store, or with a group of applications with the same bundle ID prefix.

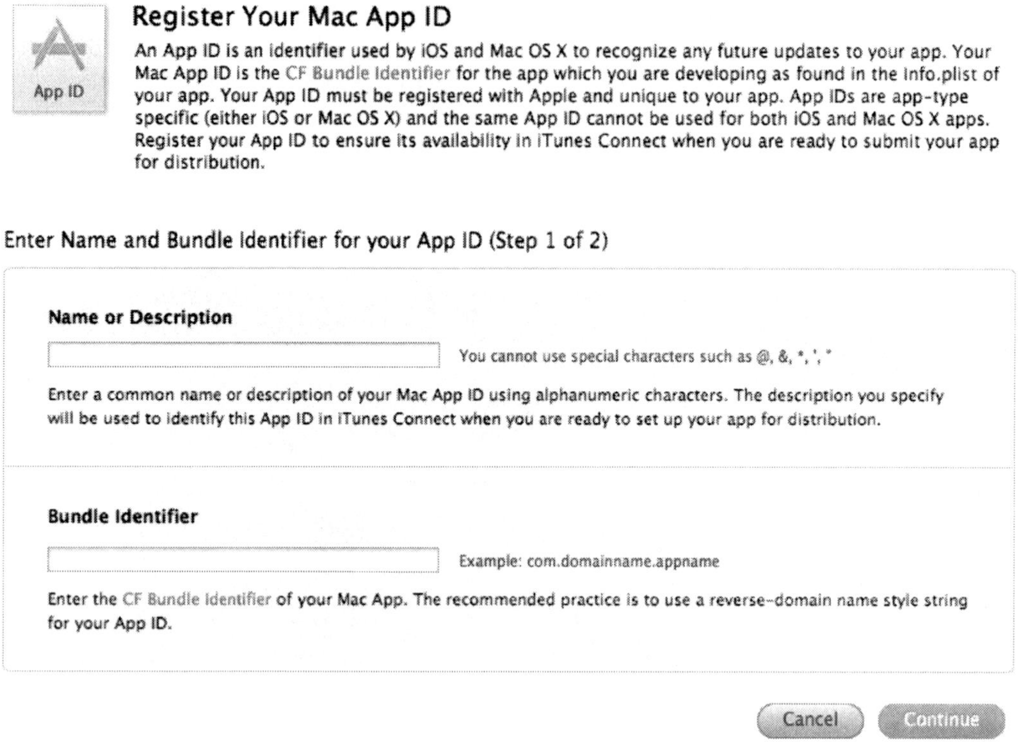

Register Your Mac App ID

An App ID is an identifier used by iOS and Mac OS X to recognize any future updates to your app. Your Mac App ID is the CF Bundle Identifier for the app which you are developing as found in the Info.plist of your app. Your App ID must be registered with Apple and unique to your app. App IDs are app-type specific (either iOS or Mac OS X) and the same App ID cannot be used for both iOS and Mac OS X apps. Register your App ID to ensure its availability in iTunes Connect when you are ready to submit your app for distribution.

Enter Name and Bundle Identifier for your App ID (Step 1 of 2)

Name or Description

You cannot use special characters such as @, &, *, ', "

Enter a common name or description of your Mac App ID using alphanumeric characters. The description you specify will be used to identify this App ID in iTunes Connect when you are ready to set up your app for distribution.

Bundle Identifier

Example: com.domainname.appname

Enter the CF Bundle Identifier of your Mac App. The recommended practice is to use a reverse-domain name style string for your App ID.

Cancel   Continue

Figure 10-2. Creating an App ID

Once your App ID is created, you have the chance to enable features such as iCloud, Push Notifications, Game Center, and In-App Purchase support (see Figure 10-3). The last two of these will also provide application-specific certificates to use when building your application: these are used to securely identify your application (or your server, for push notifications) to access the service. Usually two certificates are provided: one for the production system and another for development. The development certificate is used to interact with a different server during development, so that notifications aren't sent to all your users while you're testing an update, or so that you can verify your In-App Purchase code without actually spending money.

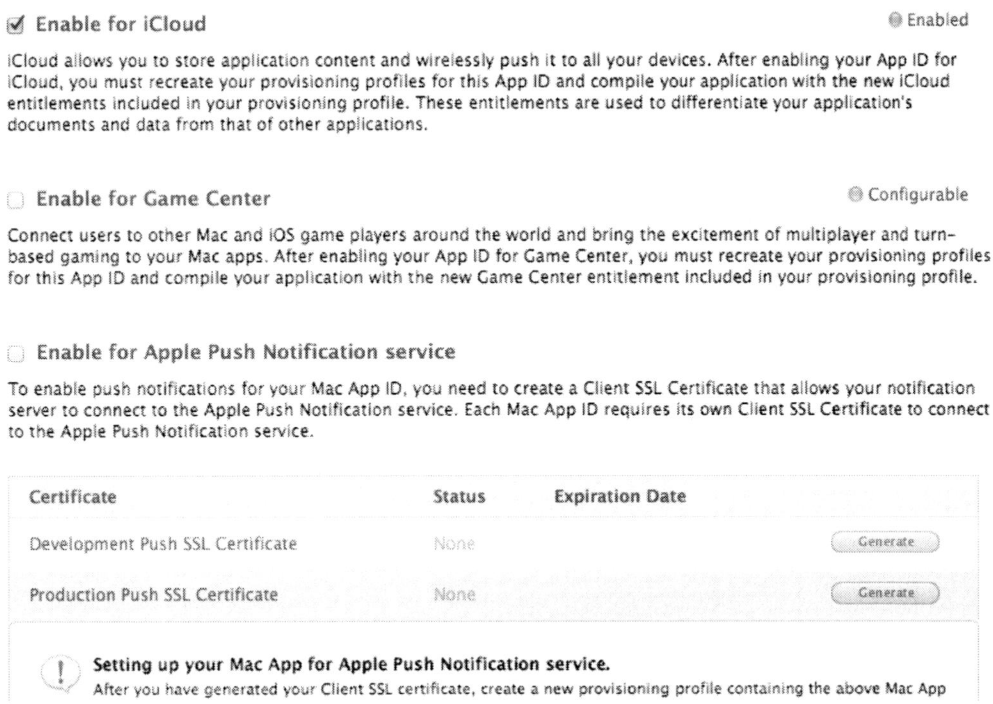

☑ Enable for iCloud   ⊙ Enabled

iCloud allows you to store application content and wirelessly push it to all your devices. After enabling your App ID for
iCloud, you must recreate your provisioning profiles for this App ID and compile your application with the new iCloud
entitlements included in your provisioning profile. These entitlements are used to differentiate your application's
documents and data from that of other applications.

☐ Enable for Game Center   ⊙ Configurable

Connect users to other Mac and iOS game players around the world and bring the excitement of multiplayer and turn-
based gaming to your Mac apps. After enabling your App ID for Game Center, you must recreate your provisioning profiles
for this App ID and compile your application with the new Game Center entitlement included in your provisioning profile.

☐ Enable for Apple Push Notification service

To enable push notifications for your Mac App ID, you need to create a Client SSL Certificate that allows your notification
server to connect to the Apple Push Notification service. Each Mac App ID requires its own Client SSL Certificate to connect
to the Apple Push Notification service.

Certificate	Status	Expiration Date	
Development Push SSL Certificate	None		Generate
Production Push SSL Certificate	None		Generate

⚠ **Setting up your Mac App for Apple Push Notification service.**
After you have generated your Client SSL certificate, create a new provisioning profile containing the above Mac App

Figure 10-3. Configuring your application's abilities

Now that your App ID is set up properly, you need certificates (see Figure 10-4). These are used to securely sign the compiled application and its resources, adding a layer of protection against modification by providing assurance that the running app is identical to the one shipped by you. It also enables Apple to cancel your certificates and, by extension, the use of all your applications if you should intentionally distribute malware. You need a Development certificate to be able to load your applications onto an iPhone or iPad, or to use iCloud, Game Center, and similar services on an in-development Mac app. To distribute your applications, you need to sign them using an App Store certificate for iOS or for Mac apps submitted to the Mac App Store. To distribute your apps yourself, you use a Developer ID certificate, which identifies your application as being built by a developer with an acceptable track record according to Apple. This is what OS X 10.8 uses to determine whether to automatically launch an app downloaded from somewhere other than the Mac App Store; it identifies it as an app from a "trusted developer." Again, if you distribute malware or violate applicable laws by, for instance, copying other developers' work wholesale, expect your certificate to be revoked and your developer account to be suspended.

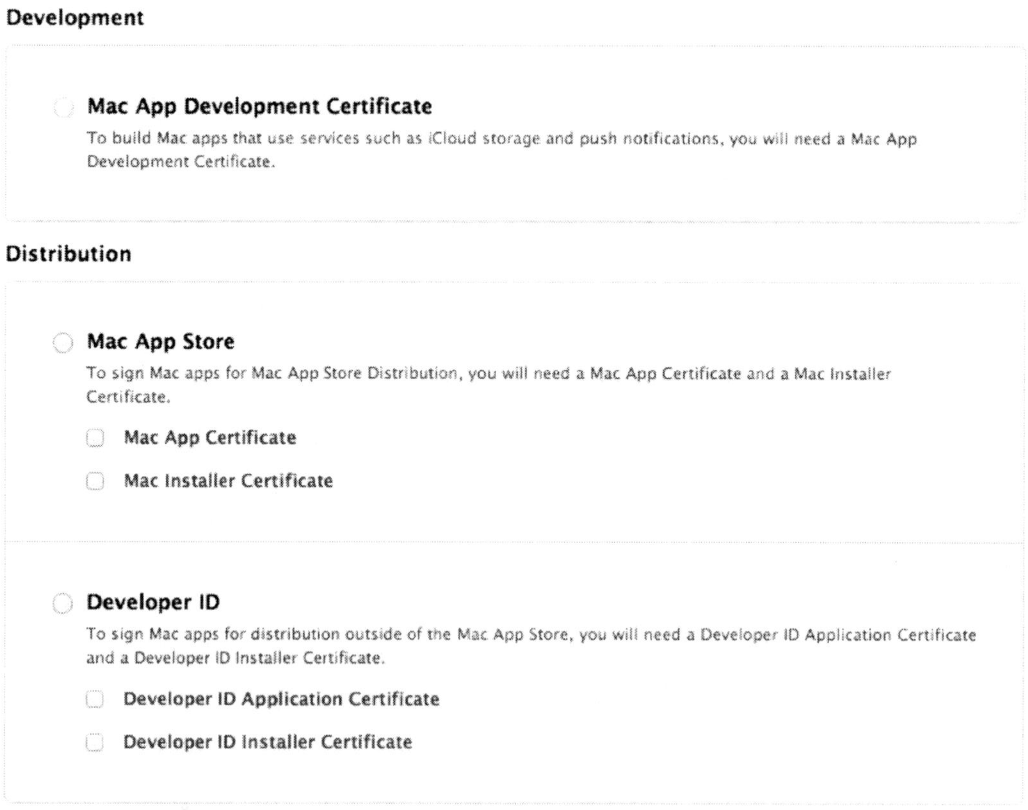

Development

Mac App Development Certificate

To build Mac apps that use services such as iCloud storage and push notifications, you will need a Mac App Development Certificate.

Distribution

Mac App Store

To sign Mac apps for Mac App Store Distribution, you will need a Mac App Certificate and a Mac Installer Certificate.

☐ Mac App Certificate

☐ Mac Installer Certificate

Developer ID

To sign Mac apps for distribution outside of the Mac App Store, you will need a Developer ID Application Certificate and a Developer ID Installer Certificate.

☐ Developer ID Application Certificate

☐ Developer ID Installer Certificate

Figure 10-4. *Creating certificates*

Note that the Developer ID section also includes the option of creating a certificate used to sign any installers for your applications. This allows the installer system to verify the integrity of the installer package, preventing the installation of packages that have been tampered with.

When you want to install your application on a device or a computer, you will need a *provisioning profile* identifying the target machine. This profile, which is cryptographically signed, will be included in your application's bundle and used by the target system to verify that the app may be used there. You first need to register the target device or system through the certificate utility shown in Figure 10-5. The UDID for each device or system is accessible through Xcode's Organize window on the Devices pane.

Register Mac OS X System

The maximum number of systems you can assign per membership year is 100. Any system added, regardless of being removed at a later time, will be counted against your 100 system maximum. You may reset your system list your next membership year upon the renewal. You can register 96 additional system(s).

Enter System Name and Hardware UUID

System Name or Description

[   ]   You cannot use special characters such as @, &, *, ', "

Enter a common name or description of your Mac Computer using alphanumeric characters.

Hardware UUID

[   ]   Example: 915A75DC-78D9-50D7-987F-A19358828029

Enter the Unique Device Identifier for your Mac computer. How do I find a hardware UUID?

(Cancel)   (Continue)

Figure 10-5. Registering a development system

Having registered your system, you can now create the provisioning profile using the interface shown in Figure 10-6. The profile will be attached to a particular certificate and, if it's a Development or Ad-Hoc Distribution profile, will include a list of supported systems identified by their UDID. Each profile can be associated with only a single App ID; Figure 10-6 shows the profile for the sample project used in Chapters 8 and 9 of this book.

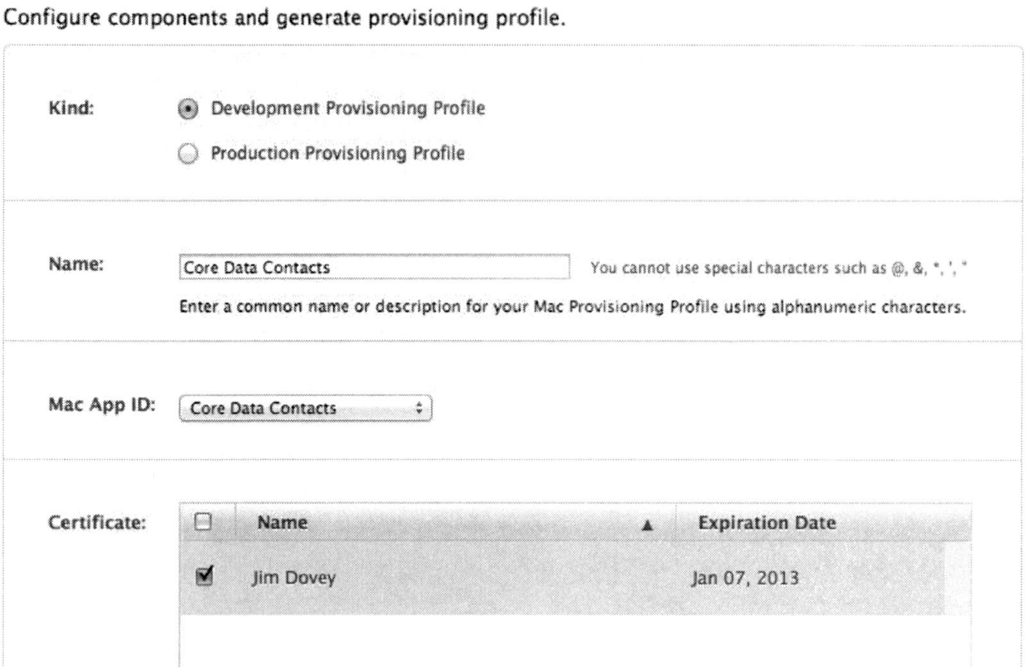

Configure components and generate provisioning profile.

Figure 10-6. *Creating a provisioning profile*

After completing these steps, you can download your certificates and provisioning profiles. The certificates will be placed into your Keychain, and Xcode will manage the profiles.

Setting Up The Application

In Xcode, select the project file in the Project Navigator and select the application's target in the editor. Switch to the Build Settings tab and scroll down to the Code Signing settings. Xcode should automatically have selected the appropriate identity certificate for you. If the certificate is for development or App Store distribution, the certificate is obtained from the Provisioning profile matching the application's bundle identifier. An example for the sample project can be seen in Figure 10-7.

Figure 10-7. *Code signing identity settings*

If you're using a Developer ID certificate, you'll likely need to pull down the list for the Code Signing Identity setting and scroll to the bottom, where you'll find your certificate listed, as in Figure 10-8.

Figure 10-8. *Choosing a Developer ID identity*

The App Store

Before you can upload your new app to the store, you need to tell the store all about it. To do so, visit http://itunesconnect.apple.com/ in your browser and log in with your Apple ID and password. You'll then be presented with the options seen in Figure 10-9.

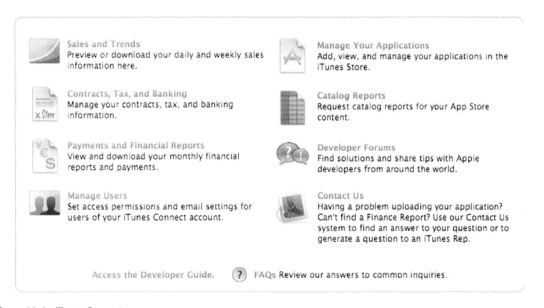

Figure 10-9. *iTunes Connect*

To create a new application, click the Manage Your Applications link to reach a list of your apps. This is probably going to be quite bare right now—click the blue Add New App button in the top left to get started.

First, you must supply a company name, as shown in Figure 10-10; this is used to group your applications together in the store.

Company Name   Objective-C Learners, Inc.

Figure 10-10. *Choosing a company name*

Select the appropriate application type in the next screen and enter some information about the app, as seen in Figure 10-11: its default language, name, SKU (this value is entirely up to you, it's only for your personal records), and bundle ID. This last ID is selected from the application IDs you set up in the Developer Certificate Center.

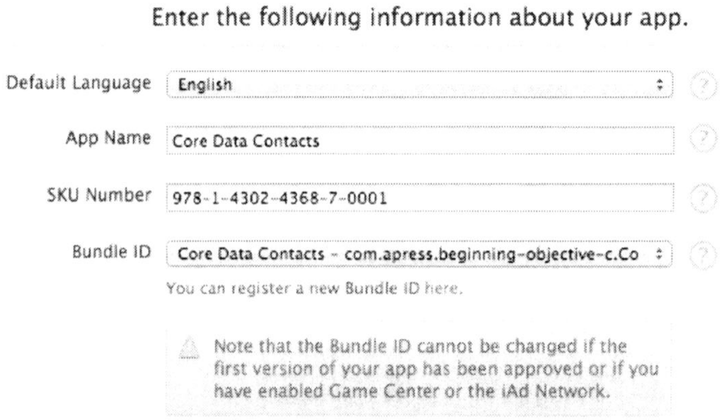

Enter the following information about your app.

Default Language   English

App Name   Core Data Contacts

SKU Number   978-1-4302-4368-7-0001

Bundle ID   Core Data Contacts - com.apress.beginning-objective-c.Co

You can register a new Bundle ID here.

⚠ Note that the Bundle ID cannot be changed if the first version of your app has been approved or if you have enabled Game Center or the iAd Network.

Figure 10-11. *Primary application information*

Next you must provide an availability date and pricing tier for the app, as shown in Figure 10-12.

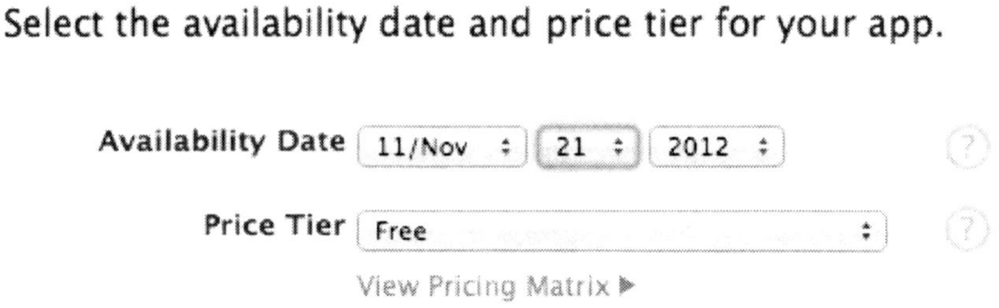

Select the availability date and price tier for your app.

Availability Date   11/Nov ⁝   21 ⁝   2012 ⁝

Price Tier   Free

View Pricing Matrix ▶

Figure 10-12. *Pricing and availability*

You also need to provide screenshots, a description, copyright information and various URLs for the application and its support and marketing sites. Once this is complete, you will be taken to an overview screen for your app, which is in the Prepare for Upload state shown in Figure 10-13. Click the similarly named button in the top right and you'll be prompted to declare whether your application implements any form of encryption. If you've implemented your own encryption in this app, say so—if you're only using built-in operating system features, you can say No. The store is now ready for you to upload your application.

Figure 10-13. *Your application's initial state*

Uploading

The first step in uploading your application to the App Store is to build the project as an archive. In Xcode, use **Project ➤ Archive** to build a release version of your application (with compiler optimizations enabled and debug symbols elided), after which Xcode will open the Organizer window to the Archives pane to show your new archive there. The archive keeps both your application and its components stored in a mirror of their installed hierarchy; it also stores the associated debugging information, enabling you to symbolicate any crash logs from this version of the app. This last is very important, as without that file available, Xcode will not be able to deduce function names, files, or line numbers for any methods within a backtrace of your application.

With the current archive selected, click the **Validate** button in the list's header pane to check your application against Apple's basic conformance criteria. This will pre-flight your application against rejection for simple things like lack of a custom icon or incorrect entitlements. The screen will show two options, as seen in Figure 10-14.

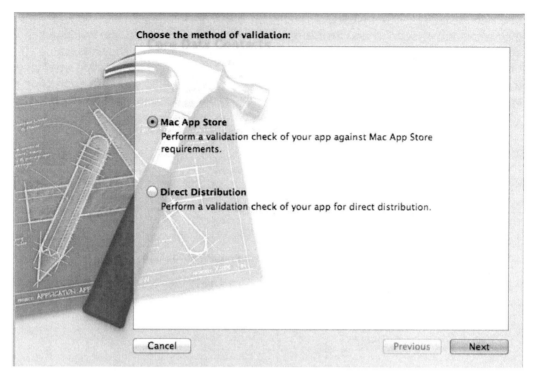

Figure 10-14. Choosing your validation method

In this case, choose **Mac App Store**, and click **Next** to be prompted for your Developer Connection login details. Xcode will log into the iTunes Connect portal for you and will locate the appropriate App Store Submission identity and Provisioning profile with which to submit your application by searching your Keychain. You'll be prompted to confirm or alter the choice, as shown in Figure 10-15.

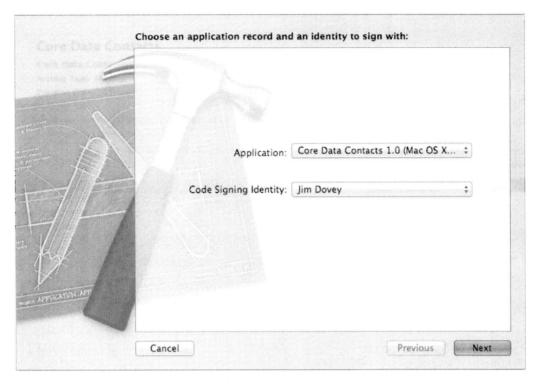

Figure 10-15. Submission metadata

Click **Next** to send your application to Apple for quick validation. If errors are reported back, correct them and create a new archive build and re-validate.

Once no validation errors occur, you can submit your application to the store. Click the **Distribute** button in the archive list and you'll again be prompted for a distribution method, as shown in Figure 10-16: App Store, Developer ID-signed application, or as an exported Xcode Archive, plain application, or a Mac Installer package.

Figure 10-16. Distribution through Xcode

Selecting the App Store option will again prompt you to log in and confirm your provisioning profile and signing identity, and it will then again validate your application before uploading it to Apple for review. If you check in at the iTunes Connect web site, you'll see that your application is now in the Waiting For Review state. You'll be notified by e-mail of any and all state changes, from here into In Review and then Ready For Sale (or, horror of horrors, Rejected). Expect it to take about a week before your app enters review, and the review itself to take a couple of hours.

At this point, you're done—your application is available on the store (or will be once your availability date rolls around).

Developer ID Distribution

Validating your app for Developer ID distribution checks only for simple items such as whether your app uses features like iCloud, Push Notifications, or Game Center, which require App Store distribution and manual screening by Apple. Distributing the app through Xcode will provide you with a re-signed application bundle (or, we assume, a Mac Installer package if your app isn't entirely self-contained), which you can then distribute as you see fit.

Summary

You've run the gamut of developing a fully functional application and distributing it either through the App Store or as a self-signed Developer ID application. This chapter took you through the sometimes-intricate experience of setting up your application in the Developer Center and managing your Provisioning profiles and your Development and Distribution certificates.

Don't forget that there are many more resources out there for you to use. The Apple Developer Forums are a great source of both information and assistance, and it is impossible to underestimate the importance of Apple's developer conference, WWDC, held in San Francisco each summer; so many great developers are there and so many potential connections to be made, that it's worth planning to be in the vicinity even if you're unable to score a ticket for the event itself. Many aspiring developers have launched their careers through acquaintances made there, your humble authors among them—it was at WWDC 2009 that the seeds of this book were first laid in a chance meeting with the Apress Mac publications' editor.

Go out and meet other developers in your hometown, too—the CocoaHeads[2] organization has chapters all over the world, and there are many other meetings where you can make connections and both learn and share your own knowledge.

You're an experienced developer now, familiar with the many facets of developing software for the Mac and for iOS. We hope that this book has given you the tools and experience you need to go further and become a world-class developer one day. If you make it there, look us up—we'd love to hear your success stories.

---

[2]Visit www.cocoaheads.org/ to find your closest chapter.

Index

D

E

CPSIA information can be obtained at www.ICGtesting.com
Printed in the USA
LVOW111709181112

307855LV00003B/1/P